ILLUSIONS OF A FUTURE

EXPERIMENTAL FUTURES:

TECHNOLOGICAL LIVES,

SCIENTIFIC ARTS,

ANTHROPOLOGICAL VOICES

A series edited by Michael M. J. Fischer

and Joseph Dumit

ILLUSIONS OF A FUTURE

PSYCHOANALYSIS AND THE

BIOPOLITICS OF DESIRE

KATE SCHECHTER

DUKE UNIVERSITY PRESS *Durham & London* 2014

Printed in the United States
of America on acid-free paper ∞
Designed by Amy Ruth Buchanan
Typeset in Garamond Premier Pro by
Westchester Book Group

Library of Congress Cataloging-
in-Publication Data
Schechter, Kate
Illusions of a future : psychoanalysis
and the biopolitics of desire / Kate Schechter.
pages cm—(Experimental futures : technological
lives, scientific arts, anthropological voices)
Includes bibliographical references and index.
ISBN 978-0-8223-5708-7 (cloth : alk. paper)
ISBN 978-0-8223-5721-6 (pbk. : alk. paper)
1. Psychoanalysis—United States—History—
20th century. 2. Psychoanalysts—
United States. 3. Institute for
Psychoanalysis. I. Title.
II. Series: Experimental futures.
BF 173.S3279 2014
616.89′170973—dc23
2014000766

Cover art: Jessica Jackson Hutchins, *Settee*, 2010.
Fabric, glazed ceramic, settee, 27 × 46 × 19 inches.
Courtesy of the artist.

CONTENTS

ACKNOWLEDGMENTS

There are far too many people to thank individually, so I will have to rest content that you each know how profoundly grateful I am for our conversations over the years. From the University of Chicago Department of Anthropology, Ray Fogelson, Judy Farquhar, and Michael Silverstein have been first-rate interlocutors, providing immeasurable support, stimulation, guidance, brilliance, and humor all along the way. Jean Comaroff, Marshall Sahlins, Sharon Stephens, Marilyn Ivy, Eduardo Viveiros de Castro, George Stocking, Jim Fernandez, Elizabeth Povinelli, Tanya Luhrmann, Jonathan Lear, Sarah Gehlert, and Irene Elkin have all taught me so much. Anne Ch'ien has been a steady, silent presence throughout my writing process; thank you, Anne, for your persistent and searching questions about psychoanalysis in Chicago. My colleagues from the International Psychoanalytical Studies Organization, particularly Robin Deutsch, Francesco Castellet y Ballara, and Glen Gabbard, have been superb in helping widen my perspective on psychoanalysis. I am grateful to Douglas Kirsner for sharing his Chicago oral histories with me and to Paul Mosher for sharing his extensive knowledge of the American Psychoanalytic Association. My dear friends Catherine Brennan, Lori Daane, Andy Harlem, Caitrin Lynch, Theresa Mah, Jane McCormack, Julia Pryce, Erika Schmidt, Laurel Spindel, Mary Weismantel, and Sharif Youssef have intervened in any number of creative emergencies, buoying me up with their acuity and enthusiasm to the very end. For the most exhilarating "book-level" conversations of all I must of course thank my editor extraordinaire, Laura Helper-Ferris; our collaboration has been utterly instrumental and intensely fun. Thank you, Ken Wissoker, both for introducing me to Laura and for your abiding confidence in this project. Finally, I am deeply beholden to my family, without whom there would have been neither motivation nor ability to tell this story.

My most sincere thanks go to everyone in the Chicago psychoanalytic community who put up with my nosiness, my persistence, and my peculiar anthropological bent over the years. I have learned so much from each of you, and from my immersion in this community; please know that any misunderstandings or mistakes here are mine alone. I will never forget how one of the most senior "classical" psychoanalysts I interviewed told me (psychoanalyzing the anthropologist, to be sure!) that eventually I would *have to* choose between psychoanalysis and anthropology. If that is the case, I have not yet reached that point. This book exemplifies my passion for each of these immensely challenging, unsettling, deeply rewarding disciplinary enterprises, and my continuing effort to pose—and oppose—them in fruitful conversation.

INTRODUCTION

"Where does she get her analytic patients?" The plaintiveness of Paul's question startled me. Paul is a respected senior psychoanalyst, and here he was anxiously wondering aloud how his colleague was managing to sustain a properly psychoanalytic practice in the quick-fix, medication-centered world of managed behavioral health that envelops them both. But it was not the question itself that struck me—it is one that is on everyone's mind in his world—so much as the pointed anxiety that surrounded his idea, perhaps his fantasy, that there was some "where," some source, some place where the patients came from, and the implication that she knew something he didn't, she had access to something he didn't. "She's never sent me a single patient in all these years," he trailed off, implying that his colleague was hoarding the goods. "She has a full analytic practice, you know." A pall fell over our discussion, one that enveloped me time and again as I interviewed psychoanalysts about their discipline, their work, their community, and as they told me, time and again, that their profession was in crisis—"though not for the relational people." Whoever they were, their situation was said to be different somehow. I remembered my interview with Paul's "relational" colleague now, how she had told me "everything I do—it's not about *technique*, it's all about the *relationship*, the real relationship. The analysis basically *is* the relationship." This figure of the relationship, *the real relationship,* loomed large in my interviews with psychoanalysts, an image of warmth and plenitude surrounded by pathos, saturated by fear of failure and by envy of the other's fortune. How might we understand the communal elaboration of a state of precarity and crisis so steadily attended by a pregnant sense of the plenty and presence embodied in this idea of the *real relationship*?[1]

For much of psychoanalysis's hundred-year history the working relationship between the psychoanalyst and his or her patient was an unmarked, untheorized, "natural" backdrop against which the transference—a distortion of that relationship composed of the patient's fantasies and projections—developed and became visible. The analyst's ostensibly technical work was reading and interpreting the transference *neurosis*, that "artificial illness" whose resolution by interpretation led to psychoanalytic cure.[2] Building on Freud's classificatory parsing of these dimensions, classical American ego psychology in the 1950s—the golden age of psychoanalysis in the United States—came to draw a sharp distinction between the transference and the underlying rational relationship between patient and analyst.[3] The transference was special, a special psychoanalytic object; the relationship was natural, unremarkable.[4] In more recent years, the relationship *itself* has come to be seen by many psychoanalysts as curative, no longer simply the silent carrier of a more valuable, distinctively psychoanalytic process. In consequence, the association between the transference and the relationship, and between the attendant ontological dimensions of artifice and reality, has shifted. In Freud's hands, intense affect in the transference was to be neutralized interpretively in and through the process of memory retrieval; in the newer view, it is precisely the psychoanalyst's ability to have a relationship with the patient, to experience, process, and contain affective intensity in that relationship, that is of the greatest therapeutic value. Many psychoanalysts complain about this shift in emphasis from transference interpretation to immediate relational experience, yet, as I will show, the most successful ones are those who espouse it in practice. The domain of "technique" has expanded to include the relationship itself.

This book examines the development of the analyst-patient relationship as an occult object, a professional artifact that psychoanalysts at once disavow and espouse. I suggest that today's psychoanalysts, in their effort to transcend their fears of irrelevance, play on the *real relationship* in a way that ends up heightening that very irrelevance. In effect, I argue, in seeking to resolve a conundrum that is central to their practice, in seeking to maintain themselves as psychoanalysts when they cannot practice what they define as psychoanalysis, they trade the *real relationship* against disciplinary failure.

Today's psychoanalysts have been laboriously trained in a craft they are almost never able to actualize in the real world of "evidence-based" medicine. Psychoanalysis has lost its footing in medicine, and psychoanalysts find themselves struggling in an atmosphere of scarce work. Evidence-based medicine (EBM), embraced by the insurance and pharmaceutical industries and by health economists and policy makers alike, stands in sharp contrast to psychoanalysis in matters of ontology, authority, and value. Health care's gold standard, EBM can well be said to be psychoanalysis's specular other. Its advocates place large-scale, randomized, triple-blind, placebo-controlled clinical trials on the model of pharmaceutical research at the top of a hierarchy of epistemic legitimacy, ranking evidence derived from other kinds of research as of limited to no value (see Sackett et al. 2000; Timmermans and Kolker 2004). The psychoanalytic case study, a qualitative narrative centered on the inner biography of the suffering individual, scarcely meets EBM's minimal thresholds of scientificity, and as professionals' clinical practices shift to accommodate the epistemic—and economic—culture of "accountability" wrought by EBM, psychoanalysis finds itself under increasing pressure to adapt to its demands for standardization and positive proof of effectiveness.

Throughout the twentieth century, psychoanalysts plied their craft independently, in private, office-based practice. Psychoanalysis was an integral part of psychiatry—a medical treatment—and psychoanalysts were, by definition, medical doctors. In 1989, a watershed civil suit required the American Psychoanalytic Association (hereafter APsaA) to change its regulations on training and admit nonphysicians (psychologists had sought for years to be trained in psychoanalysis, and in the mid-1980s finally resorted to legal remedy).[5] As a result, psychoanalysis became increasingly interdisciplinary in the 1990s, even as psychiatry was becoming increasingly biologically and pharmaceutically oriented. Today's solo practitioner, as often trained in psychology or social work as in psychiatry, faces sharp conflict with an increasingly corporatized medicine, as well as pointed disagreement in the psychoanalytic collegium over the status of psychoanalysis as a self-regulating profession and over its very definition as a practice.

"We are the last free place on earth," writes David Falk, a 2010 candidate for election to one of the executive offices of the APsaA, in a bit of electoral hyperbole.[6] The sense that psychoanalysts are precisely *not* free, that they have lost control over their work, creates a climate in which a rhetoric of exceptionalism like Falk's finds a ready audience. For years, psychoanalysts have been decrying the decline of the talking cure, the stifling of that "accepting and safe place for our patients to be themselves," and the sense that the field of mental health is being transformed from a profession into a business. As small-business persons, psychoanalysts—much like lawyers, accountants, scholars, and members of other professions—have traditionally controlled their own work through a collegial system of valuation, recognizing each others' worth through norms of mutual dependence. On the receding horizon of professional valuation in health care today, however, they have lost control of this collegial system—and of the markets in which they compete for patients, the kinds of patients they attract, and the willingness of patients to submit to psychoanalytic procedures. Surveys over the past decade have baldly demonstrated their working predicament: the majority of psychoanalysts in the United States—as in Chicago, the location of this study—have one or two patients in actual psychoanalysis. They have lost control of the exclusive educational institutes and professional organizations with which they affiliate, the pace and quality of their daily work routines, their career trajectories and satisfactions, and, not least, their status in American society. As it has been for lawyers, doctors, accountants, and other highly paid, high-status professionals who used to run their own professional lives, the very notion of professionalism that psychoanalysts have enjoyed has been dramatically transformed in the global economy of flexible specialization.[7]

Given this bleak picture, one might think that psychoanalysis would have folded under the withering gaze of an industrial managerialism derived from actuarial algorithms. Instead, as I shall demonstrate, psychoanalysts have developed their own indigenous, *relational* managerialism and their own opportunistic forms of adaptation to EBM. The historical emergence of such a *neoliberal* psychoanalysis is the subject of this study. In exploring psychoanalysts' growing attachment to the affective immediacy of the real relationship and to the unachievable fantasy of prestige, security, and the good life that it carries, I will show how deeply imbricated this professional artifact is in their effort to survive in the culture of EBM, and how central it is to this profession's effort to prevail in the face of market demands for the efficiency and standardization of mental health treatments.

Falk's deeply felt sense of psychoanalytic exceptionalism turns on what I call, following Derrida, the problematic "undecidability" of psychoanalysis.[8] I learned about the undecidability of psychoanalysis when I first started attending Chicago Psychoanalytic Society meetings some fifteen years ago. At my very first attendance at one of these public "scientific" lectures, I noted—in addition to the great age of many of those in the audience—that each person dismissed anything anyone else talked about as "not analysis." As a social worker and, then, a doctoral student in anthropology, I assumed I was witnessing a generational transition, that these old people were simply (and perhaps cantankerously) waxing nostalgic about the lost golden days of their high modernist cultural practice. I soon learned, however, that this use of the privative "that's not analysis" was emblematic, and that what psychoanalysis *is* is a durable question in the profession. Is psychoanalysis its own, qualitatively different psychotherapeutic modality, or is its difference from other psychotherapies merely a matter of degree, with psychoanalysis simply being a more intensive (and more frequent) form of "psychodynamic" psychotherapy? While there have been many changes in the organization, delivery, and practice of psychoanalysis since its heyday in the 1950s and 1960s, perhaps the principal change since the explosion of psychopharmacology in the 1980s has been the change in the scale of psychoanalytic practice. The market for psychoanalysis has contracted dramatically during this period, and most practitioners today chiefly provide psychotherapy, while continuing to prize their self-definition as psychoanalyst. While their forebears had long championed psychoanalysis's specificity—policing its boundaries to guarantee both its jurisdiction over and its purity among other therapies—I wondered what was different today. I wondered how and why today's psychoanalysts managed to maintain themselves *as psychoanalysts* when they could not practice what they preached. What was at stake in their holding on to this particular designation?

I will suggest that the aura of the therapeutic relationship—in the face of pervasive professional anxiety about the very viability of psychoanalysis as a profession, haunted by its past success and its image of present failure—governs the discourse, action, and attitudes of the group through the logic of the fetish, the denial of a feared absence through its replacement with a substitute presence.[9] A historical symptom and a modality of affective experience and practical consciousness alike, this fetishization of the real relationship can best be understood through an examination of the organizational contexts of its emergence. To do this, I draw on several modes of analysis at once: a textual analysis of the place of crisis in professional discourse; a structural account of psychoanalysis's difficult history of institutional reproduction in the United States; an ethnographic and historical reading of a group of psychoanalysts' attempts to define their protean practice in positive terms; and a political-philosophical analysis of the "resistances" of psychoanalysis that make it so seemingly impossible for psychoanalysts to organize collectively to resist health-care industrialization.

A number of anthropologists have recently turned to the concept of biopower to analyze the intertwining of medicine, technology, subjectivity, and governance in late liberalism, and in this book I extend this approach to psychoanalysis (see, e.g., Dumit 2003; Fassin 2007; Lakoff 2005; Ong and Collier 2005; Sunder Rajan 2006; Whyte 2009). Following Michel Foucault ([1978] 1990, 2003, 2008, 2009), I define biopower as the capacity to control life through a kind of scientific knowing that establishes a relationship between ontology and politics, a dynamic that places life itself—the vital characteristics of human existence—at the center of government. Contemporary analyses of biopower have centered, in the main, on either the global philosophical question of the mode of politics that biopolitics represents (see, e.g., Agamben 1990; Hardt and Negri 2001), or, more historically or ethnographically, on biotechnology and the instrumentalization and capitalization of molecular life (see, e.g., Rabinow 1996; Rabinow and Rose 2006). Foucault worried about such a macro-micro bifurcation, offering the analytics of governmentality as a way of grasping the linkages between power, forms of knowledge, and technologies of the self. Government—as opposed to discipline—draws attention to indirect dimensions of modern power where elements of freedom, conscience, and the activities of self on self are prominent (as opposed to direct power over bodies). Thomas Lemke (2005, 10), following this invitation, has argued that biopolitics may be analyzed specifically as an "art of government" so as to determine how, as Foucault asked, "the phenomenon of the 'population' with its specific effects and problems [is] taken into account by a system that endorses respect for a subject of rights and for the freedom of choice."[10] This perspective views power as operating in terms of specific rationalizations, directed toward certain ends that arise in them; it offers a genealogical mode of inquiry into the forms of local knowledge that support what Foucault referred to as "the conduct of conduct," the techniques and knowledges that underpin attempts to govern the conduct of selves and others in specific settings. Within the field of biopower, "biopolitics" embraces all the specific strategies of control over collective human vitality: discourses about the vital character of human beings, strategies for intervention into collective existence at the level of the population or species, and modes of subjectivation through which individuals are brought to work on themselves, as Rabinow and Rose (2006, 197) write, "under certain forms of authority, in relation to truth discourses, by means of practices of the self, in the name of their own life or health."

In psychoanalysis, biopower is inscribed in the working sense that psychoanalysts have of their world at risk, in their trained feel for the securitizing, risk-management powers that the doctor-patient relationship—the prized, labored, familiar figure at the center of their world—holds for them. As the capacity to cultivate deeper dependencies, thereby, in their case, literally to create analytic patients where there are none, the analyst's relational ability is under increasing scrutiny in the psychoanalytic collegium. The objectification of this relational ability, surveyed and evaluated and regulated by the analyst's peers as technical expertise—an expertise most specifically in finding, making, and keeping patients—is steadily coming to define what psychoanalysis "is" as a specific practice in neoliberal medicine. Paul's talk about his colleague (in the opening image of the book) is exemplary in this regard, for what psychoanalysis actually "is" proves to be the crux of his problem: according to the way he defines psychoanalysis, he has next to no patients, whereas his "relational" colleague has many.[11] In analysts' constant resort to the privative, to the accusation about others' work that it's "not analysis"—in and through relentless questioning about what psychoanalysis "is" and about whether the other is doing it—much of the work of its governmentalization is conducted. This discursive work expressly, performatively links psychoanalytic practices concerned with conducting the conduct of the other with psychoanalytic practices concerned with conducting one's own conduct, managing and administering one's own affective labor, as technologies of the self reciprocally come to constitute technologies of control of the other.

Chicago is a particularly apposite place for an ethnographic genealogy of twenty-first-century psychoanalytic professionalism in crisis. It is prominent as the home of several homegrown schools of psychoanalysis that problematized the therapeutic relationship per se—Franz Alexander's theory of the "corrective emotional experience" and Heinz Kohut's theory of "self psychology"—and thereby placed the enterprise of psychoanalysis into question both locally and in the broader field. Combining ethnography, history, and theory, I examine this particular psychoanalytic community in order to illuminate the intensification under neoliberalism of psychoanalysis's problematic undecidability.

This book tracks this community's history and looks closely at the way a group of psychoanalysts narrate the loss of one species of psychoanalysis and the rise of another. In following their at times contradictory attempts to restore an autonomous disciplinary space for psychoanalysis, I seek to examine the relation between a profession's crisis, a crisis in the very category of profession in the era of flexible specialization, and a moment of history that practitioners are living as simultaneously promising and imperiling. My reading of a series of moments in which the regulation of psychoanalysis came into question in local discourse will highlight some of the ways that a biopolitical logic of risk, accountability, and standardization has been installed in the clinical encounter, both in and *through* the intensely personal intimacy of the patient-analyst relationship. I will suggest that this seemingly contradictory emergence deserves special theoretical attention for (at least) two reasons. First, it challenges us to give biopolitics a positive declension (contra Giorgio Agamben or Antonio Negri), and second, it challenges us to rethink biopolitics with renovated psychoanalytic resources.

An ethnography of psychoanalysis is impossible without an engagement with Foucault, given the axial position Foucault granted psychoanalysis in the transition from classical sovereignty to liberal governmentality. An ethnography of psychoanalysis is equally impossible without an engagement with Jacques Derrida, whose problematization of the very identity of psychoanalysis offered a kind of paradigm for deconstruction. Psychoanalysis was a key category for both in their efforts to grasp the workings of power and knowledge in modernity, so their engagements with psychoanalysis are necessarily integral to my own—even though neither took on psychoanalysis as an empirical domain of cultural analysis. Psychoanalysis was one of the two great "counter-sciences" of the twentieth century (social anthropology was the other) for Foucault, notable for the grand attack on enlightenment Man that it mounted (see Foucault [1966] 1995). The science of the unconscious, of the negative, of death and desire, psychoanalysis constituted the subject of modern governance as a liberal subject, a subject that regulates itself by a sustained reflection on its freedom. Foucault gestured toward psychoanalysis over and again in efforts to understand the ways that liberalism and biopolitics are mutually inciting. In Foucault's original historicization, psychoanalysis served as a critical technico-historical hinge between classical sovereignty and liberal governmentality; as a theory of the interrelatedness of law and desire, he argued, it played a central historical role in the generalization of sexuality as the quintessentially modern site of disciplinary power. Since sex was located "at the pivot of the two axes along which developed the entire political technology of life," a means of access both to the life of the body (and its "anatomo-politics") and to the life of the species (and its "biopolitics"), its science, psychoanalysis, sat at the cardinal articulation between discipline and the biopolitical "power of regularization" (or "normalization") (Foucault [1978] 1990, 145). For Foucault, while liberalism attempted to produce freedom, in doing so it produced the very opposite. As Jodi Dean (2008, 2009) points out, psychoanalysis characterized its modal unfreedom through the story of Oedipus and his paradigmatic struggle of conscience: "In my very effort *not* to kill my father and marry my mother, I kill my father and marry my mother." In the substance and style of Foucault's arguments about neoliberalism in "The Birth of Biopolitics" and "Society Must Be Defended," psychoanalysis was at the center of the historical processes through which the norm came to supplant the law, through which normative regularization was installed in the (sexed) subject. Nonetheless, in spite of the axial position Foucault granted psychoanalysis in his account of the modern sovereignty-discipline-government complex, he never provided a sustained genealogical examination of it. Foucault did not acknowledge the historicity of psychoanalysis, and (his version of) psychoanalysis could not acknowledge the historicity of the person of desire (whether analysand or analyst). In his writings, psychoanalysis developed and generalized "a certain idea or model of humanity [that] has become normative," yet the historicity of this "model of humanity" was captive to a very particular reading of psychoanalysis (as pastoral power, as the ultimate discipline that disciplines). His readers who have attended to psychoanalysis more empirically have followed suit, even as they leveraged a psychoanalysis incompatible with the Freudian unconscious that Foucault lauded in his earlier writings.[12] I suggest, in contrast to the readings of Ian Hacking, Nikolas Rose, and Allan Young, that the rationalization of psychoanalysis over the course of the latter half of the twentieth century presents a unique biopolitical trajectory precisely because of the centrality of forces and forms of disruption, both psychic and social, to the Freudian problematic: *the negative, the death drive, ambivalence, the unconscious id, the repetition compulsion, the uncanny, the "beyond"* (as in *beyond* the pleasure principle). It is the reflexive, disruptive tendency of psychoanalysis that distinguishes its rationalization from those processes of rationalization in other professions caught up in the shifts in governance characteristic of postmodernity.[13]

Psychoanalysis's indeterminacy—what I explore ethnographically by asking "what *is* psychoanalysis if what one's colleagues are doing, always, is *not* it?"—subserves a constant sense of endangerment, for no one seems to know for sure any more what psychoanalysis is (yet psychoanalysts nonetheless claim to practice it). In reading the stories of endangered employment of several psychoanalysts, I will foreground the emergent intersubjective production of a condition of risk in the psychoanalytic collegium, demonstrating the ways that governance works among them via this very endangerment by constantly stimulating it—by stimulating the sense that what one is doing is "not psychoanalysis"—and then by intervening in its management through normalizing practices of supervision and censure. This endangerment is the collegium's very means of social reproduction, maintaining it in a state of crisis while yet serving it as a technology of "freedom" (by flagging freedom I mean to locate it in Foucauldian language as emblematic of liberalism's theory of sovereignty). I will further suggest that the reflexive governmentalization of the neoliberal psychoanalytic subject (self-government by self-doubt rather than external government by external force) affords us an opportunity to understand the freedom of the normalized subject, her vaunted flexibility, as a distinctive intersection of technologies of the market and technologies of the self.

While reading psychoanalysis in terms of biopolitics has a Foucauldian pedigree, reading it in terms of its "resistances" has, of course, a Derridean and a psychoanalytic one. For Freud, resistance was a phenomenon of the *cogito* to be treated (as it were) by psychoanalysis: it was a function of illness in the psyche. Derrida turned the Freudian notion of resistance back onto psychoanalysis itself, using it to read Freud's own logic, working with the idea of resistance to bring into view the failure of psychoanalysis to analyze itself in its own terms, analytically—and, by extension, to call attention to the aura of chronic malaise that inhabits the psychoanalytic institution with respect to its ostensible object. In turn, I offer a Derridean reading of the resistances of psychoanalysis in order to open up and ethnographically situate the very particular problem of undecidability that plagues psychoanalysis today as a problem of biopolitical governmentality—and not merely as a problem of deconstruction.[14]

By interpreting Freud's deliberate disruptions of system (in texts like *Beyond the Pleasure Principle* or "The Uncanny"), Derrida found in the Freudian corpus a psychoanalysis fundamentally resistant to its own heterogeneity—a psychoanalysis ever attempting, yet ever failing, to give itself an identity, a self-sameness.[15] "Resistance," then, was not simply a formation of the psyche. It was intrinsic to the structure of psychoanalysis and, moreover, to *analysis* itself as a concept. There is an insusceptibility to analysis, an incoherence, at its core, which Derrida set out to find at the level of the Freudian text. Resistance for Freud, he argued, defined the point at which analysis stopped. Resistance denoted the order of forces that dissimulate, its "analysis" the unbinding and dissolution of the tangled knot of obscured traces. Indeed, psychoanalysis emerged out of hypnosis, Freud's prior practice, precisely through Freud's analytic dissolution of his patients' tangled resistances to hypnotic suggestion, through his analytic conquest of those defenses that repressed the psychic representation of memory traces. But the situation was more complicated, Derrida demonstrated, for resistance in psychoanalysis is not simply a genus containing several species. Its own unity is incoherent. The resistances of psychoanalysis are of multiple orders, temporary and permanent, depending on the particular account of psychoanalysis they limit.

In deconstructively pursuing Freud's use of the term *analysis* for his science of the psyche, Derrida traced this theme from Freud's earliest "confessions" that hidden meanings—secret, dissimulated sense—exceeded his efforts to his fully developed "hermeneutic drive" to bring hidden sense under psychoanalytic reason, and then, beyond this even, to Freud's engagement with the ultimate resistance that resists analysis fully. He showed that Freud's earliest and most optimistic accounts of psychoanalysis constituted resistance as analyzable, and analysis—as this activity of untangling and dissolving—as possible. In these accounts (in, for instance, the *Studies on Hysteria*), resistance was merely contingent on the analyst's hermeneutic abilities; a fully recoverable unconscious wish or pathological idea could, on the earliest view, be discovered through an anamnesis that was, in principle at least, definitive. As Freud put it, and Derrida (1998, 7) cited, "My task was fulfilled when I had informed a patient of the hidden meaning of his symptoms." Soon enough, though, Freud discovered another order of resistance, since it appeared that the patient actively resisted being so informed of his hidden meanings. Irrational affective barriers seemed to stand in the way of the patient's rational comprehension of the hidden meaning of his symptoms (here one thinks, for example, of the Dora case). This order of resistance could not simply be comprehended by the patient; it had quite literally to be transformed. The patient had forcibly to be led to accept the analyst's reading of her hidden meanings through a more polemical hermeneutic, by way of an *erotic* transference whose interpretation would uncover these knottier resistances. Analysis was still an uncovering of meaning, but now the domain of *meaning* was expanded to include nonrational resistances to the analyst's activity of disentangling this (now expanded) domain of hidden "erotic" content.

As Freud's work progressed further still, yet another order of resistance emerged. This was one that was fully and finally resistant to analysis, an absolute limit rather than a provisional barrier, an order of resistance that Freud, in Derrida's reading, would only dimly recognize. While Freud *named* this absolute limit to analysis—he called it, variously, the navel of the dream, the unanalyzable tangle of thoughts that cannot be dissolved, the "repetition compulsion" that reigned beyond the pleasure principle—in its face he ultimately shifted his therapeutic strategy, if not his theory of cure. Derrida quoted Freud: "Besides the intellectual motives which we mobilize to overcome the resistance, there is an affective factor, the personal influence of the physician, which we can seldom do without, and in a number of cases the latter alone is in a position to remove the resistance. The situation here is no different from what it is elsewhere in medicine and there is no therapeutic procedure of which one may say that it can do entirely without the co-operation of this personal factor" (Derrida 1998, 18). Psychoanalysis had originally emerged in distinction to hypnosis, yet, Derrida noted, Freud early on smuggled into his "analysis" a fatal, personal element, adding something of a different order to the definition of analysis as a hermeneutic disentangling yet failing to propose a revised conception of *analysis* beyond "the one that has held sway in the history of philosophy, logic, science" (19). In the face of this absolute limit Freud shifted from the *analytic* to the *synthetic*, moving away from the *hermeneutic* to the *reconstructive*.

Invoking continuity with the tradition of analysis, Freud embedded in his *psycho*analysis multiple orders of resistance alongside the founding notion of analysis as, precisely, analysis of resistance (analysis of the resistance, that is, to analysis). Psychoanalysis, being thus determined "only in adversity and in relation to what resists it," can never, Derrida wrote, "gather itself into the unity of a concept or a task" (1998, 20). Left in this way to drift, with the fatal, personal element always disrupting the purity of its avowed scientificity, its disinterested systematicity, psychoanalysis developed whole catalogs of positive resistances.[16]

In this book, on the basis of this Derridean framing of the Freudian problematic of *analysis*, I read psychoanalysis's schismatic institutional history genealogically in and through just such catalogs of resistances. These offer an ethnographic entry point, a way to pursue local history in a textual and contextual mode at once. They archive institutionally and historically specific problematizations and offer access to what Derrida hinted at but did not—perhaps could not—develop: how the fatal, personal element actually *works* in a psychoanalytic collegium as an unanalyzed constraint on analysis, how the collegium is centered around this kernel of decentering, strangely disavowed, personal influence. As Derrida detailed, at the point where analysis fails, where there is no longer a separate *analysis*, there is only the personal element, only the relationship. Indeed, I show that when psychoanalysts charge that this practice or that is "not analysis," they are always talking in some way about the analyst-patient relationship. In essence, too much relationship is problematic because then the work risks being seen as unscientific, untechnical, as "merely" a kind of reparenting or as an inappropriate personal relationship of some other kind. At the same time, too little relationship clearly signals that the analyst himself is a failure; he cannot find and keep patients (and everyone knows it). At the level of the community, the scarcity of patients and the failure of the profession itself are increasingly obvious and unspoken yet palpable in their effect on psychoanalytic knowing.

I trace an institutional history over the course of which the relationship between analyst and patient becomes the consummate biopolitical object. The personal element is no longer the unremarked background of analysis but its very site. In turn, psychoanalysts now seek to regulate it, to contain it, to hedge it in with theory and claim it as a privileged technique. It has become the privileged means by which psychoanalysis, seeking to protect its autonomy, has appropriated a neoliberal discourse of regulation, positivization, standards, and boundaries through which to police the purity of practice and maintain a set of definitional boundaries: around the analyst's self-disclosure, around the correct expression of affect, around physical touch, and so on. Legal, quasi-legal, and ethical discourses have proliferated as psychoanalysts increasingly define those boundaries, both through formal laws (professional "standards") and through informal norms. In efforts to resist neoliberal medicine's regime of accountability and govern itself, psychoanalysis has, in this way, ended up redoubling the administrative thrust of audit culture (see Shore 2008).

The book is based on both archival and ethnographic field research. In terms of archival data, I examined documents concerning the history of psychoanalysis in Chicago from 1911 to the present: published papers, published and unpublished correspondence, filmed interviews with key figures, and other organizational documents connected with the Chicago Institute for Psychoanalysis.[17] Ethnographic research consisted of participant observation in the Chicago psychoanalytic community over a period of three years, including a period during which I myself underwent training in psychoanalysis. In conducting my research I immersed myself in the life of this community, attending numerous psychoanalytic conferences, seminars, meetings, and online fora, participating in the life of the field in all of its complexity. As well as my own field observations and my immersion in the history of this psychoanalytic community, I conducted in-depth interviews between 2006 and 2010 with over fifty psychoanalysts who graciously allowed me to interview them, and I held innumerable informal conversations with many more. All interviews were conducted in confidentiality, and the names of interviewees are withheld by mutual agreement.[18]

The book is organized as follows: chapters 1 and 2 describe the current situation of psychoanalysis, introducing the object of observation (the concrete social history of organized psychoanalysis), the object of cultural analysis (the "crisis" of psychoanalytic authority), and the psychoanalysts' object of desire (psychoanalysis itself, along with the central problem of its regulation). Chapters 3, 4, and 5 provide a historical ethnography, examining psychoanalysts' arguments over the place of psychoanalysis in U.S. society as they struggled to institute and to taxonomize the talking cure and reading both their resistances around the figure of the real relationship and their own readings of key organizational processes in their community from the 1930s up to the 1970s, when psychoanalysis lost its footing in medicine. Chapter 5 brings the history up to date, providing a bridge to the present via a close analysis of a historic meeting in 2009 in which a reckoning with the past took place. Chapter 6 ties these themes together in an analysis of today's "standards" movement in psychoanalysis, considering this in the context of a series of shifts in theory that refigured the therapeutic relationship.

In reading the history of the Chicago Institute for Psychoanalysis and looking closely at how this group of psychoanalysts manages an ongoing situation of collective failure, I will point to the ways that in and through an expansion of a vital politics of real relationships these psychoanalysts ratify and extend biopower without subjecting it to explicit critique, perforce without knowing about it, in two mutually reinforcing registers: a clinical technology of fostering and nurturing patients, on the one hand, and, on the other, an educational technology of surveillance centered on policing the vicissitudes of that therapeutic relationship. In tracking these, I map an array of connections between the individual and the collective, the technological and the natural, the cultural and the psychological, and the ethical and the political.

PART I

....

THE SLIPPERY OBJECT

and the

STICKY LIBIDO

AN IMAGINARY *of* THREAT *and* CRISIS

Digital Diagnostics announces its new 3 minute psychoanalytic diagnosis that integrates seamlessly into busy clinics.—Digital Diagnostics website

....

Critics, scholars, and psychoanalysts alike have understood psychoanalysis to be *in crisis* in the United States in the last twenty years.[1] Countless articles in the professional literature take up a discourse of crisis, as though this trope had not been a steady, perhaps even constitutive, companion of psychoanalysis from its founding. Crisis is the constant subject of professional conference panels, the focus of innumerable committees and task forces in the major psychoanalytic organizations, and a regular topic of talk among psychoanalysts.[2] Emblematic of this shared imaginary of crisis for those who write, read, and think about psychoanalysis today is a tragicomic cartoon image, an empty couch with a bearded, bespectacled man sitting behind taking notes, reflecting, presumably, on his own professional decline. This image of impotence is funny in part because we understand the analyst to be interpreting his lack psychoanalytically, enjoining a style of thought we know to be an atavism in today's world of auditable rational actors—one that we nonetheless embrace, if now only in an ironic mode.[3] That world, one of "managed care," is all too visible in a website for a company called Digital Diagnostics. Under the banner "We help translate your patient's responses," the company offers "automated assessment tools for detecting, diagnosing, and tracking mental health problems" that promise to help busy professionals both "save time and provide better care." The cheerful flipside of Freudian unemployment, what is on offer on the website is a "3 minute psychoanalytic diagnosis that integrates seamlessly into busy clinics."[4]

In spite of his illusions (and his theories) of autonomy, the psychoanalyst, scion of a modernist emancipatory politics of self-knowledge that is now in eclipse, is, we see, determined from without. Victimized by a feeling of scarcity, clinging to his couch, waiting for the phone to ring and the patient to arrive, he is unable to conceive the precariousness of his professional position. Peter Shapiro, a respected senior training analyst (TA) in Chicago, recited to me an account of external determination for the crisis of psychoanalysis, explaining that at bottom, "the crisis is that there are no patients."[5] He went on, "People simply don't want to do the work anymore." Where once psychoanalysis was the successful psychiatrist's mainstay, where once the typical psychoanalyst saw ten or twelve analysands in daily analysis on the couch, now, in the era of psychopharmaceuticals, managed care, and cognitive-behavioral therapy, the talking cure, left behind, engages fewer and fewer new patients in the rigors of years-long introspective treatment. Shapiro's complaint about the marginalization of psychoanalysis is a common one, echoed by many of his colleagues: psychoanalysis is too rigorous for people today; patients want a quick fix, they want symptom relief as opposed to enduring structural change. Since they want to feel better quickly they look to drugs and brief, directive (he calls them "suggestive") therapies, eschewing the hard work of daily introspection on the couch. "But it's people in the field too," Shapiro added. As a TA, Shapiro analyzes people entering the field as trainees for their required training analysis. Most of his patients, in fact, are trainees.[6] "They, too, don't seem to believe in the curative power of insight anymore." Shapiro's younger colleague, John Brandon, echoed this view about patients, adding the observation that to him, "it's a strange situation; the *meaning* of their suffering doesn't seem important to people to understand in the way it used to, even ten or fifteen years ago when I finished my training." Wavering a bit from his senior colleague's certainties, exemplifying his elder's critique of his own generation's uncertainties about psychoanalysis, Brandon went on: "I think this is part of why people are attracted to things like Pilates or yoga or physical training, or even meds—you don't have to think, you just do. I can understand it in a lot of ways. I feel that way myself a lot of the time. Analysis is hard. How it works, if it even works, is so murky and uncertain." Laughing, he paused to add that he couldn't say for sure what he got from his own analysis, let alone what his patients get from him. "From that standpoint," he continued solemnly, "it's no wonder there's such a sense of crisis around what we do." And yet, he went on, "I think we do better work now than we ever have before. We know more about what makes people better than we ever have before." Organized around a dialectic of suffering and desire, Brandon's discourse of complaint, marginality, and ambivalent belonging—of a psychoanalysis menaced and, in his word, "bashed" by external forces—is complemented by his optimism about the powers of psychoanalysis, about a psychoanalysis that works better than ever before, about a "posttheoretical renaissance of practice."

The Lacanian social theorist Todd Dufresne has commented that in the great volume of Freud-bashing that has appeared during the recent period of crisis of psychoanalysis, it "has been undeniably constructive in its self-destruction" (Dufresne 2003, 164). In the various genres of academic and popular antipsychoanalytic approbation that Dufresne tracks—as, indeed, in the worlds of popular culture that Slavoj Žižek psychoanalyzes (see, e.g., Žižek 2009)—Freud's is the death that seems to keeps on giving. Psychoanalysis is alive and well in popular culture precisely *in* its crisis, yet it has virtually disappeared as an actual clinical practice. (Dufresne cites a wonderful example of psychoanalysis's life in popular culture, an automobile ad in which Freud asks, "Vat does viman want?" and receives the knowing answer "Zero percent financing" [164].) John Brandon, to give just one example, has had only one patient in psychoanalysis since his graduation from training fifteen years ago—and it is the same patient. Nonetheless, in the professional world that Brandon and Shapiro inhabit, their shared, profound concern with the precarity of psychoanalysis, with its very conditions of possibility, is attended by what would seem to be a contradictory discourse of psychoanalytic potency. In the face of Brandon's self-doubt and his senior colleague's depiction of their field's crisis, his confidence and optimism about psychoanalysis's efficacy poses an interesting question. How might one understand their vigorous inhabitance of, and indeed expansion of, a set of earlier-institutionalized professional categories and privileges that are no longer objectively salient in the wider world of health care? How and why, in the face of a broad corporate-state-consumer demand for rationalization and accountability in health care, does a community of psychoanalytic practice and argumentation inhabit and expand on its own contrary demands, desires, fantasies, and fetishes?

"Crisis" is a central category of psychoanalysts' reflection on psychoanalysis and a recurrent mode of both explanation and experience that remains undertheorized by psychoanalysts themselves. Freud projected his movement as embattled and persecuted from its very beginning, yet despite the venerability of this theme in the history of psychoanalysis, its historicity disappears in uses like Shapiro's, where the crisis of the profession appears, unproblematized, as merely descriptive of its current external circumstances, as simply a natural effect of larger, external forces compressing their high modern cultural practice into virtual oblivion.[7] My aim in this chapter is to move beyond practitioners' descriptive understanding and to get at the way crisis is reproduced as an epistemological category with practical effects on the organization of social life. The chapter examines the crisis of psychoanalysis, therefore, as simultaneously a category in a discursive formation, a mode of subjective experience, and a social and material process of change in a social field. It delineates the work of crisis and of psychoanalysts' para-ethnographic notion of an ever "widening scope" for psychoanalytic treatment.[8] Specifically, I track how a situation of scarcity created a culture of employment characterized by a specifically psychoanalytic purgatory, a zone of work in which unregulated therapeutic activities proliferated alongside attempts at their regulation. In discussing the regulation and deregulation of psychoanalysis and the professional field occupied by Shapiro and Brandon, I unbraid three strands of the history of its construction of crisis today: the profession's evolving relationship with health insurance, its historically medical status in the United States, and its practical and symbolic division of labor through the better part of the twentieth century.

I COUNT, THEREFORE I AM (BARELY): *Crisis, Enumerated*

Peter Shapiro's and John Brandon's observations about the crisis of psychoanalysis are quantified in a set of statistics derived from a series of practice surveys taken among members of the American Psychoanalytic Association. Rendering the crisis quantitatively in terms of the sheer number of patients in analysis with members has been an increasing preoccupation of the organization's leadership since the early 1990s and the subject of a series of devices aiming objectively to describe the situation of members like Peter Shapiro and John Brandon and their colleagues, Mark Tracy, Norman Peters, and Carrie Janis, whose stories will unfold in the next chapter. They fill out these surveys and then, in turn, cite them as explanatory of their situation.

These practice surveys define psychoanalysis on the basis of the number of sessions conducted with a patient per week. Session frequency is a key criterion on which an institute's affiliation with the APsaA turns, and the Association requires that individuals trained in its approved institutes see their TA at a frequency of four or five sessions per week, just as trainees are required to see their own "control cases" four or five times per week for these cases to count toward graduation from training. When the surveys ask members about the number of cases they have "in analysis," this is what they mean; a lesser frequency means that a treatment is expressly *not* psychoanalysis but rather psychotherapy (which is not counted).[9] Surveying the field through such forced choice questionnaires and contrastively marking psychoanalysis and psychotherapy based on session frequency forces a positive, quantitative definition of psychoanalysis. Using this system of accounting to describe the crisis, the APsaA's finding is that more patients translates into a stronger "psychoanalytic identity" for the analyst. The surveys build on an earlier finding (see Brauer et al. 2008; Gann 2002) that the "professional satisfaction" of members is a direct function of the number of patients one sees in psychoanalysis.

The most recent statistics tell members that the average number of patients their colleagues who fill out surveys see per week in psychoanalysis is 3.27, a figure indicating a steady, long-term trend of decline of approximately 1 percent per year with 1976 as a baseline. A local version of this survey in Chicago puts this number at 2.4 (Shelby and Duvall 2009). In 1976 the mean number of patients analysts saw in psychoanalysis, defined in terms of four or five sessions a week, was 4.76. The organization's summary report of the 2006 survey results states that today's numbers are misleading with respect to the gravity of the crisis, for they are not accurately representative of the situation of the majority of members (see Brauer et al. 2008; see also Gann 2002). The crisis is more dire than the numbers suggest, for, broken out by *category* of membership, TAs—a minority of members at 24 percent of the organization's census—have a substantially greater number of patients in analysis than do either certified analysts (those with the additional credential to become TAs but without the requisite number of hours of *immersion* in psychoanalytic work to qualify for this status) or the majority of members, the regular graduate analysts. Trainees, those aspiring to become psychoanalysts, are the one guaranteed pool of patients. Since a training analysis is a requirement of training, and since TAs are the only psychoanalysts who can analyze trainees, they have monopoly access to the internal market. This insulates them to some degree from the more general problem of scarcity in the field. In 1990, the mean number of patients in analysis with TAs was 5.77, while it was 3.89 for certified analysts and 3.29 for regular members; by 2006 these numbers had dropped to 4.30 for TAs, 2.95 for certified analysts, and 2.72 for the majority of the membership (Brauer et al. 2008).[10]

The crisis is also enumerated in terms of the declining number of trainees. Not only is the number of patients in general dropping, applicants for training, too, are fewer—as well as older, more predominantly female, and more likely to be trained in psychology or in social work than in medicine. Only M.D.s could become psychoanalysts in the institutes of the APsaA up until the 1989 settlement of "the lawsuit," as it is known, the legal action challenging this restriction.[11] After this watershed event the demographics of trainees shifted, and classes at the psychoanalytic institutes began increasingly to be filled with members of the other professions. At the Chicago Institute, to give one example, the disciplinary numbers shifted rapidly after 1989: in the 1990s thirty-two M.D.s and twelve non-M.D.s completed training; in contrast, in the ten years from 2000–2010, twenty-five non--M.D.s and twenty M.D.s did so.[12]

As Peter continued his list of grievances, he told me, "We aren't attracting the best and brightest today, and it's not just their [disciplinary] background; the candidates today are sicker." Patients, too, he holds, are sicker now than when he trained, a shift that he implies is symptomatic of the "wider scope" of psychoanalytic practice today and the fact that those who seek psychoanalysis today have often failed in other treatment efforts. For Peter and others of his generation, those who trained in the 1960s and 1970s, a crisis of institutional reproduction has dominated the field ever since the 1989 lawsuit, and it is one that has hamstrung the profession in interminable battles over who can be an analyst and, even more bitterly, over who can be a TA. "Any other profession is proud to have an elite," he says, "and yet we are not supposed to have members who are more distinguished than other members? How would we survive if we didn't have a group who we consider masters of the trade, who define how it is supposed to be done?" The image of the empty couch thus complements that of the empty, degraded classroom, as organizational imperative and nostalgic complaint dovetail in this preoccupation with bad numbers.

The survey numbers bear out—and traffic in—these anxieties about the institutional reproduction of psychoanalysis and about the production of psychoanalytic value. In the 1950s and 1960s the average trainee was in his early thirties and was a male M.D. newly out of psychiatric residency. the average candidate in 2008, in contrast, is a forty-nine-year-old, significantly experienced, midcareer female psychotherapist coming to her psychoanalytic training less for a core credential than for further professional development. She is more likely to be a psychologist or social worker than an M.D. Shapiro said, "These people are—some of them—very sensitive therapists, but how can they diagnose a medical condition that is giving rise to the patient's symptoms?" Prior to the lawsuit, almost 100 percent of those trained as psychoanalysts were, like him, psychiatrists. In the period between 1996 and 2002, 37 percent of individuals admitted for training were psychologists, 13.4 percent were social workers, and only 41.6 percent were M.D.s. And the age of non-M.D. applicants entering training was significantly higher than the age of medical applicants during this period: M.D.s were, on average, 39.9 years old on matriculation, psychologists 45.7, and social workers 48.7. (This concern is additionally significant to the APsaA's organization health, since "emeritus" members are no longer dues-paying.)[13]

The crisis of succession that troubled Peter Shapiro has further developed in the past five years. Whereas over the previous twenty or so years this motif of deskilling that he drew on has centered on the field's absorption of the other, lower status mental health professions—in essence its demedicalization and feminization—now, he told me, "we have to worry about people who aren't even social workers, let alone M.D.s, who want to call themselves analysts." He was referring to movements in several states to regulate psychoanalysis as a master's level (as opposed to doctoral level) profession. Three states so far, New York, New Jersey, and Vermont, have begun granting a separate professional license in psychoanalysis, wholly distinct from the licenses granted to members of the existing mental health professions. He told me, "This is exactly what I predicted. Now everyone wants to get ahold of the title of psychoanalyst, and we have no way of stopping it. You laugh, but the barbarians are inside the gate."[14]

Peter's despair about the transformation of psychoanalysis at the hands of not only nonmedical but, even worse, non–clinically trained individuals is seconded by Sheila Gray, a founder of the Consortium—an organization that draws together the four largest psychoanalytic organizations in the United States to develop guidelines for psychoanalytic education—who writes that it is imperative that "we," the members of the Consortium, band together with the state in an umbrella of other "mainstream" psychoanalytic organizations in order to fight for the exclusive privilege to accredit psychoanalysts, since several other accrediting bodies have now arisen to offer independent credentials to practitioners trained in a penumbra of different practices "we" would scarcely call psychoanalytic.[15] Shapiro's and Gray's comments about the deskilling of mainstream psychoanalysis demonstrate an anxious concern that psychoanalysis divorced from the mental health disciplines will have no hope of maintaining any purchase whatsoever in health care.

Another crisis of commensuration, meanwhile, worries would-be psychoanalytic entrepreneurs, like Bob Bosch, who concern themselves with the relation of psychoanalysis to the disciplinary languages of evidence-based psychology. "We have to operationalize our concepts if we want to function in the real world. We need to start speaking the language of evidence-based psychology," he told me, pointing to an American Psychological Association (APA) publication on the desk in his office (the APA had deemed 2000–2010 the "Decade of Behavior") and citing the plethora of new studies that translate psychoanalysis into the terms of empirical research (see Shedler 2002). Historically, many psychoanalysts have viewed quantitative and behavioral research with disdain, seeing efforts to study observable behavior as trivializing and as reductive of the richness and complexity of the psychoanalytic exploration of the inner depths of subjectivity. Now a veritable industry of writings by psychologist-analysts seeks to render psychoanalysis in positive terms and to demonstrate its efficacy in the languages of controlled trials, Q-sorts, chi analyses, and dose-response relationships. Glen Gabbard, a prominent author, writes that we are "faced with a demand for research efforts that demonstrate the efficacy of psychoanalysis to prevent it from disappearing entirely" (1999, n.p.). Robert Wallerstein (2002b, 1247) urges the profession to "strengthen the credibility of psychoanalysis as a science of mind, amenable to growth through empirical research in accord with the canons of scientific method," while Peter Fonagy (1999, 196) notes an imperative to produce such research given that "we live in a culture where a form of treatment that is 'without substantial evidence' may well be thought of as 'without substantial value.'"[16]

These mounting concerns about the crisis of psychoanalysis evidence the psychoanalytic community's deepening ambivalence toward neoliberal regulation, with its simultaneous allure and repulsion, containing as it does both a promise of survival by adaptation to a hostile world and—at the same time—a threat of subjective dissolution and betrayal of an ideal. Enumerating psychoanalysis in these ways, surveyors and researchers act as if psychoanalysis is decidable. Analysts respond accordingly, filling in questionnaires that ask about frequency and number, reinforcing the idea of a quantifiable positivity for the talking cure. As techniques of reduction, the surveys lend themselves to audit culture, and, through the performativity of this reordering by the numbers, a homogenizing regulatory power expands. One kind of reality is replaced with another, seemingly more transparent. Such practices of commensuration and boundary-making address, incite, and circulate an imaginary of scarcity where the desiring professional longs for something to which she has no access—something she attempts to stabilize by translation into other, more powerfully legitimated disciplinary languages.

INSURING THE PURITY OF PRACTICE: *Code-Switching and Practicing without a Trace*

We used to define denial as a primitive or early defense mechanism by which an individual unconsciously repudiates some or all of the meaning of an event; the ego thus avoids awareness of some painful aspect of reality and so diminishes anxiety or other painful affects. Now, in the words of the *Aronson Managed Care Dictionary*, denial is a process whereby a managed care organization cannot recommend payment of a claim for services.—Paul W. Mosher, "Managed Care for the Perplexed"

On its face, today's "crisis" appears overdetermined by the millennial consolidation of industrial biomedicine that has amply been documented by medical sociologists and historians of neoliberalism (see, e.g., Mechanic 2007; Stevens 1998). Over the past two decades, health-care industrialization has shifted flows of capital and other forms of value from individual private purveyors of socio- and psychotherapies to corporate purveyors of insurance products and pharmaco-therapies, with their widely advertised promises of cheap, quick, rational, empirically validated, evidence-based treatments. American psychiatry has been corporatized during this period, the "personal problems" domain over which it claimed jurisdiction from roughly 1930 to the mid-1970s definitively biologized and behaviorized, as risk management languages of accountability, optimization, and quantification have taken hold across medicine.[17] Rapid and hegemonic yet at the same time contingent and contested, this industrialization is reflected as much in pharmaceutical advertisements that promise rapid relief for depression and affect consumer demand for medications as in counterhegemonic para-clinical practices like switching insurance codes to get a higher reimbursement rate for one's work, as much in the profusion of secondary markets for drugs as in the changed time-valuation of the clinical "hour" by both patients and doctors.

John Brandon's nervousness about the "murkyness" and untranslatability of psychoanalysis—its failure to produce the hegemonic kind of scientific evidence—is symptomatic of the changes in the legal, regulatory, and market structures that organize the conduct of behavioral health in EBM.

John himself wonders the inevitable: does psychoanalysis do something therapeutically beneficial that can be empirically validated in these terms? As the third party mediation of medical work-processes has encroached on the phenomenal purity of the face-to-face clinician-patient relation through utilization reviews, quality control audits, pay-for-performance reimbursement algorithms and the like, "denial," formerly a property of the profession—a cultic epistemic object, as it were—has migrated under corporate control. Stripped of its majesty, it is now merely an economic device wielded to enhance the fungibility of health-care dollars, and Paul Mosher, in his satirical tract "Managed Care for the Perplexed," gives dark, comic-theological weight to this resignification (Mosher 1999). Alluding to the famous twelfth-century guide of the great Jewish philosopher and medical doctor Maimonides, Mosher depicts the psychoanalyst today as minoritized, persecuted, and in exile; the demedicalized, re-Judaicized psychoanalyst no longer owns his own work—or even his own lexicon.

One can only understand these shifts in terms of a conjuncture of factors and events. For the first half of the twentieth century, most psychiatric patients paid for the psychiatrist's services out of pocket, so psychiatrists were not generally accountable to any third parties (Horwitz 2003, 38–56; Mayes and Horwitz 2005, 255). Organized psychoanalysis first threw in its lot with insurance after World War II, in an era when state and private employers provided generous health benefits, and for several decades the insurance industry and government programs funded psychoanalysis because it was the only treatment for anxiety and depression that was available. During the 1960s, many medical insurance plans had begun to include mental health coverage, and private insurance paid for about one-quarter of outpatient treatment; in the 1960s the Federal Employees Health Benefits Program, underwritten by Aetna and Blue Cross, reimbursed psychiatric care dollar for dollar with other medical treatments. During the 1970s, the rate of private insurance coverage for outpatient treatment continued to rise, and Medicaid and Medicare also became major sources of payment for therapy. Insurance companies quickly came to view psychotherapies as a financial bottomless pit that would require potentially uncontrollable resources, since patients could spend years in therapy. The Blue Cross vice president Robert J. Laur summarized the views of many third party payers in 1975: "Compared to other types of services there is less clarity and uniformity of terminology concerning mental diagnoses, treatment modalities, and types of facilities providing care. . . . One dimension of this problem arises from the latent or private nature of many services; only the patient and the therapist have direct knowledge of what services were provided and why" (cited in Mayes and Horwitz 2005, 253). Neither policy nor industry maneuvers to allow medicine to audit and regulate itself succeeded in trimming expenditures, and already by the mid-1970s Aetna had cut back mental health coverage to twenty outpatient visits. By the 1980s, with costs in medicine exploding and numerous new and more seemingly cost-effective pharmacological treatments for anxiety and depression emerging, psychiatry's earlier mandate to run its own economic affairs ran out. Employers scuttled expensive indemnity insurance plans in favor of the new risk-management products of managed care. Postwar welfarist assumptions about the need to expand health care were also reversed during this period as policy makers, insurers, and pharmaceutical manufacturers all discovered that certain treatments were financial losers while others were winners. As medicine defaulted to the market, psychoanalysis was one of the major losers.

During the 1970s and 1980s, managed care organizations (MCOs) took over the medical marketplace, promising to diminish deductibles, limit demand-side cost-sharing mechanisms (i.e., patient co-pays), and control costs. The first MCOs limited mental health coverage relative to general medical coverage, but when the 1996 Mental Health Parity Act mandated that mental health benefits offered by employers and insurers be on a par with physical health benefits in both dollar limits and reimbursement rates, MCOs rushed to augment their medical contracts with separate mental health and substance abuse (MHSA) contracts with managed behavioral health organizations (MBHOs). These "carve-out" firms provided specialized mental health coverage at a great discount, and they remained legally and administratively apart from the firms managing general medical care. Management of MHSA care by MBHOs has since become common in both the public and private health-care sectors (Grazier and Eselius 1999). Under this system, an employer, health plan, or Medicaid or Medicare program contracts with a single MBHO to administer all necessary MHSA care to enrollees. The rapid change away from the fee-for-service arrangement of indemnity insurance and toward "specialty care" through MBHOs has been driven by the robust finding of health-care economists that MBHOs reduce mental health spending by as much as 40 percent.[18]

Since MBHOs assume all of the costs of both inpatient and outpatient MHSA care for the MCOs with which they have contracts, they have strong financial incentives to limit services, reduce "medically unnecessary" spending, and enforce provider accountability. Many MBHO plans retain responsibility for prescription drug costs, adding additional financial incentives to encourage the use of pharmaceutical treatments, since these then do not appear on the MCO's budget. Enrolling providers in closed networks, capitating their fees, incentivizing the use of pharmaceuticals, and then linking the costs of inpatient and outpatient MHSA care under contractual payment structures has further encouraged the substitution of inexpensive outpatient services for more costly hospitalization and long-term treatments ("very long episodes of outpatient care" in the 2010 Patient Protection and Affordable Care Act, popularly known as Obamacare), generating additional corporate profits. Finally, MBHOs have generated further profit by linking patients' use of these health services to clinical algorithms, information technologies, pay-for-performance tools, and other forms of selective contracting (prepaid group practices, for instance)—on top of unabashedly reducing people's benefits and obstructing their access to them.

The dominant tool for implementing the corporate medical model in the MHSA domain has been the classification system of the *Diagnostic and Statistical Manual of Mental Disorders* (DSM), which psychoanalysts and other mental health workers use alongside the American Medical Association's procedure codes (current procedural terminology [CPT] codes), fractionation tools by which insurers can count and commensurate "medical episodes" by time spent and procedure conducted. Competing representations of mental suffering have consolidated around the DSM's touted atheoretical—yet nonetheless medical—taxonomy of mental disorders, composed of discrete and (what the DSM's authors dub) purely descriptive categories of debility.[19] As an instrument of commensuration, the DSM allows diverse parties to tally unlike values—forms of suffering become diagnoses, forms of helping become coded services—for transactions along idealized, frictionless exchange surfaces. If critics view the DSM as the apotheosis of medical neoliberalism, the insurance industry promotes it as a neutral, descriptive medium that diverse parties can use in forming contracts for services, allowing for greater accountability in MHSA. Psychoanalysts, psychiatrists, social workers, psychologists, cognitive therapists, family therapists, psychiatric nurses, and internists alike can use the same coding system for the commodified medical services they provide, while the burgeoning specialties of researchers and administrators—case managers, utilization reviewers, insurance auditors, and administrative psychotherapists—can survey and monitor the field of exchanges.

Whereas DSM II maintained a place for psychoanalytic diagnosis—diagnosis based on underlying psychological dynamics thought to lead to suffering—DSM III expressly shifted the classification of psychopathology from a "depth" view of psychiatric symptoms to a frankly behavioral, descriptive, categorical view of human suffering as a matter of discrete diseases. The rise of third party payers contributed to pressures to change the approach to classification because the qualitative continua and the symbolic mechanisms of psychoanalysis did not fit an insurance logic that would only allow payment for the treatment of discrete diseases in discrete episodes. The DSM III removed the quintessentially psychoanalytic diagnosis *neurosis*, as well as developmental or adaptive psychopathology, from its purview altogether, since these implied a theoretical perspective. The DSM IV pushed psychoanalytic diagnosis and depth psychology out of the system altogether (Mayes and Horwitz 2005).

At issue for health-care professionals in general, not least for psychoanalysts, has been the matter of their autonomy, defined as their power to keep their relationships with patients relatively unmediated by outside parties. With the increasing involvement of both government programs and private insurance companies, the economic basis of the therapeutic relationship has become increasingly mediated. Corporate and state interests have demanded diagnoses and treatments that are demonstrably effective and financially accountable, and outpatient care in office settings, the primary venue for most psychotherapies, has come under attack as ineffective, unaccountable, and wasteful. Health-care conglomerates and multinational pharmaceutical companies thus have reconfigured earlier-established relationships among professionals (now "providers"), patients (now "consumers"), companies, universities, private training institutions, and the state in order to privilege themselves. These changes have succeeded in downgrading the formerly privileged, relatively unmediated, "real" and "private" relations between patients and those who take care of them.

Cast by psychoanalysts as traditional, an image of their autonomy and of the privacy of their relations with patients is self-evidently a nostalgic ideal that John Brandon and Peter Shapiro share, a reaction to the growing imperialism over the course of the twentieth century of a vision of medicine in which the doctor can act on the patient's behalf to the degree to which the patient's body can be integrated into the webs of technology that constitute him as a member of a health population and, as such, as visible and tractable to medicine. Until the 1980s, doctors' organizations were able to leverage this (modern) image of the traditional—and strictly clinical—doctor-patient bond to create expert enclosures that allowed them to hold onto their strategic position as gatekeepers, to avoid subordination to corporate interests, and to maintain their practices despite escalating costs. No doubt they could do this in part because patient dependency, thence allegiance, made professional mediation in financial exchanges over the payment for care seem indispensable.[20] Beginning in the 1980s, non–medically trained case managers and utilization reviewers, using the discourses and accounting techniques of health economics, began to assume prerogatives to make decisions over such matters. As governmentality theorist Nikolas Rose has written, "management, mathematics, and monetarisation were to tame the wild excesses of a governmental complex in danger of running out of control." These managers and reviewers' collective judgment—based on large-scale, randomized, triple-blind, "horse-race" style clinical trials—was that psychoanalysis was neither "empirically validated" nor "evidence-based" nor, above all, cost-effective (Rose and Miller 1992). In contrast, the growing volume of findings in the new, quasi-academic field of health services research indicated, on the same epistemic grounds of large-scale trials on "health populations," the relative efficacy (not to mention the greater cost-effectiveness) of pharmaceuticals and short-term cognitive-behavior therapies in treating such psychoanalytic mainstays as depression, anxiety, and obsessive-compulsive disorder.

Psychoanalysts overall take issue with this kind of proof and this epistemic universe. Their stance is that people are not only biological systems but growing beings with complex internal worlds of meaning that cannot readily be captured in large-scale trials. For them, even in instances where drugs *are* helpful, the drugs aren't seen as bringing about emotional growth and meaningful change, just the capacity for sufficient calm to ground the work of looking inward to gain insight and grow psychologically. Nonetheless, psychoanalysts have had to find ways to negotiate with insurance companies that will allow them to preserve their practices and their sense of autonomy. They have sought, in effect, to fit into the system somehow. When insurance paid for psychoanalysis, psychoanalysts accepted insurance; now that insurance does not pay, or does not pay much, most psychoanalysts have attempted to avoid joining the insurance system as "in-network" (or "preferred") providers. If they are able to establish themselves in working referral networks, most decline solicitations to list themselves on insurance panels in an effort to retain the ability to set their own fees and in an effort to reduce the involvement of third parties in the content of their work. Those who are for one reason or another less able to establish themselves in collegial referral networks join insurance panels and become in-network, accepting reduced fees and utilization auditing so as to maintain their practices. Others simply cut their fees in direct negotiation with patients who, they know, can, but for the patient's dependency within the relationship, go elsewhere. Others still accept "out-of-network" payments and write off patient co-pays so as to maintain their sense of autonomy. They want to maintain themselves in what they think of as private practice, so they dance around to preserve being both in and outside the insurance system at one and the same time, providing their patients with billing statements that have DSM and CPT codes on them that the patients can themselves submit for out-of-network benefits.

Many find themselves pulled into perplexing, often unwitting contractual arrangements with corporate entities, arrangements that come into being in a variety of ways, such as by cashing insurance checks that have come to them instead of their patients, or by requesting electronic information online. Penny Gould, one of the Chicago analysts I interviewed, described having received phone messages from a representative of a subsidiary of Aetna called Global Claims Services. They wanted her fax number so that they could fax her what she said they called a settlement offer, hoping to persuade her to accept less than half the amount she had billed. They described themselves as—she showed me a letter from this company—"a cost containment company that specializes in repricing claims and negotiating payment agreements between payers and providers." If Penny had agreed to the "repricing" offer—and they promised to send her a check right away if she did—she would have thereafter been bound by contract to accept whatever amount Aetna paid out, regardless of her usual fee. She said that later that same week a patient had asked about whether she had gotten the promised check from her insurance company, the patient having received a voicemail message saying that his doctor was out of compliance with the plan's benefit limits. "But I never signed a contract," Penny vituperated as she described this scenario. "Yes, I'm 'out-of-network,' so my billing is completely between me and my patient. And now my patient is in the position of being told I'm out of compliance?! It's obvious how this kind of thing undermines the transference, so it comes into the analysis in these menacing ways when one isn't expecting it." Note that Penny had given her patient a bill with insurance codes on it, even though she did not herself send it to the insurance company. She is "out-of-network," but she has willingly placed herself in the DSM system she complains about nonetheless. Penny uses her story of the insurance company's insinuating itself between her and her patient to demonstrate how these new and multifarious forms of "denial"—repricing offers, settlement offers, blind contracts—add up to the same thing: an increasingly negative proportion between her own productivity and the insurance company's profit.

Carrie Janis, another Chicago analyst, similarly described her solicitation over the phone by a company called SubmitPatientForms, whose stream of brochures cheerily announced that they are "an Internet service that allows medical practices to have an unlimited number of patients fill out their HIPAA form, personal/insurance information and medical histories online (for a low price of $49/month). If desired, for a one-time setup fee of $995, a doctor's original custom forms can be converted to SubmitPatientForm's software. Once submitted, the forms are available in four formats for downloading to practice management software—PDF, Excel, JPEG and TIFF. You no longer have to scan any forms!" SubmitPatientForms offered in this friendly, upbeat tone to provide a helpful service to clinicians who wanted to reduce their administrative tasks. However, these conveniences, Carrie went on to say, were double-edged because they got the clinician "into stuff way outside the relationship with the person in front of [her]." She added, "That *can't* be good for her therapy, even if it *might* save me a few hours a month, or a few headaches." Like Penny, she emphasized how these new technologies of insurance interfered in the one-on-one relation between patient and clinician, although she emphasized the damage this interference inflicted on the *relationship*, whereas Penny worried about its undermining the *transference*.

Carrie also described another product she felt ambivalent about, a pricey American Medical Association newsletter for "coding professionals" called CPT Assistant, touted as a way to help busy clinicians "appeal insurance denials, validate coding to auditors, train their staff and answer day-to-day coding questions." She needed something to guide her with coding dilemmas, since she felt constantly perplexed about the accuracy of her coding: "It's very discouraging, and I'm thinking I need to take myself off the panels because their values aren't in synch with my own. I don't think its ethical to tell the reviewers I am doing behavioral treatment when I'm not, so I go back and forth about how to handle it and which codes to use for what."

I mentioned to her that I had read a posting on an internet discussion group in which a colleague reacted against people seeing these dilemmas as in any way "ethical" ones. He had written:

Indeed, I am barred from using 90807 as it does not speak to *medical* thinking or *understanding*, but licensure as a physician. It was created after a long debate with the AMA, which creates these unscientifically based codes for proprietary use (profit and market place control), when psychiatrists (for the greater part, NOT psychoanalytic physicians) became concerned that if they used the same codes as doctoral level psychologists their reimbursements might recede as they were doing the same treatment, some of them with far less training in 90806; but with 90807 they felt they would more safely maintain a modicum of financial security vis a vis their *non-medical* counterparts. Since the US diagnostic nomenclature as well as procedure codes are controlled by proprietary organizations who gain great profit in publishing their manuals, and requiring payment for their use (if done properly & legally) and as 501c3s or 6s are exempt from *restraint of trade regulations* rather than a system more scientifically based and in the public domain, as all medical/psychological dx & TX codes should be, it's just hard for me to see how one can have an ethical dilemma in using a code that is neither scientifically derived, nor ethically sound.[21]

I asked Carrie whether she didn't agree with the writer's view that these so-called coding dilemmas were political ones and pertained to power contests between the various professional groups more than to ethics per se. "I struggle with it," she responded, warily, only marginally acknowledging this other perspective. On a given day, she explained, she might engage a patient in a blunt discussion of behavior change, "so I can maybe see coding it that way," but in the subsequent session the discussion might never touch on behavioral change, "so it really does stretch things to call it anything other than insight-oriented." Some people were more comfortable with that than she was, she noted, but she felt it was lying to code a session one way when she knew she was doing something other than what the code was supposed to stand for. Was it that she was afraid of getting caught, I asked her? No, she said, "it's more my internalized sense that it's lying. I try to develop that sense of honesty in my patients and to live by it myself. It's just not something I'm comfortable with." She went on to say that the more genuinely troubling issue for her was an inner conflict over the value of her work; she questioned how much her work really *was* worth when the patient's insurance company valued it at $65, about half of what she charged. "There's no way that doesn't get inside you and make you wonder, deep inside, whether you really are doing something that is helping—especially when it takes so long and the patient is constantly challenging you and voicing this sense they're not getting better." In contrast to Carrie's more resigned perspective, another analyst angrily blogged:

> The way I've experienced the scum-bag insurance companies in [name of state] since MH parity passed, is they ask intrusive questions to see if the treatment is "medically necessary," in which case they give 8 or 10 or 15 sessions, after which more paperwork is required; or is the treatment just "self-improvement," in which case they don't cover. I think the "self-improvement" is their way to deny longterm psychotherapy. As for insight-oriented therapy or psychodynamic psychotherapy, they act like they never heard of it. I won't go into all the shocking aspects of how I was treated during this review. What is important for you to know, is that the reviewer stated outright that the company only covers therapy that sets "specific measurable symptom-focused goals." I said that my treatment method is psychodynamic psychotherapy, which does not focus directly on symptoms. The reviewer referred to psychodynamic psychotherapy as "just talk." I was assigned to consult with the patient's psychiatrist for a referral to a behavioral out-patient intensive eating disorders program.[22]

This person's view is more like that of Norm Peters, whose attitude was typical of many of the M.D.s I interviewed: "Fuck them, I mean I would rather just do medication than deal with that baloney; they don't question medication choices I make, whereas I lift a finger to talk to someone in a way I think is incredibly helpful and all of a sudden my same judgment is in question?!" In any case, the result is a strange one. These analysts insist among one another that they are doing psychoanalysis, but nonetheless they code for psychotherapy because (most) insurance plans will cover psychotherapy (90801) but not psychoanalysis (90845). Note that psychoanalysis has a code of its own, but because it is not an empirically validated treatment for most DSM categories it is not considered sufficiently evidence-based to count as "medically necessary" (which means it is not reimbursable).

Organized psychoanalysis has responded in several ways to the rising hegemony of DSM valuation in corporatized health care and the demands of insurance companies that only empirically validated treatments pegged to DSM diagnoses and CPT codes are to be performed by their contracted providers. One of the APsaA's formal responses to the growing hegemony of EBM has been to produce a series of "practice bulletins." Like the aforementioned practice surveys, the practice bulletins are a way the organization has sought somehow to align the profession with the commensuration practices of EBM. The practice bulletins address the following topics: informed consent, charting, external review of psychoanalysis, appointment records, interacting with third parties, and psychoanalytic clinical assessment (American Psychoanalytic Association 1994, 1996a, 1996b, 1999, 2001, 2003, 2006). These documents, revised several times since first crafted in 1991, address "the proliferation of managed care and other cost containment systems [that have] intensified concern about the effect of ongoing third party claims review on the therapeutic alliance and ultimately on the outcome and effectiveness of a psychoanalytic treatment" (American Psychoanalytic Association 2003).

The practice bulletins evince an ambivalent and at various points contradictory reaction to this proliferation of threat. The Committee on Peer Review asserts that MCO consent forms do not adequately explain the risks to patients posed by third party review, so, they warn, "consent may be considerably less than informed." Yet they nowhere spell out these supposed risks beyond repeatedly asserting that third party review will "degrade" psychoanalytic treatment or that treatment "may end prematurely or may suffer major distortions of the therapeutic alliance." The notion of informed consent itself is not problematized (interestingly, for how can the consumer "choose" psychoanalysis if psychoanalysis deconstructs the consumer's sovereignty?). Similarly, "the APsaA opposes all methods of quality assurance review," since "the psychoanalytic method is uniquely vulnerable to significant alteration or even destruction by the introduction of observers into the psychoanalytic situation," yet, contradictorily, while APsaA recommends that "oversight by 3rd parties should be limited to pre-authorization," the practice bulletins also say that a third party may be engaged to review a treatment to determine the merit of ongoing payment for the treatment when it "extends beyond the usual and customary length as established by statistics." (The document wisely advises that "in some instances, continued subsidy for treatment is not contractually available, in which case the psychoanalyst and patient should recognize that circumstance" [American Psychoanalytic Association 2001, n.p.].)

Documenting the content of a psychoanalysis "seriously alters that treatment process and conflicts with fundamental clinical psychoanalytic skills," so the guidelines recommend that psychoanalysts refrain from creating session-by-session progress notes. Yet in another seeming contradiction the practice bulletins say that documenting the *overall* analysis does not alter the treatment process. "Practice Bulletin No. 6, Interacting with Third Parties," says that "the mean duration of a properly completed psychoanalytic case is approximately 1000 sessions; therefore a psychoanalysis may be considered to extend beyond usual lengths at plus one standard deviation from the mean, or beyond 1575 sessions" (American Psychoanalytic Association 2001, n.p.). These are very precise numbers for a qualitative practice; even though they belie an effort to resist the push of "cost containment systems" to quantify psychoanalysis, they are responding essentially on their terms.

As if their professional and collegial system of valuation were still operative, as if it had not been taken over by the economy of flexible specialization, the APsaA practice bulletins underscore the threat that third party review (as opposed to peer review) will "degrade" the psychoanalytic treatment process and the treatment alliance between doctor and patient.[23] They underscore the importance of peer review versus outsider review. Peer review is "a collegial process conducted in the ambit of a professional organization" whose "ultimate aim is to assure that the professional services are appropriately selected and performed." Peer review would support the notion that "psychoanalysis is a single procedure from start to finish," not a series of discrete medical episodes or encounters. It is "by definition open-ended" and should be viewed, in this sense, "much as one views a surgical operation as a single intervention" (American Psychoanalytic Association 1994, n.p.). The practice bulletins also underscore the importance of not documenting session-by-session progress, for "the damage done to the alliance by the requirement to create notes for external review may be seen as comparable to the contamination risks introduced into a surgical situation if the surgeon were to break aseptic technique by writing chart notes with one hand while performing surgery within the patient's chest cavity with the other" (American Psychoanalytic Association 1994, n.p.). In the very period when psychoanalysis is no longer an exclusively medical profession, these surgical metaphors are striking, harking as they do back to some of Freud's own early language (though Freud himself abandoned the surgical metaphor in his later writing).[24] The implication is that surgery is visibly a science, with observable and measurable results, and psychoanalysis is similarly scientific. While psychoanalysis should not be fractionated by reimbursement technologies that contaminate its surgical purity by allocating payments on a per session basis, the practice bulletins recommend that the CPT code 90845 be used when submitting insurance claims—and, again contradictorily, this is a code for the individual session.

In view of these practice recommendations on how psychoanalysts can best ensure the purity of their practice, the third and fourth of these emphases are perhaps most telling about how insurance "is likely fatally to degrade the psychoanalytic treatment process." The practice bulletins describe the way underwriters, as part of risk management, urge psychoanalysts to keep records that demonstrate that appropriate care was provided to the patient and indicate that the absence of such records may be considered evidence of malpractice. The Committee therefore recommends *against* keeping detailed records (this practice is known in the malpractice world as *negative charting*) because it believes "that documenting the content of a psychoanalysis seriously alters that treatment process and conflicts with fundamental clinical psychoanalytic skills. In addition, since a dynamic recollection of the psychoanalytic interaction reliably exists in the minds of psychoanalysts and patients and can be retrieved as needed, health care charts are not needed for good psychoanalytic care" (American Psychoanalytic Association 1994, n.p.). The "technical features" of the psychoanalytic process directly conflict with the conditions imposed by third party review. Psychoanalytic listening, for one technical feature, involves the creation of a vast database stored in the preconscious or unconscious areas of the clinician's mind, created out of an "evenly hovering attention" that can't be squared "with efforts to select items to be documented." Such selection efforts would distort the process of psychoanalytic attention because the analyst's unconscious mind constantly organizes and reorganizes this database throughout the course of treatment. So, say the recommendations, *any* documentation—because it is selective—will create distortion in the analyst's memory. Only *after* the analysis is over is this unconscious archive subject to the kind of conscious, "secondary process" scrutiny that might be utilized in creating documentation. "We believe this is an absolute problem apart from that of confidentiality" (American Psychoanalytic Association 1994, n.p.). That patient communications are continuously inscribed, organized, and reorganized in the mind of the psychoanalyst derives from the notion of psychoanalysis being a unitary treatment; by definition, one listens neutrally to all of the patient's communications and makes them part of one's own memory. In essence, the practice bulletins locate psychoanalytic evidence firmly beyond the reach of insurance, pushing it deep into the analyst's unconscious mind where it can organize itself without a trace—without, that is, an auditable trace.

Another, related means by which the Committee says that psychoanalysts may resist the subsumption of psychoanalysis into insurance is through maintaining total confidentiality. The secret quality of psychoanalytic communication is explained in the practice bulletins as stemming from a metapsychological precept: that "no analysand succeeds in divesting himself of all defenses unless he can be certain that the derivatives of his id will not become known beyond the analytic situation" (American Psychoanalytic Association 1994, n.p.). Since harm will come to patients' treatment if ever they read any representations of it, patients' urges "to have their analyst champion efforts to obtain subsidy for treatment . . . should be the subject of analysis and not the impetus for collusion in action" (American Psychoanalytic Association 2001, n.p.). The analyst's frame of mind and emotional disposition toward the patient are significant technical considerations, so if there is a chance that the prospect of third party participation might affect these, analysts should avoid third parties altogether because analysts must not enter into any contracts with the expectation that they will not be fully honest in all communications. What is clear throughout these practice bulletins is that psychoanalytic evidence, while organized *beyond* insurance, is nonetheless being organized *in relation* to it, and that terms and practices and ways of understanding psychoanalysis are shaped by the very "other" that the practice bulletins attempt to define the domain of psychoanalysis in opposition to (and, indeed, to resist).

John Brandon explained that he felt that his senior colleagues were confused about all of these matters having to do with managed care and insurance. He quipped that the confusion of senior people as to what to write on insurance forms reminded him of an old joke where a man asks "Is this the line for foreign passports?" The question reflects the man's confusion about the difference between visas and passports, playing on the motif of travel to foreign territory where the rules that hold at home are no longer useful guides. The joke points to a "confusion between the meaning of our procedures to others and to us, with the implicit idea that we'll value our work in currency unknown to us." The unknownness of the currency, the mystification of the exchange rate, is what John and his colleagues are working against. John's explanation highlighted a fear that analysts would undervalue their work with respect to its intrinsic craft worth and a simultaneous fear that they might be overvaluing it based on a growing suspicion among them that their craft is not that valuable in the world anymore.

REGULATING COMMERCE, PURIFYING TECHNIQUE: *Exclusion, Monopoly, and the "Problem" of Lay Analysis*

We doctors could not give it up if we wanted to, because the other party to our methods of healing—namely the patient—has not the slightest intention of doing without it.—Sigmund Freud, quoted in John Forrester, *The Seductions of Psychoanalysis*

The statements discussed in the previous section are essentially defensive, but the defense is crafted in the language of medicine and insurance. Put another way, EBM and insurance have hooked into and brought to the fore a long-standing insecurity in psychoanalysis. It is precisely this definitional anxiety—in what way is psychoanalysis a medical science?—that has shaped the profession's American history.

If the history of psychoanalysis in France or Argentina can be written as the history of a cultural and intellectual movement quite independent of medicine, psychoanalysis in the United States has a thoroughly medical genealogy (Forrester 1990; Gellner 2003; Hale 1995; Luhrmann 2000; Roudinesco 1990; Turkle [1978] 1992). The disciplinary status of psychoanalysis had been a question on Freud's mind as he attempted to manage the institutionalization of his ideas and (ultimately) the matter of his succession; he warned, famously, that bringing psychoanalysis ("the plague") to America would lead to its subsumption into psychiatry and medicine. He insisted instead on its autonomy as a kind of secular care of the soul. In Freud's view, medical training was less the deciding factor in the matter of who could become a psychoanalyst than was a certain psychological outlook and disposition, but from the late 1930s until the 1989 lawsuit, generations of the APsaA's leadership, under the twin banners of preserving standards and making psychoanalysis scientifically respectable, held firm to the view that psychoanalysis was a medical science and that only physicians should practice it.[25] The "1938 rule" of the International Psychoanalytical Association (IPA), passed at the last international congress before World War II, granted the APsaA both an exclusive franchise on training in psychoanalysis in the United States and "total internal autonomy" to determine training standards. This was a unique arrangement, testament to the strength of American doctors in arguing for the strategic necessity, on the eve of war, for the IPA leadership to concede to these doctors' intentions to secure the future of the psychoanalytic movement in the United States.[26] The APsaA was to be the guardian of the movement's rigor and purity, and the APsaA's leaders invoked the 1938 rule to decree that in the United States only physicians could become psychoanalysts.

While defining what counts as psychoanalysis was a key feature of Freudianism from the very start, a particular division of therapeutic labor consolidated in the United States around ego psychology in the 1950s.[27] Freud provided the definition of psychoanalysis, on the grounds of technique, that American ego psychology institutionalized: in "Lines of Advance in the Path of Psychoanalysis," Freud wrote that "the large scale application of our therapy will compel us to alloy the pure gold of analysis freely with the copper of direct suggestion" (Freud 1919, 167). Because of the medical status of this "pure gold," in the United States both psychoanalysis and the mental health professions that were to administer its large-scale application became centrally organized around the question of access to training. At midcentury, during the decades of psychoanalysis's reign at the center of psychiatry and ego psychology's reign at the center of psychoanalysis, the APsaA defined psychoanalysis in sharp contrast to *psychotherapy*. The gold and the silver of Freud's alchemic metaphor were two decidedly different value-producing labor forms. The gold of analysis was reserved for psychiatry, while psychotherapy, the baser derivative, was granted to the penumbra of professions that developed around psychiatry: the social workers, clinical psychologists, psychiatric nurses, teachers, and human resources professionals whom the APsaA designated to *apply* psychoanalytic ideas in psychotherapy for the masses, if not themselves to practice it. Different publics were projected as the recipients of these treatments and different professions as their practitioners. Patients who could afford to come to a psychiatrist four or five times a week and were considered analyzable could be seen in psychoanalysis, while psychotherapy was available for those who either were sicker ("unanalyzable") or could not afford the psychiatrist's fees. Since psychotherapy was conducted at a lesser frequency and by a less elite professional, it was less costly and could be made more available.

Under the gold/alloy vision of psychoanalysis's exceptionalism that the APsaA institutionalized in the United States in a multitiered training system ("full" training in psychoanalysis for psychiatrists, "applied" training in psychotherapy for the auxiliary professions), Heinz Hartmann, Jacob Arlow, Charles Brenner, Merton Gill, Leo Rangell, Robert Knight, David Rapaport, and their students systematized Freud's structural model, the model of id, ego, and superego.[28] Psychoanalytic institutes around the country embraced their brand of ego psychology. (This is the psychoanalysis that registered in pop culture from Hollywood to *Mad Men*, and versions of it linger in corners of the profession as "classical" psychoanalysis.) In ego psychology, the distinction between psychoanalysis and psychotherapy turned on an understanding of language that privileged reference over pragmatics.[29] A paradigmatic statement of the psychoanalysis/psychotherapy distinction can be found in Kurt Eissler's famous 1953 paper "The Effect of the Structure of the Ego on Psychoanalytic Technique."[30] Eissler's definition of psychoanalysis was based on a distinction between cure by what he called "interpretation alone" and cure by the use of what he called "parameters." Parameters were "non-interpretive" interventions by the analyst, by which he meant such things as reassurance, advice, support, behavioral guidance, face-to-face discussion, direct suggestion, and the like. Interpretations, in contrast, were finely crafted propositions about the patient's "intrapsychic" functioning and its roots in his history.[31] The use of parameters Eissler deemed *manipulation* of the transference, as opposed to the interpretive *analysis* of the transference.

The patient who could be analyzed via the model technique was a high-functioning person with a normal ego, usually a professional, someone who was capable of a contained "therapeutic regression" to earlier emotional themes. This regression would be induced through the use of daily—or nearly daily—sessions. He was someone who was capable of making "maximal use of the insight which is conveyed to him" (Eissler 1953, 115). The normal ego, Eissler quoted Freud as saying, "is one which would guarantee unswerving loyalty to the analytic compact" (120). The analyst would be for the most part silent, a blank screen for the patient's projections, and the treatment would be conducted under conditions of "privation and in a state of abstinence." The rationale for abstinence, in Freudian drive theory, was that (the analyst's) deprivation of (the patient's) drive satisfaction was necessary to facilitate the emergence into consciousness of the patient's repressed instinctual wishes. These would emerge over time in his associative material and, through the analyst's interpretive work around these repressed wishes and the patient's growing insight about his functioning, the patient would be freed to achieve sublimation or renunciation.[32]

Patients who could not tolerate the blank screen approach and the stringent *techne* of interpretation alone—those who needed more warmth, reassurance, or direction from the doctor—should, for the most part, be seen in psychotherapy instead. Since they were already regressed in their real-life functioning, frequent sessions would be inappropriate for them.[33] In Eissler's words, this kind of patient cannot use interpretation because he cannot surrender to the voice of reason. He "behaves like someone who has in his grasp all the riches of the world but who refuses to take them and must be forced to do so" through a more directive procedure (Eissler 1953, 116). By giving pride of place to "interpretation alone" Eissler was attempting to isolate the most potent, most valuable element in Freudian technique, as well as to distinguish this technique from the mutations he and other self-consciously orthodox leaders of the APsaA associated with their contemporary Franz Alexander, in Chicago. The ego psychologists found Alexander's approach of giving the patient encouragement and advice anathema, frank manipulation, and they routinely dubbed it unanalytic (Eissler 1950).

The concept of analyzability that Eissler and others embraced was first introduced by Elizabeth Zetzel, one of the most authoritative representatives of ego psychology in the United States. Though she viewed analyzability as theory free, it turned on concepts specific to ego psychology. In order to be analyzable, the patient had to have adequately negotiated the pre-Oedipal phases of development and to be able to establish an Oedipal transference neurosis in the analytic situation. Zetzel deemed patients who had not done this to be, in essence, unanalyzable.[34] Analyzability depended on two capacities of the patient, understood to be the signal developmental achievements of the earlier, pre-Oedipal stage: the capacity to trust and the capacity to distinguish reality from fantasy. Translated into clinical terms, these added up to the patient's ability to form with the analyst a "therapeutic alliance" and then, on the basis of this, to allow a transference to develop. The therapeutic alliance was the basic, real, underlying relationship formed between the patient and the analyst; the transference, in contrast, was the special structure of fantasies that the patient projected onto the analyst, the symbolic material the analyst was to interpret. Zetzel's starting point was the idea that pre-Oedipal object relations were of a dyadic type (Mommy and me), as opposed to the more advanced triadic object relations of the Oedipal phase of development (Mommy, Daddy, and me as one triangular relation). These "phases," understood to unfold sequentially, corresponded to the periods from birth to age three or four, and then from age three or four to age six. By definition, what had failed in the neurotic's development was the resolution of the triangular, Oedipal situation—the "family romance" of the child who wishes to compete with the same-sex parent for the love of the opposite-sex parent but to retain the love of both despite these conflicting passions. The child's anxiety about the imagined consequences of his Oedipal wishes (e.g., castration, loss of love) and his erecting of defenses against this anxiety led to the development of neurotic character. The textbook neurotic, whether a hysteric (usually female) or an obsessional (usually male), suffered from "Oedipal level" difficulties with inhibition, sexual frigidity, passivity, compulsiveness, guilt, and the like— despite a general capacity to function well in life. Unlike "unanalyzable" narcissistic and borderline characters, a patient of this kind could "split" his ego into an observing part and an experiencing part.[35] The observing part of his ego could develop a trusting, reality-based therapeutic alliance with the analyst; the experiencing part, in contrast, could experience the Oedipal wishes and conflicts anew in the transference, with the analyst experienced in terms of the faulty logic of the child. Over the course of analysis, through the analyst's steadfast interpretation of the patient's transference neurosis, the patient could be helped to find new, nonneurotic solutions to his emotional difficulties and to resolve the Oedipal situation at last.

To the ego psychologists, analyzable psychopathology was a pathology of intrapsychic conflict, not a pathology of ego abnormality, and expertise in the treatment of the conflictual relations of id, ego, and superego was a matter of skill in interpretation. The ego psychologists were ambivalent, even pessimistic, about the "direct" molding of the patient's psyche via interpersonal influence. The idea was that other sorts of therapies imposed prescriptions on the patient, impinging in this way on his freedom, whereas "interpretation alone," in its (supposed) austerity, merely *exposed* what was already there in the archive of memory, the patient's conflicts and defenses. In this imagining of what took place between doctor and patient in psychoanalysis, the here-and-now historical relationship between the doctor and the patient could be parsed out from the transference. The analyst's biographical person could be seen as largely irrelevant to the process; he was a blank screen for the patient's projections, master of the technique of evenly hovering attention, able to interpret the Oedipal neurosis from a vantage point of neutral authority. The analyst, unimplicated in what unfolded, could stand outside and merely survey and interpret the scene. From this authoritative place, he could read the analysand's projections unambiguously; through his training analysis, the analyst could eradicate his own "countertransference" and see without distortion what the patient distorted. This skill was cast in medical terms: the analyst was like a surgeon who, consequent on his successful training analysis, could calibrate his "analyzing instrument," his attention, to the neutrality required in proper technique.[36] Parameters and other unanalytic techniques were only to be used with those patients whose deficits prevented their being able to tolerate this model technique. Otherwise unanalyzable, these sicker patients, while theoretically interesting, belonged to what Eissler's colleague Leo Stone dubbed the widening scope of psychoanalysis.

RISING RESIDUALS / CHARISMA REDIVIVUS: *The (Medical) "Problem" of Lay Analysis and Its (Legal) Solution*

The same period saw the consolidation of a formation of lower paid, less skilled, largely female mental health workers taking up positions in hospital and community settings around the country, working under psychiatrists, and their exposure to psychoanalysis in these environs tapped into the upwardly mobile aspirations of many of them.[37] Psychoanalytic institutes began to court social workers and psychologists in the 1940s and 1950s, but not for psychoanalytic training. Instead, many institutes developed "applied" programs in psychotherapy for these ancillary professions, while excluding their members from full training. These professionals were not only a natural audience for the outreach efforts of institutes but also a natural pool of patients, for they were high-functioning, neurotic, psychologically oriented, professionally motivated, upwardly mobile, and in need of their own trials of treatment in order to work with their clients. During this period, a trickle and then a stream of social workers and psychologists, having been trained in the practice of psychotherapy in the psychoanalytic institutes' auxiliary training programs, began to set up their own private practices and to compete directly with the psychiatrists for private paying patients. Many requested training in psychoanalysis but were denied as a matter of course. As I have indicated, the ego psychologists had posited as their counterideal the analyst's direct emotional involvement with the patient, his influencing of the patient through active, charged, intimate, relational participation. While the institutes of the APsaA maligned such modifications of interpretive technique as unanalytic, the ability to utilize such parameters to help patients enabled the nonmedical psychotherapists to treat a broader range of patients than analysts did. Reading theorists whose writings were excluded from the ego psychology canon—principally the "interpersonal" theories of Harry Stack Sullivan and the "object relations" theories of Melanie Klein and others in the United Kingdom who had opposed Anna Freud's ego psychological teaching—the social workers and psychologists (and, to be sure, a number of psychiatrists) opened their doors to these "sicker" people. In other words, in the 1950s the excluded therapist began seeing the excluded patient using the excluded theory, and as the scope of psychoanalysis widened in this way, the austere notion of treatment by interpretation alone was placed in contrast to a more informal praxis of supportive responsiveness, understood as the provision—to patients with frank emotional deficits—of needed, developmentally missed learning experiences.[38]

At the same time that social workers and psychologists, with their nonmedical approaches to human suffering, were beginning to attract psychotherapy patients away from psychoanalysis, insurance companies were beginning to discover that these clinicians could conduct many of the same therapies physicians could, at cheaper rates. Lobbyists and consultants for these professions rapidly succeeded in winning them privileges previously reserved for M.D.s—insurance reimbursement for psychologists and social workers, prescription privileges for R.N.s (psychologists have also now been seeking prescription power for at least the past fifteen years). During the 1980s the wholesale retreat by insurance companies from the funding of intensive long-term talk therapies led to a steep decline in patients for psychoanalysis; this, in turn, was followed by decreased interest in psychoanalysis among psychiatrists and by the rapid biologization of psychiatry.[39] This placed an even greater pressure on psychoanalytic institutes to admit non-M.D.s, because, with fewer patients to treat and fewer students to train, their organizational survival was at stake. Finally, in 1989, after almost two decades of pressure to provide "full training" to psychologists and social workers, the APsaA and IPA agreed to open psychoanalytic training to nonmedical personnel.

In a lively account of this pivotal moment, Robert Wallerstein (1998) describes how the settlement of the lawsuit ushered in a discourse of having "solved the problem of lay analysis" at last, putting a celebratory spin on what had been a politically necessary concession, tying it rhetorically to events of longer duration and greater historical moment for the psychoanalytic movement. The problem of lay analysis was, after all, one that Freud himself had struggled with. In alignment with Freud's own intentions, in this one dramatic gesture the APsaA could now relinquish its medical pretensions and admit other qualified individuals for training. On the one hand this opening up of the institutes was talked about as the death knell of psychoanalysis, much along the lines of the comments of Peter Shapiro quoted at the beginning of this chapter. On this view, psychoanalysis was losing its medical core, and the worry was that physicians would no longer be attracted to it if training were available to others; that nonphysicians would now be competitors with physicians; that a loss of affiliation with medicine would translate into loss of income for physicians; that physicians might soon lose control of the professional membership organizations; and that institute classes might suffer in quality. On the other hand, for the proponents of the opening of the institutes to non-M.D.s, the hope expressed was that these formerly exclusionary, authoritarian, socially conservative, largely male bastions of medicine could become the home for a rejuvenated, liberalized, democratized, nonmedical, humanistic American psychoanalysis. Combined with a growing critique of the cultural authority of medicine in general and a post-1970s antipsychiatry movement that sought to treat the personal problems of the suffering self as opposed to the pathologies of the mental patient, with the settling of the lawsuit in 1989, the autonomy of psychoanalysis was definitively shown up. As in other professions, the inability of an elite to protect its privileges, maintain its enclosures, and prevent the degradation of its emblems of status led to the inflation of titles and degrees, to the proliferation of practitioners and credentialing enterprises, and to a crisis of social reproduction. Horizontal and virtual labor integration have since replaced the Fordist vertical integration that had maintained both private psychiatric practice and the hierarchical midcentury division of mental health labor. In replacing Fordism, the new forms of labor also displaced the relations of authority that maintained a particular epistemic culture.

RELATIONAL "ACCOUNTABILITY" AND POST-FREUDIAN MUTUAL FUNDS

Prior to the 1970s, when there were enough patients and enough trainees to sustain the exclusivity of American psychoanalysis, psychoanalysts shared a narrow definition of their trade and of the analyzable neurotic who was its beneficiary. Many suffering individuals did not make the grade; analysts were to refer them elsewhere (whether for treatment or for training). The term "unanalytic" found its grounding by cordoning off noninterpretive therapeutic procedures under the debased notion of the parameter or the "modification" and then grouping these under the contrastive category psychotherapy, a baser practice. But it began to appear during that era as though the medical monopoly that underwrote psychoanalytic exclusivity was, in effect, putting psychoanalysis out of business. Over the past thirty years, psychoanalytic theory has steadily come to include as "analyzable" more kinds of patients, blurring in practice the previously drawn distinction between psychotherapy and psychoanalysis. At the same time, the institutes of the APsaA have retained the distinction, instituting it in formal training standards now emptied of their earlier referents. This has allowed analysts to maintain a *sense* of the exceptionalism of psychoanalysis in spite of the fact that so few of them are actually able to practice what they hold to be psychoanalysis. With the illusion of a unity, and with the name "psychoanalysis," they can still perform the boundary work of dubbing what they don't like "unanalytic," effacing the corrosive effects of ongoing exclusionary practices.

In offering a genealogy of ego psychology's signature categorical opposition relationship/transference and plotting the work of this binary in relation to the division of labor in the mental health field in the latter half of the twentieth century, I have provided a schematic overview of developments in the psychoanalytic theory of technique. Briefly, these developments have sustained an omnivorous vision of a "psychoanalytically" governable reality in the face of a situation of growing scarcity. The crisis of psychoanalysis that psychoanalysts like Peter Shapiro and John Brandon refer to does not, in this view, describe the failure of a prior regime of success but is, rather, a phantasmatic placeholder, a frame through which psychoanalysts can render unbearable structural contradictions bearable through enactments around the very intelligibility of a cultural practice. Construed by them as a natural effect of larger, external changes in the world, crisis is a systemic artifact: a para-ethnographic hermeneutic that functions performatively, reflexively, to mediate analysts' relations with patients, with health-care third parties, with themselves, and with one another. By supposing an identity for psychoanalysis as something that many fail to uphold, the notion of crisis works to purify the problem space, binding these psychoanalysts through a triangulated relationship to a third thing, a slippery thing they can sometimes hold stable. The image of a widening scope for the application of psychoanalysis is, then, a way for analysts to bundle economic and epistemic forms in a single imaginary, a way, cognitively, to manage and map a landscape that has decidedly outstripped their control. This "wide" vision of psychoanalytic powers is one that many hold firmly, in spite of the virtual collapse of psychoanalysis as a concrete social practice.

The story that can be told is a collective story about the personal, a story of promise and hope and flexible specialization that can conceal the shame and sense of failure embedded in the experience of being structurally marginalized and professionally dispossessed. Far from being neutral terms that represent an external reality, crisis and pluralism have constitutive powers at the hub of self- and world-making practices. These motifs allow one to experience one's own story as part of something larger, even if one's relation to that larger thing is ambivalent. Crisis thus holds analysts in thrall, extending the life of psychoanalysis both notionally and spatially with an autosuggestive appraisal of its—and of their own—significance. The widening scope works both with and against this crisis as a kind of stop-loss order, a way to organize diverse elaborations of expertise in a single provisional enclosure. Within this enclosure, the professional standard—that to which one is supposed to be accountable—holds the place of a structural impossibility while simultaneously disavowing it.

· 2 ·

ANALYSIS DEFERRED
(or, THE TALKING CURE
TALKS BACK)

Does the actual state of psychoanalysis include, in its dominant schools (and by school I mean both school of thought and the apparatus of training and reproduction), an element that is unanalyzed but in principle analyzable, an occlusion, as I was saying a moment ago, that prohibits the effective emergence of an ethics and a politics contemporary with psychoanalysis? This occlusion distributes forces in the following way: on one side, theoretical advance troops incapable of giving rise to institutions that integrate them . . . ; on another side, an empirical proliferation of discourses and practices, of micro-institutional affiliations, of suffering or triumphant marginalities, an improvisation left to drift as it will according to the isolation, the places of biographical, historical, political inscription, and so forth.—JACQUES DERRIDA, *Psyche: Inventions of the Other*

....

Mark Tracy, Norman Peters, and Carrie Janis are colleagues on the faculty of the Chicago Institute for Psychoanalysis, one of the nation's oldest and most established centers for psychoanalytic learning. The Chicago Institute is famous in the history of psychoanalysis in the United States for the influential work of Franz Alexander in the 1930s and 1940s and, several decades later, of Heinz Kohut, with their respective theories of the corrective emotional experience and of self psychology. Mark, Norm, and Carrie, trained in this institution, all identify strongly as psychoanalysts, even though they have, respectively, zero, one, and "four and a half" patients in analysis. All three suffer a passionate, unfulfilled devotion to an impracticable ideal, and their stories of precarious labor and impossible identity exemplify three very different strategies for coping with the dearth of patients they all lament, three different forms and understandings of (under)employment, and three different responses to wider structural limitations on professional self-determination. The problem-space they operate in is extremely complex, for Mark, Norm, and Carrie lack a vocabulary—beyond the notion of crisis—that would allow them to translate their divergent views of psychoanalysis. Indeed, the very question of what psychoanalysis "is" proves, for them, to be the crux of their problem—and it is one that is exacerbated by the situation of scarcity in which they practice.

Mark, Norm, and Carrie experience deeply troubling dilemmas stemming from the paucity of psychoanalytic work, and in narrating the fragility of their situations and the definitional problem at the center of their professional life they participate in an intensive collective venture of parsing and demarcating "psychoanalysis" from "psychotherapy" on the one hand and "transference" from this other conceptual object, this ostensibly more personal "real relationship" on the other.[1] In polemically evaluating one another's positions on "what works" in psychoanalysis, they endorse (now with hostility, now with affection) a set of more and more personal, less alienable qualities of expertise—qualities of work on the self intertwined with work on the other—that are embedded in the notion of the real relationship.

What is at stake for Mark, Norm, and Carrie is the intensification of a systemic predicament of indeterminacy in the psychoanalytic collegium, a form of disciplinary instability that maintains the psychoanalytic institution in a constant state of crisis while at the same time serving it—productively—as a technology of freedom. In developing a solution to his or her own predicament of scarcity, each of these three psychoanalysts finds a psychoanalysis *un-disciplined* by its current crisis. Each, in his or her marked unease about psychoanalysis—about its identity, stability, and transmissibility—articulates a higher order narrative of disciplinary immunity, mediated through a personal narrative of precarity, foreclosure, and failure. As their stories of dispossession indicate, their realities of practice are anxiously cast in terms of nostalgia about a psychoanalysis past, a lawful, stable psychoanalysis. Their talk about the present, in contrast, showcases the lack of success at the heart of psychoanalytic self-fashioning and institutional reproduction. In examining their stories, what becomes evident is the degree to which the economic tie—the patient's ability literally to be in analysis, the analyst's anxiety about this—has become a primary site of problematization in psychoanalysis today. In this psychoanalysis two risk discourses permeate each other, the patient's and the analyst's, and the verisimilitude of the real relationship highlights their entanglement.

POLICING THE BOUNDARY: *"Triumphant Marginalities"*
in the Biopolitical Zone of Enterprise

Mark, Norm, and Carrie identify strongly as psychoanalysts, in spite of their limited practice of their more specialized and more beloved craft. Like the majority of psychoanalysts in the United States today, Mark, Norm, and Carrie spend their days working chiefly as psychotherapists. As I have indicated, these terms are sharply opposed yet inextricable—charged referents whose distinctive features, in practice, are increasingly underspecified, even though everyone continues to use them. Mark, Norm, and Carrie are successful professionals in private practice, yet each of them suffers a passionate, unfulfilled devotion to an impracticable ideal. In their sixties, while no longer beholden to their own former TAs, they still do not have power in their psychoanalytic institute. Norm and Mark are M.D.s who went through analytic training thirty years ago, in their thirties, just after residency, the age that M.D.s were traditionally trained in the era when psychoanalysis was an exclusively medical field. Carrie is a psychologist, a beneficiary of the lawsuit that opened up psychoanalytic training in the late 1980s to non-M.D.s. While roughly the same age as Norm and Mark, and with the same number of years of prior experience as a psychotherapist, Carrie was only able to train as a psychoanalyst in the 1990s, while in her fifties. The powerful analysts in their community are in their seventies and eighties, some in their nineties, male M.D.s who continue to conduct the training analyses of current trainees and to define psychoanalysis on the basis of a model that last mirrored realities of practice in the 1970s.

Though Mark, Norm, and Carrie graduated from training in the 1980s, early 1990s, and early 2000s, respectively, all allude to being locked out of the central institutional source of power at their institute by virtue of their lack of "immersion." Conflict and contradiction simmer in their talk of failed immersion, evoking a climate portrayed in a paper given by Steven Stern, who offers a startling image of the humiliation, shame, and desperation these exemplary professionals suffer in their failure to progress. He writes:

> The prerequisite for progression to Training Analyst is "immersion" in psychoanalytic work. I picture a cartoon of a swimming pool with the water rapidly draining out of it. In fact most of the water is already gone and there's maybe a foot or two left in the bottom, a few feet more in the deep end. A little water is trickling in through a hose that says "analytic

cases," but the water is draining out faster than it is trickling in. All the new graduates are crowded in the emptying pool in their bathing suits, straining to get immersed. Some are lying on their backs on the bottom; some are kneeling with only their heads submerged; others are lying on their stomachs or sides. All are struggling to get underwater while the water continues to drain. (Stern 2008, n.p.)

Mark, Norm, and Carrie all swim (or sink) in this pool. *Ressentiment* bubbles up in their talk about relations with professional colleagues, with the insurance auditors who have pretensions to monitor their work and its reimbursement, with clinicians of other stripes, with patients (most of whom scarcely recognize the all-important distinctions between psychoanalysis, psychotherapy, psychology, psychiatry, counseling, etc.), and, tellingly, in the interview situation. These individuals literally cannot practice what they preach, yet they seek to maintain themselves as, specifically, psychoanalysts.[2]

They inhabit three distinctive performativities in the interview situation. Mark has little to say: he is the silent analyst, analyzing the other without allowing any real otherness; he carries the mark of psychoanalytic immunity in his omniscient stance. Norm is chatty, normalizing his crisis with an eclectic approach to staying afloat. Carrie carries the conversation forward, risking herself by throwing herself into the impossible unknown, doing the interview much as she does her work with her patients, "together." Each maintains a definition of psychoanalysis against the others' definitions. I read each of them through their own readings of psychoanalysis, and then through their implicit readings of each other's readings of psychoanalysis. A central finding about the ethnoepistemology of their collective culture is that these psychoanalysts cannot but psychoanalyze. From the standpoint of ethnographic method, I suggest that it is crucial to read their narratives in this reflexive way, therefore, and not, as an ethnographer, to "psychoanalyze" them in turn.

THREE CASES

MARK: THE BABY AND THE BATHWATER

Mark calls himself a classical Freudian analyst. He's reserved, conservatively dressed, austere in his expression. Sitting with him in his formal, steel-grey office I felt like my breathing was too loud, my questions too sloppy. My words reverberated off the walls and reentered my ears as chastisements. His skilled analytic silence was deafening. Why was I there, what could I possibly want from him? The analyst waits for the patient's desire to emerge, and he waited for my questions. I sat on his analytic couch, where his patients recline, and he sat in his leather armchair. He was clearly accustomed to being the interviewer and not the subject. I felt a pang for us both for having to go through this awkwardness. I thought of John L. Jackson's "anthro man" and the mask of confidence the anthropologist dons to interrogate his consultants.[3] I asked Mark about his practice, and as we talked, he returned over and over again to what he called the "postmodern, anything-goes" mentality he sees in psychoanalysis now. "When I was in training, people were not supportive. They were helpful, perhaps, but definitely not supportive. They'd tell you if you had a problem, if you had a learning block and you needed more analysis. Analysis wasn't meant to be supportive. It was a one-person approach," as opposed to an intersubjective, or two-person, or relational approach. "There's been an enormous change in the whole character of the profession. People used to wear ties. I think someone who's a doctor, someone who's seeing patients, should. Something has changed."

I asked Mark what had changed and how he understood this change, and he referred several times to a loss, or decline, of "standards." "Casualness has a seductive appeal, like the idea of being more democratic. Some people want to be loved and appreciated, and they will change the standards to do that. It's not that it's evil. By some criteria it's unethical, it's probably illegal, but it's motivated by vulnerability, by issues that people have that they haven't resolved, chiefly their need to be loved. The larger group pays the price for this in its sense of cohesion, in terms of lowered standards."

When I asked Mark how many patients he had in analysis he became visibly uncomfortable and looked away; when he looked back toward me I saw that he was pale. You'll note in his response that he evaded my question, that his evasion was in a sense his answer, even though I attempted to provide reassurance by providing context, by letting him know that I had interviewed several dozen analysts and that the majority of them had zero, one, or two patients in analysis. As already noted, these numbers are borne out in a recent survey of the members of the APsaA, the largest national membership organization of psychoanalysts in the United States, as well as in a similar, local study in Chicago.

I'd want a full-time analytic practice if I could have it, but it doesn't seem like it's going to happen. I've always had my main professional connection with medicine, and it's not going to happen from within medicine.

It would have even ten years ago, but now the internists want to treat the patient themselves. You've heard of a concierge practice? My internal medicine colleagues who used to refer patients to me now want to set that up. They want to do everything for the patient, to keep the patient for themselves. Of course what they do works by transference, but they don't know the first thing about interpreting transference, they don't have a theory of transference. You know, after you emailed me about talking, I also thought about how many of my referrals have come from analysts other than from my own analyst, and I realized very, very few.

He drew a breath. "As far as the analytic community goes, I've been a donor not a recipient." Again I pressed my question about his actual practice as an analyst. "It's shifted over time," he grimaced, reflecting back on when he first started working as an analyst.

After graduation I was running two or three patients for a while. Then I decided to become a TA. You have the immersion requirement, and at one point I got up to seven patients for that. It's gone down again the last couple years, but in an odd way, with people drifting off, not formally terminating. One woman moved and we continued by phone. It didn't terminate with setting a date, but I could see it coming. She was increasingly freed up in her life, was able to marry and have a fulfilling relationship, so I could see it coming. I don't know if she saw it coming in the same way I did; I think she just saw it as she had to move. Then I had a guy who left and started with another analyst. Then I had another person that got transferred; he's also by telephone now and that's terminating now. I have some people with an analytic process but that are not using the couch. I have one guy in therapy who was in analysis before, but he's also not using the couch now.

I could see how uncomfortable Mark was at having basically just told me he didn't have any patients in analysis in the way he defines analysis— the use of the couch, the four/five times weekly frequency, plus "an analytic process"—and that most of the people he has had recently have left him "in an odd way," without formally resolving the transference (transference resolution being the sine qua non of a completed psychoanalysis in his view). Mark exemplifies a common defensiveness brought on by the re- definition of the status of psychoanalysis in the field of psychiatry in which his practice is embedded. Psychoanalysis is no longer given much pride of place in psychiatry. His charge is that the field of psychoanalysis has been perverted by an epidemic of *niceness* and *supportiveness* deriving from the doctor's unanalyzed *need to be loved.* He also alludes, in his comment about the internists setting up concierge practices, to the doctor's need to hold onto patients. Mark does not change his definition of psychoanalysis, or of analyzability, despite his colleagues' acceptance of a "widening scope" of clinical indications for the talking cure. Far from it. In contrast, he tells of resigning from committees and walking away from teaching and supervising appointments in protest over this epidemic of relationships, this epidemic of colleagues' "needing to be loved," that is now standing in the way of true psychoanalysis.

Mark tells a story in which he is both a victim and a hero, heroically facing his social negativity. He is punished by his professional peers who withhold referrals, but he perseveres. He preserves the ideal, he secures the fixed form of analysis proper. He is the properly analyzed analyst who does not "need to be loved," the self-denying analyst of the structural closure, willingly subjecting himself to the law of correct practice in the face of a postmodern, interdisciplinary erosion of the formal standard. Changing the rite is not an option for Mark, only noble submission to its disappearance. He would rather throw out the baby with the bathwater (or silently preserve it in his withering criticism of his casual, relational, postmodern colleagues). Mark, alone among the three, claims to give a "Freudian" reading of the emptying swimming pool. In effect, he says, the others haven't been adequately analyzed; they suffer (and then they inflict on their patients) their overweening "need to be loved." They haven't renounced their infantile longings; they act them out, compulsively, with patients and with one another. "And the larger group pays the price." I use Mark to point up the way that the distinction between psychotherapy and psychoanalysis turns on the distinction between transference interpretation and relationship and to suggest that the mark of analysis, its decidability, circulates through precisely the metapragmatics of such characterizations. The Derridean ordeal is avoidable for Mark; the double bind of simultaneous divisibility and identity of psychoanalysis can be mastered by proper adherence to a law of practice: four weekly sessions, the use of the couch, the interpretive resolution of a transference neurosis, a proper termination.

NORM: WATERING IT DOWN

Norm announces right off that he is an Eagle Scout (the highest rank attainable in the Boy Scouts of America); he's cheerful in the extreme, garrulous: "Whenever there was an opportunity to excel, to go for the next badge, I would go for it—until I reached the point where the next step was Certification." "Certification" is a grueling prerequisite to becoming a TA, a national test in which examiners from the APsaA's Board of Professional Standards (BOPS) read the applicant's cases and then interview the applicant on her or his clinical work over a period of several months. Historically, Certification served as an affirmation of the fact of an analyst's graduation from training; the authority to determine an analyst's clinical competence was housed in the institute that graduated him. In the early 1990s Certification was delinked from plain membership in the APsaA and made a national prerequisite for becoming a TA.[4] With Certification now a mechanism for determining eligibility for TA appointment, its supporters started to claim its necessity as a "national indicator of clinical competence" above and beyond graduation from an institute, saying "that such an indicator [was] necessary to assure that the analysis of new trainees will be in the hands only of analysts whose 'competence' has been confirmed."[5] Certification has had an additionally fraught aspect since the 1990s, since many applicants suspected that they were turned down for Certification not for the quality of their work but for its failure to conform to the values of ego psychology and the vision of normality and health enshrined therein.

So it was at the point of considering whether to go for Certification that, Norm exclaimed, "I got really turned off of organized psychoanalysis." Unlike Mark, who was cautious and vigilant in the interview situation (not to mention theoretically orthodox and duly Certified), Norm was expansive, instantiating his depiction of himself as an energetic guy who likes to grab the ball and run it down the field, to get hold of a problem and innovate a solution. He used stories from sports, from his navigation of the rigors of training, from the slings and arrows of his professional organizational life, and from his marriage and family experience to illuminate his way of working as an analyst.

> The psychology I'm trying to explain to patients comes alive in parables and stories; I try to present myself to the patient as a fellow-traveler and use examples from my life. My wife's always surprised I can sit and listen to people all day because in a lot of ways that's not me; I'm really more of a do-er. And I have more of a task-oriented approach now than I used to. That's WAY different from my analyst. He was changing my personality, and the other stuff—behavior change—would just follow naturally. But it doesn't. People have learned these klutzy or offensive or rude or

not-effective ways of relating and they don't just change, so I often engage people directly in discussions which really amount to education stuff. The danger [with this] from an analytic standpoint is it gums up the transference. I do think it interferes with more negative transference stuff developing, but that doesn't stop me.

Norm is eclectic in his use of psychoanalytic ideas, but—notably—he doesn't define this other "stuff" that he does as psychoanalysis per se.

I ask Norm how his change to what he called a more task-oriented approach, a here-and-now, you-and-me approach, came about. "I think that the Certification thing was my adolescent rebellion that I'd never had. I acted out." He "blew the whistle" on the reliability and validity problems with the Certification process. The whole standards process, he felt, had no reliability or validity, and he went out and made that point publicly.

After that I was basically censured. I'm the guy in class who the teacher's ambivalent about 'cause I call 'em like I see 'em. I decided after getting called out on that that I didn't want to turn over some sort of further evaluation of me to some other guys. Also, this was a huge outlay of time for something that is not even valid. And then there's the whole thing of identifying with the idea that the Certified guy is the ideal guy. I thought the whole thing was a huge mistake for the field. I'd been in all these high-pressure schools and never felt that scrutinized before. So that was the first time I decided hey, maybe I'll stop shy of Eagle Scout this time. A lot of people feel pissed—"I've had all this training and I don't get to do any actual analysis." I have this one guy in analysis now, and I use what I learned with everyone I work with in therapy. I think about everything in terms of interlocking transferences, but I mostly do this other therapy stuff now and not analysis. Basically people just aren't up for that.

Norm takes a commanding stance in the interview with me. His "task orientation" to the therapeutic relationship comes through loud and clear in our time together: "You'll want to know that I'm doing less and less transference work, more and more interrupting, more talking, more direct shaping of behavior." Norm's not waiting to see what I put out there; he's not allowing his behavior to be shaped by me. He doesn't change analysis to fit the times, or to fit the patient (indeed, I don't hear much about the patient). He just does "this other thing." He's assertively "not a victim" of the hysteresis of psychoanalysis, but I'm left wondering why, in the end, having dispensed with the transference and given over to the direct use of coaching, he continues to identify as an analyst, to write papers and teach classes on psychoanalysis when he doesn't practice it, to participate in conferences and meetings as an active psychoanalyst. What is at stake in giving up the name, as he appears unable or unwilling to do? I selected Norm here to show a shift in the field from the mark or law of pure psychoanalysis to this newer norm of eclecticism or applied psychoanalysis, in his case the adaptation of a kind of personal influence that he calls interrupting behavior, or behavior-modification, to more strictly psychoanalytic techniques like Mark's prized "interpretation alone."

CARRIE: BACK IN THE DEEP END
(EXTENDING THE ENTERPRISE FORM)

Carrie is tentative, unsure. She alludes to a permanent struggle with self-confidence. I remembered that a senior analyst in her eighties had confided to me once about Carrie that "she's still got a touch of shyness that hasn't been fully analyzed." Carrie herself doesn't seem like someone who would describe another person as not having been "fully analyzed"—in fact, I get the feeling that the notion of being fully analyzed is not even on her radar. More than Mark's or Norm's, her story is open to revision, halting. She uses parallelisms and multiple voicings to build a description of her practice in terms of cases and examples. She doesn't seek mastery in the interview as they did—instead she keeps testing out and then commenting on her comments, framing and reframing them.

> I'd been in practice for twenty years already when I started analytic training so I was pretty sure of myself in my work, but it's isolating; I always needed more connection and stimulation; it had been annoying dealing with managed care all the time and I wanted to get out of that; Jeanne Brewster [pseudonym] convinced me to do the training; first I said I can't do that, it's not for people like me, it's for people from [an exclusive suburb]. Ultimately she got to me. I remember thinking there was this way the analysts thought that I could see was really different from how I was thinking as a therapist, and I wanted to be able to look at things in that kind of depth. I remember thinking, "Well, if there's a conflict between helping the person, being a good therapist, and doing a proper analysis, then I'm definitely going to be a good therapist." I saw them in opposition then, as different, which I don't now.

Carrie subjects her definition of psychoanalysis to constant revision deriving from introspection on what she does with her patients; her definition is elastic, not based on either the frequency of appointments, the use of the couch, or the resolution of transference neurosis. (This is in keeping with being "self psychological," as she identifies herself: self psychology explains psychopathology as a condition evolving from historically unmet developmental needs rather than from conflict between drives or agencies of the mind). In consequence, unlike Mark or Norm, she has "four and a half" patients in analysis. But what is a "half" patient, and why and how does she define *as analysis* what Norm happily enough calls psychotherapy? We talked at length about what she called "depth," what it is and how you see it, circling around what she meant when she said she had four and a half patients in analysis until I finally blurted out my question: "What is a *half* patient?" She responded:

> Well ... there's some people who—it's hard to look at themselves deeply—they kind of report things. They're anxious, they're like "she said this then she said this then she said this." It's hard to get them to look at their own reactions, they're so overwhelmed with stuff in the world and that's what they end up talking about. I'm thinking about one person I had in analysis. I hadn't realized how much in the hole she was getting financially, and she suddenly cut back to once a week and was feeling like I was trying to control her, tell her what to do. She was angry and didn't want to come in. I mean, this is exactly her family history of being told what to do. That's the transference right there. So, it's interesting. It's much less intense at once a week, but there's still the transference, so we're working with that. It feels less intense, but it's still an analytic process. It's still analysis.

Here Carrie began to clear her throat with a thoughtful, slightly wounded look. Moving back and forth between *an analytic process* and *analysis*, she seemed uncertain of the distinction she was groping for. "In fact," she went on,

> towards the end of the time when we were doing four times a week it had stopped feeling like an analytic process. I wasn't aware of what was going on with her at the time 'cause she wasn't talking about it, and part of the enactment was my not addressing it directly, my not addressing it as I was starting to get frustrated. I felt stuck, and I guess she felt stuck. She was really mad, intensely negative. Finally we talked about it and she said, y'know, she said she'd been feeling like she had to do what I said. Meanwhile all she was talking about during that whole time was her job,

asking me what she should do, what she should do. This was a way of engaging me, how she'd do it with her best friend, like she was the one who was a mess and the friend would tell her okay do this, try that, try this, and would help her and give her instructions and ideas and advice. The friend helped her, but she resented the friend and felt she couldn't do anything on her own. So, I think this was an enactment on her part to try to get me involved in the only way she knew how, and then I'm sure she got frustrated at "I have to be the stupid one and ask you what to do all the time," so we were both extremely frustrated. I felt like I should have picked up on it; I felt I was so stupid, how could I have missed it; I felt I'm not a good analyst; I really felt awful, but I think even that was part of the enactment, and maybe even a necessary part.

Even Carrie's *own* sense of insecurity, her feeling *stupid* and *blind* and *anxious* was part of the enactment? And maybe even a *necessary* part? Carrie described a kind of affective labor in which her own precarity was out front, her own dependence on her patient. The prominence of uncertainty, risk, and affective participation in Carrie's narrative is in some respects unremarkable; with her great focus on flexibility and adaptation in the therapeutic relationships, her enfolding into herself the anxious undecidables of her patient's economic situation, her patient's struggles with passivity and resentments about being "told what to do," Carrie probably *is* the "too nice," too personal, too casual, postmodern, anything-goes, relational analyst Mark denounces. Carrie told a story now of how she presented a case to a prominent New York analyst. "He took me as one of those Chicago people. The kind of critiques he made—well, for months my patient—this was my lady with the [identifying feature]—she didn't think it was helping, she thought she should leave, I tried interpreting it as her seeing me as the parent who's not responsive and she was like 'Yeah, you are!'" As in, 'Yeah, you *are* the parent who's not responsive.'" At this point in her story Carrie laughed warmly. The recollection seemed to hearten her, steeling her earlier sense of uncertainty about what was happening with her patient and in the interview with me.

She was ready to leave every minute. She felt worse and she blamed me. We were both in crisis mode. She finally sat up and told me she was gonna stop. I said, "Well, I think it *has* been working, but I know it is hard for you to trust me." I said, "I know you've jumped in the deep end and I won't let you drown." He [the New York analyst] said, "You can't say that." That's acting like you have a magical relationship with the lady. But that was exactly what helped. It shifted things. He said, "You're promising magic; you can't promise magic. It's too supportive. You're being too nice. You're supposed to be giving an interpretation." Well I think that *was* an interpretation. I had a visual image, the deep end, and that was the interpretation. It wasn't like "Oh I thought of a good interpretation." And plus I think I'd already tried everything else he was saying. A different *kind* of interpretation was needed. She [the patient] was intensely anxious and I was intensely anxious and it was the only thing I could do—and it was what turned things around.

The New York analyst said she was being seductive in promising something "real," something she could not really give. She, in contrast, feels what she did was an emergency response, that it worked as such, that nothing else had worked, and that really extending herself in this way was the only thing that did. She offers an image of a kind of heroism of desperate maneuvers. As she describes them, her appointments with patients involve intense affective entanglements that enfold within them multiple virtual entanglements with others not physically present, in which the ethical relations of each to all are at stake. Her appointments intensify these ethical relations with an express introduction of risk, chance, and freedom. They mobilize affects of shame and guilt, challenging expectations and obligations. They activate Carrie's own conflicts and uncertainties (Care? Guidance? Authoritative interpretation? *What do I do?!*) and implicate her in the very undecidables that possess her "lady with the [identifying feature]." For Carrie, in contrast to both Mark and Norm, there is no external rule to be followed, nor even a consistent set of norms. There is simply the real relationship between analyst and patient and her depth of involvement in it, something she sees as reparative in its own right. Where Mark fails to take account of what in his analysis resists analysis, Carrie's analysis literally suspends itself in order to *do* analysis.

THE "RESISTANCES" OF PSYCHOANALYSIS, OR, WHAT'S IN A NAME?

These three individual narratives constellate a collective project of mourning an unattainable ideal. Several motifs are indissociable, and together they define a situation of productive misunderstanding. There literally *are* next to no patients, yet the mark of "real analysis" flies around, the accusation hovers, proliferates. Her New York analyst tells Carrie "That's not analysis." Mark says "They want to be loved; that's not analysis." Norm says about his interrupting behavior that "a lot of people wouldn't call it analysis." But what I'm doing, Carrie falters, it is analysis, isn't it? Isn't it, she asks? It is, isn't it?

The worry and suspicion surrounding the ambiguity of analysis, what is, what isn't analysis, is publicly traded as if it were a normative matter: this is therapy, that is analysis, goes the routine. In her recent paper "That's Not Analytic," Carol Levin discusses how central such censure was to her training but repeatedly slips into utilizing the distinction as a gloss for and as a way to oppose the terms "certainty" (which she views as *not analytic*) and "uncertainty" (which she views as *analytic*) (Levin 2007). A search for the neologism "unanalytic" in the Psychoanalytic Electronic Publishing archive (a database of all of the putatively major psychoanalytic journals) turned up the following plethora of similar uses in recent articles: "The idea that childhood events create adult psychopathology in a linear, direct fashion is profoundly unanalytic" (Robertson and Paris 2005, 343); "Unthinking commitment to the 'rules' can express just as unanalytic an attitude as rationalized compromising of those rules" (Furlong 2005, 383); "Ferenczi's formulation here is remarkably unanalytic, and it disregards the child's own impulses and unconscious fantasies. He knew and did not know that abused children may have intense guilt and shame consequent to unconscious complicity as well as identification with the feelings of the abuser" (Blum 2004, 10); "Countertransference responses by analysts that show frustration and retaliation, and that lead to unanalytic interventions, are not uncommon. These reactions often play into the unconscious wishes of the patient, whereupon enactment ensues instead of working through" (Marill and Siegel 2004, 679); "Analyst and analysand traveled through the traumatic moment together. Would it, then, be unanalytic to not acknowledge the shared reality of the situation?" (Cabaniss et al. 2004, 730); "In supervised analyses conducted by my candidate-analysand, for example, repetitive patterns of acting out, stubborn countertransference-influenced blind spots, and unrecognized unanalytic interventions constitute in part that candidate-analysand's report on me and on his or her analysis" (Orgel 2002, 432); "An overly austere and abstinent technique, as Gill (1984) has pointed out, represents an unacknowledged and unanalyzed manipulation of the transference, and is therefore unanalytic" (Inderbitzin and Levy 2000, 208); "We know that some analysts appear to be more successful than others in engaging prospective patients, often engendering in rivals suspicions concerning their use of unanalytic collusive measures" (Levy and Inderbitzen 2000, 749).

I have instead described a kind of suffering from experiential contradiction that stems from a community not being able to live up to its own ideals. Attempting to bring analysis under control, to render it calculable, to contain and institute its "theoretical advances" (per Derrida) in standards—standards, in such commentaries, stands as a transcendental referent—indubitably fails. This chapter suggests a Derridean diagnosis of the failure: an unrecognized double bind leads to a failure to analyze analysis—an apotropaic defense, as it were, a displaying of the penis to ward off its loss—rather than a confrontation with an ethico-political problem of psychoanalytic responsibility.[6] In a situation of intensifying competition, Mark and Norm take the question of what analysis is to be decidable. Psychoanalysis has a fixed meaning. The constitutive Derridean ordeal of aporia is avoidable. The double bind of the simultaneous divisibility and identity of psychoanalysis can be mastered. The therapeutic can be pinned down without taking up the critical. Crudely put, analysis *is* its time-tested postural and temporal clinical requirements. One can see how (and why) these two analysts suffer from (and inflict on others) their lack of patients. Strictly delimiting the exceptionalism of his own brand of psychoanalysis, each produces the boundary anew through his classificatory work—even in the interview.

Mark, the avowed Freudian among the three, resorts in the end to delivering medications to his patients, all of whom he describes as either unreceptive to his analytic advances or, in his assessment, "unanalyzable." In a metapragmatic commentary on the ethnographic interview, he silently awaits his interpretive opportunity, his moment for psychoanalysis to turn the tables on its interlocutor. His psychoanalysis is designed as a criticism of others', and he advances it through the administration of silence, through his abhorrence of the eclecticism, informality, and relational Being Nice of his colleagues. In this sense, his crisis serves as the very mode of transmission for his psychoanalysis. With Freud bashers at every turn and the only imaginable future a partisan one, it is apparent that Mark preserves intact his trained conviction that psychoanalysis is the preferred treatment for neurotics by conceiving of his problem epidemiologically. For Mark there are no neurotics anymore: "Patients are sicker now." As a consequence of this transcendental shakedown, changes in referral patterns that disadvantage both psychoanalysis and Mark himself, and the fact that other, "relational," analysts are keeping all of the patients for themselves, Mark is an analyst with no patients—but he holds tight to the exceptionalism of psychoanalysis and, in this, to his honor. From his vantage point he alone is a real analyst; the others are merely doing psychotherapy under the guise of psychoanalysis.

Mark's psychoanalysis bears the mark of death—the mark that does not outlive the presence of its original author, "Freud." Ironically enough, Mark fails to give up where Freud himself gave up, at the moment where one can only set aside the interpretive and "work to the best of one's power," via the relationship, via one's personal influence. Mark holds fast to an alternate true reality—a purely theoretical, or theoretically pure, psychoanalysis—rather than submitting it to an expedient pragmatism. His is a master discourse, a discourse of truth unveiled. For Mark, proper rendition is possible, a record of original events to which a full interpretive return is possible. Mark refuses the spectral space between original and copy, the radical otherness that opens psychoanalysis to impure repetition. The analyst can be properly analyzed in a circular hermeneutic return to Oedipal origins and can, ultimately, no longer "need to be loved." Analysis can be freed of its relational impurities, freed of the personal influence of the physician. Indeed, Mark himself is the properly analyzed analyst, in possession of the whole story. What he calls "the group" can be properly diagnosed: its pathology of casualness, of needing to be loved, is a primal fixation.

Norm, in turn, has developed an array of psychotherapeutic activities, all of them undergirded by what he calls a "psychoanalytic psychology" that, he says, "I couldn't do if I hadn't been psychoanalytically trained." Psychoanalysis informs all of these activities but is not the same as all of these activities. Consequently, he says, "I have one patient in analysis per se at any given time." Like Mark, Norm believes in the exceptionality of psychoanalysis, reproducing the psychoanalysis/psychotherapy boundary through his classificatory work in the interview. Unlike Mark, though, he, seemingly proud of his adaptability, does "all these other things" that he couldn't do if he weren't trained as a psychoanalyst; he doesn't simply bail on psychoanalysis and resort to providing medications, he practices "psychoanalytic" therapies, integrating "psychoanalytic" ideas into other practices. Norm's practice also purifies the category of psychoanalysis, this time in a metaphysical gesture of auto-affection; he teaches his patients how to live *his* way. He may not *do* psychoanalysis, but he deems what he does "psychoanalytic." Taken in by its repetition compulsion, his "psychoanalytic" intervention, his interrupting behavior, is commanded by a certain status quo, inscribed in a relation of forces Derrida describes for the personal element under the law "choose my solution, prefer my solution, take my solution, love my solution" (Derrida 1998, 9). Norm's norm disarticulates the life and death drives of psychoanalysis, purifying the doctor-patient relationship of any otherness. Norm wrests sovereignty from "some other guys" and their "reliability and validity problems," but, alas, he has no patients (or, rather, he has one "at any given time").

Carrie's improvisatory behavior (there is no external rule to be followed, or a single, consistent set of norms to guide all decisions) is, to Mark, exemplary of the failure of standards he laments—the very failure that in turn sustains his failure to get referrals. To Mark her elasticity is a classifiable and circumscribable psychopathology, a problem of analysts being "too nice." Unlike him, Carrie, whether she really is "too nice" or not, has a full(er) psychoanalytic practice. The meaning of her *half* patient lingers beyond their mutual mistranslations, though, for, from her standpoint, it is precisely Mark's failure to analyze his analysis that is the sickness of analysis; he is caught in the aporia of his own obsessional project of mastery of an unmasterable situation, using an ahistorical (and ahistoricist) ideal. He does not take account of what in his analysis resists analysis. In contrast, Carrie's "psychoanalysis" suspends itself in order to do psychoanalysis. Autodeconstructive, it carries the day. Analyzing her analysis, resisting her resistances, she evades the impulse to classify her practice. Anxiety and frustration and risk are objects of desire for her, just as they are objects of disavowal for her New York analyst. They hover around the mark; they dissolve the norm. As she emphasizes over and again, "We were both anxious; we were both frustrated."

Mark and Norm each take the crisis of psychoanalysis as descriptive, an external, statistical event of underconsumption that is independent of their own activity. Unlike in classical Freudian thought, where conflict, crisis, and contradiction are integral to an analytics that aims to disclose the inextricability of seemingly opposed terms, for these (post-)Freudians, crisis is an accident that befalls the subject, not an integral moment in a theory of history. Psychoanalysis, for them, is a possible profession. (Or maybe we should say it's possible, just not for them.) Each, in his own way, assumes policy (qua "standards," "reliable and valid" standards) to be the avenue through which he might overcome his situation. Carrie, in contrast, grapples with inherent instabilities in the identity of psychoanalysis and attempts to embrace these. Her relationship with her patient reads as an attempt to embrace the logic of vulnerability, to defer these instabilities if not deny them, an attempt at survival, and responsibility, in a situation of crisis. Carrie defines "the relationship" against the symbolic (against, literally, *analysis*), favoring an immanentist vitalism that works through affect.

A back-and-forth movement between flexibility and security is evident as she negotiates with her patient their interdependence, their relationship, mediated as it is by shared anxiety about their tie. In her relational ontology, the figure of primary vulnerability is central.

In banishing the real relationship from proper technique, psychoanalysis has historically sought to guarantee its scientificity and thereby its legitimacy as a "medical" practice. These three analysts are all dancing around the topic of the personal element, the relationship between the analyst and patient, whether attacking it (Mark), failing to engage it (Norm), or capitalizing on it (Carrie). It is evident that the emotional habitus of the real relationship is peculiarly fitted to the need to survive—to survive *as analyst*—in neoliberal medicine. Carrie's "four and a half" is about precisely this situation of mutual implication. It is a form of flexible specialization. The fact is, for her to have a practice at all, she must be flexible. She must take risks. She must "be nice." In doing this, she steps out of the Freudian structural closure and into economy, the space of what Derrida calls "the impossible." The real relationship can thus be seen as the idealized expression of an economy of life "in crisis" that constitutes the parties as infinitely indebted. In Carrie's ontology of psychoanalysis, we are now firmly in a world of *need* and *provision* rather than a world of wish and defense. In a return of the repressed, the relationship's rise is a response to—bound up with and a solution to—the crisis of psychoanalysis. Now *its* crises can become focal problems for psychoanalytic work. Open to the other and to the event, the message of Carrie's "half" patient seems to be an invitation to inhabit the double bind of analysis as a figure of risk beyond sovereignty. Emblematic of simultaneous peril and promise, the half patient is a message of neoliberal enterprise, a guarantee of limitless work that carries risk into the heart of the cure, binding the life and death tendencies of psychoanalysis in a simultaneously suicidal and self-transformative retrenchment. As Mark says about his relational colleagues (as about his internal medicine colleagues), "they want to keep the patients for themselves." They promise magic. Their analysis has no limit.

Without this double bind of analysis there would be only the failure of a sovereign scientificity; in its circular logic, self-preservation and entropic decline are woven together into an acephalous psychoanalytic power that takes hold of more and more objects (and more and more patients), that eventuates in longer analyses that treat more and more elements of the life process as being in need of supervision and management. The impulse to bind analysis instead fragments and extends it in diverse forms, in halves and in quarters, in deeper dependencies, in circuits of ever-intensifying competition. Because equilibrium is impossible under such conditions, the result is a kind of freedom—but it is freedom as entrapment in a contest of entrepreneurship, a contest, that is, rather than a collaboration. An unstable truth of hyperindividualized expertise is achieved within a pervasive pathos of professional organizational life. For Carrie what happened "originally" is (or was) traumatic; the original event cannot be repeated as such. The childhood trauma is polymorphously present, serving as the bait for work while generating what she calls "enactments" between herself and her patient. In these enactments around the bond between them she risks her own professional survival. The ultimate meaning of these enactments is always out of reach for her, for they are, quite literally, *about* risk (both her own and her patient's). Here is a psychoanalysis whose definition is permanently deferred. At the point where analysis fails, where there is no longer a separate analysis, there is only the personal element, only the relationship. As the heart of this real relationship, Derrida's fatal, personal element has become the consummate biopolitical object, progressively thematized (and, to a lesser degree, theorized) over the course of the institutional history I shall trace.

Thrown into infinity, Carrie's psychoanalysis is an enterprise form, a zombie psychoanalysis, the hyperbolic paradigm for a potentially endless series of mutations. "In terms of how you think about analysis," I asked her, "what is *not* analysis?" "That's a good question," she responded, with a worried look. Precarious, fragile, flexible labor becomes "psychoanalysis" in a political economy of uncertainty. "I guess if you put it that way I can't think of anything." To echo Derrida, to defer to Edward Sapir's (1949) discussion of the psychiatric "pitfalls in the business of getting a living"—in which he anticipated the impact the practitioner's anxiety could have on the actual content of psychiatric work—one may now ask about Carrie's embrace of the plasticity psychoanalysis, Is not *this* double bind the very question of analysis itself? "I can't think of anything," she repeats, analysis deferred.

PART II

....

THE PROBLEM
of
PSYCHOANALYTIC
AUTHORITY

INSTITUTING PSYCHO-ANALYSIS IN CHICAGO

Two Pedagogies of Desire

It was all to be seen from the first, although I would not permit my heart to acknowledge it. We were there for the entertainment of a sick, lonely, gifted man. Sitting up in his huge bed, Lionel held forth on every subject imaginable that related to human creativity. He talked brilliantly, fluidly, endlessly, while his auditors listened, sipped tea or coffee or a liqueur, bit into a cracker or sandwich, laughed or smiled when signaled to do so, or scowled when necessary. The strange thing was that so many were envious and wanted desperately to belong. But the numbers had to be limited. Lionel did the choosing and he did the eliminating.—STUART BRENT, *The Seven Stairs: An Adventure of the Heart*

The first human being who hurled an insult instead of a stone was the founder of civilization.—SIGMUND FREUD

....

So far I have given a fairly general account of the problem of the undecidability of psychoanalysis in a moment of crisis, but this is a mystification, since Mark, Norm, and Carrie conduct each others' conduct through historically specific assemblages of symbolic and pragmatic resources. These assemblages originally coalesced around two distinct images of the place of psychoanalysis in society—an image of its disciplinary autonomy and an image of its integration within psychiatry—and articulate divergent representations of the analyst's authority, divergent pedagogies of analytic treatment, divergent modes of transmission and legitimization of psychoanalytic knowledge, and divergent psychologies of analytic desire.[1] These assemblages descend from the distinctive projects of sovereignty of two apical ancestors, Lionel Blitzsten and Franz Alexander, the antagonistic founders of the Chicago Psychoanalytic Society and the Chicago Institute for Psychoanalysis, respectively.[2] Blitzsten and Alexander each claimed a Freudian pedigree, but their efforts to institute psychoanalysis in Chicago derived from markedly different and fundamentally incompatible visions. Even though the Chicago Institute, virtually alone among the major psychoanalytic institutes in the United States, never split apart, a permanent polemic between the lineages of these two men is visible to this day in the tensions I presented in the previous chapter: over what psychoanalysis is, over what form psychoanalytic authority should take, over the relationship of treatment to training.[3] Mark and Carrie draw on these assemblages in their efforts to legitimize their construals of—and practices of—psychoanalysis (his paternal law of the father, her norm of self-doubt). In competitive attempts to regulate an always at-best provisionally stable image of the talking cure, to ascend to a pure form and at the same time to control the real, daily conditions of their work, they leverage a quasi-metaphysical opposition: the real relationship versus the transference. This was precisely the site of struggle for Blitzsten and Alexander, who defined the terms of their argument around a contradiction between theory and technique.

THE DESIRE TO REPLICATE AND THE REPLICATION OF DESIRE:
From Genesis to Structure in "a Swampy Excrescence"

As historians of medicine have documented, late nineteenth-century American psychiatry was a thoroughly marginal specialty practiced by alienists in custodial asylums isolated from medicine's main currents. "A keenly felt sense of professional inferiority" underwrote the alienists' ambitions, charging with purpose a collective effort to extend psychiatry's jurisdiction beyond the institutionalized psychopath to the socially maladjusted, the neurotically miserable, and the plain unhappy (Lunbeck 1994; see also Abbott 1988, 2001; Caplan 2001; Rothman 2002; Scull 1989; Shorter 1997). Early twentieth-century psychiatrists envisioned great possibilities for their developing discipline, and through their endeavors in the new fields of eugenics, criminology, juvenile delinquency, mental hygiene, and psychoanalysis they set out to refashion their work in alignment with Progressive Era ideals of science, progress, expertise, efficiency, and control. Helen McLean, a founding administrator of the Chicago Institute for Psychoanalysis, placed the work of institute-building in Chicago in precisely this context, what she described as "the whole problem of trying to make psychiatry a first-class specialty."[4] This was a problem that her husband,

Franklin McLean, dean of the University of Chicago Medical School, sought to solve, in collaboration with the university's president, Robert Maynard Hutchins, by bringing in a leading European psychoanalyst, Franz Alexander, to the University of Chicago in 1931.

The trajectories of psychiatry and psychoanalysis were tightly interwoven in the first decades of twentieth-century America, and their relationship provides a particularly apt entry point for examining the institutionalization of psychoanalysis in this country, for it was through the play of two contrasting efforts at institutional legitimation in psychiatry that a handful of psychoanalysts around Franz Alexander succeeded, in the period between World War I and World War II, in instituting a disciplinary enclosure whose normalizing doxic and taxonomic projects would ramify across the international psychoanalytic movement.[5] From the standpoint of "the movement," the official history of psychoanalysis in Chicago began in 1911, the year Ernest Jones, a Welshman, founded the APsaA with the strategic intention to stem the influence of Abraham Brill, Jones's rival in the early effort to implant Freud's ideas in the United States.[6] As part of Jones's entrepreneurialism on behalf of the Freudian cause—as part of his formidable personal aspiration to be Freud's favorite—the Welshman set out to convert the local medical profession and intelligentsia in Chicago to Freudianism. As he wrote to the master in 1908, just before Freud's own visit to the United States, "I am not very hopeful of the present wave of interest, for the Americans are a peculiar nation with habits of their own. They shew curiosity, but rarely true interest (it is the difference between the itch of a neurasthenic and the desire of a normal lover). Their attitude towards progress is deplorable. They want to hear of the 'latest' method of treatment, with one eye dead on the Almighty Dollar, and think only of the credit, or 'kudos' as they call it, it will bring them."[7] On his return to Europe from Chicago, Jones deemed the city "the most hideous excrescence on God's earth," although he remarked that he had met some charming men there, several of them receptive to psychoanalysis.

The Jones-Freud correspondence lingers only briefly on Jones's Chicago junket, just one of his many missionary ventures for the cause. Jones's barnstorming trips represented his efforts to establish an *id-centered* psychoanalysis in the New World, in contradistinction to the more ego-centered visions of his fellow "Secret Committee" members, Freud's other emissaries in the band of brothers whose internecine rivalries defined the early movement.[8] In Jones's id-centered imagining of the conversion of the Americans, the "itch of the neurasthenic" had to be converted to "the desire of a normal lover" in order for psychoanalysis to take hold. His February 8, 1911, letter to Freud emphasizes the puritanical prudishness of his American audience. He wrote that his most interesting case was that of a businessman whose wife "took the upper position" in coitus, rendering the man neurasthenic and incapable of performance at work.[9] Not only did Jones seem to feel his American audiences were similarly inept, he seemed sure they envied his proximity to Freud. Jones's self-definition was that of the consummate insider, envoy for a daring cause (he tells Freud he even needed to take a security guard to protect him from critics while in Chicago!). His is a story of courting converts and fending off fools and foes at every turn. In the end, he averred,

> My trip to Chicago was very successful and enjoyable. . . . Dr. Patrick, the chief neurologist there, who opposed us at Washington last May, is practically converted, thanks, so he says, to the talks he had with me then, and has an assistant in his private practice who devotes all his time to it. My address was well received, except by Sidney Kuh who made a very aggressive onslaught. It was extremely stupid. "He couldn't agree with the logic of Freud's argument that because Frauenzimmer in German = Frau, therefore to dream of a room means something sexual." I was in bad need of some Abreagieren [abreaction] . . . and as he fortunately laid himself open in most obvious ways, I let myself go at him in a way I have never done in my life (as a rule I am rather a man of peace). Luckily he is very unpopular, so the others greatly enjoyed it. I could write a great deal about Chicago, but will spare you.[10]

Jones sowed seed on this trip, for Chicago's first native psychoanalyst would be a student of the aforementioned "practically converted" Dr. Patrick, a young man named N. Lionel Blitzsten. Blitzsten was a University of Chicago alumnus of Russian Jewish parentage who had grown up on Chicago's North Side and gone to Rush Medical College and then on to Northwestern University for his residency.[11] According to one of his own future students, "as early as 1915 Blitzsten was already discussing the new field with classmates at Rush" (Gitelson 1961, 10), and by 1920 he had concluded that neurology and neuropsychiatry were limited, makeshift fields and that "the future of psychiatry would include the 'new' theory and practice" (Orr 1961, 25). By the 1920s a steady stream of Americans were going to Europe to study psychoanalysis directly under Freud. Freud had stopped producing case histories by this point and was devoting himself almost exclusively to the lucrative, expansionist enterprise of analyzing his students from abroad. When his closest followers followed suit, a veritable cottage industry for American aspirants was established in Europe for the Freudian cause.[12] Blitzsten joined this fellowship of impassioned early Freudians as its first midwesterner, and between 1921 and 1929 he went off to study psycho-analysis in Berlin, Vienna, Munich, London, and Zurich, undergoing periods of analysis with both Otto Rank and Franz Alexander (see Roazen 1975).

There is a certain scandalousness around Blitzsten's training, since Blitz-sten always claimed to have been analyzed by Freud, while Freud denied "ever having known anyone by that name." It seems from the various ac-counts of Blitzsten's Freudian pedigree that he scheduled an initial ap-pointment with Freud but arrived somewhat late, dismissing his tardiness as a logistical mishap. Apparently Freud was not amused. As Blitzsten's stu-dent Robert Knight later wrote about this momentous meeting, "before he could go on Freud insisted that he analyze this as a resistance to starting analysis with him. Lionel was surprised and shocked. He was most eager to see Freud and to work with him. In spite of all arguments, Freud remained adamant; that was the end of his experience with Freud" (Orr 1961, 25). This, it seems, is how Blitzsten ended up in analysis with Franz Alexander.[13]

Franz Alexander, the man Freud would call "my best pupil in the United States" (Saul 1964, 422) was one of Freud's earliest, greatest hopes for his cause. Alexander was the celebrated first graduate of the first psychoana-lytic institute, the Berlin Institute.[14] It was with Alexander's blessing that Blitzsten, on his return to Chicago, organized the city's first seminars on psychoanalysis, listing himself as TA under the auspices of the IPA. Estab-lishing a private practice and joining the psychiatry faculty at Northwest-ern University Medical School, Blitzsten was the first—and for over half a dozen years only—psychoanalyst west of New York City. From this position, through teaching, training, and analyzing hundreds of young psychiatrists from across the Midwest and the central states, Blitzsten became a key fig-ure in what William Menninger called the "de–New Yorkating" of Ameri-can psychoanalysis (see Menninger 1946; also Gitelson 1953; Jones 1957).

Blitzsten's Monday evening seminars in Chicago were glittering avant-garde affairs attended by the Chicago intelligentsia during the 1920s and 1930s, welcoming philanthropists, academics, medical colleagues, artists, students, writers (Ben Hecht would carry Blitzsten's image to Hollywood in his celebrated filmic representations of the talking cure) to explore the world of Freudian ideas. Karl Menninger (in Orr 1961, 44) described "a kind of salon which was often distinguished by wit and brilliant discus-sions in which he was always at the center." The Chicago publishing maven

Stuart Brent (1989, 66) celebrated Lionel in his book about the city's literary scene as "the man with the golden couch," a man who "required constant stimulation to avoid falling into melancholy."[15] As Dorothy Blitsten described her husband's psychoanalytic salon in her unpublished memoir, "it was a kind of underground movement with high morale," and "one was flattered to be included in this circle where one was sure to meet interesting people from various professions, to hear good music and conversation, and to eat and drink well."[16] A dazzling speaker, a gourmand and oenophile, Lionel was well known for his oriental robes, his epicurianism, and his connoisseurship of all things classical and literary.

From his Monday evening seminars Blitzsten went on, in 1931, to found the Chicago Psychoanalytic Society (its original members were Blitzsten, Thomas French, Helen McLean, Margaret Gerard, Leo Bartemeier, and Karl Menninger). This was the same year Franz Alexander, Blitzsten's former analyst, arrived at the University of Chicago to take up Robert Maynard Hutchins and Franklin McLean's invitation to join the faculty as the country's first professor of psychoanalysis. Hutchins projected psychoanalysis as an integral part of the University of Chicago, which he envisioned would be centered not on a worldly "vocational realism" but rather on the soaring idealism of the Western canon of great books (see Hutchins 1995). Alexander had hankered after a prestigious academic berth, and the Chicago invitation seemed a perfect opportunity. On Alexander's invitation to Chicago, Blitzsten, until then "the one analyst west of New York" (Gitelson 1961, 10), would have to share the field he had so carefully cultivated (and with his own former analyst, no less). Thus began a friction and rivalry that developed over the course of the next two decades into an outright contest of faculties as younger psychoanalysts and psychiatrists settled into the gravitational fields that developed around these two men, with their very different temperaments and very different visions of psychoanalysis.

In the course of Alexander's first year at the University of Chicago he attracted the admiration of several prominent members of the social science and law faculties. It was his presentation on criminality and the castration complex at the 1930 Mental Hygiene Congress that had originally gained President Robert Maynard Hutchins's attention, and the prospect of applying psychoanalysis to the understanding of social issues held significant promise for some scholars in the social sciences. The sociologist Harold Lasswell and the political scientist John Dollard met frequently with Alexander as they began to develop their ideas about the role of psychological expertise in sustaining a modern democracy. They were particularly interested in the potential of psychoanalytic testing "for answering the question of who can be trusted with power" (Lasswell 1946, 2). However, while collaboration with Alexander held some real appeal for these social scientists, he rapidly and decisively alienated the members of the new Department of Psychiatry. He held that specific psychological conflicts underlay specific symptom presentations, and these "psychosomatic" hypotheses offended their biological understanding of psychiatric symptoms. Moreover, they were concerned that Alexander's was not an experimental but merely a clinical science. On the occasion of his very first lecture the doctors staged a walkout. As reported by Roy Grinker (1994, 220), who became a close colleague of Alexander at the Chicago Institute for Psychoanalysis,

> it was at the University of Chicago where Dr. Alexander was placed in the rather unfortunate position of giving a seminar concerned with the relationship of psychoanalysis and medicine to members of the Department of Medicine and . . . essentially hostile guests. On one particular day Alexander recounted a case history illustrating the dynamics of constipation. At that time, and perhaps even yet, he contended that constipation was based on a syllogism, "inasmuch as I do not receive, therefore, I do not have to give." He told the story of a young lady who had developed constipation shortly after her marriage to a man who paid very little attention to her. In his management of this case Alexander spoke to the husband and pointed out that her constipation was a reaction to his lack of attention. Whereupon the guilty husband immediately became solicitous, purchased a few red roses and gave them to his wife. Immediately after she received the first gift since their marriage her constipation miraculously disappeared. This was too much for the Department of Medicine and marked the beginning of Alexander's end at the University of Chicago![17]

The members of the Department of Medicine were, furthermore, committed to a vision of psychiatry that centered on the treatment of the more severe forms of psychopathology, those seen in hospitalized mental patients, rather than a psychiatry focused on the "functional" pathologies that psychoanalysts like Alexander or Blitzsten intended to treat in private practice. The question of the location of psychiatry, of its jurisdictional domain, was central to the doctors' protest; the location of psychoanalysis was, in turn, central to that question.

In Grinker's account, this was a year of "formal defeat for psychoanalysis" (1975, 220). The defeat was not merely due to Alexander's Freudian misfirings from behind the podium; he had also become involved in a scandal over fee-splitting, the practice of taking healthier, wealthier patients out of the hospital and into one's private practice, an activity that was roundly frowned on by the psychiatry faculty and viewed as a sign of self-serving opportunism that was destructive to the profession's aspirations to be a first-class medical specialty.[18] Until then, medical students had been treated for free on a gentlemen's agreement between the generations; Alexander had breached this custom and begun charging a student privately for psychoanalysis. The psychiatrists' ire boiled over at this combined offense to their jurisdictional pretensions and their younger confrere.

Freud himself attempted to intervene in the situation from afar, for he had taken a special interest in Alexander's efforts in Chicago, believing strongly as he did that psychoanalysis belonged in the university as a proper discipline rather than in a medical school as merely a part of psychiatry. Nor would psychoanalysis fare well, Freud feared, if it were hived off in the kind of autonomous institutes that were developing in Europe. Freud went so far as to recommend that Alexander try a rhetorical gambit with the doctors: ask them whether they considered astronomy or paleontology real sciences, since, after all, one could not experiment on stars or fossils (Alexander 1960, 102). Did they not think psychiatry could stand firmly as a science on purely clinical foundations? Whether Alexander tried Freud's approach is unknown; what is known is that his University of Chicago appointment was soon terminated, and the chance of housing psychoanalysis—whether as its own discipline or as a formal part of psychiatry in the medical school—was foreclosed.

After this fiasco, Alexander spent the following year in Boston working with William Healy, a proponent of psychoanalysis and leading American reformer in the area of juvenile delinquency. Psychoanalytic criminology had been one of Alexander's earliest research interests, even before his interest in psychoanalytic psychosomatics, and his work with Healy that year resulted in the widely read book *Roots of Crime*. From the standpoint of Roy Grinker, looking back on this period, Alexander's year in Boston was a period of "exile" whose result, in the end, in the form of Alexander's triumphal return, was everyone's gain—for "eventually the Chicago Psychoanalytic Institute developed from Alexander's desire to establish psychoanalytic training and investigation on a level equivalent to the standard of university departments" (1994, 343). Alexander's view of psychoanalysis, which Grinker shared, was that psychoanalysis, if it was not part of the university, was certainly to be instituted in the image of the university because, as Alexander put it, it was "a part of medicine in so far as it is a therapy, and a part of social science in so far as it deals with human relationships" (1938, 600). This ambitious, transdisciplinary vision of the broad applicability of psychoanalysis in society, from the psychiatric to the political, from the somatic to the legal, from the clinical to the applied, was very different from Blitzsten's narrower vision, which held that psychoanalysis was solely for the treatment of an individual's neurosis, a treatment conducted one-on-one, in depth, in the analyst's office.

When in 1932 a group of wealthy philanthropists wished to set up the first formal psychoanalytic institute in the United States—along the lines of, though, as noted, not in affiliation with—a university, it was Alexander they called. Alfred Stern had been cured of a long-standing stomach ulcer after a few months in psychoanalysis with Alexander, and he brought together a group of philanthropists to serve as board members and to inaugurate the freestanding Chicago Institute for Psychoanalysis in 1932.[19] Stern commanded significant wealth and power. He was married to the heiress to the Sears fortune and was closely connected to the Rockefeller Foundation's Alan Gregg through their shared interest in psychosomatics. Psychiatry had been a major focus of the Rockefeller Foundation's activities through the 1920s, and funding Alexander's Chicago Institute would be an integral piece of Alan Gregg's overall plan for what he called psychobiology, "an interdisciplinary amalgam of the clinical, biochemical, biological, and psychodynamic aspects of psychiatry and neurology" (Brown 1987, 156–157).[20] The faculty was to function on the model of a Prussian research institute, similar to the biological Kraepelin Institute, running research studies and generating and disseminating scientific findings.[21] In addition, a training program was to be set up on the Berlin model of psychoanalytic training, reflecting Alexander's tenure at the Berlin Institute. Under the Berlin "tripartite" model of training, a candidate in psychoanalytic training underwent a personal training analysis, attended a series of academic seminars, and treated a number of "control" cases (cases under close supervision). Alexander's intention in establishing the training program was to offer training for a "limited number of psychiatrists," focusing his greater effort on the development of the science of psychoanalysis and on experimenting with its application in a controlled fashion.[22] Under Alexander, the institute would have a small, closed, tightly controlled, quasi-tenured, full-time faculty (known as "the Staff") to carry out this scientific work and to conduct the training of candidates.

Alan Gregg viewed psychoanalysis as a potential bridge between the biological and social sciences. He planned to develop centers for psychosomatic research at various strategic locations around the country and to fund the development of regional foci in the field of psychiatry.[23] In the Midwest, his plans included a substantial grant to the University of Chicago's Department of Psychiatry, to be directed by Roy Grinker. Grinker had been analyzed by Freud on Rockefeller funds, and Gregg encouraged him to work closely with Alexander, since, Gregg hoped, "we would prefer to see some sort of univ. connection for the Inst" (quoted in Brown 1987, 169). Gregg was cautiously optimistic about the independent Institute's scientific potential but felt that "its members have plenty of winnowing to do to have something definite to contribute to the study of somatic diseases" (Brown 1987, 169–170). By working closely with Stern and Gregg, Alexander was able, during his tenure as Institute director, to lead the Chicago Institute for Psychoanalysis to prominence as the premier U.S. center for the study of psychosomatics. Via the success of psychosomatics, he was also able to propel the Institute to the forefront of the burgeoning national (but still New York–centered) psychoanalytic movement.

Franz Alexander's style was, in Grinker's (1977, 91) words, "a distinctive combination of authoritarianism and experimentalism," and in spite of Gregg and the Rockefeller Foundation's steady pressure to secure a university affiliation for the Institute, Alexander, with Rockefeller funds in hand, increasingly steered the organization by his own lights, branching out from Gregg's prime interest in psychosomatics to his own other interests in criminology, politics, and, most contentiously in the domain of psychoanalysis, therapeutic technique itself.[24] This last interest—in speeding up therapy and making it accessible to more people—ultimately got him in big trouble with "the Blitzstenites" (Emch 1961, 16). Alexander was part of a national movement in psychiatry that sought to incorporate the findings of psychoanalysis into psychiatry and to make it as efficient and effective as possible; in this view, psychoanalysis could offer psychiatry powerful new clinical tools, and it could in turn be modified through its interplay with other disciplines in medicine and the social sciences. On the other side of the divide was the national movement to which Blitzsten belonged, centered in the APsaA, which sought to affirm the disciplinary primacy of psychoanalysis, understood as an autonomous, coherent whole.[25]

While Alexander and the Rockefeller Foundation had been courting one another, Blitzsten, prevailing on his own followers, vociferously objected to Alexander's efforts to popularize and streamline psychoanalysis. He felt that Rockefeller Foundation and "lay" patronage threatened the integrity of psychoanalysis by implicating it in external agendas. Blitzsten had no interest in *applying* psychoanalysis to social issues, and no interest in research. He simply wanted to conduct—and to teach—the pure craft of psychoanalysis. In the Chicago Psychoanalytic Society *all* qualified psychoanalysts—whether Institute Staff or not—were members in equal standing, and with Blitzsten holding forth at the Society, it grew in prominence as an outlet for those opposing Alexander's ambitions to streamline psychoanalysis. A growing resentment of Alexander and the Staff's power at the Institute strengthened Blitzsten's voice in the Society (see Brent 1989).

Blitzsten's antipathy toward Alexander stemmed in no small part from the experiments with "flexible technique" that Alexander had initiated at the Institute following the publication of his 1946 book *Psychoanalytic Therapy: Principles and Application.* For several years Alexander and his colleague Thomas French had worked to develop shorter, more directive forms of symptom-focused psychoanalysis that could maximize the therapeutic potential of the doctor-patient relationship. Their efforts won them the opprobrium of the ego psychologists at the annual meetings of the APsaA in New York. Blitzsten, along with Alexander's opponents in APsaA, criticized Alexander's efforts to shorten psychoanalysis and to emphasize the reparative experience the patient could have in his or her relationship with the doctor (Alexander referred to the "corrective emotional experience") over the insight the patient would gain from proper interpretation of his or her conflicts. These critics dismissed Alexander's work as watering down psychoanalytic technique, rendering it, in the words of one, "little more than old-fashioned habit training with especially strong suggestive influencing" (Greenacre 1954, 675–676). Principally, they accused Alexander of "manipulating" the transference rather than "analyzing" it, referring to his teaching of flexible technique as a "Chicago School" in efforts to deride all that was unacceptable to them in his tendency to alloy the gold of pure analysis, interpretation alone, with baser forms of influence (the use of the doctor-patient relationship as a reparative technology in its own right). Blitzsten's friend Kurt Eissler warned that "Alexander reverts to magical treatment in psychoanalytic phraseology. It is exactly that which Freud had warned against and which we made a supreme effort to keep out of psychoanalysis. . . . This does not mean that magical therapy is ill-advised;

it means that a physician using magical therapy should know that he is outside the bounds of psychoanalysis" (Eissler 1965, 150). In Eissler's view, Alexander's notion of the corrective emotional experience was "the acme of distorted psychoanalytic technique."[26]

FROM INSULT TO INSTITUTE: *A Structural Anthropology of Founding Acts*

In writing about his teacher, Leon Saul described Lionel Blitzsten as "hostile to strong men." This is an example of the kind of political rhetoric that was in vogue among the Blitzstenites. In the case of Karen Horney, who Saul also declared had this tendency, her hostility to strong men was a function of her "failure to work through her anger towards her father" (quoted in Quinn 1987, 273). Saul's "psychoanalytic" reading of Blitzsten's issues with authority turns on a similar assessment, exemplifying a style of reflecting on the group through the motif of the family romance, a habit of understanding psychoanalytic politics ad hominem, in terms of the faulty analysis of the analyst. By encasing an idealized image of a successful psychoanalysis in an assignation of its empirical failure in the individual case, the value of psychoanalytic purity was passed down along the Blitzsten line, analyst to analysand, master to apprentice. Blitzsten's own person invited just such "psychoanalyzing," just as his approach to technique did, and indeed this came to be the specifically Blitzstenite form of political discourse. Alexander and his compatriots refused to engage it. Indeed, Alexander addressed Blitzsten's tendency to personalize theoretical differences: "The inclination to seek the author's motivation is a legitimate problem in psychology but if not kept in its proper place can easily vitiate scientific criticism. . . . The 'deviationist' from established theory . . . must defend himself against the tacit or open charge that he proposes his views not because of factual evidence or intellectual conviction but because of some ulterior, although unconscious, motives" (Alexander and French 1946, 4). But what *was* the proper place of psychoanalysis? Alexander's un-self-conscious effort to place a prevalent—and virulent—discursive genre outside the realm of proper political discourse points us toward the Blitzsten-Alexander classificatory battle royale.

In his memorial address for his teacher Lionel Blitzsten, Robert Knight wrote that "the student entering supervision with him, already supposedly finished with his training analysis with someone else, soon felt he was in analysis again—or at least that he was now, in the supervision, being confronted with aspects of himself that he had somehow escaped facing hitherto" (1961a, 5). Blitzsten's effort to extend psychoanalysis, his "aggressive intrusiveness," his "clairvoyance," his "aggressive yet benevolent unmasking," and his special capacity to use "some not yet identified antennae" in "verbally denuding" the "masks, hypocrisies, and hidden motives of all" constituted—and instituted—a practice that ran beside and below the level of theoretical discourse marked as such. It captivated his followers with its uncanny naturalness, speaking to—while at the same time crafting—their intuition they had stumbled onto the secret truth of psychoanalysis.[27] Further inscribing Blitzsten's monopolistic impulse with his own apologia, Knight wrote that "no student who carried through with this supervision felt it to be sadistic or intrusive, but those who quit quite often felt it necessary to justify their termination by critical attacks. They had failed to qualify for the Order of S.O.B.s. (sons of Blitzsten)" (1961a, 6). The symbolic struggle for the pedagogical imaginary, the struggle to craft a psychoanalytic common sense, is most readily evident here in the insult that divides the local psychoanalytic world into the "S.O.B.s" and those, in Knight's terms, who "failed to qualify." Blitzsten's theory of politics turned on the development of a web of intense pair bonds. Alexander did not cultivate pair bonds as the political unit par excellence but the organization as a whole, the Institute as a scientific organization, emphasizing its relation to the broader cultural surround. Alexander had his eye on the institution as an abstract unit, whereas Blitzsten had his eye on the sets of *particular* relationships and the affectively charged web of affiliations at whose center he was. These were two very different theories of institution and of political belonging. The one relies on an appraisal of the colleague as essentially trustworthy; the other sees him as pathological and in need of "psychoanalysis."

Blitzsten's followers, working thus to establish a monopoly on symbolic violence, turned the "Blitzstenkrieg" against Alexander again and again.[28] Hedda Bolgar, for example, commented that Alexander's theoretical conviction that the patient's dependency on the analyst should be kept to a minimum—in Alexander's view, this was to prevent patients from substituting the therapeutic relationship for real-life relationships—was actually a function of his personal "repudiation of his own dependency needs" (in Schmidt 2007, n. 28). Similarly, Frances Hannett, also "psychoanalyzing" Alexander, wrote that "Alexander had a six month analysis with Hanns Sachs. He was proud of the fact that he was considered so normal that no more treatment was deemed necessary. Today we know that one barely gets into analysis within the first six months, let alone completes one, especially with such a complex individual as Alexander" (Hannett 1983, 175). Blitzsten's was an "epigrammatic pedagogy," not a systematic one, writes the psychoanalytic historian Jerome Kavka. "It was not in the nature of his character to establish a cohesive metapsychology" (1991, 214). Kavka does not question the idea that a pedagogy derives from the nature of a person's character; this is a given from the standpoint of a certain psychoanalytic common sense. And it was just this "character" that established Blitzsten as a figure of fascination for generations of Chicago psychoanalysts. The "character" that first appeared in the Monday evening seminar as a personal quality—Stuart Brent's man with the golden couch—was passed into the disciplinary field as an effect of style, as something imitable, as a technology of treatment.

Franz Alexander established his legacy with a prolific output of work, publishing dozens of books and articles on the science of psychoanalysis, lecturing and lobbying throughout the country on matters psychiatric. In contrast, Blitzsten's published record is minuscule given his stature in the profession: he reputedly analyzed more presidents of the APsaA than any other TA, and it was his photograph that served as the frontispiece for the inaugural issue of the *Journal of the American Psychoanalytic Association* in 1951. He exercised his influence almost wholly through personal contact, one-on-one or in small groups. Discipleship was not only a means but was itself a direct effect of his teaching, and his personalist pedagogy magnified this effect as his students objectified his charisma into a methodology. His seminarians carried his personalized teaching throughout the country, becoming leaders at the Menninger Clinic, the Austin Riggs Center, the Sheppard and Enoch Pratt Hospital, and Chestnut Lodge, as well as founders of institutes in Seattle, New York, and Los Angeles (Rubins 1978). In, around, and between these psychiatric sites, oral testimony about the personal relation to Blitzsten circulated the doctrine of personal influence; testimony circulated alongside the doctrine, and testimony wove itself deep into the heart of the doctrine.

These different technologies also carried competing and differently embedded assessments of the scope and potency of psychoanalysis, which one can use to reconstruct their doxic battle. Blitzsten's was fundamentally a practice theory, a theory of the case, transmitted personally in intimate, one-on-one clinical supervision. As his analysand Minna Emch wrote about his inductivism, "his ability to 'stick to the clinical material,' which was his by-word, made him a superior analyst, but stood in the way of his ignoring detail long enough to write anything more than the briefest of clinically oriented communications."[29] The fortunes of this kind of teaching are dependent on the capacity of the master to produce disciples, disciples who will in turn achieve legitimacy by producing works for each other, resisting more public forms of success. Alexander, in contrast, cleaved to the formal, generalizing metapsychological language of Freudian drive theory, a theory that—used deductively—could illuminate individual cases but was not itself derived from them. He was a publishing powerhouse and popular lecturer who would express in public fora around the country his conviction that psychoanalysis's period of isolation was over. He believed that psychoanalysis had reached scientific maturity and no longer needed its defensive avant-gardism, that it could leave the isolated space of the consulting room and join the sciences in a wider conversation among the disciplines. As he conceived this moment of expansion, integration, and scientificization, "this new era required a change in our attitude toward the nonpsychoanalytic world, particularly the field of medicine in general and psychiatry in particular. At the same time it required a change in attitude toward our own knowledge, our methods of teaching and treatment.... First of all ... an emphasis on systematic collective research based on recorded clinical material, on the comparative study by different workers of cases belonging to the same category ... and on the testing of our formulations by the technique of prediction" (Alexander and Ross 1953, 20–21). However, went the complaint of his Institute colleagues, for all his missionizing Alexander was just "too darn busy" being the public face of psychoanalysis to concentrate on the actual psychoanalysis of trainees, on their supervision and cultivation at home (McLean and Tower n.d.; see also Quinn 1987, 441). His seminars focused on the interface of psychoanalysis with the wider world and with the other disciplines, with enhancing the calculability of psychoanalysis, with translating it into other disciplinary languages, and with confirming Freudian theory clinically.[30] Blitzsten, in marked contrast, worked close to home, producing an esoteric discourse for insiders; he was an analyst's analyst, and this was the ultimate value in the eyes of his students and colleagues. Blitzsten never hesitated to expatiate about Alexander's disciplinary promiscuity, always focusing his critique on issues of "narcissism" rather than of "science," pointing up a gaping, deeper and more deeply constitutive pathology of psychoanalytic community with his infamous Blitzstenkrieg.[31]

A virtual hagiography surrounds the figure of Blitzsten to this day. In a 2009 case conference on the subject of "Failed Cases" in which a psychoanalyst un-self-consciously displayed his erotic appreciation of his patient's feminine beauty, an elderly analyst offered his younger colleague a sharp corrective, bringing silence on the seminar: "Blitzsten," this old man offered, "said that the experience of fascination with a patient is a sign of countertransference."[32] Blitzsten's view was that problems in the conduct of analysis stemmed from unresolved issues in the analyst. From this viewpoint, the measure of a successful analysis is the success of the analyst's analysis, and the focus of training should be the perfecting of the analyst, the focus of the institution the perfecting of its membership. Here is the psychoanalytic *mysterium ministerium*, the mystery whereby the charismatic illusion operates such that the "representative of the group receives from the group the power to make the group" (Bourdieu 1985, 739). In the canonization of Blitzsten, psychoanalysis became capable of imagining itself a self-sufficient universe, capable of imagining its survival as a matter of operating on its own membership.

What psychoanalysis offered for Blitzstenites, then as now, was a penetrating immersion in personality, "the thrill of discovery that comes with seeing the most characteristic facets of a human personality arise out of the debris of the subject's initial and restricted self-knowledge" (Eissler 1965, 101). Dismantling this debris required a passionate, reflexive knowledge that could not be generalized. Here was a craft understanding, a pedagogy, and a political philosophy all in one, an understanding of craft that pushed the ideal of disciplinary autonomy to its limit. An indistinct boundary between institutional space and the private space of the analyst's office made it easy to fix the moral qualities of psychoanalysis on the person of the analyst. Metonymically related to the group, "Blitzsten" became the sign of its personalist pedagogy, its fundamental academic necessity, and its reflexive regime: analysis of the colleague and of the self of the analyst—especially his "countertransference"—were ever more intimately interconnected.

While the Blitzstenites ranted about Alexander, Alexander, meanwhile, had nary a word to say about them (in print, at least). Encouraged to strike back by his student and former analysand Karl Menninger, he expressly declined to comment, beseeching Menninger to steer clear of the personal insult, to keep it in its "proper place," outside science. Science must not be so personal; it must not be so defensive, so indecorous. Alexander's neo-Kantian focus on the maturity of the Oedipal subject in rational public discussion belied his effort to ground a psychoanalytic politics in rationality. His failed attempts to impose restraints on verbal conduct belied a hope to ground the disciplinary legitimacy of psychoanalysis on a transcendental cognitive standard and thus to constitute a rational political community. However, despite his great success as a spokesman for psychoanalysis in the wider world, the technologies of organizational reproduction that he had at his disposal simply did not allow him to leverage the strategic insinuation that gained Blitzsten such power *inside* the profession. By means of the insult, the systematic attack on character, Blitzsten crafted that very inside/outside boundary around "real" analysis.

Against Alexander's normalizing push for scientific legitimation of psychoanalysis, Blitzsten specialized in "the emergency interpretation."[33] Just as he would castigate colleagues, he would castigate his patients for their narcissism, accusing them of acting like babies, of regressing to pre-Oedipal neediness. The Blitzstenkrieg came in several varieties. One story with many variants has it that Blitzsten told a suicidal patient who was threatening to jump out the window that if he did jump he should pin a note to his breast saying "Dr. Blitzsten's patient." In another he threw a phone book across the room and when his patient tremulously asked, "What was that?" replied "Well, it's not my dead body" (implying that the patient was treating him as though he weren't there).[34] In another Blitzstenkrieg, this one described by Robert Knight,

> a concert singer presented in a panic regarding a sudden loss of voice, with a concert scheduled for that night. She was only able to whisper that her symptom appeared in the morning following sex with a new lover. This led the practitioner, a reputable analyst of the time (Lionel Blitzsten), to surmise that she had spent the night with a new lover and that their sexual play had probably included an abortive attempt at fellatio to which she had reacted with repulsion. . . . "[He] decided on an action interpretation which would in a professionally ethical way reenact the traumatic episode. He excused himself from the consulting room and went to the kitchen where he procured a frankfurter which, by good fortune, was available. He returned to the patient and approached her with the frankfurter, insisting that she take it into her mouth. She let out a clear mezzo-soprano whoop of protest and her voice was back." (Quoted in Apfelbaum 2005, 165–166)

If it is Blitzsten who defines the emergency interpretation, it is his apprentice Robert Knight's rendering of these idiosyncratic interpretations as a general theory of practice that constructs the Blitzstenite teaching. Knight normalized into routine the "emergency" exception, instituting the Blitzstenite hermeneutic of suspicion with the idea that the analyst can "fall into the patient's trap," the analyst can be "fooled by the patient," the patient "engulfs the therapist" and feeds him "pap" (Sklansky 1991, 230–234). The analyst must at all times be vigilant, be suspicious. As an Alexander partisan wrote about this episteme, "this attitude toward a patient, of seeing him as an adversary rather than a partner in the therapeutic alliance, influenced the analytic stance of many of Blitzsten's admirers" (Sklansky 1991, 232). As Knight would say admiringly about Blitzsten's teaching, "one felt there was no place to hide from his intuitive perception of what one at first would have wished to conceal" (1961a, 5). The effort to routinize the rigors of aggressive intrusiveness as psychoanalytic method would be the problem Blitzsten would finally take to the national leadership, appealing to the APsaA to bring censure on Alexander for his infidelities.[35]

Alexander's project of publicizing psychoanalysis involved streamlining the process in order to bring it to wider audiences beyond the community of connoisseurs; toward this end, he argued that treatment should focus directly on the patient's symptom rather than on a thoroughgoing analysis of his overall personality. His buzzword was *flexibility* of technique. Among Alexander's many flexes away from classical technique, perhaps the most notorious in the psychoanalytic world was his proposition that psychoanalysts could provide the patient with a corrective emotional experience. This was something Eissler and Blitzsten—and then the leaders of the APsaA—deemed frank manipulation, as opposed to "analysis," of the transference. In Alexander's view, since transference interpretation alone wasn't enough to help the patient get better, the analyst should provide the patient with a new and different relational experience, one that would correct the pathogenic experience of childhood (intentionally being warm, for example, with a patient who had had cold parents) (Alexander and French 1946, 66).

The Blitzstenites objected to Alexander's deductive method of decoding symptoms into a set of relations known a priori to lie behind them (i.e., "cold parents" means the analyst should "be warm"). They objected to the analyst purposely providing new relational experiences. In contrast to Alexander's approach, which they deemed formulaic, theirs was what they called "genetic." It involved the lengthy, painstaking unraveling of the layers on layers of emotional events that lay buried behind the manifest psychiatric symptom at the level of character structure. All of the links had to be excavated and reconstructed, all of the mediations mapped, in order to bring about the *insight* that was curative. This insight was what defined psychoanalysis as a special therapy. Alexander objected that detailed "genetic reconstruction of the past is less important for the patient than for the physician" (Alexander and French 1946, 22), but as Blitzsten pointed out over and again, Alexander's technique relied on the trustworthiness of the patient's ego, on viewing the patient's ego as fundamentally sound. Blitzsten, in contrast, treated the patient's fraudulent ego itself, pushing beyond the patient's neurotic symptoms to open up his narcissistic character. Penetrating the depths of character inevitably stimulated intense regressive reactions, so these, too, needed to be unpacked lest they stood in the way of further analysis. Such a careful genetic uncovering—such a careful hermeneutic linking of insult and injury—took years of daily work on the couch. *This* was the gold of real analysis.

While Alexander's "corrective emotional experience" became notorious among analysts, in the end it was Blitzsten's difference with Alexander on the matter of session frequency that brought the local conflict of faculties to national attention. "Reducing the frequency of interviews," argued Alexander, "is one of the simplest means of preventing the transference from becoming too powerful an outlet for the patient's neurosis; if the dependent tendencies are frustrated, they are thrown into relief and the patient is compelled to resist them consciously" (1948, 284). Blitzsten found this so offensive—genetic uncovering could not be streamlined, nor should dependent tendencies be frustrated—that he appealed to the APsaA for formal censure of the Chicago Institute. In 1955 the APsaA sent out two emissaries, Lawrence Kubie and Clarence Oberndorf, to review the Chicago situation, and they decided definitively for Blitzsten. A reduction in session frequency was an unacceptable modification. This was no longer psychoanalysis.

As the Chicago member of the Executive Board of the APsaA, Lionel Blitzsten had been a key player in the 1938 reorganization of the APsaA that limited the IPA's power over training in the United States; now, in the early 1950s, he used his association with the national organization to bring it to bear on the matter of Alexander's heterodoxy.[36] Alexander had wanted to loosen the relationship between the Institute and the Society, hoping ultimately to embed the Institute in a university rather than a private fellowship of psychoanalysts. Blitzsten, as the Chicago ally of the powerful New York–based ego psychologists who led the APsaA, wanted to strengthen that tie in order to use the Society to control training at the Institute and to guarantee that the Institute upheld "good standards." He doubted the possibility of an institute maintaining good training standards if there were no Society to keep it in check—especially if that institute were linked to a university and thus subjected to "academic regulations which might be irrelevant to analytic training" (Knight 1953, 203).

Here was a strange situation. Freud had feared that psychoanalysis would be diluted in the United States, and deploying Alexander as his movement's representative had been his response to that threat. Yet now Blitzsten and his network were accusing Alexander of revisionism while casting Blitzsten—about whom Freud had said "I never knew such a person"—as the traditionalist. Objectifying one another's objectifying practices, asserting rival teachings grounded on different assertions of necessity (the one a disciplinary necessity, the other a broader social necessity), Blitzsten and Alexander each laid full claim to the Freudian legacy and to the process of its institutionalization in Chicago. Without means for brokering multiplicity, they staked out mutually exclusive positions.

The sticking point, it could be said, was the relationship between theory and technique. For Blitzsten, adherence to correct technique defined psychoanalysis; for Alexander, psychoanalysis was fundamentally a (psychosexual) theory of human motivation, applicable to multiple human problems, in various settings and at various scales. In a scathing indictment of Alexander, Blitzsten wrote to Karl Menninger that at the very beginning of his career he had started to distinguish sharply between "the theory of psa [*sic*] and the technique of psa, the latter so far removed from the former." He wrote, "If you recall, I dubbed the former—which I repeatedly recognized *in statu flagrante* at the C.I.P. [Chicago Institute for Psychoanalysis]—'the penis-penis-who's got the penis' brand of psa. I have hopes that some day my voice will be heard in the outer darkness so when I receive a letter like yours my hopes rise."[37] If Blitzsten's prickly polynomasia is a visible trace of the struggles for the power to, quite literally, name the Institute, Blitzsten's and Menninger's epistolary gossip is indicative of the larger problematic of instituting psychoanalysis. Blitzsten questioned central aspects of Freudian drive theory, but remained rigid in what he called technique: the analyst was to see patients daily, using the couch, and to interpret the patient's anxieties as they emerged in the transference. As a teacher and supervisor his focus was on the analyst's countertransference, the analyst's resistance to analysis. This had to be rooted out. In contrast, Alexander adhered to the Freudian thesis of psychosexual fixation but taught a pragmatic, flexible, symptom-focused technique that utilized "noninterpretive" interventions like encouragement, support, and the provision of new relational experience with a quasi-parental other. In this, he offended the purists, eroding the axial distinction between psychotherapy and psychoanalysis in applying "psa" to other enterprises. In his view, it made sense to adjust session frequency, office furniture, and the focus of clinical discussion, for in all this he was only modifying *technique*. These were at most technical variations that did nothing to the core of psychoanalysis. "Psychoanalytic theory," he wrote, is, after all, "the common property of the whole [of] psychiatry," not the sole possession of a psychoanalytic guild (Brown 1987, 171).[38]

While Alexander would become the public face for a postwar psychiatry rapidly becoming psychoanalytic, Blitzsten's technical purism would hold the attention of the connoisseurs, those members of the "C.I.P." and the APsaA who believed that Franz Alexander was "undoing the work of Freud" (Eissler 1965, 95). In an earlier letter to Karl Menninger, Blitzsten spelled out the connoisseurs' complaint in his inimitable way.

> By sheer accident I espied the latest concoction of the C.I.P., called, humorously enough, *The Vector*. As it happened to be in the hands of Peggy Gerard [a child analyst Alexander had invited to Chicago] the moment I espied it, I asked her if I might glance through it. It served two purposes—1st, it enabled me to divert my attention from the irritating mental B.M. which Tom [French, Alexander's closest collaborator] was trying to achieve to the accompaniment of many ehs—ahs—ohs, etc; the end result being only a feeble fart; the 2nd, well, if you perchance have seen it you'll know what I mean. Comparisons are odious I know and this one might be called odorous. All of which is my awkward way of telling you that your Bulletin is ace high and *The Vector* is somewhere else. Or if I must stick to comparisons—then your opus is Casin's Sweet Pea—[while] *The Vector* is what the other fellow's crap smells like to anybody but the crapper. Ye Gad. I'm waxing anal-ytic.[39]

In the Chicago Institute's early battles to taxonomize the talking cure it was not only the winners and losers who were in constant dispute; so were the stakes and the criteria of success. These institution builders mobilized a complex cooperative network with shifting internal and external boundaries, circulating ideas, people, cases, funds, facts, staffers, texts, and referrals, to build up a chiastic structure of organization. Housed in the broader field of psychiatry, itself housing an internal hierarchy organized by degrees of prestige, the Institute came to enclose and incorporate a system of value precisely obverse to its external valuation in wider medicine. Waxing analytic about the C.I.P., Blitzsten and his fellows installed the odorous, seductive illusion of a pure psychoanalysis. In the Blitzstenite cosmogony, psychoanalysis was born ex nihilo of the clinical situation, and on the basis of this origin story the Institute would erect its distribution of dominance. In his hermeneutic of suspicion all was transference, so all was fair game. Thus was the insult instituted, as an insider's hierarchy of values inverted the public's appraisal of psychoanalysis as a tool of medicine. Behind these walls, the master of analysts was above all common healers.

While these tensions between the two factions strained the Institute's cohesion in the very process of its founding, Alexander and Blitzsten seem to have been resolved not to split. A group of Blitzstenites discussed breaking away and forming their own institute, but their movement was quelled by Maxwell Gitelson, rising star and Blitzsten's heir apparent.[40] The two sides' rivalry persisted for decades, shaping talk about method, theory, training, and institution.

Alexander's long tenure and experiments with flexibility brought the Institute success while inaugurating the firestorm that led to his own banishment. In the early 1950s, in the face of his persistent experiments with flexible technique, the APsaA began to consider withdrawing the Chicago Institute's accreditation. Now the Blitzsten group made its final move. They were hardly willing to suffer expulsion from the national organization because of Alexander's indiscretions. They had steadily infiltrated the core Staff of twenty powerful TAs, and from there they engineered Alexander's departure. Sorely disappointed by the Staff's failure to support reform, in 1956 Alexander quit Chicago and psychoanalysis in one gesture.

Forty-seven years after his initial barnstorming of America, a querulous Ernest Jones revisited Chicago, that "swampy excrescence" where he'd been rebuffed in early days. He had not forgotten his first Chicago experience. Acidulous, depressed, elderly, ailing, this last remaining lion of the movement maintained his anti-Americanism to the end.

Blitzsten's heir apparent, Maxwell Gitelson, described the visit and the compliment bestowed on him by this lion of the psychoanalytic movement. "We were on tenterhooks," Gitelson wrote. Though Jones's bitterness about the shape of the Freudian legacy remained rife, Gitelson wrote, "the one compliment I received from him was a propos his hearing . . . that though I had taken an open and uncompromising issue with [Alexander's] Chicago 'School,' I had also been alone opposed to the solution of the problem by way of a split. His parsimonious comment to me was 'Good man!' But from him it was much."[41]

PROFESSIONALIZATION
AND ITS DISCONTENTS

The Theory of Obedience and the
Drama of "Never Splitting"

It would be nice if some of the wrangling about the pros and cons of Freud were to cease.—GRACE BAKER to WILLIAM C. MENNINGER, December 2, 1947

$Vs \times Ss$? $Ad / F \times R / P$? T / E ? N, where
Vs = Specific emotional vulnerability; Ss = External stresses, esp. in relation to specific emotional vulnerability; Ad = Difficulty of adjustment, internal and external; F = Flexibility, adaptability, including capacity for temporary and partial regression; R = Regressive forces, including fixation (toward childish dependence or infantile attitudes or reactions); P = Progressive forces (toward independence, responsibility, productivity, maturity); T = Emotional tension; E = Ego strength (especially control and integrative capacity); N = Degree of neurosis—LEON SAUL'S formula for the quantification of "analyzability"

....

At the outset of World War II, Chicago Institute for Psychoanalysis graduate William Menninger was appointed director of the Psychiatry Consultants Division of the office of the surgeon general of the U.S. army. Trained by Franz Alexander, Menninger had a definite vision for the place of psychoanalysis in psychiatry, and his vision for psychoanalysis was an integral part of his vision of the place of psychiatry in general in American society. Brigadier General Menninger held Chicago Institute graduation certificate number 14 (his brother Karl had been the Chicago Institute's very first graduate), and on his assumption of office he ordered that every doctor in the military learn the basic principles of psychoanalysis so that military recruits could be psychiatrically evaluated before commission and so that psychiatric casualties of war could be treated.[1] He felt that "the necessity to understand the many milder disorders and the combat casualties in the military reënforced the importance of the need of all psychiatrists to have a dynamic orientation that can be provided only through indoctrination by those familiar with psychoanalytic theory and practice" (Menninger 1946, 413). Next, Menninger chaired the committee that produced the revision of the classification of mental disorders that was adopted by the armed services.[2] Soon he was nominated by his psychoanalytic colleagues to lead the APsaA, and at the APsaA's annual meeting in 1946, controversially, he urged the full integration of psychoanalysis into psychiatry, in effect championing its dissolution as an autonomous discipline (Hale 1995; Plant 2005). With government money flowing into psychiatry departments—in 1946 Congress passed the first National Mental Health Act, to support psychiatric research and training—and a deepening sense of urgency in Washington about the country's mental health needs, Menninger and his reformist compatriots felt that psychiatry needed to cull the "queer birds and eccentric individuals" from psychoanalysis and regularize the profession to meet the national need.[3] "Never have we had a more pressing need for experts in human engineering," Menninger read from a statement written by President Truman to the American Psychiatric Association in 1948. "The greatest prerequisite for peace, which is uppermost in the minds and hearts of all of us, must be sanity. We must continue to look to the experts in the field of psychiatry and other mental sciences for guidance in the evaluation of our mental health resources," Truman concluded.[4] For Menninger, psychoanalysis, though it was not the only tool available to psychiatry, was one of the most vital. Menninger and his compatriots were convinced that "the psychoanalytically oriented psychiatrist and not the psychoanalyst per se represents the greatest hope in providing for [the nation's urgent public health] needs" (Menninger 1946, 414). In view of the country's great need for the psychiatrist to be trained in psychoanalytic techniques and the limited pool of senior psychoanalysts available to train him, Menninger proposed, in the interest of marshaling the country's psychiatric resources, that the psychoanalytic training institutes do away with the "lengthy, costly" training analysis requirement for psychiatrists so that all efforts could be focused on the public welfare (Plant 2005). He held a strong conviction, he said, "that psychoanalysis will and can reach fruition only when it becomes an established section or department of the psychiatric faculties in our medical schools and general psychiatric training centers. Highly valued and worthwhile as our Institutes have been, I am sure that they must strive for eventual integration with medical centers and not continue indefinitely as isolated units" (Menninger 1946, 414).

Medically oriented, psychoanalytically trained psychiatrists like William Menninger spearheaded the rapid buildup of psychiatric forces during and after the war, and they soon found themselves at the top of a pyramid of mental health manpower and resources, directing research programs, university departments, and hospitals with large staffs of auxiliary mental health workers under their charge. Psychoanalytic training was a professional necessity for ambitious young psychiatrists who wanted to excel in these settings, even if they did not wish to practice psychoanalysis per se. The exponential growth of psychoanalysis in the postwar period was in this way intricately linked to the broader expansion of psychiatry, an expansion that carried institutes like Chicago's ambivalently into the heart of medical psychiatry, pitting purists whose institutional homes were in the independent institutes—people like Maxwell Gitelson, along with his Blitzstenite colleagues—against hospital-based and university-based reformers and integrationists, people like Franz Alexander's younger colleague Roy Grinker. Grinker, like his colleague William Menninger, was a leading figure in this new political alliance between psychiatry and the state, as well as a spokesman within psychoanalysis for a campaign to medicalize, popularize, and, perhaps above all, Americanize it. Notably, despite Grinker's stature at the helm of the Psychosomatic and Psychiatric Institute at Michael Reese Hospital, the "Athens" of midcentury psychiatric training in the Midwest, his colleagues from the Institute murmured against him nonetheless. "We didn't think of Grinker as a real analyst," said one senior psychoanalyst I interviewed who trained during that period. Maxwell Gitelson, in contrast, "was the last word at the Institute, the voice of orthodoxy. Gitelson analyzed a lot of the older people that are still around here."[5]

The two groups of psychiatrists competed to define psychoanalysis going forward, the one pushing for its autonomy and the other pushing toward its full integration in the new "psychodynamic psychiatry." Under the pressure of these competing views of the place of psychoanalysis in psychiatry, the theme of "not splitting" became prominent in Chicago in the waning years of Franz Alexander's tenure as director. With prominent European émigré nonmedical analysts seeking new professional homes and waves of young American psychiatrists also pressing for entry into training around the country, psychoanalytic institutes elsewhere had experienced schisms. "Not splitting" had become a banner concept in the APsaA as it tried to adapt to the rapidly expanding fortunes of psychoanalysis, and institute leaders around the country worked to professionalize, normalize, and hold together psychoanalysis. While other institutes split apart, Chicago was able to maintain its cohesion, and its faculty held "justifiable pride in having maintained unity in discord, by neither suppressing 'dissenting' viewpoints nor permitting disruption through isolation."[6] How did this happen, when one by one the APsaA's institutes in New York and Los Angeles (and the IPA institutes in several European cities) became divided?

For the psychodynamic psychiatrists, psychoanalysis was one among the several tools in psychiatry's toolkit. While integrationists like Menninger and Grinker wanted to get rid of the eccentrics and émigrés they associated with the institute culture of psychoanalysis (that is, with, literally, the Chicago Institute, where they had trained), they wanted nonetheless to embrace what was potent and curative in psychoanalysis, the psychological perspective and the clear effectiveness of talking, listening, interpreting, and understanding as ways to help patients. They wanted to integrate these practices with the biological perspective of organic psychiatry and to streamline them so they could be made more widely available. Psychoanalysis had allowed psychiatry to expand its purview beyond the severely ill asylum patient to "milder" cases, and now the integrationists wanted to push the techniques further in their ambition to achieve greater success and greater effectiveness. Several mutually reinforcing factors thus came together to cement psychoanalysis into a postwar psychiatry that would experience dramatic success in America: a "pragmatist" belief among many psychiatrists that psychoanalysis could be shortened, its powers harnessed to symptom-focused treatments; a broad anti-émigré, anti-European, and anti-intellectual sentiment among leaders in the field; the medicalization of psychoanalysis from within through its dalliance with psychosomatics; the increasing social attention being given to the study and treatment of war casualties; and increased public sentiment against the dehumanizing conditions of mental hospitals and in favor of the more humane methods of talking to patients that were associated with psychoanalysis. The reformers' efforts would greatly enhance the fortunes of the psychoanalytic institutes, as young psychiatrists vied with one another from the 1950s to the 1970s for the opportunity to train in psychoanalysis for what promised to be a lucrative career in psychiatry.

In this postwar moment of contestation, however, a group of analysts at the Chicago Institute looked on the new psychodynamic psychiatry with disdain. They were intent on maintaining the privileged status of psychoanalysis within psychiatry. They were suspicious of the quasi-analytic therapeutics enjoined by the new psychodynamic psychiatry. Menninger had protested "against the direction of . . . our best analytic teaching power into the intensive training analyses of a handful of candidates, when those same brains could give a helpful, working, dynamic orientation to ten times the number" (Menninger 1946, 414). The analysts at the Institute, however, were wary of popularization. Menninger felt that the war effort had made the strengths of psychoanalysis as a treatment so clear that "the verities of analytic theory in practice seem to me far past the need for constitutional or legislative protection." His view was that "inter-society political maneuvering" over these verities was wasting the profession's energies (414). Four sessions a week or five, must the patient free associate or can he speak focally about his concerns—these did not matter to him. In contrast, Gitelson and his Blitzstenite compatriots felt that the verities—insofar as they pertained to training standards—were fundamental, and they set about to sharpen, systematize, and preserve these. They geared their efforts to further developing ego psychology and to solidifying a school of thought they felt was truer to Freud.[7] They did not want to split off from the wider field, even though they wanted their own autonomy within it. In the Institute a self-conscious shift from movement to profession was in full force, and Gitelson and other Institute insiders sought to consolidate psychoanalysis as such by routinizing and centralizing control, by strictly defining its own form of knowledge, and by making sure it was, according to its own lights, a "science."

The Chicago Institute's Board of Trustees, cognizant of these tensions over the place of psychoanalysis in psychiatry, carefully selected a moderate and, they hoped, noncontroversial figure to replace Franz Alexander as director. Gerhart Piers was to oversee a shift in the structure of authority at the Institute from the charismatic model of the period of its founding to the formal, bureaucratic administration the Board felt a mature profession required.[8] Maxwell Gitelson, in the spirit of Thomas Kuhn, announced that the psychoanalytic "movement" was at last to become a "normal science," through organizing its training system. Two strands of practice—and of thought and writing about practice—are centrally relevant to understanding "not splitting" as a principle of government for this newly normal local science in Chicago. The one strand centered on the framing of a new clinical problematic, that of *ego autonomy*, through the creation of a new figure of pathology, the "too normal" trainee. The other strand centered on the place of psychoanalysis in medicine, for this "too normal" trainee was, after all, a psychiatrist. He was a man who, through medicine, was bound to—not autonomous from—society's postwar hopes for psychiatry. The "too normal" trainee was in a sense a symptom, in his very person, of the impossible autonomy of psychoanalysis, and in the ego autonomy theorists' project of working out the implications for the psychoanalytic *profession's* autonomy, the trainee's psyche became the place par excellence of struggle over the social location of psychoanalysis.

TRAINING ANALYSIS AND THE PATHOLOGY OF THE "TOO NORMAL" TRAINEE

In 1956, when Gerhart Piers took the reins, the Chicago Institute was viewed as something of a pariah in the APsaA because of Franz Alexander's experiments with flexible technique. There had been rumblings at the national level that Chicago might be expelled from the APsaA (indeed, this was in large part why the faculty ultimately turned against Alexander), and Piers was in the unenviable position of helping the Institute recover from the political trouble Alexander had gotten it into. Piers facilitated a delicate compromise between the rival Chicago groups by installing an Alexander collaborator, Thomas French, as director of research and a Blitzsten collaborator, Joan Fleming, as dean of education (Kirsner 2000). Joan Fleming had suggested this division of labor in an effort to help Piers "organize" the institute.[9] Among Fleming's many educational interventions it was perhaps this very division of labor that would remain her most far-reaching political legacy, since thereafter a line between *research* and *education* would mark an impasse between the efforts that were geared toward mediating psychoanalysis to an outside public ("research") and the efforts that focused on the internal, professional universe and its social reproduction ("education"). In the research department, Thomas French would explore the efficacy of psychoanalysis in treating a range of problems, from schizophrenia to anxiety to ego weakness. The education department, meanwhile, would also carry out a kind of research on psychoanalysis, but here the population of concern was the psychoanalytic candidates themselves. By separating research and training, the three leaders were able successfully to steer the organization back into the APsaA mainstream in the late 1950s; at the same time, this new division of labor further inscribed the Institute in a domain of practice separate from the wider world.

Piers delegated much of the daily work of administering the Institute's affairs to Fleming, under whose watchful managerial eye, it is said, "political games were endemic and institute leaders disapproved of independent thinking" (Kirsner 2000, 115). A single woman with administrative leanings, married to psychoanalysis—reportedly she was "saved from her lone-liness by her analysis with Blitzsten"—Fleming was perfect for the job.[10] From the 1950s to the mid-1970s this "smart, bossy" leader of the "Jew-boys" worked overtime to update the Prussian curriculum and bring the Institute's unorganized syllabi, uncoordinated supervision, and unmoni-tored training analyses under firm, centralized control. "Gerhard was the director," said a senior analyst about the period of Fleming's tenure, "but he counted on Joan to do everything—and she did, she ran the place. You'd make or break it with Joan. The group around her was very loyal to her, and they wrote a book, articles, developed a lot of ideas. Lou [Shapiro] was one of them, Sol [Altschul], Max [Forman]. They were Blitzstenites."[11]

Piers's directorship fell squarely within the golden era of psychoanalysis, the period when psychoanalysis reached the height of its power and pres-tige in the United States and psychoanalysts' practices were full to bursting. With a raft of applicants wishing to be trained and with veritable bottle-necks in assigning TAs for those who matriculated (one told me "I waited several years to get assigned a training analyst"), the issue of what was called applicant "selection" came prominently to the fore. Fleming led a large-scale research project from within her education department into the quali-ties of character an analyst should possess. The intent of her project was to develop a framework for the standardization of selection that would scien-tifically pick out "on an ego-psychological level as opposed to just behavior" the ingredients that made up what she came to term the "work-ego" of the analyst. Marshaling these twinned forces of standardization and division in her quasi-scientific notion of selection, Fleming's life work would be that of surveying, routinizing, dividing, and defining the limits of analysis—with significant entailments for the field's understanding of analyzability that her close colleague Maxwell Gitelson would further work out.[12]

In an era of systematization, where—as Heinz Hartmann and Rudolph Loewenstein wrote (1962, 44)—"we find two trends, one of which tends to underestimate the role of the superego compared to that of the ego, while of the second the opposite is true," Fleming's central effort was to theorize the psychoanalytic work-ego, and she became, through her own work-ego, one of a series of strong establishment figures based in Chicago who shaped the field from within.[13] Steering the Institute squarely back into the APsaA's mainstream, she soon became the nation's premier "peda-gogue of psychoanalytic education," the ideological spokesperson for the APsaA's BOPS and the chair of the APsaA's Survey Steering Committee, which produced the "Rainbow Report" on the state of psychoanalytic education (American Psychoanalytic Association 1955). This report created the field study of psychoanalytic education carried out by Bertram Lewin and Helen Ross (1960). Deemed by the psychoanalytic historian Robert Wallerstein "comparable to the impact of the famed Flexner Report in the structure and conduct of medical education in the United States early in the century" (1987, ix), it led to the establishment of the Committee on Psychoanalytic Education (COPE), which was dedicated to studying and promulgating recommendations on the standardization of both psychoanalytic technique and psychoanalytic training.[14] To cope (as it were) by *selection* was vital, since applications for training were flooding into the Admissions Committee of the APsaA, and one of this committee's central problems had now become (or was now going to be framed as) that of "the normal candidate."

This new problem was thematized in the following broadly circulated 1953 APsaA President's Statement made by Robert Knight.

> In the 1920's and early 1930's those who undertook psychoanalytic training were of a somewhat different breed from the current crop of candidates. There was, in those days, less emphasis on selection procedures and many analysts were trained who might today be rejected. Many training analyses were relatively short, and many gifted individuals with definite neuroses or character disorders were trained. . . . In contrast, perhaps the majority of students of the past decade or so have been "normal" characters, or perhaps one should say had "normal character disorders." They are not so introspective, are inclined to read only the literature that is assigned in Institute courses, and wish to get through with the training requirements as rapidly as possible. Their interests are primarily clinical rather than research and theoretical. Their motivation for being analyzed is more to get through this requirement of training rather than to overcome neurotic suffering in themselves or to explore introspectively and with curiosity their own inner selves. Many have had their training largely paid for by the federal government, and this factor has added to training problems. (Knight 1953, 217)

For their teachers, Knight's gifted generation, who "tended to be highly individualistic" (Knight 1953, 217), it became supremely important that the trainee, the candidate, be trusting of the Institute and of its servants, those TAs whose passionate intent was to foster psychoanalysis. The literature on psychiatric normalization devotes great attention to the theme of manifest behavioral normalcy (sexual normalcy especially, since so many of these authors follow Foucault), neglecting this other dimension of "normalcy," trust in authority, the principle at the center of Joan Fleming's pedagogy.[15] She and her compatriots were not as interested in normal behavior in the usual sense of the word as they were interested in "the normal ego" as defined on ego psychological grounds. As one 1950s applicant for training at the Chicago Institute explained,

> I remember they started doing these group Admissions interviews. I remember this one young guy in particular, we were talking about our interest in applying. We were both really quaking. He had just found out that "group interview" meant a group of TAs would interview each of us—and you really had to talk personally about yourself. He'd thought it would be a group of candidates being interviewed by one person! His lack of trust [in the interview procedure] was a problem, and I think that was the end of him.[16]

But Fleming didn't stop at rendering scientific and measurable the "special qualifications" required in the individual applicant at the point of selection. She also studied those more developed "ego skills" that were required at the several points of "progression" along the way in training, thematizing the "ego abilities" that needed to be manifest at each juncture: when a candidate could begin didactic seminars, when he could start his first control case, when he could start his second control case, and, finally, at the end of training, when his fully molded work-ego had crystallized.[17] According to Fleming's 1961 article "What Analytic Work Requires of an Analyst: A Job Analysis," the analyst's work-ego centrally consists in the capacity to withstand the deprivations of analysis because "the analyst must devote all of his energies to . . . the patient rather than to achieving gratification of his own impulses. The only gratifications for the analyst in this special kind of relationship are altruistic, vicarious, and sublimated" (Fleming 1961, 723). He must maintain free-floating, evenly hovering attention (also called "controlled daydreaming"), tolerating the patient's regressions while maintaining his own integrated state, controlling the discharge of his affects and living simultaneously in two worlds "with no loss of reality contact or of his own identity." Fleming's (1961, 729) core intuition was that "in correlating these performance criteria with selection criteria, the latter could be sharpened and refined to increase our skill in recognizing the indicators of good or poor potentials in applicants."[18]

Several other Blitzstenites worked closely with Fleming to develop these managerial methods of selection and standardization of training; among her colleagues, Minna Emch, Maxwell Gitelson, and Theresa Benedek each published important papers on these subjects. In Blitzsten's own swan song, a final article coauthored with his favored analysand, Joan Fleming, the two delineated the terms of what they called the "supervisory analysis" (Blitzsten and Fleming 1953; see also Grotjahn 1954). They conceived of clinical supervision—the close discussion of a case—as the direct continuation of the student's own training analysis, in which the teacher would interpret the student's neuroses, sending the student back for more precise analysis as needed. Kavka wrote that "they emphasize that no therapy occurs for either patient or student if the patient's transferences are attended to while the student's countertransference is neglected. The technical suggestion offered is that the student be asked if he has taken up the countertransference issue in his own analysis; even more, a conference between the personal analyst and the supervisor is suggested as a valuable collaboration working in the best interests of the student in training" (Kavka 1991, 222). Minna Emch, another of Blitzsten's analysands, added the idea that one could perform a veritable calculus of the personnel and their crosshatching transferences, which should put us "in awe of the many psychically represented members of the psycho-analytic family who silently participate in our . . . supervisory setting" (Emch 1955, 304). The whole "family," in this sense, must be attended to in the "supervisory analysis," along the quasi-mathematical lines of the model presented in the epigraph to this chapter.

> If, as we know, the seven elements are personified, we also know that they are far from being the conveyors of a unitary or single primary (non-ambivalent) attitude. If, then, each of the seven is taken as conveying at least one clearly accepting and one clearly rejecting attitude, we find by the same formula that our seven persons will provide us with the staggering total of 1,183 different combinations of positive and negative feeling among and between all the 2-groups in our system. And if this is not sufficient to indicate the potential for complication, we should for the moment consider that all the possible juxtapositions and arrangements (permutations) of our original seven elements reach the tremendous total of 5,040. (Emch 1955, 299)[19]

The vision of psychoanalytic pedagogy that Fleming and her compatriots were developing extended well beyond the assessment of the clinical results of trainees' cases, beyond monitoring their "integration" of the various elements of psychoanalytic education, to the evaluation of the candidate's training analysis itself. Meeting minutes throughout the 1960s are full of intense and often acrimonious debate on this subject, the phenomenon that Bertram Lewin and Helen Ross, in their monumental 1960 study of psychoanalytic education, called "syncretism." As framed by Lewin and Ross, syncretism was the thorniest problem psychoanalytic training had to contend with, a murky blending of educational and therapeutic motives and activities. As one senior analyst described his experience in supervision with Fleming (baring his soul, as it were),

> if you were honest with her you'd be fine. People were terrified of her, but I got on well with her. She was a real moll. I dunno how else to describe it. I'm saying this because [one time] she said, "C'mon out to the country this weekend, I'll see you out there." This was a holiday weekend. I said, "I have the family." She said, "Well, bring the family." So I had these two kids, it's one of hottest days of the year, and we get there and she doesn't even give 'em a cold drink. Didn't have any maternal quality. A tough mien. But she believed if you told the truth about what you were doing then you were doing it right, and I did, and I got on well with her. She was a good supervisor, really devoted to analysis and to the Institute; that's why she got promoted to that big office in The American.[20]

In calling Fleming a "moll" he was referring to her relationship with Blitzsten—she was a moll to Blitzsten's gangster. She pushed for explicit reporting on the progress of trainees' analyses to be a part of their formal academic record, a position that many of even the most orthodox analysts of the APsaA felt went too far in its intrusiveness into the trainee's personal life. The guidelines that she recommended TAs use in assessing their analysands in written reports to the Progression Committee included:

— Is the candidate able to associate freely? If so, this usually accompanies a good working alliance and demonstrates some ability to regress.
— What is the stage of transference development? Is the transference neurosis still being resisted? If so, this form of regression can be interfered with by matriculation. The responsibilities and conflicts associated with courses and cases can very easily be used to avoid the transference neurosis by mobilizing a flight into health and/or success. Is the transference itself so entrenched as an erotized [sic] resistance in defense against narcissistic injury that the analysis appears stalemated or in danger if matriculation occurs? If so, it may be that the candidate is not analysable. Has the candidate experienced

negative transference? Has triadic transference material appeared or is it still dyadic? This bears on the strength of the narcissistic core, the level of object relatability achieved, and the solution a given candidate found for his Oedipal conflict.

— Has the transference meaning of matriculation been worked on in the analysis?[21]

Embedded in Fleming's managerial optimism was the omniscient fantasy that it was possible to create a pure field of observation into the psychic life of a student that was free of institutional "artifacts" or power relations. Science, after all, did not truck with such matters. Disavowing its own administrative thrust, this conviction presupposed and entailed two related theses: first, that there could be a neutral, fully analyzed analyst, and second, that the mark of a successful analysis was the development of an autonomous ego free of "the culture."[22] Again, the target of her attention and worry was the ego of the trainee—and by extension the future of psychoanalysis itself. Trainees had become the privileged site of operation for psychoanalysis, the "subjects" upon whom the developments of ego psychology were elaborated. Regular psychiatric patients, the kinds of people whom Thomas French's research studied, were no longer so important to Fleming and Gitelson; for them, the most important issue was the transmission of correct psychoanalysis. Fleming's move to hive off research from education effectively marginalized French and his research on the broader efficacy of psychoanalysis, and, with him, almost all of the outside world.

The askesis of "the normal candidate" would reach its apotheosis in the writings of Maxwell Gitelson, who wrote in an article by that title that "psychoanalytically we are compelled to look on 'normality' as a defense" and, relatedly, that "it appears to be a hopeless task to set up normality as a basis for the selection of potential analysts whose training would [then] be presumed not to take too much time" (Gitelson 1948, 206). Normality—by which he specifically meant an individual's adaptation to surrounding culture—was a defense whose undoing would take a very, very long time. This message of length and thoroughness was precisely contrary to William Menninger's plea to the profession for an expedient utilitarianism in the service of the national need for a healthy populace. Gitelson was blunt: undoing the defense of normality would take "in some cases as long as the individual has lived already" (Gitelson 1948, 207). Manifest normality was the façade of a pernicious narcissistic character disorder promoted by "our culture," and Gitelson stood in staunch opposition to those in psychiatry—

like William Menninger—who subscribed to those surface indicators of normality as arguments for the wisdom of shortening, or God forbid, removing the requirement for, the training analysis. "The recent history of the psychoanalytic movement has literally dropped th[is] problem at our doorstep," he wrote (1954, 176), since the success of psychiatry was attracting to psychoanalytic training young psychiatrists for whom the training analysis was just one more step in a successful adaptive process whose goal was money, social acceptance, and status. "Very sick and almost unanalyzable," this generation of ambitious young people "approach analysis as another task to be mastered in a search for recognition. This façade, culturally determined, is itself a resistance, preventing the individual from achieving the true freedom essential for the practice of analysis" (Gitelson 1954, 183).[23] Clinically, Gitelson argued, these "normal" candidates had more distortions and anxieties than those who presented with a downright neurosis, so that "with such candidates it is necessary to mobilize a conflict made latent by the culture, [because] only thus can one analyze the libido itself." Still, he noted, writing to his TA colleagues, some TAs despaired altogether about the suitability of normal candidates for a career in psychoanalysis, since their pervasive, "ego-syntonic" narcissistic defenses—submissiveness, intellectualization—meant that in them "the 'paranoid' and 'manic' defenses [were] more extensively elaborated" than in the neurotic trainee of yore; these "normal" patients literally did not—and constitutively could not—know how sick they really were.[24]

In view of the difficulty of exposing the narcissistic core of the pathology, the normal candidate required a longer, deeper, and invariably more difficult ("if not impossible") analysis than the neurotic candidate had required, and, contra the Alexander people's desire to streamline analysis, "whether we like it or not, there is no short cut. Those modifications of technique which have been proposed, such as selective therapeutic planning, denial of dependency, circumvention of the transference neurosis, dilution of the analytic schedule, and fractionation of the entire course of the analysis have yet to demonstrate their psychoanalytic validity" (Gitelson 1973, 149–150). Thus the paradox of the normalization of psychoanalysis. Since "to no other symptom does such a large quota of secondary gain attach," the analyst must simultaneously stand in for authority while working to dissolve in the patient the transference to him qua authority (Gitelson 1954, 178).[25]

Around this fragile claim—deemed authoritarian by its adversaries—a battle crystallized for ownership of the candidate's psyche, one that would strengthen the walls of the bastion and menace the psychiatric assimila-tionists. Which was to be the proper site of psychoanalysis, the normal can-didate's psyche or society's "pressing need" for expediently trained psychia-trists? In determining that "our candidates, as we find them, are the future of psychoanalysis," Gitelson, gathering together the strands of what others had noted about the current generation of trainees (Knight, for instance, in his Presidential Statement), sounded an alarm to the profession. For Gi-telson, libido had to be disimbricated, and he delineated a new theoretical object toward this end, pathological "normalcy." It was a paradoxical pa-thology, a pathology of paradoxical autonomy. Shifting the field's attention in this way from neurosis to the problem of "normal character," he pushed the Institute beyond the problem of mere "selection" and into a full con-frontation with the perils, for psychoanalysis, of normality—the perils of, indeed, success.

In direct contrast with Hartmann's much-remarked-on idealization of healthy adaptation, Gitelson's monstrous "normal" lived "in terms of a fa-çade patterned by his environment, providing him with an opportunity to gratify his instincts by virtue of their imbrication with the demands of his environment" (Gitelson 1954, 183).[26] In articulating his revision of metapsy-chology, Gitelson pushed to place the problem of narcissism—understood as the trainee's problem with accepting, literally, his patienthood—at the center of ego psychology. This would be a program from which there was no turning back, for, as Gitelson had anticipated, in light of the postwar popu-larity of psychoanalysis, "the normal candidate" would keep showing up for training. Since this would be the candidate of the future, "our future," and since "we cannot sidestep our responsibility for trying to insure that future," theorizing the normal candidate's psyche was essential (Gitelson 1954, 183).

INTERLUDE. BEYOND THE PALE: *Building the*
"Other Scenes" of Psychoanalysis

Unsurprisingly, with such intense scrutiny and rigorous criteria for "se-lection," the Institute deemed many young psychiatrists unanalyzable and turned them away during the Gerhart Piers years. This was a point of great shame for many who were rejected for behavior that fell outside the acceptable definition of maturity. Homosexuals were of course ex-cluded, and unmarried individuals of either sex were especially scrutinized because "genital" normality was considered an essential feature of matu-rity.[27] By excluding numerous aspirants to psychoanalytic training at a time when certification in psychoanalysis was a necessity for the ambitious young psychiatrist—whether he did or did not want to practice purely as a psychoanalyst—the Institute contributed to building an "other scene" for psychoanalysis, a space of exclusion where psychoanalysis lived a dissident life.[28] Several psychiatrists who were excluded from Institute training, as well as several others who had been trained but were excluded from moving up to full TA status, formed study groups outside the Institute, sites of unofficial, informal, and often interdisciplinary training. These groups began to develop subcultural styles of practice beginning in the late 1950s. While the Institute's curriculum was strictly ego psychological, members of these outsider groups—led by Peter Giovacchini, Gene Borowitz, Erika Fromm, Merton Gill, and Bruno Bettelheim—began to read Melanie Klein, Donald Winnicott, Harry Stack Sullivan, and other writers whose work fell outside the canon. These were the first psychotherapists in Chicago to take up British object relations ideas. The groups also brought together the growing number of psychologists and social workers who were interested in psychoanalysis but were prevented from formal training. It was these nonmedical therapists, in their conversations with one another and with the dissident psychiatrists, who first began to incorporate these foreign ideas into psychotherapy practice. These heterogeneous groups held some strong beliefs in common (along with their outsider status). Many resented the APsaA's "medical monopoly" on psychoanalysis, and they also found that institution's preferred theory of ego psychology to be authoritarian, proconformist, and overly individualistic in orientation. Crucially, they were interested in social interaction and interpersonal communication more than they were interested in the endogenous drives of a Freudian closed system.[29]

But exclusions proliferated. Even as the Institute turned away potential trainees during this period, the Institute's clinic, too, rejected many applicants for treatment. This clinic had a waiting list that was often a year long, as upwardly mobile, aspiring young professionals, academics, lawyers, teachers, housewives, students, business people, and doctors all desired to experience psychoanalysis for themselves. Like the Institute itself, the clinic used strict criteria of analyzability in determining who was an acceptable patient, rejecting many of those who desired treatment as too sick for psychoanalysis. It referred these "unanalyzable" patients out, in many cases to the private practices of the psychologists and social workers, for psychotherapy.

In this way, the Institute, attending to its boundary work, began inadvertently to support these other scenes.[30] Arguably, Fleming's and Gitelson's purifying practices of standardization, selection, and training analysis enhanced rival practitioners, rival professions, rival practices, and rival theories, extramural scenes of psychoanalysis that were all developing their own psychoanalytic languages. The Institute, meanwhile, offered programs in "applied psychoanalysis" intended to allow the auxiliary mental health professional the opportunity to partake of psychoanalytic ideas, albeit in modified form. The more vocal of these would ultimately articulate claims on formal psychoanalytic training.[31]

Meanwhile, a subgroup among the Institute's faculty began to assert its own claims, and this group's efforts to expand the range of analyzability to include *children* would decisively change the relations among the mental health professions arrayed around the Institute. Mainstream psychoanalysis in the United States had always marginalized child psychoanalysis, and psychoanalysts at the Institute regularly questioned the child psychoanalysts' central conviction that children could be analyzed as well as adults. The majority of psychoanalysts felt it crucial that a patient have a well-formed "repression barrier" (the ability to repress primitive wishes), which they considered a developmental achievement of later adolescence. For most psychoanalysts, therefore, younger children were, by definition, unanalyzable. Among their colleagues, the child analysts were dogged, therefore, by the question of whether they were "real" analysts or not.[32] At the same time, the child psychoanalysts' mission to the wider world on behalf of psychoanalysis had been quite successful because they had managed, beginning in the 1920s, to establish themselves as consultants in child guidance and juvenile protection clinics around the city. Chicago had a well-established culture of such clinics and agencies, and Institute analysts served as respected pedagogues in these organizations. These were the institutional places where most child therapy was performed, so it was *outside* the Institute that the child analysts found their bailiwick.[33]

From the standpoint of the Institute's leaders, if child psychoanalysis were not real psychoanalysis—if what the child analysts did was merely a form of supportive psychotherapy—then psychoanalysts were not needed to conduct it. "Lay" therapists could do it just as well. This created a thorny problem for the Institute, a problem of jurisdiction that was beginning to worry leaders of psychoanalytic institutes around the country. As Robert Knight put it, "there are at least two unrecognized institutes in New York City which openly train nonphysicians . . . for child analysis. . . . This latter training activity, which violates the training standards of the APsaA, is defended by those who participate in it on the ground that more child analysts are badly needed."[34] The problem was that child analysts might encroach on the domain of psychoanalysis proper. "It is well known," Knight went on, "that child analysts tend in time to abandon the more arduous work with children and to limit their practice to adult patients" (1953, 213). The real problem, he pointed out, was that the child analysts were going to compete for adult patients, abandoning their supposedly "more arduous work" to do so and blurring the boundary around what was true psychoanalysis. In other cities, émigré analysts had been the ones to raise the jurisdictional "problem of lay analysis." In Chicago it was, instead, the child analysts and their nonmedical collaborators, the child therapists.

All of these tensions—over the status of child analysis in relation to adult psychoanalysis, over the question of who could practice it, over whether it was indeed psychoanalysis or just psychotherapy, and over whether children were even analyzable—became evident when the Institute established its Child and Adolescent Psychotherapy Training Program in 1962 (CAPT).[35] This program was the Institute's response to the child analysts' growing recognition that social workers in agency settings were providing most of the psychotherapy to children in Chicago, and their concern that these individuals had had little systematic training. The program succeeded the earlier Child Care Course, which had provided social workers and teachers with classes on child development but no direct clinical training. In the words of one of the CAPT's first graduates whom I interviewed, the leaders of the Child Care Course had "made no bones about telling people that they were not there to do therapy"—they were there to learn about child care, period.[36] Another first-generation student of the CAPT program described the "strangeness" of some of the consultations that Institute faculty would conduct in the social welfare agencies. These experts ventured forth from their tony Michigan Avenue practices to social service agencies in poor neighborhoods to listen to social workers describe what they were encountering in their cases. Poverty and powerlessness were eclipsed in their pronouncements that the families being described were "primitive."[37] Such authoritative pronouncements about the poor seem nonetheless to have created a mystique for agency workers around this "impenetrable notion of 'analyzability,'" said one respondent. "I don't think they had a clue about the cultural context of these kids," he continued. "They'd lecture us about pregenital personality and it was a total contortion we'd go through to fit ego psychology to the families we were working with."[38] The social workers had been trained in a psychoanalytically inflected casework that reflected the ideas of Harry Stack Sullivan and centered on understanding psychological distress in terms of interpersonal relations and social context (including issues of power, poverty, race, social marginalization, etc.) rather than in strictly intrapsychic terms of the one-mind psychology the analysts were steeped in. Amazingly, in spite of these broader horizons, said this man, the social workers seemed to "accept this situation much like blacks accepted segregation." This was his metaphor, and he went on to say, "We had been brainwashed, me and all my colleagues. The higher status conferred on a person in analysis then, it was like it was magical."

The CAPT trained a generation of social workers, many of whom would later leave their jobs in social welfare agencies to establish private practices competing with the analysts (precisely as Knight had warned).[39] The CAPT curriculum was, indeed, a virtual replica of the training in psychoanalysis, so they were quite well equipped. An early group of CAPT graduates, having achieved the status upgrade from "Care" to "Psychotherapy," soon went on to found their own institute, the Institute for Clinical Social Work, setting up a training program that would mirror the Institute's psychoanalytic program while offering a credential the Institute didn't, a Ph.D. Faculty at the Institute worried that these graduates might begin to call themselves psychoanalysts. A common complaint was that these therapists were keeping child patients for themselves—keeping them in psychotherapy, that is, and not referring them on for "full" psychoanalysis. Some Institute faculty members also feared that the APsaA might expel the Institute if it were seen to be training nonphysicians as analysts. The CAPT program flew under the radar of both the APsaA and the American Medical Association; despite the beginning development of these other scenes of psychoanalysis in Chicago, and all of the Institute's concerns and compromises with them, at its apex psychoanalysis remained firmly ensconced in psychiatry.

PSYCHIATRIC BONDAGE / PSYCHOANALYTIC AUTONOMY

The "medical" identity of psychoanalysis—its place within psychiatry—was nevertheless very much under discussion in Chicago as elsewhere. Should psychoanalysis be coextensive with psychiatry? Should it be an independent profession? How should it be regulated? In a series of polemics, Roy Grinker—close collaborator and former analysand of Franz Alexander—went after Maxwell Gitelson, Blitzsten's heir, as the two faced off over these questions about psychoanalysis's institutional location and scientific status. "Which institute?" Grinker would blithely ask, on hearing a colleague mention "the Institute." For Grinker, director of the psychiatric Athens that was Michael Reese Hospital—with its extensive research budget and his own extensive clinical experience with veterans—psychoanalysis was indubitably a part of medicine; psychoanalysis, in fact, provided medicine with (and theorized) what he called the crucial "transactional matrix" that medicine required in order to help trauma sufferers. For Gitelson, whose career was centered at the Institute, the relationship of psychiatry and psychoanalysis was much more problematic. It came down to "a marriage of convenience," one that had already been profoundly damaging to psychoanalysis in "diluting" and "watering it down" (Gitelson 1973, 147, 244). Gitelson lamented the way the war had "breached the ivory tower of the psychoanalyst" as well as the fact that "[psycho]dynamic eclecticism had become the psychiatric vogue" (241). Though he wrote sympathetically about the personal pull that psychoanalysts might feel to do "practicable" work that would address "the social problems of our time," he pressed for relative isolation from psychiatry, filling his publications with emphatic statements that began "Freud says," "Freud emphasized," "Freud envisaged." What Freud apparently emphasized above all (to Gitelson at least) was that "deepening analysis rather than shortening it must be the first consideration" (146). He therefore adamantly opposed "modified techniques" or "trends in the direction of so-called liberalization," reiterating that while he was not depreciating psychotherapy, "it is not psychoanalysis, even when it is psychoanalytic" (247).

Grinker, who, in contrast, began *his* polemics with statements like "I can't read papers that begin with 'Freud said,'" denounced Gitelson and his Institute compatriots for making up a "dogmatic orthodoxy," for having "not yet entered the 20th century of psychiatry" (Grinker and Grinker 1995, 176). Grinker's lifelong investment in medical psychiatry led him to found the American Academy of Psychoanalysis, a "progressive"—read medical—association of psychiatrist-psychoanalysts united in their commitment to psychoanalysis residing squarely within psychiatry. He was instrumental in establishing the Combined Psychiatric Faculties of Chicago, a dual psychiatry-psychoanalysis training program in which his synthetic vision of psychoanalysis was formalized. Nearly all trainees from the late 1950s through the 1970s would enter the Institute through this portal, yet Gitelson, for his part, was strongly critical of it, arguing that psychoanalysis occupied an important vanguard position that it would lose if it were to merge with psychiatry. He avowed: "There are those whose special capacities lead them to devote themselves to the psychoanalytic method, and to some of those it is given to advance the discoveries begun by Freud" (Gitelson 1956, 253).[40] Freudian psychoanalysis was a basic science in its own right, his argument went, whereas psychiatry was a pragmatic and applied hodgepodge of techniques anxiously in search of a theory (similarly, he wrote, "accounting and mathematics [a]re not to be confused") (Gitelson 1956, 241).

Entangled in the debate between Grinker and Gitelson and their followers were two distinctive understandings of social relations as these shape psychoanalysis: one that we might call ecological (with a nod to Gregory Bateson, since Grinker's discourse is centered on the motifs of ecology and transaction between ecological levels), and another that we might call egological (with a nod to Freud, since Gitelson claims to follow Freud's view of social relations as expressed in *Civilization and Its Discontents* and *Group Psychology and the Analysis of the Ego*). These different visions of psychoanalysis are most clearly manifest in Gitelson's 1963 and 1964 papers "On the Present Scientific and Social Position of Psychoanalysis" and "On the Identity Crisis in American Psychoanalysis," and in Grinker's 1965 rebuttal, "Identity or Regression in American Psychoanalysis?"

A Freudian language does the heavy lifting in Gitelson's interpretation of psychiatry's investment in psychoanalysis. He writes that an intellectually bankrupt psychiatry "projected" its own extravagant hopes on psychoanalysis and then "fell in love with the image." Or, again, that "the child has turned against its father while yet accepting its birthright"; or yet again, that psychiatry carried psychoanalysis along "for its own purposes" and is now "disappointed to discover that the real thing is more of a burden than the idea of it." Gitelson reserves his most bitter suspicion for those colleagues who pursue *applied* psychoanalysis, whether in the form of psychotherapy or social analysis. These people, he writes, are after "secondary gain"—like government money. "I think," he writes, that "analysts are being tempted to back away from the uniqueness and isolation characteristic of their work" (Gitelson 1973, 351). Their "science envy" prompts those who can't tolerate their anxieties about their procedure's "competitive inferiority" to depreciate—thus to betray—psychoanalysis. His diagnosis? Their "fear of being controlled by machines" leads to the fantasies of "mergence" that are evident in the very fact of interdisciplinary participation.

The totalitarian trends of our time affect us from several sides. We ourselves have become fearful of what I have called the "cruel robot" of the unconscious as we see it operating with apparently inexorable force in the world around us. Perhaps the clearest example of the reality which stimulates our free-floating anxiety is to be found in the calculating machines the new applied science of cybernetics has produced . . . for such machines may be used by human beings to increase their control over the rest of the human race. Such participation is the basest conformism there is. (Gitelson 1963, 350)[41]

Gitelson's use of Freudian language and his concern to psychoanalyze "the problem of the mental hygiene of psychoanalysts," the very anxieties about psychoanalysis of psychoanalysts themselves, made him a hero among Blitzstenites. On Gitelson's reading, the analyst's occupational social deprivation, his immersion in the unconscious, produced a kind of "agoraphobia" that led inexorably to an urgent, driven need for narcissistic supplies—for recognition—and to a "compensatory wish for participation in and control of the external world." All of this, plus the guilt and disappointment attached to the difficulties of the work and the frequency of failure, led him to conclude that it would be surprising indeed if analysts did not experience a strong need for validation in the eyes of others, did not hanker after fraternity and worldly respectability, did not wish to be safely bound by "that need for compliant belonging which characterizes our generation" (Gitelson 1973, 155). Against Grinker's eclecticism and thrust into the wider world of Cold War medicine—what Gitelson viewed as, precisely, a flight from analysis—he instead prescribed interminable askesis, for we "are responsible for passing on the torch of self-knowledge which we received from Freud" (359). The structural contradictions inherent in a psychoanalysis now popular are evident in his prescription that analysts continue to work on themselves in the face of whatever threats the outside world presented.

Grinker's retorts would as often as not start with an invocation of Franz Alexander. "What bothered Alexander," he wrote, were the interminable analyses conducted by his colleagues, "the year after year vainly wasted by Blitzsten, Gitelson, Emch, and others in attempting to reorganize the total character structures of their patients" (Grinker 1977, 83). Instead of holding in thrall a closed cadre of interminably self-analyzing partisans, he wrote, "a majority of my staff are analysts, but they are analysts who are able to see the broader spectrum of psychiatry as a biopsychosocial field and not limit themselves entirely to analytic theories or analytic techniques" (Grinker 1975, 220). Psychoanalysis had become "a cult atmosphere," separated from the biological and social sciences, and the Blitzstenites were willfully neglecting the principles of hypothesis testing, experimental control, prediction-making, and rigorous reliability and validity checks that would make it rational (Grinker 1965, 114). At the center of Grinker's cybernetic, transactional view of psychoanalysis was the horror of the closed system.

> I must say that the worst, hardest job that I've done in teaching is supervision. It's virtually impossible. In the first place you don't know the patient; . . . the resident tells you what he wants to tell you to stay in good with you; he will probably not tell you enough about what he said because it might be a mistake. Secondly you don't know the various situations in which the so-called therapy occurs, you don't know much about the therapist, and then your own reaction to him or her becomes important. So you've got so many transactional variables that it was like a piece of lead sinking into the water when I first used it at the psychoanalytic meaning. They said "we can't understand those words." Well, then what's happened is there's a group of youngsters now working at the Institute who recognize that analysis cannot stand on its own as a research technique, . . . different from your friend Gitelson. . . . You don't throw analysis away, it's an important technique. Together with [other tools] it forms a total understanding of the human being. So many of the things I've done have had a delayed impact on the field because I've been so antagonistic to traditional analysis, and I've never seen any of these people quote my work.[42]

He vituperated against Gitelson's claim that "adaptation to culture" had no place in psychoanalysis, claiming that "analysis can not be conducted in gravitationally free outer space, nor can intrapsychic processes be understood apart from behavior in life" (114). Adaptation—as the ego's relation to social norms—was indeed central to health. For Grinker, adaptation, far from being a pernicious narcissistic resistance, was the desirable endpoint of a successful analysis.[43] He argued that a psychoanalysis centered on communication systems in constant reciprocal interaction could become "a genuine cybernetic science." As Grinker wrote (however elliptically), "progressive evolution does not occur in isolation but only through partial separation (specialization) to concentrate the genetic pool (conceptual formation) and by transaction with other groups to add gene symbols (communication) and to test them through natural selection (scientific method). This I hope will be the future course of psychoanalysis" (Grinker 1977, 93).[44] To Gitelson, Grinker's focus on communication and transaction was frank behaviorism asserting itself against unconscious meaning, and he rallied the Institute to push back against systems theory, ecology, and "sociological role theory" for the Freudian cause.[45]

THE PARADOXES OF NORMALIZATION

The ambitions and anxieties of these Chicago analysts were given their determinate form by structural contradictions stemming from the postwar success of psychoanalysis in America. Success led to crisis, stimulated by the arrival on the psychoanalytic scene of the normal candidate. The solution the Institute's leaders sought—normalization, after a fashion—would reorganize the structure of psychoanalytic authority and, in doing so, transform the wider field of professional relations in a variegated process of rationalization and routinization.

As incumbents in key roles in the IPA and the scientifically oriented Academy of Psychoanalysis, Gitelson and Grinker had a final dispute that exemplifies their markedly diverging visions of psychoanalytic authority and of the disciplinarity of psychoanalysis. The dispute developed as follows, printed in the *Bulletin of the International Psycho-analytical Association*. In 1964, Grinker joined his former mentor Franz Alexander and several others in mounting a reaction to Gitelson's (1962a) broadside "Communication from the President about the Neoanalytic Movement," which was printed in the *Bulletin of the International Psycho-analytical Association*. Gitelson, as president of the IPA, had condemned "the 'liberal' psychoanalytic movement" and its "galaxy of diluted and distorted improvisations which have the rationalized purpose of extending its therapeutic limits" (Gitelson 1962a, 373–374). What set off Grinker and his compatriots was Gitelson's concluding exhortation. As Grinker and company read it, Gitelson was prescribing a standard for psychoanalytic authority that devalued the wider world of science. What Gitelson wrote was this:

> If we ask ourselves what may be at the root of such dissidence as presents itself in the phenomenon of the neoanalytic movement, we must come up with answers bearing on the problem of our selection of candidates, and on those qualities of the training analysis and of the supervisory system which eventuate in failure of resolution of pathological narcissism.... Our failure to be uncompromising in the application of our psycho-analytic insight into our authoritarian roles as teachers and educators may have something to do with the fact that at least some of our

colleagues and students find solace for narcissistic injury in alliance as dissident coteries. There is reason for interminable self-analysis for each of us not merely as individuals, but also in our function as members of groups which are responsible for passing on the torch of self-knowledge which we received from Freud. (Gitelson 1962a, 373–375)

Members of "dissident coteries" like Grinker championed the need for institutes to have "open windows" and for the professional associations to serve as open forums for the exchange of scientific ideas. Not only specific institutions and associations were at risk, they felt, but also the fate of the entire enterprise should psychoanalysis turn its back on society. This risk was heightened by leaders who justified their authoritarianism on the grounds of deeper insight into the nature of authority itself. But what is most striking about the 1964 rebuttal from the "dissidents" is the way the referent, psychoanalysis, through the question of what is and is not "analytic," floats free from any semantic mooring in a frenzy of reportage.

Nothing demonstrates better the need for a free scientific society than the lament in Gitelson's Presidential Communication that teaching and education have not been "authoritarian" enough! This lament amounts to an advice to intensify the policy of dogma and self-serving regimentation. Contrast this advice with [Siegfried] Bernfeld's statement made ten years ago: "Now if anyone has to frustrate his power drive . . . it is certainly the psycho-analyst during his workdays. And so, in consolation, we are burdened in our international, national, and local organizations with committees over committees; on rules, on standards, on laws and the multitude of their qualifications; we have the whole rigmarole [sic] of big business, the army, and any bureaucracy in order to govern a little band of a few hundred generally civilized and pleasant individuals, most of whom are seriously interested in helping themselves and their patients, and in doing some research in their spare hours. But unfortunately, the writing of laws and their application and enforcement turns into a hobby with a vengeance. It takes the life out of psycho-analysis by imposing on it, as we have seen, more and more nonanalytic regulations." (Grinker et al. [1963] 1964, 620)

Grinker deploys "Bernfeld," known for his work on psychoanalysis and social change, against the proliferation of "rules, standards, laws" so that he can censure Gitelson for authoritarianism on the grounds that Gitelson claims to possess an analytic authority that derives—unacceptably, in

Grinker's view—from "nonanalytic regulations"! Thus a tacit law is born (again). The disposition of psychoanalysis—what it is, what it isn't—is, as it were, rewritten as pure performativity.

Each man operated in the orbit of ego psychology, yet their valuations of the adapted ego differed dramatically. Unlike Theodore Adorno or Jacques Lacan, who were developing their post-Freudian critiques of the ego in the same period, neither of these Americans had any nostalgia for the prebourgeois subject. Admittedly, the problem of the subject escaped Grinker's instrumentalism altogether. He preserved the self-identical, adapted ego as a norm, whereas Gitelson's diagnosis of the pseudo-autonomy of the normal candidate gestured at the possibility of freedom from norms. Gitelson claimed that autonomy was fostered by analytic authority and that it is "our failure to be uncompromising in the application of psychoanalytic insight" that leads, via "narcissistic injury," to schism (Gitelson 1962a, 375). It is on that proper "application" that analytic authority stands. The analyst should draw to himself—not decline—the transference to authority, since psychoanalytic cure results in autonomy, the shift from the subject's vulnerability to external authority to his full capacity for internally motivated self-determination. Gitelson repositioned the ego in its relation to the wider world, presenting this relation as the object of psychoanalytic treatment. If the ego is fully submerged in the world at the beginning of such treatment, fully adapted to the contours of the world, by its end reason has conquered the ego's narcissistic illusions of normalcy. He assumed, however, that the subject would be capable of freely choosing a bureaucratically administered world as the system of values most suited to its own life. (Note also that the form of self-determination Gitelson is championing is, fundamentally, self-constraint, anonymity.) Far from abetting adaptation, in his view the analyst's inhabitance of the abstract position of authority aimed to free the "normal" subject by purifying authority of its personal dimensions altogether. In his formulation, a mature psychoanalysis *should* be maladapted to its environment, its gadfly not its servant, the veritable doctor for its diseases of normality.

This crisis of organizational authority exposes several contradictions of rationalization. The solution in the Institute was to impose a stricter curriculum, a stricter askesis, a sharper effort to render the analyst's work-ego pliable and calculable in an effort to place psychoanalytic authority on firm grounds. Thus was the Institute able to celebrate the maturity of its never splitting. As Gitelson's wife and fellow faculty member Frances Hannett would write, singing his praises by contrasting Chicago's situation with a

European schism she adjudged an instance of "adolescent rebellion," "the Chicago situation serves as an example of a successful Oedipal solution in which a pivotal figure, deciding that he could not participate in the parental differences, left them to themselves and found his own controlled narcissistic solution outside the main arena, but well within the system where an impact could be made" (Hannett, in Joseph and Widlocher 1983, 172). The dissidents saw the "Oedipal solution" of never splitting as an authoritarian solution. But it nonetheless represented a tacit agreement that was, in a sense, beyond law—for the bastion had failed to notice its metastases (the dissident groups that had sprung up during this normalization). If Gitelson and Fleming succeeded in elevating the illusion of a psychoanalysis free from any external determination, substituting a craft necessity for a broader social necessity, it was the unintended collusion between psychiatric opponents that succeeded in establishing the power of psychoanalysis at midcentury. Whereas institutes in other cities split apart over basic training privileges (who could train?), over the TA designation (who could be a TA?), and over Certification (should there be a separate board certification for psychoanalysis?), Chicago, maintaining its self-consciously mature integration, without prominent émigré lay analysts to roil the waters, with a strong child guidance culture to absorb the interest of the nonphysicians, had only to cope with the threat to its integration from within psychiatry.

That threat was temporarily neutralized by the very popularity that the normal candidate represented, but Gitelson's ideal of the analyst's authoritative incognito—that vital passage point between the analyst's authority and his patient's autonomy—would soon collapse as the normal candidate came of age and as enrollment in psychoanalysis, along with its ambiguous success, collapsed as well.

PART III

....

PSYCHOANALYSIS

and the

DECLENSIONS OF VERISIMILITUDE

THE PLENTY OF SCARCITY

On Crisis and Transience
in the Fifty-First Ward

The leader of the group is still the dreaded primal father; the group still wishes to be governed by unrestricted force; it has an extreme passion for authority. —SIGMUND FREUD, "Group Psychology and the Analysis of the Ego"

Increasingly crises are coming on top of each other.—GEORGE H. POLLOCK, "What Do We Face and Where Can We Go? Questions about Future Directions"

....

Simultaneously the head of the American Psychiatric Association, the APsaA, the Illinois Psychiatric Association, the Illinois Psychoanalytic Association, and the Chicago Institute for Psychoanalysis (this last as Gerhard Piers's successor), George Pollock aggressively promoted psychoanalysis in the 1970s and 1980s. He was a program builder and a dynamo of expansionist entrepreneurialism self-consciously in the mold of Franz Alexander, and his many publications centered on the themes of transience, temporality, scarcity, mourning, and depression. These were themes he returned to over and again, exhorting his colleagues to attend to the impending "crises of our time," for increasingly, he said, "crises are coming on top of each other" (Pollock 1972, 576). Medicare had recently been passed, and many Americans expected universal health care to be next (whether a single-payer, tax-based system, Kennedy's approach, or a market-based approach building on the private insurance system, Nixon's plan). A rapid increase in health-care costs followed the passage of Medicare as hospitals and physicians raised their rates, and the Nixon administration sought reform through price controls and other limits on health-care expenditures; Nixon hoped for a structure for permanently monitoring and containing health-care costs. "We must adapt," was Pollock's mantra. We must change. The world is changing, health care is changing, and so must we. "Whether a national health insurance program will be a panacea, a placebo, or a Pandora's Box only time will tell," he wrote in 1972; but "can we avoid recognizing that the next decade may be filled with so many transformations and crises that we may not survive as a profession?"[1] Freud had written in his 1916 meditation "On Transience" that "transience value is scarcity value in time" (1916, 305), and Pollock returned to Freud's ahistorical theory of value over and over again in his efforts to make a historical argument to his colleagues about the need for psychoanalytic organizations to look outward, to change in order that they could adapt to "the current crisis in health care" (1972, 577).

On his election by the Board of Trustees in 1971, Pollock immediately reorganized the Chicago Institute's administration, replacing the elite permanent staff (a quasi-tenured group of a select few) with an elected Education Council and opening up consideration for TA status to every graduate in good standing.[2] A youthful stalwart of ego psychology, he championed psychoanalysis as a general science of adaptation, he suggested that its clinical application in the form of the classical, four-days-a-week psychoanalysis on the couch was only one among its many potentialities, and he urged his associates to break the "antithesis between the clinician and the researcher" that had created a "lock step" preference in the field for matters of guild over matters of science.[3] He even flirted with the idea of opening up training to allow in non-M.D.s, bucking his colleagues' view of psychoanalysis as a medical specialty. Pollock suspected that economically driven changes in workforce dynamics would decisively affect psychoanalysis, and he wanted the Institute to shape the trend rather than be led by it. At the same time, he suggested that the profession mourn its earlier success, in the Freudian sense of putting a love object psychically to rest after death. He was giving his people mixed messages, however, for they could only mourn if psychoanalysis had indeed died, while they could only adapt—change to suit the times—if psychoanalysis were still alive. Moreover, without a way of conceptualizing psychoanalysis's predicament beyond ideas about individual psychology, both mourning and adaptation would prove impossible.

Despite his extraanalytic excesses, Pollock was for many years forgiven by a faculty that benefited from his political efforts. A stellar fundraiser—at one point during his tenure the budget of the Chicago Institute was larger than the budget of the APsaA itself—he expanded the Institute's programmatic offerings by seeking alternate sources of funding. Ever-attentive to the threat from without, Pollock always came through, assuring the faculty that their committee work, their teaching, their research, and their supervising would be well remunerated. With perquisites flowing in the forms of grant money, teaching appointments, berths on select committees, publication support, and patient referrals, it seemed that little could go wrong. Under Pollock's guidance, driven by his expansive vision of psychoanalysis's universe of application, the Chicago Institute became America's richest center of psychoanalytic learning in the 1970s, even as the wider world's stock in psychoanalysis was beginning to fall. Why (and how) was Pollock growing the Institute under conditions of crisis that he himself worried (and theorized) so much about? What kind of "adaptation" was this patronage system, and how did his benefactors understand their own participation? (One of them described the political culture at the Institute under Pollock as being "like Chicago's Fifty-First Ward," referring to the city's infamous machine politics.)

The hegemony of ego psychology in American psychoanalysis had held firm throughout the golden era of psychoanalysis. Now the appearance—in Chicago—of Heinz Kohut's new "self psychology" threatened its stature. With a new focus on narcissism that sidelined Freudian drive theory, Kohut's psychology of the self captivated a vocal segment of the younger Chicago Institute faculty. Pollock tried in vain to limit the growth of what his colleagues feared could become a rival school. As Kohut and self psychology rapidly gained adherents in the Institute and around the country, Pollock strove to keep up, self-publishing more and more articles and promoting the efforts of his ego psychological confreres to advance their canon in ways that could both contest Kohut's teachings and show up Kohut's narcissism. For his ego psychological colleagues, Pollock strove to provide a bulwark against the subversion of Freudian theory arising from within their ranks. By patronizing their work, he provided what was, for them, an even more necessary disavowal of the larger social and economic realities that were beginning to press their kind of psychoanalysis into virtual oblivion. Invoking a discourse of the university in his grand efforts to remake the Institute as an interdisciplinary center of learning, Pollock built a patronage system that came to stand as an image of an active, growing, vital field, distracting everyone from what they could not acknowledge.

In his own effort to grasp the larger situation and translate the crisis of psychoanalysis into psychoanalytic terms for the group, Pollock proposed that "creative or successful psychosocial transitions are accomplished by individual and group when a normal mourning process can take place. When this is not the case, we detect what has recently been called the mortality of bereavement—the apparent harmful effects of the unresolved or deviated mourning process" (1977b, 26). Pollock used Freudian language to explain the crisis of psychoanalytic authority stimulated by Kohut's revisions, extending the Freudian theory of individual mourning in order to prescribe a healing process for the group. One can read this as a theory of "scarcity value" with institutional implications, a symbolic resource these Chicago psychoanalysts used to make sense of the failure of psychoanalysis that they participated in—and, in a backhanded way, embraced—in the 1970s and 1980s. I contrast Pollock's theoretical formation with a trend that was developing in Kohut's own work, one that equally but differently disavowed from psychoanalytic theory any place for social relations. In different ways, on utterly different grounds, each reinscribed Freud's thesis that the events of history are but a reflection of the dynamics of individual psychology writ large. Both, in this sense, reaffirmed the epistemic authority of the psychoanalyst—even as his social power crumbled.

Whereas the bulk of the chapter reads the group's efforts to stave off the crises that Pollock noted were "coming on top of each other" in the 1970s and 1980s, the last section examines their present-day reflections on the implosion of psychoanalytic authority that ensued in the wake of Pollock's ouster. Scandalous events led to it—the discovery of an illicit funding scheme that emblematized how he propped up the Institute's great success in that era—but the group could only process them decades later, and only in terms of its own psychoanalytic rhetoric of history.

INSTITUTE U.

Pollock's aspirations were universitarian. Like his forebear Franz Alexander, he envisioned an institute that would be more like a university than a vocational school, a multidisciplinary hub of scholars and clinicians producing research as well as training students to become analysts and therapists, and he set about to make this happen. Some of his colleagues understood his aspiration to establish a "university" culture for the Institute as his way of compensating himself for not having received the chairship of the Department of Psychiatry at the University of Illinois. One said, "He was very intent on getting that, but Mel Sabshin got the job, and that was a very, very painful event in his life. Following that, he asked the staff to vote itself out. The plan was that we would have a council of seventeen people and all the members of the council would have professorial titles, such as associate and assistant professor, and so on."[4] The titles were important. Whatever his motivations, Pollock's plan to remake the Institute on the image of the university had many beneficiaries. The Center for Psychoso-cial Study was founded and funded; it would draw university scholars to seminars on psychoanalysis and culture, politics, and history. A clinic dedi-cated to childhood grief was founded and funded, as was a new journal, the *Annual of Psychoanalysis*. A host of other programs were founded or were strengthened with new funds: the Adult Psychotherapy Program, the Busi-ness Executives Program, the Continuing Education Program, the Teacher Education Program, an expanded library with a new literature index, and a film archive, named after Max Gitelson. Research money was funneled into faculty projects on such subjects as the selection of candidates for training, the psychology of separation and loss, the psychology of music (one of Pollock's own research interests), and the treatment of narcissistic pathology (Kohut's research). There was even, for a brief while, a Ph.D. program in psychoanalysis, the country's first.

Among the beneficiaries of Pollock's largesse were several non-M.D.s whom he sought to introduce into his patronage economy in efforts at ex-ogenous recruitment. Not only was Pollock eager to enhance the growth of scholarship in "applied psychoanalysis" in the arts, humanities, and so-cial sciences (the idea behind the Center for Psychosocial Study) but also his vision for the Institute-as-university included addressing head-on the "changes in health personnel categories [that] will have an impact on health delivery systems" (Pollock 1972, 582). Pollock framed his aspiration to include non-M.D.s in terms of the field's need to expand its territory in the face of the broader changes in health care that, he warned, would soon affect funding for training for psychoanalysis. He recognized that young psychiatrists were beginning to turn away from psychoanalysis as promising new drugs appeared and the academic profession was starting to focus its attention on biological approaches to mental health. "We too are part of the health care 'industry,' and our profession has societal responsi-bility," he argued—although his colleagues worried that he was putting the medical basis of psychoanalysis at risk.

> We must recognize we cannot rest on Freud's laurels. We cannot remain isolated from the rest of medicine, including psychiatry. We cannot re-move ourselves from the field of scholarship, the arts, the humanities, the biological and social sciences. We must recognize that our excellent clinicians alone may not be the researchers we need to further our sci-ence. We cannot be content to say our critics have residual problems. Freud himself noted in a communication to Jung, "let each of us pay

more attention to his own than to his neighbor's neurosis." . . . If we face the issues directly, we can work together toward creative solutions. (Pollock 1977b, 25)

Pairing the notion that "we must recognize we cannot rest on Freud's laurels" with the seemingly contradictory "Freud himself noted," Pollock crafted a form of self-immunizing political speech. Manipulating the intertextual gaps between multiple "Freuds," Pollock's paracritical rhetoric of change-amid-continuity would produce an increasingly hollow image of the analyst's authority. His dissenters couched their opposition to his rhetoric of change in the twinned languages of *standards* and *scarcity*. As psychiatry departments were becoming less friendly to psychoanalysis and as prestigious university appointments were less available to them, some of those who had previously sought the full integration of psychoanalysis into psychiatry looked to the Institute for their professional rewards and worried about the inclusion of potential nonmedical competitors. The Institute might be "over-run by barbarians" if Pollock's Chicago Plan and later Chicago Proposal came to pass. (This was told to me by the first anthropologist trained at the Institute, who reported that he'd been told on admission that the faculty feared a flood of anthropologists would follow.) As with Pollock's talk about opening up training, so with his plans to open a clinic for bereaved children. A steady stream of consultants urged a slow and cautious approach to change to avoid being overwhelmed by applicants. Benjamin Garber, director of the Barr-Harris Children's Grief Center, noted in a 2006 report on that clinic's history that "there was always an underlying anxiety of being overwhelmed by large numbers of patients." Garber's report referred to this as a "schizophrenic attitude towards outreach." The idea of outreach was alluring because it might bring welcome patients and new trainees to sustain a profession in crisis. But it was also repellent because the prospect of the opening up of the Institute might lead to an unmanageable flood of people that would tax the Institute's capacity and threaten its way of life—a nightmare of abundance (Garber 2006, n.p.). In the 1950s, there really had been such a crowd at the gates, and the boundary defining who could train served to uphold the profession's status. Now the boundary had to move, Pollock suggested, even as the group's fear of imaginary hordes helped them maintain their sense of exclusivity.

During Pollock's tenure as director, from 1971 to 1988, a steady stream of psychologists and a smaller group of social workers approached the Institute in the hope of receiving clinical training in psychoanalysis. By APsaA policy they were to be denied admission, though Pollock did allow a few to apply as research (as opposed to clinical) candidates, as long as they signed a waiver stating they would not pass themselves off as analysts and actually see patients. Concurrently, under a new, national-level APsaA program with a similar stricture, several academics who wished to "apply" psychoanalysis in their scholarly research were allowed to matriculate into research training through the Committee on Research and Special Training program of APsaA. The hope was that these scholars would bring psychoanalysis back into the universities and that this would strengthen the presence of psychoanalysis in the academy. To be admitted to this program, a scholar had to be "senior" and hold a position of "strategic importance," possess a significant publication record, and be at no risk of leaving academe for the allure clinical practice might offer; applicants were made to go through extensive vetting to ensure their intentions were, indeed, purely scholarly, and then to sign a waiver stating that they would not see patients.[5]

Pollock exhorted his colleagues that an even greater opening to the world was needed, for "changes in health personnel categories *will* have an impact on health delivery systems" and the scope of the Institute's educational activities was inevitably going to need to change as well.

> Are we going to be involved in the educational programs of these groups? Physicians' assistants will not become analysts, but they may become members of the pool that delivers some form of mental health care.... Will psychoanalytic institutes and educators participate in the training programs of these individuals or will we let others, who may be less qualified, do the job we should do? I do not believe we will be "taken over" by the new systems of educational emphasis. If we do not examine our possible active cooperation in these new ventures, however, we can be permanently "bypassed." (Pollock 1972, 583)

Pollock's proposed plan therefore called for the training not only of dedicated senior scholars in applied psychoanalysis but also of "young students from nonmedical backgrounds, with scant clinical experience," through "an experiment in establishing a university that could grant the degree 'Doctor of Psychoanalysis.'" As the minutes of a national meeting read on this matter, "Chicago made it plain that the experiment aims at training clinical psychoanalysts and not Ph.D.'s who are tied to their own disciplines. The Chicago proposal approaches the question of whether carefully selected people who are not physicians might be able to become competent and contribute significantly to psychoanalysis in a carefully controlled program"

(American Psychoanalytic Association 1974, 442). The prospect of such disciplinarily un-tied Ph.D.s—however carefully selected and controlled—led to a backlash. Some APsaA members already saw the research training program as a way of sneaking in "lay" people to fill institute coffers, and Pollock's plan was perceived as yet a further step beyond this. After much discussion over many months, APsaA finally rejected Pollock's "Chicago Plan"—though not before he had admitted several individuals to begin earning Ph.D.s at the Institute.[6]

The interdisciplinary cohort of 1973, Pollock's pet project, contained an equal number of M.D.s and Ph.D.s. One of the Ph.D.s, a historian, spoke glowingly of his experience at the Institute.[7] "They fully included us in all the classes and it was right when Kohut was starting to talk about self psychology and taking off from Freud, so it was a really interesting time." In contrast, one of his M.D. classmates resents to this day the way "the academics" seemed to take over the seminar discussions, all the while being critical of the teaching. With a pained look, he recounted an episode in which the Ph.D.s confronted a senior analyst, saying, "Look, if you don't know how to teach, why are you teaching?"[8] Another of his Ph.D. classmates, an anthropologist, reported that "in many cases we knew more psychoanalytic theory than the teacher did, we had read more Freud and so on, so it was often awkward. At the same time, I think we also felt privileged to be there."[9] The M.D. I interviewed felt that criticism of the teaching at the Institute was unfair, since the instructors were not Freud scholars but practicing psychoanalysts who were dedicating their energies to passing on to the next generation the clinical practice of psychoanalysis. In his view the teachers had no particular reason to know about pedagogy; they were doing what their own teachers had done, teaching by case and by clinical anecdote. This style of teaching was foreign to the Ph.D.s., expectant as they were of a lecture to contextualize the assigned readings. Instead, readings were merely used as a jumping off point for discussion that would rapidly move away from the written text and into stories—stories about patients, stories about Freud, stories about other analysts. One of the Ph.D.s, a psychologist, added that classes would start late and end early, saying (perhaps a bit cynically) that "it was often clear the teacher had nothing to offer and just wanted to get through it alive." He said he suspected the M.D.s weren't even reading the assigned texts, despite regularly referring to what Freud said. The historian added, less cynically, that "it was a certain kind of thrill to get to listen in on what went on in the analyst's office, like I was getting a privileged glimpse of something I would never have gotten from reading the text. That said, the treatment of the literature was shockingly thin." According to the M.D. I interviewed, his fellows were "relieved" the following year when Pollock's proposal was denied by the APsaA. The experiment in interdisciplinary dialogue had "created a hostile climate having these two really different groups in the same class. We just wanted to learn about psychoanalysis; it seemed like they just wanted to attack it." After this short-lived effort and another failed attempt to build a degree-granting program (this time one offering a "Doctor of Psychotherapy" degree, a debacle that mired the organization in a lawsuit), Pollock steered back to safer waters, and from that point up until the 1989 national lawsuit that formally opened training to non-M.D.s, the Institute would train a mere eight non-M.D.s, while eighty-one M.D.s were trained during Pollock's tenure.[10]

INFLATION AND GRANDIOSITY IN THE EMPIRE OF NARCISSISM

Concurrent with Pollock's fervid expansion of programs and personnel in the 1970s, the Institute's clinic was beginning to register a decline in the number of applicants for psychoanalysis, as well as something that one of the clinic's social workers described as "a change in the *kinds* of patients applying."[11] A discourse of scarcity and devaluation was subtly taking hold, and the clinic's frontline workers—the social workers who performed the intake assessments on those who applied for treatment—were among the first to witness the shift in the Institute's asset structure.

Unlike many other institutes, Chicago's had a small staff of social workers who conducted the screening of applicants for low-fee psychoanalysis. Under the supervision of a senior TA, they sent those they deemed "analyzable" into treatment with the Institute's trainees, for whom they counted as training cases. The clinic staff thus had a unique vantage point on the (supposed) changing pool of patients and the simultaneously changing discourse around analyzability. Specifically, they conducted extensive, multipart evaluations of these individuals to determine their analyzability, using a complicated system that scored the prospective patient on several "potentials" that, in combination, qualified him as either analyzable or unanalyzable. The clinic's social workers screened applicants for their "background potentials" (defined as cultural background and basic intelligence), their "ego potentials" (defined as their "superego functioning and defense system functioning"), and their "libidinal potentials" (defined specifically as an absence of pre-Oedipal fixation). As one of the intake social workers remarked in an interview about her work in the late 1970s, describing the way Institute psychoanalysts thought about analyzability during her tenure, "up to this point everything was Oedipal." She had been sitting in on Institute classes while working at the clinic and had noted the growing sense of concern among the trainees about the dearth of "good patients."[12] The analytic candidates needed Oedipal-level patients for their control cases, and they would complain when the clinic sent them "so-called good hysterics" as opposed to "true" good hysterics. The diagnostic distinction between good and "so-called" good patients was based on two widely read papers, Zetzel's (1968) "The So Called Good Hysteric" and Easser and Lesser's (1965) "Hysterical Personality: A Re-evaluation." Zetzel maintained that hysterical women could be differentiated into good (analyzable) and bad (unanalyzable) hysterics.[13] Though her work referred specifically to feminine hysteria, her own area of interest, Institute psychoanalysts used it to define criteria that marked the limits of analyzability in general. These two papers, manifestos for a seemingly disappearing condition, posited a spectrum of pathologies ranging from the neurotic to the quasi-psychotic, from the Oedipal to the pre-Oedipal, and from the analyzable to the unanalyzable. Utilizing these categories, clinic staff agreed that the patients who were presenting for treatment had greater difficulties with reality testing and with object relations, especially with trust, than had patients in the past. They were "sicker," with developmentally earlier, pre-Oedipal problems. In spite of some theoretical interest in these patients, all efforts were made to find control cases for the candidates who still made it into the "analyzable" category. But if the trainees were complaining that the social workers were sending them "pre-Oedipal" patients who were too sick to be taken on as control cases, the faculty overseeing the trainees were complaining that the intake workers were being too restrictive and preventing the trainees from getting cases.

In Chicago, patients with these "pre-Oedipal" disorders were considered beyond the reach of psychoanalysis proper until Heinz Kohut's theories opened up the "pathologies of the self" to psychoanalysis. Trained by Ruth Eissler, Kohut had earlier been a veritable spokesman for ego psychology and was dubbed "Mr. Psychoanalysis" in the early 1960s (Strozier 1985, 3). He, Joan Fleming, and Louis Shapiro "had reestablished orthodoxy in the curriculum and ferreted out the Alexandrian heresy of shortening psychoanalysis" (Strozier 1985, 8). Later in the decade, however, he began to redefine the limits of the talking cure with a new theoretical system he called self psychology, one that soon polarized the Institute's faculty. Funded by Pollock, Kohut had begun to write about his work with a group of patients for whom the technique derived from drive theory was proving fruitless. Focusing on their subjective experience (its integrity, continuity, and phenomenal transparency), Kohut would draft a new, first-person epistemology for psychoanalysis that was centered in the patient's conscious experience of herself. His intention was that this first-person epistemology would supersede both the Freudian postulate of the neurotic subject's constitutive self-deception *and* the methodological complement of that condition, the hermeneutic of suspicion that inclined the analyst to view the patient as an adversary whose resistances needed to be attacked.[14]

Kohut began with a statement placing empathy at the core of the clinical process: empathy alone—defined as vicarious introspection—was to delimit the domain of depth psychology (see Kohut 1959). This represented a major shift, since it moved the analyst from his classical objectivist stance to a thoroughly subjectivist stance vis-à-vis the patient's experience. He followed this with a 1966 paper placing narcissism on its own line of development, building on Anna Freud's widely accepted model of separate "developmental lines" for the different psychological capacities (Kohut 1966). In his framework, "narcissism" was not a pathological self-centeredness that the analyst should debunk (as per the Blitzstenite—and classical Freudian—approach). Rather, it was a healthy, expansive force for growth that the analyst should nourish in analysis.[15] "Narcissism," in Kohut's rereading of the idea, referred to the emotional investment a person has in himself; the developmental line of healthy narcissism, then, moved from the rudimentary sense of self in earliest life through the child's capacity for effective assertion and for pleasure in accomplishments, and toward the durable self-esteem of the adult who is confidently able to pursue aspirations with enthusiasm and joy. Problems along the way were what led people to seek treatment, and the work of treatment centered on reengaging development in this area where it had left off—"narcissistic" development or development of the self.[16] Kohut's theory held that the new, supposedly "pre-Oedipal" patients suffered from what he called self disorders or disorders of narcissistic development. When these people were not accurately recognized or understood by others, they were vulnerable to injured self-esteem, what he called narcissistic injury. Their fragile self-esteem and ready vulnerability to narcissistic injury qualified them as having disorders of self. Kohut thus repurposed an old psychoanalytic term, one with a significant history, and put it to entirely new (if not, in many ways, opposite) ends. While *pathological* narcissism might still entail arrogance, greed, and self-centeredness per the common use of the term, Kohut used the term neutrally to describe the psychological dimension of the self's emotional investment in the self. Healthy narcissism, in contrast to vulnerable narcissism, was durable, buoyant, and agentive.

Rather than focusing on the patient's intrapsychic conflicts—the unbalanced relations of id-ego-superego—Kohut instead foregrounded the immediate experience of a nonconflicted "I" that was struggling to grow, a fragile "I" struggling to fulfill itself without sufficient inner resources. This was a sharp break with drive theory's third-person objectivism. His thesis was that psychoanalytic theory should not explain clinical phenomena on the basis of abstract, unobservable agencies (drives, egos, superegos, etc.). His was, he claimed, a strictly *psychological* phenomenology, based only on data the analyst derived by immersing himself into the felt experience of the patient. Kohut's theory admitted of the analyst's contribution to the patient's experience through his activity of observing and interpreting the patient's productions, but he emphasized the patient's subjective experience of this, not the interpersonal or interactive aspects of the relationship. While the analyst was not a blank screen for the patient's distortions and projections, he was nevertheless a dispassionate, scientific observer. He was not (theoretically) a participant.[17] From his standpoint, not only the biological concept of drive but also what he derisively called "sociological" or "social psychological" concepts (notions of transaction, interaction, environment, adaptation, dependence, or autonomy) had no place in psychoanalysis, for these all approached the suffering individual from the outside, from an external, "exteroceptive," third-person perspective. As he put it, "we speak of physical phenomena when the essential ingredient of our observational methods includes our senses, [and] we speak of psychological phenomena when the essential ingredient of our observation is introspection and empathy" (Kohut 1959, 460).

Frustration remained the vehicle for psychological growth for Kohut, but he conceived of such growth not in terms of drive neutralization and mature adaptation to a pregiven reality (as per the ego psychologists) but in terms of the development of the patient's capacity for "narcissistic equilibrium." He sharply distinguished *optimal* frustration from traumatic frustration: optimal frustration, small amounts of benign, daily frustration—whether a mother's kind but firm "no" or an analyst's imperfect understanding of a patient's communication—was necessary for the internalization of "selfobject functions," the hallmarks of psychic health that grow over the course of development, whereas traumatic frustration stymied such growth. The core selfobject functions that he identified as defining of the intact self were the ability to calm oneself (this he viewed as deriving from the childhood experience of having been soothed by an empathic parent); the ability to aspire to goals and pursue desired ends (this he viewed as deriving from the experience of having had an admirable, accomplished caregiver to look up to and rely on in childhood); and the ability to feel oneself to be normal, understandable, human (this, he viewed as deriving from childhood experiences of likeness with others, of smoothly fitting into a matrix of relations). Countless small instances of optimal frustration were central to the building up of these functions as enduring, structured capacities of the self—whether in childhood or, if that did not go so well, in adulthood in the experience with the analyst.[18]

Kohut distinguished these optimal, incremental, growth-producing frustrations from another, more malignant kind of frustration that he referred to as traumatic. In traumatic frustration the child's normal needs for love, understanding, care, protection, stimulation, and so on, are either not met or are actively thwarted by a parent incapable of empathic attunement, incapable of "seeing" the child accurately. These unmet needs are split off, showing up as the symptoms of depression, anxiety, low self-esteem, addiction, or general emotional instability that a patient with a self disorder brought to treatment. Because the patient's painful emotional need-states have been split off, they are effectively unmeetable in real life, so the goal of treatment was to facilitate the reintegration of these split off need-states into the patient's core self so that he or she can pursue fulfillment in the activities of real life. Kohut's theory presupposed that pathology resulted from the specific, actual failures of parental responsiveness to the needs of the developing child, whereas in Freud's drive theory frustration was viewed as a condition of scarcity per se. In spite of this marked departure from Freud's ontology, Kohut, by emphasizing this motif of frustration and sharpening Freud's methodological individualism, kept his theory of technique in line with classical theory. Recall that for Freud impulses were conceived to be sexual in origin, so the notion of their "real" gratification in the relationship with the analyst carried an unacceptable connotation that analysts of virtually all schools have avoided at the risk of being seen as "unanalytic." The concept of the "selfobject" allowed Kohut to maintain an intrapsychic, one-mind perspective, thereby to address the patient's childhood deprivation while at the same time avoiding the opprobrium associated with the idea of the analyst actually gratifying the patient through their relationship.

On this basis, Kohut proceeded to define a new taxonomy of transferences and expectable countertransferences above and beyond the Oedipal triad of competitiveness, fear of castration, and sexual possessiveness. These "selfobject transferences" included a mirroring transference (the patient's seeking to be recognized and appreciated), an idealizing transference (the patient's seeking to form a link with an idealized figure), and twinship transferences (the patient's seeking to experience a sense of likeness with the analyst), interpretive foci that significantly expanded the analyst's interpretive range and opened up new pathologies—newly tractable pathologies—to the talking cure.[19] Where classical psychoanalysis had conceptualized transference as the patient's projection of childhood imagos (of the parents) onto the analyst, repeating the past and displacing it into the present, Kohut understood selfobject transference as *both* containing repetitions of the past *and* being shaped in the present by the observing and interpreting activities of the analyst.

Kohut framed the impetus for this expansion of psychoanalytic theory in terms of stimulating new clinical quandaries, though his friend and ally Charles Kligerman described a more pernicious, more local influence on Kohut's work. "A stifling influence came from a branch of the Chicago group led by Blitzsten that had an enormous interest in narcissism," Kligerman said. "They acted as if all narcissism were pathological, a regressive obstacle to the development of object love. One of the favored ways of dealing with the typical narcissistic grandiosity was to adopt a joking, ironic stance. I am sure this stance caused Heinz [Kohut] a good share of pain, although he manfully went along with the rationale, and even tried the technique himself" (Kligerman 1984, 12).

In placing narcissism on its own line of development, in viewing it as a psychic force sui generis, expressions of the patient's grandiosity (viewed as obnoxious by the Blitzstenites) and expressions of idealization or admiration of the analyst (viewed as sycophancy by the Blitzstenites) could now be viewed as positive, growth-seeking phenomena to be welcomed. The patient's seeming grandiosity expressed his expansive hopes for self-actualization rather than his envy, destructive superiority, or resentment. With these proposals Kohut, former president of APsaA and vice president of the IPA, previous heir apparent to Anna Freud and Heinz Hartmann, was well on his way to being shunned by the psychoanalytic establishment.

In specifying the implications for treatment technique that stemmed from his theoretical innovations, Kohut would over and over again contrast his view of healthy narcissism with the "hypocritical" attitude of the Blitzstenites.[20] "The overcoming of a hypocritical attitude toward narcissism is as much required today as was the overcoming of sexual hypocrisy a hundred years ago. We should not deny our ambitions, our wish to dominate, our wish to shine, and our yearning to merge into omnipotent figures, but should instead learn to acknowledge the legitimacy of these narcissistic forces as we have learned to acknowledge the legitimacy of our object-instinctual strivings" (Kohut 1972, 365). He urged his generation of analysts to accept the motivational primacy of narcissistic strivings in the same way an earlier generation had come to accept the motivational primacy of sexual and aggressive drives. As an example of his difference with the Blitzstenite view of human motivation, Kohut offered the interpretation of parapraxes (Freudian slips). For him, these classic Freudian pathologies of everyday life were mortifying to the speaker who uttered them because of the welling up of the speaker's understandable rage and shame at his failure of verbal/mental control. The traditional view held, in stark contrast, that slips of the tongue were mortifying because they revealed hidden, embarrassing Oedipal wishes that the speaker did not wish to have pointed out.[21] Another example of Kohut's difference with the Blitzstenite view, now on the grandest of scales, turned on their different readings of aggression. For Kohut pathological aggression (even in large-scale violence) was reactive; it was secondary to *actual* historical injury and trauma, not a function of an endogenous primary aggressive tendency (as Freud had posited).[22]

In "The Two Analyses of Mr. Z" Kohut graphically contrasted the ego psychological view of narcissism that he himself had taken during "Mr. Z's" first analysis with the revised, self psychological view that he adopted in a second analysis with the same patient.

> This phase in the second analysis was quite similar to the corresponding one in the first. What was different, however, was my evaluation of the psychological significance of his behaviour. While in the first analysis I had looked upon [the patient's idealization] in essence as defensive, and had at first tolerated it . . . and later increasingly taken a stand against it, I now focused on it with . . . respectful seriousness vis-à-vis important analytic material. I looked upon it as an analytically valuable replica of a childhood condition [an unmet childhood need] that was being revived in the analysis. This altered stance had two favourable consequences. It

rid the analysis of a burdensome iatrogenic artifact—his unproductive rage reactions against me and the ensuing clashes with me—that I had formerly held to be the unavoidable accompaniment of the analysis of his resistances. And—a reliable indication that we were now moving in the right direction—the analysis began to penetrate into the depths of a certain formerly unexplored sector of the patient's personality. (Kohut 1979, 12)

The core of Kohut's revisionist theory was expressed in the Mr. Z case, which his biographer and his students have understood as an autobiographical account of his own first, unsuccessful ego psychological analysis with Ruth Eissler, followed by a second, imaginary *reanalysis* based on what he had learned in the intervening years through his own work with patients. In writing an entire case history that was essentially an autobiography, in implicating his own "narcissism" at the core of his theoretical intervention, "nothing he ever did more clearly marked his heroic sense of himself" (Strozier 2001, 308).

Put most concisely, Kohut wrote in the Mr. Z case, "My theoretical convictions, the convictions of a classical analyst who saw the material that the patient presented in terms of infantile drives and of conflicts about them, and of agencies of a mental apparatus either clashing or co-operating with each other, had become for the patient a replica of the mother's hidden psychosis, of a distorted outlook on the world to which he had adjusted in childhood, which he had accepted as reality" (Kohut 1979, 16). Note what he has argued here: the classical *theory* wielded by the analyst functioned as a replica of the patient's mother's *psychosis*. The theory had become a replica of the psychosis to which the patient had, in childhood, adjusted, with sequelae in the form of the deformations of character and the phenomenal suffering that had brought him into treatment. Recall now that Kohut is the patient, and the account therefore reads like this: my own earlier theory had become, to me, a replica of my own mother's psychosis. My own previous theory—classical psychoanalytic theory—was, in essence, psychotic. It was a replica of my mother's psychosis. In contrast, my current theory, my self psychology, is no longer experienced by my patient (me) as a replica of his mother's (my mother's) psychosis. My current theory is not psychotic (unlike my own first analyst's classical theory).

"Mr. Z's" two analyses kicked off a wave of second analyses by younger analysts returning to the couch to throw off the destructive effects of their first, classical analyses with the Blitzstenites. The narrative theme of doubling is central to the stories of the two analyses of Mr. Z, the two analyses of Ernest Wolf, the two analyses of Marian Tolpin, the two analyses of Jerome Beigler, and the two analyses of numerous others. Their stories are emplotted along much the same lines: a first, compromised, harsh, official training analysis with a classical analyst and then a second, helpful, voluntary, "this one was really for me," private analysis with Kohut or one of his followers. The qualities of the dualism are posed in terms of oppositions: cold/warm, harsh/kind, intellectual/emotional, artificial/real. In an example of this local genre, Ernest Wolf compared his official training analysis, conducted by Gitelson, to his second, elective, "personal" analysis.

> I was appalled by the apparent contempt and lack of empathy [Gitelson] showed for his analysands. . . . A repeated interpretation was "You don't want to be analyzed, you just want to be an analyst without being analyzed." . . . Once he complained to me about my wife. "Yesterday, when you left, I thought I finally had you where I want you," he said. "But today you come in as before because your wife has put you all back together again." . . . Indeed, the analysis was a failure in terms of the then current ego psychological theories. One of the country's most respected psychoanalysts had not been able to get through my resistances and we had ended with an unmistakable feeling of mutual and reciprocal hostility. . . . I experienced the cold, detached, almost brutal objectivity with which Gitelson conducted the analysis as a contemptuous nonacceptance of me. . . . Kohut's Psychoanalytic Psychology of the Self entered into my psyche like germinating seeds into fertile soil. The analytic ambience was one of trying to understand rather than condemn. (Wolf 2002, 132–133)

Doubling down, throughout the 1970s, Kohut focused his theoretical attention on such symptoms as anomie, low self-esteem, emptiness, meaninglessness, alienation, psychic fragmentation, and addiction, none of which had had any place in the received model of Oedipal psychopathology and all of which were increasingly being seen in the patients who walked into analysts' offices. His notion of the incompletely formed self afforded a view of these problems in terms of deficits in functioning consequent on failures of early child development. As he put this, "I relinquished the health and maturity morality that had formerly motivated me and restricted myself to the task of reconstructing the early stages of his experiences, particularly as they concerned his enmeshment with the pathological personality of the mother" (Kohut 1979, 416). Many of the younger analysts now followed Kohut in renouncing the "health and maturity morality" of Gitelson and his group and embracing the hopefulness of Kohut's image of restoring growth by picking up on derailed development. Along with the "health and maturity morality"—the Blitzstenite technique of telling the patient to grow up and stop acting like a baby—Kohut's theory displaced the centrality of the Oedipus complex, the telos of psychosexual stages (oral, anal, genital, phallic), the armature of defenses, and the economy of cathexis (with its various vectors of displacement, projection, and condensation), along with the drives of libido and aggression. Now the psychoanalyst was to recognize and encourage the patient's hopeful strivings for growth and development. Far outstripping his ego psychologist colleagues in productivity, popularity, and sales, Kohut's books were top sellers in the field.[23] While his ego psychologist colleagues looked on, saying, with anger, "good psychotherapy, perhaps, but not psychoanalysis," Kohut's study group blossomed and grew, developing in short order from a local discussion group of his immediate students into a large annual conference attended by both analysts and therapists from around the country and, later, around the world.[24]

NARCISSISM AND THE EGOTISTICAL SUBLIME:
Expanding the Ego's Pathography

For some of the older Chicago faculty, the therapy Kohut was prescribing was simply not psychoanalysis; several went so far as to claim that Kohut's was a new "Chicago school," a new Alexandrian doctrine of corrective emotional experience that was operating illicitly outside the APsaA's reach. By the time of Kohut's 1977 book it had become clear to them that his was an entirely new metapsychology, one free of drives altogether. The following exemplary critique is from a censorious review in 1979.

> Beneath the series of . . . newly coined terms is a basically simple system, far less complex than psychoanalytic theory as we know it. It is indeed very appealing to minimize or even virtually to do away with the role of infantile sexuality and of aggression. To put to the side, at the same time, ego and superego development, the central roles of the Oedipus complex, of castration anxiety and penis envy, of the intricacy of the dream work, would seem to satisfy many of the objections which have been directed toward psychoanalysis. . . . From one point of view it might be argued that some of the appeal is the derogation of the role

of defense, i.e., permission to support the resistances, always a tempting maneuver in conducting an analysis, but not as a rule productive of the more profound insight which we tend to value. Is the search for insight and recovery of unconscious material a mistaken, perhaps futile, goal in the treatment of so many of our patients? It is an arduous one, which may arouse a good deal of annoyance, if not worse, on the patient's part, and fatigue and discouragement on ours. Shall we therefore discard it, in favor of a more comfortable philosophy and technique? (Stein 1979, 679)

Seeking to cleave to that arduous philosophy and the uncomfortable technique that Freud had promised would "disturb the sleep of mankind," several of Chicago's ego psychologists began now to craft baroque additions to the Blitzstenite canon in efforts to restore Freudian theory to its pride of place. With their ideas of "phallic narcissism," the "defense transference," and the "diatrophic bond" they directed their efforts at restoring the transference neurosis to the heart of psychoanalysis proper by expanding the ego's pathography (see Forman 1976; Gitelson 1962b; Kavka 1976; Schlessinger 1990; Schlessinger and Robbins 1983). Reviving the ontology of endogenous inner forces in the face of what they perceived to be Kohut's interpersonal perspective—and this despite Kohut's constant efforts to avoid the opprobrium associated with the interpersonal or the social—they sought to contain his narcissism in a larger hierarchy of psychoanalytic values, one in which Oedipal resolution reigned supreme. They sought to resignify Kohut's narcissistic pathology, then, as phallic conflict, to reduce his broad metapsychological system to a mere redescription of pre-Oedipal pathology, and to demote his technique of interpreting selfobject transferences to the status of a preparatory "pre-analysis," at best a phase of psychotherapy before the real work of psychoanalysis could take place. Their summation was that Kohut was pandering to the patient with his humanistic emphases on the first-person perspective and the lifelong need for selfobject experiences. They argued that by valuing the "experience near" he was actually *promoting* the patient's narcissism (in their "negative" sense of the term, the patient's immature self-centeredness) rather than enhancing his "autonomy" and his mature capacity for "object love" (as opposed to immature self-love). Kohut, they felt, was producing selfish, appetitive, dependent babies rather than mature, autonomous, renunciative adults.[25] The ultimate value in their view was what they referred to, following Anna Freud and Heinz Hartmann, as ego autonomy, a combination of the two qualities they viewed as defining maturity: the capacity to control one's baser instincts and the capacity to control (not be controlled by or dependent on) one's environment.

Gitelson had warned that the appearance of a warmer, more active, more personal, and more supportive kind of therapy, in conjunction with "disappointment in their own therapeutic results," was tempting the younger analysts to move toward "modification and innovation as well as outright repudiation of psychoanalysis" (Gitelson 1973, 329). Attempting to reinscribe the moral, paternal meritocracy of Blitzstenite descent, he and his associates attached to Kohut the specter of Alexandrian heresy, insinuating that any such repudiation of psychoanalysis (i.e., ego psychology) must be a function of the analyst's personal inadequacies, and suggesting that the younger analyst's ambivalence toward his elders' stricter version of analysis was a result of his being unqualified as such to practice it. Some speculated that Kohut was homosexual (this ultimate expression of unmasculine narcissism always rumored, never confirmed), others charged that he denied his Jewishness, all part of a mounting critique of his flagrant demotion of the phallic adult's moral and developmental supremacy.

Meanwhile, Gitelson's younger colleagues faced a problem that was apparently not an issue for Kohut: patients' aversions to a wholehearted dependence on them. It seems that this was a growing problem the ego psychologists faced: their patients did not trust them, and something (theoretical) had to be done. Their proposals turned on Gitelson's seminal idea that a patient whose problems centrally included a defective capacity to trust the analyst in fact needed the analyst to provide a "diatrophic" (literally, "entirely nutritional") initial phase of reparative therapy. This phase of work, understood as fundamentally maternal, was meant to install trust and induce cooperation, and it was necessary before the rigorous work of Oedipal interpretation could take place. "It is my position," Gitelson had written in his celebrated 1962 paper, that "the patient who presents himself for consultation, and who we see in the first phase of analysis, is like the child we must lift to a secondary level of development" (Gitelson 1973, 317). Gitelson was reclaiming for *psychoanalysis* some of the functions that had previously been categorized as *psychotherapy*; he underscored, however, that this was not the *real* work of analysis, and that what he was proposing was far from Alexander's doctrine of the corrective emotional experience. Rather, what he was doing was merely the necessary, preparatory phase of dealing with the patient's mistrust, attaching the patient to the analyst before the real work of attacking the patient's defenses could begin.

Freud, Gitelson recognized, had taken for granted the work that took place during the beginning of an analysis. In Freud's view, nothing had to be done but to give the patient time. Now, though, with analysts reporting increasing difficulties in beginning new analyses, the problem of attaching the patient to the person of the doctor seemed urgently in need of explicit theorization. Following the developmental psychologists Rene Spitz and Margaret Mahler, Gitelson argued that "the so-called good hysteric" had a deficit in her capacity for trust that had to be remedied; indeed, all patients needed a "built-in parameter in the very nature of the first phase . . . a parameter which moves toward resolution" (Gitelson 1973, 341).[26] Instituting such a nonanalytic but analytically resolvable "built-in parameter" preserved the notion of analysis *proper* by sequestering it—temporally, technically—from the more primitive, "pre-Oedipal" problem of basic trust.

In many ways, Gitelson's conception of this preparatory work takes off from some of Kohut's ideas about the silently operating transferences that stabilized the patient, a similarity Gitelson both recognized and dismissed. "I do not depreciate the humanistic trends," wrote Gitelson depreciatively, but they are misrepresented if they are represented as new discoveries, since their dynamics are already identifiable in—and intrinsic to—the classical analytic situation, in Freud's implicit work with the patient to "link the doctor up with one of the imagos of the people by whom he was treated with affection [in childhood]" (Gitelson 1973, 315). In the words of one of Gitelson's analysands, himself now a faculty member in his eighties, "what was good in Kohut really wasn't new, and what was new wasn't really good."[27] One of this man's original classmates found Kohut outrageous, interpreting him as castrating those with whom he disagreed.

> Kohut's whole emphasis was on disqualifying the ego autonomy folks. Fleming hated him. She felt he was trying to promote a cult. What did bother me was the way Kohut tried to press his case about the Oedipus. "We never see it; did you ever really see it?" "Yeah," I said to him, "my son just said to me 'next week we're gonna have roast meat, Dad, your penis!'" Kohut said to me "See, your kid's sick; the Oedipus only comes up like that in sickness, it's not a normal thing." If Kohut thought you were challenging his ideas he could cut you off at the knees—or cut your cock off, if you prefer.[28]

Yet it was ego psychology, not Kohut's new self psychology, that found penises (and attacks on them) everywhere. Again, ego psychologists could only understand Kohut's theory (and Kohut himself) as feminine or anti-masculine (two sides of the same coin).

The ego psychologists argued that people start off in a state of dependency, leaning on the people and things around them, but that as they mature (if they mature) they become autonomous, independent from others and from the environmental surround. The adult renounces his earlier dependency for hard-won autonomy, becoming a monadic closed system, no longer vulnerable to outside forces. In contradistinction to Kohut's supposedly overgratifying, overly personal approach, recognizing nevertheless their need to do something to get their patients to depend on them—so they could, paradoxically, help the patient through analysis to develop his autonomy—they conceded that the analyst might well need to provide the patient with a receptive, maternal attitude for a while at the beginning of analysis. They conceded that *some* "humanistic" techniques might be necessary to *establish* the psychoanalytic situation proper, to *induce* the necessary movement from the "environmentally contingent state of infancy and early childhood" to that higher level of development characterized by the mature "autonomy of a closed system vis-à-vis the environment" (Gitelson 1973, 316). This maternal attitude must not involve direct suggestion, however (for example, suggesting to the patient that he should depend on the analyst), and indeed the analyst would establish it essentially through silence. If the analyst approached the patient wishing only to analyze and not to influence (aspiring to influence the patient would be narcissistic on the analyst's part), he brought the essential diatrophic attitude. This state of trained nondesire was the analyst's "qualification for his work," that alone by which real analysis could proceed (329). The analyst's silent wish to analyze would foster the dependency that in turn would allow for the work that would bring about the patient's ego autonomy. This stance toward the patient's dependency renders legible Gitelson's accusation of Ernest Wolf in his cutting remark to the young trainee/patient, "You don't want to be analyzed, you just want to be an analyst": from Gitelson's perspective, Wolf was refusing to submit to his ministrations. Gitelson didn't need the patient, but he needed the patient to need him, or, as he parsed this resistance, he couldn't do his work of analyzing.

Stemming from Gitelson's idea that the analyst could serve a diatrophic function in order to cultivate the patient's dependency, two younger faculty members next developed the notion of the "defense transference." Sharing their teacher's discomfort with the Kohutians' downplaying of the Oedipal transference neurosis, Nathan Schlessinger and Fred Robbins argued that the problems a patient presents are not Oedipal *or* pre-Oedipal. Indeed, they wrote, analysts had formulated some cases purely in terms of the Oedipal paradigm only because they had paid "inadequate attention to earlier developmental derivatives." Their studies emphasized "the need to attend to such [earlier] psychopathology not simply as a regressive defense against Oedipal conflict but as a significant focus of interest in its own right and a critical determinant of the outcome of the process" (Schlessinger 1990, 10). The patient's attempts to pull the analyst into an interpersonal—"open-systems"—encounter, to turn him from analyst into therapist, to invite him into a relationship of mutual influence, was his *defense against* the transference, not his transference proper. The patient's pull for a real relationship was his generalized, "characterological" way of avoiding transference, of avoiding analysis. Character was, in a sense, the avoidance of transference.[29] An analyst's first step, then, must be to build up an "analytic alliance" in which he could render the analysis-avoiding character traits ego-dystonic (ego-alien). He would need to tackle the entire character structure first, *before* the neurosis it sheltered could be revealed for analysis proper. Unless this armored system were addressed and an analytic alliance established, an entire analysis could proceed on false grounds, in the framework of the "defense transference" rather than the true, libidinal, Oedipal transference.[30] Vigilant attention to the defense transference would thus open up "systematic access to and influence over pathological aspects of the analytic alliance" (Colarusso 1985, 285). As one can see, the pathologies of *alliance* between patient and psychoanalyst were now front and center for the ego psychologists.

Kohut's new way of thinking about psychopathology and its treatment provoked two of his colleagues to develop another way to protect the psychosexual trope at the heart of their analysis. Max Forman (1976) and Jerome Kavka (1976) offered "phallic narcissism" as an effort to contain Kohut's desexualized narcissism within the psychosexual picture of drive maturation. If the Freudian explanation of psychic turmoil turned on the notion of diverted sexual instinct, these writers proposed that narcissistic patients were essentially fixated at the dawn of the phallic, unable to turn the dial from narcissism (feminized self-love) to (mature, masculine, heterosexual) object love. Kavka describes a patient who guards the emergence of his transference neurosis by being extremely sensitive to criticisms from the analyst; he writes that "within the context of this walled-off neurosis was contained both active castration wishes towards the father [analyst] and the patient's reactive castration anxiety" (Kavka 1976, 276). The distinction can be confusing diagnostically, Forman agreed. He offered a diagnostic schema in which the two orders could co-exist "as mutually exclusive," as long as the phallic were accorded its place on top: "Seeming exceptions occur where initially the picture in an Oedipal neurosis is strongly narcissistic because of specific childhood traumata during the Oedipal period, which have determined the outcome of the Oedipus. Metapsychologically, these contributions are primary transference neuroses in which secondary narcissistic regressive defenses are very prominent. I say secondary narcissistic defenses because they derive from penis envy or phallic narcissism" (Forman 1976, 73).[31] What we see in these baroque additions to the local canon of ego psychology is the reaction that Kohut's ideas set off, for Kohut had dethroned the Oedipus (or, if you prefer, "cut off the cock of the ego autonomy folks"), reducing it from its role at the center of a universal drama of human subject formation and granting it only secondary status, the secondary status of occasional pathology. Displacing the entire psychosexual explanatory framework, he had left penis envy and castration anxiety—and masculine individuation as such—without a home. Gitelson (with his "diatrophic bond") and Schlessinger and Robbins (with their "defense transference") had each sought to incorporate but subordinate a zone of Kohutian analysis within Oedipal interpretation by expanding the ego's pathography to include pre-Oedipal problems in need of maternal attention. In seeking the sublime with their idea of "phallic narcissism," Forman and Kavka sought to go farther, granting self psychology only a bit of room at the dawn of the phallic, "where the level of narcissism that is disturbed is on a more primary narcissistic level, not having reached the developmental level of the Oedipal neurosis" (Forman 1976, 73). Hereafter narcissism would haunt the Oedipus, in pathology and in health. Which was primary—and which secondary—was now decidedly up for grabs.

MOURNING, AND ITS DISCONTENTS:
On the Abjection of the Social

In the same year Kohut had published his first paper, George Pollock, fresh out of training, published his first as well. Like his ego psychological confreres, Pollock would soon be responding to the crisis that self psychology would create for ego psychology, but in a different realm. His focus was neither individual psychopathology nor the problems with the "alliance" that worried other ego psychologists but the survival of psychoanalysis itself. He sought to shepherd the profession, and the Institute, past the challenges posed not only by self psychology but by medical reform; he engaged in institution-building and social intervention, cloaking his leadership in the language of psychoanalysis. Launching a writing career that would be as prolific as his administrative career would be (by its end) ignominious, he theorized the role of a new figure: the psychoanalytic *consultant*, the powerful individual who brokered referrals. As it would turn out, this paper would be the charter for the role Pollock would occupy at the center of a patronage system in which he controlled the flow of capital, consulting, referring, and assigning patients, candidates, committee spots, and the like to his beneficiaries. This consultant role needed a psychoanalytic epistemic anchoring, and Pollock found this in the notion that the consulting analyst had a privileged vantage point from which to arbitrate central dynamics: the consultant adjudicated reality (ferreting out its nemesis, "unconscious resistance"), purity (sniffing out its "contamination"), and semiotic legibility (while the patient's transference was "distortion," the consultant, in contrast, operated from an "explanatory level" of communication free of "suggestion") (Pollock 1960, 634).

"The consultant," Pollock wrote, "has to decide what can be done for this person with his particular difficulties in a specific reality situation based on his individual developmental pattern. The amount of time needed for this evaluation varies; however, if it extends beyond two to three sessions, subsequent referral may be contaminated" (1960, 634). The original referring source—the family physician, the prospective patient's parent or spouse— often "has an unconsciously hostile attitude to analysis, [so] sabotage of the therapeutic planning may be anticipated. Further referral for psycho-analysis may arouse competitive feelings." Pollock sutured together the elements of the consultant's toolkit with the notion that the patient's hesitation in accepting referral for analysis "may be posed as reality-anchored, but since the consultant has considered reality factors in arriving at his decision, these ['reality factors'] may be viewed as . . . resistance" (1960, 634). Rationalized in this way, Pollock-the-Consultant kept ego psychology on life support through referrals to his favorites, maintaining the idea that outsiders envied the valuable interpretive activities psychoanalysts could do that they could not. Still, while his close associates received the referrals of trainees, Pollock, reality's arbiter, knew well enough that recent grads, freed from the required training analysis, were going on for second, personal analyses with the self psychologists. In both camps it was already becoming clear that the internal market for psychoanalysis—the treatment of psychoanalytic trainees and other mental health professionals—would be the reliably durable one going forward.

As Pollock drove on, producing and storing more and more surplus, achieving a mirage of eminence through auto-citationality, the decline of an external market for psychoanalytic publications quietly reduced his flagship journal to the status of a vanity press. The organ of Pollock's publishing empire was the *Annual of Psychoanalysis*, published by the Chicago Institute, and for two decades nearly every issue contained at least one article authored by him, with many of the others authored by his immediate beneficiaries. Institute monies were involved on both ends of the publishing process. The Institute published the *Annual*, and then, under Pollock's direction—unbeknownst to (or unacknowledged by) all—bought up all the issues of the *Annual*. Strong sales and good circulation (as it were) were thus guaranteed.[32] Meanwhile, in the larger world of psychoanalytic publishing, Kohut—working a reward system that distributed merit according to the freshness of ideas—was winning the field for self psychology, getting his name attached to the last great systematic metapsychology of the twentieth-century.

Pollock, having launched the psychoanalytic rationale for his patronage system in his early paper, after a brief foray into Fleming's old problem of trainee "selection," turned his attention to the topic of mourning, the central theme of his voluminous writing over the next twenty-five years. Inspired by a minor essay by Freud, Pollock produced a recapitulation theory in the Freudian mold to apply the idea of mourning to the profession's crisis; his version centered on the idea that "organizations grow up like people do as we know clinically [*sic*]" (Pollock 1977, 7). In Freud's drive theory of mourning the ego over time "decathects" (withdraws the libido from) the deceased (or lost) love object; through the mourning process, the ego becomes able, in time, to cathect a new love object. Pollock recycled this classic Freudian tripe in an effort to point out a path toward the profession's health after a normal process of adaptive recathexis. Diagnosing rampant denial in the profession, he prescribed the mourning of Freud's death. "We cannot rest on Freud's laurels" forever, he wrote. *Denial* was the defense he liked best to note in the profession at large. (Gitelson had—it seems—preferred to find *devaluation* in his colleagues.) He suggested that "in addition to the customary categories of pathology with which psychoanalysts were familiar, e.g., developmental, neurotic, and psychotic configurations, one might additionally consider 'transition pathology'" (13). In the case of psychoanalysis, the symptoms of transition pathology were "nepotism (symbolic and direct), elitism, compliance, and/or submission," and above all an unwillingness on the part of the profession's aging custodians to give up the reins to the younger generation (13). His "Freud said" collages are animated by the confident claim that psychoanalysis can grasp any human topic, individual or social. Yes, psychoanalysis as a *profession* must move toward a realistic recognition of its current crisis and grapple with the transience of its clinical forms—but as a *basic science of man* its interpretive potential was limitless. Psychoanalysts might fail, but psychoanalysis never would.

Freud's group psychology presupposed the individual; it was, in this sense, an individual psychology all the way down. Indeed, nowhere in Freud's writing is the primacy of the individual more pronounced than in his theories of group psychology and civilization, in which social solidarity is explained in terms of the relations between ego and superego. Pollock recapitulated precisely this asocial, ahistorical reading of the group in his vain efforts to grasp the profession's crisis. His prescription was a mourning process, but, in a reading devoid of any kind of social structural account of the "crises coming on top of each other," this was impossibly cast as an individual, psychological process. Good leadership, he hoped, would draw the profession toward a healthy adaptation; the political vision "of a Mao or a Lenin" was a pathology of leadership, a longing for an "ideal commonwealth where disharmony and inequity no longer prevail" (Pollock 1977, 13). The current profession of psychoanalysis represented a similarly pathological effort to secure a utopia, he wrote, an unrealistic effort that stemmed from the unconscious wish to regress and to merge symbiotically with the pregenital mother.

> Symbiotic reunion with this maternal, genderless god-figure allows entry into the pregenital heaven and paradise, if life has been in harmony with the superego and ego-ideal system. . . . Regression to this earliest state, where there is little differentiation of self and object, is accompanied by the loss of objective reality testing, inability to distinguish between self and all else, magical animistic thinking, and omnipotence resulting from the archaic narcissistic symbiosis. The belief in animism, magic, and omnipotence goes unchallenged. Cultural reinforcement of these beliefs allows man to put aside his reality testing when confronted with the stress of nonexistence and gives rise to many cults which, though bizarre, are understandable. (Pollock 1975, 341)

It is apparent here, in his effort to talk about the profession's transition by way of adaptation and the role of the leader in assisting this, that the "cultural reinforcement of beliefs" is crucial. "Culture," in this usage, does not constitute the individual, it merely reflects (in this case reinforces) him. Pollock offered a hopeful message nonetheless about how environmental adversity—environment construed in Hartmannian terms—might offer hope, for after all "there is permanence in change." No, we can't return to the good old days, but "what is valuable endures, and so we can have our permanence as well as our changes" (Pollock 1977b, 32).

"We must not act like the Viennese neurological hierarchy," he counseled the profession. Instead, he wrote (rather paradoxically in view of his counsel that analysts should mourn Freud), we should *be like Freud*, for whom "adversity play[ed] a constructive role; if Freud had been comfortably welcomed, accepted, encouraged, and supported by the clinical neurological establishment of Vienna, would he have discovered the unconscious and founded psychoanalysis?" (Pollock 1977b, 31). Exhorting his compatriots with an injunction to bury the dead, offering his own hopeful frustration theory (adversity can be our friend, just like it was Freud's!), Pollock undergirded his adaptationist pieties with a bold claim for ego psychology's power as a social hermeneutic. Pointing to a universal value that exists apart from the cathexis of its transient, historical forms ("What is valuable endures"), his platonic view of adaptation further heightened the contradictory status of an ego pinned between the motifs of autonomy and dependency. At the same time, psychoanalysis was not (in fact) dead, not yet anyway, and his recommendation of mourning as an adaptive strategy fell on deaf ears; his colleagues were still getting too much out of the referral system he was propping up to adapt to (unthinkable) eventualities.

MAKING SENSE OF AN ENDING: *Family Secrets and the Psychoanalytic Rhetorics of History*

Ultimately Pollock's fundraising became too creative for the faculty's taste. Accepting money from a wealthy patient for both the Institute's coffers and for his personal projects, in 1988, after three full terms and an additional several years, he was ousted from the directorship for what the group understood to have been clinical and ethical malfeasance. The faculty felt that Pollock had too much power, that he had abused it, and that the structure of the organization needed to change so as to avoid such a concentration of power in one person's hands. In Pollock's wake, a "Committee on Committees" was established to make the teaching and supervisory and committee assignments that Pollock had doled out by his own lights. With this innovation, and the intent to observe term limits, the Institute was, by its own lights, "democratized" (Kirsner 1999, 432).[33] As the APsaA site visitors noted in their glowing 1991 report on the Institute's functioning, congratulations were deserved for a successful effort "to replace an over-centralized, top-heavy monarchical system and move to a democratic system with a balance of powers" (Kirsner 2000, 135).

In spite of these plaudits, over the next twenty years, a succession of relatively impotent directors administered an institution with a dwindling student base and little external funding, levying substantial faculty dues to fill in for the tuition shortfall and to sustain the daily functioning of the organization. Meeting minutes are filled with the ceaseless efforts of the group to find the necessary handful of trainees each year that would allow the doors to remain open and the faculty to continue functioning as such. (During several of these years no class could be started because there were no applicants.)[34] The students who did matriculate struggled on their own to find patients who would come at the required four-times weekly frequency (the clinic no longer had cases to send them), and it became more and more difficult for the Institute to adhere to the official APsaA training standards. Not only did trainees struggle to find cases but faculty, too, struggled to meet the "immersion" requirement for rising to the status of TA. The majority of the faculty were reduced to practicing psychotherapy, as patients for psychoanalysis—other than those few trainees in need of a training analysis—had all but ceased coming.[35]

A full twenty-one years later, in 2009, still in this situation of scarcity, the faculty held a meeting to make collective sense, for the very first time, of the ouster of George Pollock and its ending of a working, if ultimately corrupt, patronage system. A recording of this meeting, held on May 27, 2009, at the Chicago Institute, was made with the permission of its organizer, James Anderson, who also made a copy for the Institute's library.[36] Convened by a psychologist faculty member who in the 1980s had been one of the first beneficiaries of Pollock's efforts at opening up the Institute to non-M.D.s, the agenda for this meeting featured three elderly analysts who had been key players in the drama of Pollock's professional demise. Two had been members of the ego psychological "troika" Pollock had installed to administer the Institute's daily training functions while he attended to his larger political mission of public speaking, fundraising, and program development. I call them Drs. S and H. The third was the man who had been head of the Ethics Committee that, as its very first mission, had charged Pollock with violating the community's fundamental principles by taking large sums of money from a wealthy patient. I call him Dr. B. "We were a band of brothers," this man choked out on the verge of tears at the beginning of the meeting, alluding to Freud's mythical primal horde who organized to overthrow their tyrannical father at the dawn of civilization (Freud 1913, 142). Justifying and excusing his betrayal of his "brother" in the same breath, his spearheading the bringing of charges, he emoted, "I liked George, I felt close to him; but what he did was not right. We had to do something."

Why revisit this history now? In the spring of 2009, the Institute's director—structurally disempowered since the leveling of the administrative structure twenty years earlier—had proposed opening up training substantially farther than the 1989 lawsuit had, permitting individuals currently in analysis with non-TAs to train. Recall that the lawsuit had opened training to mental health trainees who were not M.D.s; it had not challenged the TA system. Now the director was proposing to allow trainees to enter training regardless of whether they were going to be in analysis with an official TA. "It's survival, folks; we won't have a class if we don't do this," had been his refrain. A new backlash was gathering force to keep the official TA system in place, to preserve the guardianship of psychoanalysis by an elite, even though the world had moved on, even though other, expressly nonmedical, expressly non-ego-psychological competitor institutes were attracting most of any potential trainees that might be out there. In the face of such further leveling of its historically hierarchical system of valuation, the Institute faculty had, it seemed, decided that they had to make sense of the fall of its last great leader, its last great protector, a man who had, in spite of his excesses, done so much to preserve their world. It had to open up a ritual space for the group to reflect on itself as such.

Here was the faculty, straining against the tide of its decades-long diminution of status to work out a politics of authority that might support its ongoing viability. Here were its members, mounting their effort to transcend a real structural contradiction, foregrounding the enabling fiction of a pious desire to uphold justice conceived in terms of prior property relations, attacking Pollock's "unbridled ambition" and his "instinct for power," citing Shakespeare, redirecting one another to keep a "psychoanalytic" perspective on Pollock's behavior. With little hint of the larger structural dislocation of psychoanalysis in the health-care system (apart from the director's effort to acknowledge Pollock's efforts to keep the Institute afloat), the group underscored the heroism of the "band of brothers," giving the elders—the former analysts of many in the room—the floor for one last (it seemed) Promethean moment. But what about the theoretical factions, the proponents of self psychology and those of ego psychology? Had they reached a settlement? Let's see what happened, according to the elders. Let's see what they did, in 2009, with "what happened" in the late 1980s.

> Dr. B: George Pollock was a very, very complex person. He was a good man. A kind man. An intelligent man. And a good analyst, and a good contributor to the field in his own research. I feel a little bit like I'm Mark Antony [Dr. B was the head of the new Ethics Committee, and in that role he was the person who had initiated the formal proceedings that had led to Pollock's ouster], but he was too ambitious. Power grew on him. [*Nervous laughter from the audience.*] You must remember, what George did was change [the Institute] into a more democratic institution. . . . But George wanted to be president—and he was president of many things. He was president of the Illinois Psychiatric, the Illinois Psychoanalytic, the American Psychoanalytic, the American Psychiatric, the American College of Psychoanalysts, and so on. . . . What happened was I was at a wedding reception at the South Shore Country Club for a friend of ours whose daughter had gotten married. Both Nate and Leo came up to me, as chairman of the Ethics Committee, and asked me in private to listen to a disturbing story. Leo had heard from the couch [i.e., from a patient] that there was some unethical behavior going on in George's practice. And Nate had received from his two sons, who were both attorneys, information . . . proving that George had appropriated monies from [a] lady to the tune of either eighty-seven thousand or eighty-nine thousand dollars per year for ten years and also had set up a research fund totaling five million dollars. And the trustees of that trust fund were people who had been his analysands. . . . It's a troubling situation, what power does to people—what Lord Acton says—that power corrupts and absolute power corrupts absolutely.

Dr. B's narration of the events that ensued to bring Pollock down begins with an epiphany at a wedding, a dramatic hinge point when an abstract idea—George wanted to be president of everything—became a real problem for the Ethics Committee. Sparked by Leo's information "from the couch," kindled by Nate's information from his sons, attorneys both, in a moment George's ambition became an actionable offense. Time was transformed, in this moment of the story, from the habitual to the mythic: Pollock's patronage economy was about to come crashing down.

Dr. S: His career as director of the Institute has the inexorable quality of a Greek tragedy, under the heading Power Corrupts. He was appointed by the staff of the Institute as a rising star. Ambitious. Very full of ideas about how to expand the Institute. And he proceeded to do so, quite successfully, adding new programs.

Dr. S, who had been one of Pollock's "troika" of lieutenants who administered the Institute while the director was off politicking and fundraising, now listed these new programs at some length, describing, with no small degree of reverence, the richness and great variety of activities that created "the very thriving situation" of the Institute in the 1980s.

It was a favorable milieu for his will to power to flourish. One of the first things he did was to dispense with the staff, ostensibly in the interest of democratizing the Institute. But it had the effect of eliminating a supervisory function that had been exercised by the staff. In the interest of democratization, he was actually engaged in centralizing the power in his own hands. He created a faculty, controlling very carefully its agenda and membership. Sort of a division of power. Distributing power, but maintaining control. He also appointed, eventually, a troika, Dr. A, Dr. H, and me, distributing power safely and freeing himself to pursue his own political ambitions and national pursuits. By the end of his second term, he had created an administration that was tightly in his own hands. He rewarded his supporters and punished any critic. And at the end of the second term, he posed the idea of a third term, to which the council acquiesced. And the board approved it. Incidentally, he had appointed his former patients to be on the board so that he had a loyal set of supporters that would approve whatever he would present. He raised a lot of money for the functions of the Institute; his patient [and later victim] Mrs. Lederer contributed a generous annual sum to enlarge and support the library. [Another former patient] supported the teacher's education program and the Barr Harris clinic. But what developed then was some confusion about who the fundraising was for, whether it was for the Institute or for himself.

Now the convener opened the floor to questions and comments, and the audience quickened to criticize the "nonpsychoanalytic" Caesar and Lord Acton ("power corrupts") readings of what had happened with a plethora of psychoanalytic accountings for George's behavior in the various terms of psychopathology—the self psychologists emphasizing his vertical split and his disavowal of narcissistic rage, the ego psychologists pointing to his phallic narcissism. The first to speak was one of the leaders of the current effort to preserve the TA system against a newly proposed relaxing of national standards. "This episode points to the difficulty of the transference and how analysts have to be extremely sensitive to what patients do or don't do. That's what we need to keep in mind in terms of our own learning from such a terrible experience. I think obviously George seduced this woman to give the money, in some way, and she was like most everybody here that was involved with him, she complied." The lesson, in his view, was that we should not comply with the current director's seductions, his promises of success with the newly proposed changes, for what the director was proposing denatured psychoanalysis, if psychoanalysis is the constant and extremely sensitive effort to grasp and to interpret—and not to act on—the difficulties of transference.

"That's fine," added another older analyst, a veteran author with many articles published in the *Annual*, "but how did George get away with it as far as *he* was concerned, for himself? One of the things I remember him saying was, 'I saved that woman's life. If that woman had not been in treatment with me, she would be dead by now.' And that became a, what we say now, excuse. But for him, it was a justification." Now the current director interjected: "Like all the favors he did all these other people here, right?!" The audience laughed at the director's allusion to the beneficiaries of Pollock's patronage machine who were present in the room, as the speaker went on, swatting away the director's effort at humor with a gesture of mock indulgence mixed with real irritation.

> *This* was something very special though. *This* was something that was really tremendously important, that could be balanced. He could, he deserved it, because he had really *done* something [in helping this woman patient] that was momentous. But one of the things we are interested in psychoanalytically is how to understand the behavior, not just to prevent anything like it ever happening. How does one *do* something like that? How does one *get away* with it? You say, well both of you quoted Lord Acton, which in a sense is true, but it doesn't, it's not a terribly *psychoanalytic* point of view. Is it that the ego expands so much that anything that you do is all right? You don't have to face a kind of shaming or guilt-ridden superego because it's not present anymore? You are justified in what you are doing because of your own grandiosity? That would be one way of thinking about this.

The group lingered on whether George had or had not been a favorite child to his parents, and if he *had* been a favorite child what the implications of this were in terms of his psychology. "It was incredible to me that he needed to be the president of this, that, and the other, all at the same time," said one middle-aged faculty member, now a leading light, taking a developmental object relations view of the situation and mustering what he called "what we now know from current psychology" to strengthen his argument: "When one is a favored child, genuinely favored, there is a time when enough is enough, that you actually get filled up, you may even need *less* to get filled up. George, as it turned out, needed more and more to fill him up. I just wonder whether the antecedents of that could be seen in the early days, or did he actually change?" Dr. H, the other member of the erstwhile troika, now brought up the wounding that everyone knew George had experienced on being denied the chairmanship of the Department of Psychiatry at the University of Illinois. He pointed at George's compensatory efforts to remake the Institute in the image of the university in order to deal with this blow. This time the group roundly rejected the explanation, since it turned on "adult life occurrences." They drove instead toward the events of George's emotional development in childhood that must have been decisive for his political behavior. The director now jumped in to tie together George's two sides. "We can speculate about a deep injury which led to a split. Here was this grandiose portion of him which was more and more stimulated and could never be satisfied, and somewhere else was a malnourished child, depressed, God knows what—Arnold [Goldberg] could speculate about that probably better than I—that never got integrated, it never got nourished. And we all paid the price. And we all helped." At last, "we all helped" was on the table. As the meeting reached a crescendo, two octogenarian gentlemen who both happened to be named Arnold—one of them the Institute's leading exponent of Kohut's self psychology, the other the Institute's staunchest Freudian—finally stepped into the ring. Now the Freudian Arnold [Tobin]—not the Arnold whose speculations the director had just invited, but the other, rival Arnold—took the floor to talk about "the role that George Pollock played in terms of group psychology."

> The question is not just those individuals that benefited, but how he functioned, played a role for the whole group. We learned later that George was giving Kohut money. And it was the assumption of many of us that he did that so that there would not be a split, so that Kohut would behave himself and not be carried away himself and challenge

George but rather be part of the group. So, what I'm saying is that in many ways, I think George *served the purposes of the group*. And I think this is the hard part to look at because, while it's important what kind of personality George had, I'm willing to settle for the idea that that was his personality and that made him ideal to be *a tool of the group, to do what we wanted done*. And that was, for example, *not getting split, and raising money for us*. We knew, for example, many of us knew, that Glen Miller and Jackie Miller (Glen was the librarian, Jackie was George's secretary), that the two of them entertained Mrs. Lederer [George's wealthy patient and patroness] on a regular basis. And when George said he saved her life, what he did was structure a life for the poor lonely woman. That's true, and many of us knew about it, but no one thought to question what he was doing. So there was a lot of that kind of stuff that went on. *George was serving purposes*. And that fits then, Jim, with what you brought up at the beginning [of the meeting, by way of introduction], and that is that we need to look at what happened *afterwards* and how we have continued to do the same kind of thing in different ways. I have my own personal experience which goes along with what people have said. He was a brilliant man. He brought, for example, culture to this Institute. He was the one who talked about art and so on. So he played a number of different roles, which different people appreciated. It was not as simple as it's been presented so far. I emphasize Freud's *Group Psychology and the Analysis of Ego*, and how the leader of the group is as much a leader as he is captive of the group itself. I would think we would need another meeting to explore that, and to look at what happened afterward, when there were many things about the organization that took place. We had a more of what we call, what's been referred to as, a classical approach, then it became more of a Kohutian approach. And this was in the organization of the curriculum, for example. I know personally, I was asked not to teach anymore because I was too old, at the same time that many others, my age or older, continued to teach. So there were *violent changes* that took place after George left, changes we were protected from *by our own agreement* that he should remain in power.

Political metaphors structure Freud's discourse on the ego, and this speaker was taking up these metaphors in his reading of Pollock; he was marshalling Freud's theorization of the leader's function as that of holding the group together and holding violence at bay. Here the psyche is an arena of conflict based on an economy of scarcity, as is the group.

The Kohutian Arnold was next. Urged on by both the meeting convener and the director, his fellow self psychologist, Goldberg disagreed with his Freudian counterpart; he instanced the group's collective refusal to attend to "the purposes of the group," to own the "violent changes" that had taken place, to see the leader as "a tool of the group," to analyze the collective purposes Pollock was serving. He pushed on toward that apotheosis of the empathic perspective, a theoretically rationalized tendency to privilege the individual "I" of discourse and to disavow any unconscious motivation other than the restoration of individual narcissistic equilibrium, any third-person perspective on events, and group psychology itself. The group that matters is the original family group of Pollock, not the current group in the room, which Arnold Tobin felt was in need of another session. He nudged the meeting to conclude on this less conflictual note.

> [George] had a real, real disavowal, a real, real blind spot that I think goes along with the kind of vertical split that he had.[37] On one hand he was generous, fun, charismatic, and on the other hand he was totally blind to what he was doing. One other interesting fact is that George would not leave the Institute, so when I became director we had to devise a way to get rid of him. So we decided that everyone who was a member had to sign an agreement that they had no ethical violations outstanding against them, or history of ethical violations, since, as Dr. B said, his was never [formally] exposed [because the legal case was ultimately settled *in camera*]. George refused to sign, and thereby we managed to get him to leave the Institute—but only after this particular thing. The last thing I remember about George is that I wrote him a note saying that, being director, I recognized all that he had done for the Institute, all that he had accomplished. It was amazing what he had done for the Institute, in spite of—and you have to divide these—his autocratic style and his terrible, terrible fall from grace. He wrote me back a one-liner: Thank you.

Self psychological Arnold had the last word, with his reading of "George" that emphasized the pathological individual (viewed empathically of course) and that eclipsed any wider collective function that the individual leader might (as the other, Freudian Arnold put it) have been "serving." In the Freudian reading, the individual leader was a function of the group's need to constitute and maintain itself as such (granted, the group was imagined on the lines of the individual writ large, the leader mediating its organic solidarity). Self psychology could only imagine the socius in terms of a kind of mechanical solidarity, the group as a collection of fully separate, empathically understood, narcissistically motivated individuals. "George," then, mediates a common culture, even if the group can't imagine such a thing; he serves the group's interest in abolishing the larger situation in which it finds itself and in which Pollock found himself director. In the absence of other collective resources to make sense of *what happened*, "George" is trafficked between symbolic orders as the group posits and attempts to reconcile a lower sphere of narcissistic self-aggrandizement with a higher sphere of eternal psychoanalytic values. Thus is the group's appropriation of the individual completed, in the collective rite of (as it were) mourning.

But strategic games of self-aggrandizement are so intrinsic to the projects of institutional and cosmological reproduction that I have described here that it's impossible fully to disentangle them. Without the first Arnold's Freudian idea of intergenerational strife to bind its members into a contractual—if conflictual—fraternity, left only with the other Arnold's Kohutian idea that "George never saw he was doing anything wrong, he could not see what other people could see," the group could banish the communal order—could banish its groupness—in favor of the purely individual pathological act. Unrecognized would be the objective structural fact that there literally was no money without the communal contract founded on paternal gift giving, without the leader's risky speculations on scarcity (his vanity publishing, his theorizing the need to "decathect" the image of Freud, his strategic referrals to friends), without the contingent games of prestige between rival "brothers" that ensued to snap up the froth of appointments and referrals, without the constant efforts to adjudicate proprietary claims over *real* psychoanalysis. These phenomena of individual and collective misrecognition oriented, and orient, real practices, especially those aimed at reestablishing the objective value of the psychoanalytic credential—*then* in the instance of accepting the non-M.D. on the basis of the judiciously applied *numerus clausus*, *now* in the instance of accepting the applicant in analysis with the "non-TA."

CODA: *On the Plenty of Scarcity*

George Pollock propped up the Institute with an array of foamy patents and indulgences, a speculative bubble on the future of psychoanalysis, while at the same time theorizing (or trying to theorize) *value* as something that especially attends scarcity. Scarcity, by Freud's definition, was precisely what gave an object value. Pollock's efforts to open up the Institute forced his conservative colleagues to step up their investment in the TA system so as to maintain the relative scarcity of their own qualifications, so as to maintain their overall position in the hierarchy. Proximity to "George" in the circuits of patronage thus became one of the key stakes of intragroup competition, the entitlement by which fractions of the group constituted themselves vis-à-vis other fractions. But Pollock was also playing it safe with his gambling habit, keeping a cartel of ego psychologists in charge while placating Kohut at the same time. He knew that the Institute needed to reach out to the world even though he didn't accept that its core product needed to change.

The 2009 struggle around exogenous recruitment—"we should open up training" versus "we should only train those in analysis with TAs"—is a further instance of collective resistance against the devaluation of the psychoanalytic credential. The psychoanalysts use "George" symbolically, as diagnostic of a current political pathology of adaptation (to the culture of managed care). "George" places on display the threshold that defines the perimeter of the Institute, the boundary where it meets the nonpsychoanalytic world, a boundary that all now recognize to be "in crisis." The name of this last, primal father stands as an internal critique of the naturalness of the institutional boundary. In the event, Pollock was trying to articulate a theory of scarcity value, but without the political capital or the concept of the group he would have required in order to do so effectively. Pollock's referral—privileged token of paternal excess in his regime of scarcity—was as much a mitigating force in the impending crisis as it was corrosive of the group's fraternity, and, in the end, impolitic.

ON NARCISSISM

"Our Own Developmental Line"

We see the patient enter into analysis with a reality attitude to the analyst; then the transference gains momentum until it reaches its peak in the full-blown transference neurosis which has to be worked off analytically until the figure of the analyst emerges again, reduced to its true status.—ANNA FREUD, quoted in Arthur Couch, "Therapeutic Functions of the Real Relationship in Psychoanalysis"

If the home atmosphere is ungiving . . . the child will be impressed with a "feeling of scarcity" and may well develop the "anal" characteristic of hanging on to what he has because there may not be any more.—CLARA THOMPSON, *Psychoanalysis: Evolution and Development*

....

The director had attempted to open up training, proposing that new candidates be admitted to training regardless of their analyst's status, as long as their analyst had himself or herself completed training. Under this thinking it didn't matter when their analyst had graduated, or whether he had passed the national certification test and become an official TA. This proposal met fierce opposition, and a settling up of old accounts—personal, theoretical, political—ensued: a final reckoning with Pollock and his legacy. Those arrayed against the director insisted on conservation, aggressively flying the flag of "standards." They didn't like the figure of the analyst that was emerging now, reduced, as it were, in status. In one blow, with this new proposal, the hierarchical system of social reproduction would be leveled— along with (they felt) any standards whatsoever. And as the standards flag snapped in the Windy City breeze, the director pressed his case, saying they didn't have the luxury of disagreeing, that this was a matter of survival.

But what were these vaunted "standards"? And how did they correspond with the set of newly popular, post-Kohutian relational theories of therapeutic action that centered on the therapist's curative indispensability, that target of Mark's complaint in chapter 2 about his colleagues being "too nice"?[1] This chapter engages the intimate relation between the formal regulation of psychoanalysis (through objectified standards) and its informal regulation (through collegial moral and aesthetic standards), both organized in relation to the sublime figure of the real relationship. The director's proposal condensed these, authorizing (and finally provoking) a neoliberal solution to the crisis of scarcity that all labored under. Here I examine at last the movement from law to norm in psychoanalytic governmentality, mediated by an ever-present, specifically psychoanalytic reflexivity, a particular set of "games of freedom and security" that shapes the ways professional psychoanalysts evaluate, check, and conduct the behavior of one another and of themselves (Foucault 2008, 65). This normalizing reflexivity—at once a manner of reflexive thinking, an attitude toward reflexivity, and a system of representations *of* the reflexive self—constitutes an ethnographically distinctive biopolitical assemblage.

THE FORCE OF FREQUENCY: *On the Mystical Foundations of Authority*

The director's proposal outraged the descendants of Lionel Blitzsten, for whom power was to be embodied in specially analyzed persons. Peter Shapiro (the senior TA whose interview was discussed in chapter 1) promoted his esoteric definition of psychoanalysis, referring to the "supposed" scarcity of analytic patients and citing Blitzsten's credo.[2] "It is normally a matter of the *analyst's own resistance* to analysis that keeps him from getting the patient to come at the proper frequency. These are countertransference problems *in analysts* that need to be worked out analytically," he maintained, replicating an authoritative discourse with particular communicative care. "I never had a problem getting patients to come four, even five times a week, because I *believed in* what I was doing. I'd tell them, if you want to address the underlying cause of your problems and not just the symptoms then you have to come with sufficient frequency for us to be able to work at that level." Denying outside reality in his rendition of the crisis, he added, "I saw the results, and the results always confirmed my recommendations." The others, he felt, were politicizing their own personal difficulties finding analytic patients, showing their faulty commitment to psychoanalysis (and, presumably, their incompetence as well). They were indulging in a nonpsychoanalytic notion of necessity, an economic notion of necessity, and in pursuing this understanding they were putting the Institute at risk of devolving into a mere psychotherapy school.

Not so, countered the director, in turn citing Franz Alexander's innovations of over half a century earlier in a much-talked-about letter to the *International Journal of Psychoanalysis* (Terman 2009). The 2009 International Congress was about to be held in Chicago for the first time in history and would bring the world's leading psychoanalysts to town. In the months leading up to this event the director invoked Alexander over and again, saying that the Institute was finally on the verge of accomplishing some of the reforms that his great forebear had sought to achieve way back in 1954. In his tightly crafted letter to the membership of the International, styling himself as Alexander's Kohutian epigone, the director secreted his decisive innovation away in a laundry list of other, more innocuous, strategies of recruitment he called "outreach." "We have admitted several of these [individuals who are in analysis with members of our faculty who are not TAs] with the proviso that they will spend some time with a TA at some point during their clinical work. So far, these candidates have been excellent students, and we are in the process of devising evaluation procedures to more systematically compare their performance and progress with candidates in analysis with TA's. *Our opening our training to such candidates has permitted us to have two consecutive first year classes*" (Terman 2009, 206, emphasis mine). He emphasized the sheer necessity of such changes for the Institute to draw some trainees. He also celebrated the paramount integrity of the therapeutic relationships these potential new trainees had with their "non-TA" analysts over the official training analysis system, in which only a specially vetted group of analysts could analyze the next generation. "Forcing people to change analysts in the middle of a good analysis is non-analytic," he argued, invoking the privileged privative in a meeting on the subject of his proposal. Rupturing these relationships would be destructive to the individuals who had come to depend on them. The self-styled dissidents, the standards bearers, pointed out that he was still requiring trainees to switch analysts at some point in order to spend this required "some time with a TA," and they pressed him to clarify *when* these new trainees would make the move (not to mention pressing him on the seeming contradiction between dismantling a system and maintaining it at the same time). He reiterated: "We didn't specify when, because we decided that would add something non-analytic." What he meant, apparently, was that creating a rule that specified when trainees had to switch from their regular analyst to a TA trampled the integrity of their analyses, imposing from without on the privileged, confidential analytic process. His preference for a "flexible" approach hearkened back to Alexander's faith in communicative rationality and in the trustworthiness of the patient's ego (in this case the trainee's ego) in the face of Blitzsten's suspicion of that ego's claims to self-knowledge. These were the kernels of two very different political imaginaries, two very different pedagogies of professional desire. One posited a dyadic world that could rely on the trustworthiness of analyst and patient to decide on the effectiveness of their work on the patient's behalf; the other posited an authoritative system of laws that could determine true psychoanalysis from without.

Mark Tracy was one of the members of the group opposed to the director's proposal. "*Some* time with a TA?! What exactly does *some time* mean?" he asked, his tone mounting in anger. "Either you do or you don't believe in standards. If you do, then you don't have people in analysis with whoever they want," for however long they want. If you don't, he continued, you take the system down with you. Summoning the rhetorical power of the personal insult, he listed several colleagues "who should not be analyzing candidates. Would you want [name] to teach the next generation? You really wonder about what [name of colleague] did for [name of another colleague]; of course that whole group of people [analyzed by this aforementioned colleague] is like that. If I had my preference none of them would be TAs."

What's their deficiency, I asked him? "They're not doing analysis," he confided. "I'm sure [name] is seeing his patients less than four times a week." One of Mark's compatriots expressed her related impression that "what some graduates practice as analysis has little resemblance to any theoretical school I've ever studied. Supportive psychotherapy and plain old judgments seem to pass muster." In response, Mark and others were trying to reinstall monitoring of session frequency and of the duration of the training analysis, some centralized control over this most important element of training. Such reporting had ceased in the 1980s, as had reporting the actual *content* of the trainees' analyses. Since then it had become apparent to Mark and his colleagues that some trainees were seeing their analysts below the required frequency, while others were terminating their analyses, they thought, prematurely. They sought to have the Institute install oversight in the interest of standards, to render psychoanalysis decidable by authority. Their strategy was to elevate a calculability that turned on powers of form, number, and transparency. As another of Mark's confreres said, "we reject the unsubstantiated assertion that the conditions of a candidate's analysis is [*sic*] the barrier to robust classes every year" and, going further, "arguments like 'studies show that experience doesn't make any difference' are a ruse for justifying the goal of no standards at all." In essence, "they want to make it so that our own local committees decide these things rather than use a national standard, which I think overestimates the ability of colleagues to be impartial about one another's work." Mark's group of standards bearers felt that the director was placing self-interest and false "reality-concerns" above the integrity of the educational processes that should be the Institute's sole focus. Specifically, they charged that the director's move to modify training was embedded in base financial motives, not in psychoanalytic ideals (the unspoken assumption being—always—that psychoanalytic ideals were of an altogether different order from financial motives).

Mark's group galvanized the national organization's BOPS, which promptly sent out a memo, "A Clarification Regarding the American Psychoanalytic Association's Training Analyst System" (American Psychoanalytic Association 2009, n.p.). Signed by BOPS officers, the memo said that "the phrase 'in analysis with a Training Analyst for a substantial period of time,' has been used to evade the Training Analyst system, to create a system with the primary analyst being a non-Training Analyst and [only] a small, unspecified amount of time required with a Training Analyst.... This change in policy is out of compliance with APsaA standards.... The failure of an approved institute to enforce these standards will lead the COI [Committee on Institutes] and the BOPS to follow the procedures outlined in the Bylaws concerning noncompliance." Institutes that failed to comply with the TA system, that failed to insist that trainees see a designated TA, were at risk of being expelled from the APsaA.

On the director's side, self-consciously that of "liberalization," Norm Peters, in sharp contrast to Mark, felt that in any case it was not such a bad thing if the Institute *were* to become, in effect, "a psychotherapy school." In the discussion period after a colleague's research presentation at the Institute on May 13, 2009, Norm spoke up and said he felt like analysts were avoiding "a real problem with not very many analytic cases." He said "there was laughter at me earlier for talking about it, but we have to talk about it." He cited an article that said that the French analysts don't use session frequency as the definer of analytic identity. "This is reality, folks." A colleague dismissed his argument, comparing psychoanalytic training to surgical residency, arguing that "if you don't do enough angioplasties they won't let you in the operating room." Norm soldiered on in the face of the vaunted surgical referent, holding up his own medical pedigree in this room of aging male doctors and middle-aged, mostly female, psychologists and social workers. "That would be like if we were a surgical institute and we just focused on one rare kind of surgery that there were only fifteen people in town who needed and who were willing to pay for. Why wouldn't we broaden it to all kinds of surgery training?" Disentangling therapeutic labor from psychoanalytic purity, Norm envisioned a form of recognition and belonging that analysts could enjoy in a psychotherapy school free from conflict. As another of his compatriots said about the elitist ethos of what they called the standards movement, "for many prospective candidates, that stance suggests fundamental disrespect for their capacity to make critical decisions about their own lives and contributes to our image as arrogant, inflexible, and patriarchal."

The frequency of sessions—it had become clear—was central to the problem of decidability; central, that is, to the "standards" upheld by the official TA system. It was central to the authority embodied by the category of the TA in that system, central to the very possibility of an official psycho-analytic authority. Psychoanalysts identified this measure as the site where the truth of their practice took calculable form (recall Carrie's struggles over the determination of her "half" case in chapter 2).[3] Freud had originated frequent sessions as part of drive theory: analysts needed repeated, regular time with the patient in order to establish an analyzable transference neurosis. Cultivating and then resolving this transference neurosis was intimately bound up with a work routine—a daily schedule—that in turn created the very condition for analysts' social belonging outside the treatment room. This work rhythm provided a theoretically rationalized identificatory framework that served as a social coagulant. It told analysts who they were and what they did. With the waning of drive theory, however, psychoanalysts have found it more difficult to justify frequent sessions on theoretical grounds, though they nevertheless assume their necessity to cure. What is at stake for analysts in the erosion of the work routine of the daily hour, just as in the absence of psychoanalytic work writ large, is not only their relationship to their own labor time but also their very rationale for daily labor. What is at stake in the issue of frequency is the stability of one's world of belonging, with all the benefits and securities that used to come with that: the self-understandings, the rationalizations, the recognition, prestige, financial comforts, and self-esteem of success. What is at stake is the shared image of productive selfhood and of privileged membership in a socially esteemed profession.

Given the theoretical underdetermination of frequent sessions in post-classical psychoanalysis, and given that the official definition of psychoanalysis still turns on the frequency of sessions, theorists have had to posit a supplementary construct to stave off total dilution of the form. This supplementary process, called "conversion," bridges the dichotomy between psychotherapy and psychoanalysis in practice while at the same time inscribing it more deeply in theory. A psychoanalyst nowadays has to "convert" a case (from therapy) in order for it to *be*—to be counted as—analysis, in order, importantly, for the person who conducts it to be conducting psychoanalysis. The notion of conversion is needed today since the majority of patients who come in to analysts' offices today come in for psychotherapy. They don't know they need psychoanalysis, but their analyst does, and he sets about to convert the case to analysis by deepening the patient's involvement in the work. When the psychoanalyst is at last conducting the case at a frequency of four or more weekly sessions, he has converted it to psychoanalysis. Now the analyst can count the case toward training, or if he is a graduate hoping to move up to TA status in the TA system, toward the requirement of immersion. Conversion is thus a purifying practice, preserving the defining line between psychotherapy and psychoanalysis. For analysts like Mark, Norm, and Carrie, the ability to convert cases, as well as the sheer number of cases, carries prestige and status, membership and esteem.

Alongside the TA system and the law of frequency enshrined in standards, another element is central to psychoanalysts' present efforts to preserve their authority to decide what psychoanalysis "is" (or "does"). This is the shared idea that the patients whom they are seeing today are no longer "Oedipal" patients with structured internal conflicts amenable to a strictly interpretive cure; they are patients with deficiencies of basic trust in need of a new developmental experience in a real relationship. To grasp this shift in the norm, one must decipher more clearly some of the transformations of "narcissism"—culturally, semantically, over time and through discourse. If for Freud narcissism was self-love, an intermediate stage of development between infantile autoerotism and mature object love, something to be grown out of as one matured, for Kohut narcissism was an entirely separate developmental line, the line of investment in the self (as discussed in the previous chapter). Indeed, Kohut had enlarged the area of analyzable psychopathology beyond the traditional neurosis to disorders of (his) "narcissism." The goal of treatment on this understanding was for the patient to develop a stronger self, a greater self-esteem—not to resolve Oedipal issues and become capable of mature (read heteronormative) "object love." Kohut had earlier taught that work with these patients would be punctuated by cycles of disruption and repair, exchanges in which the analyst's inaccurate understanding of the patient, who needed a kind of exquisitely attuned recognition, led to a disruption of the patient's "narcissistic equilibrium" (put most simply, her self-esteem). The analyst's "empathic failures," the patient's outbreaks of "narcissistic injury," and then the interpretive repair of the patient's painful states of shame or despair would be at the center of treatment. The analyst was to handle this process interpretively, by pointing out to the patient what had happened in her experience of the misattunement in such a way that she now felt understood, felt restored, gained an increment of insight about her selfobject functioning, and grew thereby. Multiple micro-instances of the healing of such narcissistic injuries would build up the durable self over the course of treatment. Kohut's emphasis had been on what happened *inside* the patient in these inevitable moments of misattunement and restoration, not *between* patient and analyst. He took great pains to emphasize that it was the analyst's *interpretation* of these frustrated selfobject needs and not his direct *gratification* of them in the relationship that restored the patient's cohesion and promoted emotional growth. The analyst didn't have to cultivate the patient's dependency on him; this arose naturally as the patient experienced the healing effect of being accurately recognized and responded to.

A number of Kohut's successors, including David Terman, the director who had proposed liberalizing the TA system, drew on Kohut's theoretical reframing of narcissism to propose new ways of treating these new patients. Since they were traumatized at a preverbal level, interpretation—even interpretation of ruptures in the experience with the analyst—would not cure them; their deficits were preverbal, and analysts could not treat them with yesterday's logocentric techniques. John Gedo, for example, specified that if analysts used a theory limited to pathologies of *symbolic meaning*, they would miss the most crucial psychoanalytic data, those "biological observables" that were beyond words, repetitive behaviors stemming from traumatic early developmental experiences that had been encoded nonverbally (Gedo 2005). Patients *enacted* these observables in session—they precisely did *not* (they *could* not) talk about them. Such behaviors were, functionally, "apraxias," dysfunctional patterns without content. They were "beyond interpretation," so the analyst could only modify them in the therapeutic relationship through a "noninterpretive" praxis (by instructing or advising the patient, for example, in how to live). Through theorizing the treatment of such patients, the erstwhile parameter—the noninterpretive intervention that had once been a temporary stopgap for the emergency moment or the sicker patient—would grow into the very centerpiece of analysis. This would be a talking cure that demoted symbolic talk in favor of the healing action of the real relationship.

The director's new proposal would take *both* the therapeutic centrality of the relationship *and* its economic base into consideration in one maneuver. The proposal rested on his awareness that few potential trainees could afford the fees of the TAs (typically around $200 to $250 per session, $800 to $1,000 per week, or approximately $50,000 per year) and that for a variety of reasons, including financial, many younger therapists in the community were electing to see more junior analysts for private treatment. In attempting to achieve immersion or simply to fill their practices, the more junior members of the faculty were willing to work at a discount (it should also be noted that the "junior faculty" were people in their forties, fifties, and sixties, hardly youth, while most of the TAs were in their seventies and eighties). As he said, "the people we have already accepted in analysis with non-TAs would not have come if we had demanded that they change analysts." His new proposal would thus support the therapeutic primacy of these relationships while at the same time opening up the channels to career progression in the field for analysts like Norm Peters or Carrie Janis.

The standards-bearers initially responded by hardening their position. The BOPS planned a "summit" to call for renewed standards, sending out advance emissaries to Chicago to warn that "the danger is that institutes will decide on their own what they are doing and there won't be a national standard for psychoanalysis."[4] The BOPS planned to meet with representatives of the Institute during the IPA Congress with the intent to censure the organization. But in a surprising turn of events, several members of the BOPS suggested a compromise that would allow them to retain their power, a "two-track system" that would add to the current TA pathway an alternative "developmental" pathway for the non-TA analysts who might be seeing potential trainees; this would keep them in the fold, placing them in a subordinate position on a "developmental" gradient. Both tracks would, they underscored, maintain the requirement of session frequency at "five (or four)" times a week.[5]

Emphasizing the strict necessity for a national system of standards, one of the BOPS emissaries specified that "*A lot* of supervision is necessary so people don't go back to a non-analytic stance, to interpreting reality. If we can find a way of evaluating that, it would help because *that's* what's different about analysis."[6] As Mark's group had argued, "reality" was getting in the way of analysis. The standards bearers felt that training and supervision (*a lot* of supervision) were crucial to maintaining an "analytic" stance, a stance focused on *psychic* reality rather than *external* reality—in this case the APsaA's very existence. (Chicago's representative to the APsaA said he "could think of no better example of human irrationality than APsaA's inability to address its own survival needs.") *A lot* of close supervision was necessary to maintain "what's different about analysis."

The director's proposal, reshaped by the BOPS to preserve the Board's authority to determine proper psychoanalysis, was finally entextualized in a set of new "Standards for Education and Training in Psychoanalysis," published in January 2010 (American Psychoanalytic Association 2010a). John Brandon, Penny Gould, and others remarked that in a backhanded way it offered regulations that were seemingly stricter than the current ones. Nonetheless, they saw the new standards as a victory for liberalization. Why?

The standards revision document contained the following option, under the heading *Waiver of TA Requirement*: "To enable individual institutes to request a waiver from the existing requirements for a Training Analysis with a Training Analyst (TA) for an individual candidate applicant. This change would allow institutes, on a case-by-case basis, to request of BOPS a waiver allowing individual candidates to continue personal analysis with a non-Training Analyst" (American Psychoanalytic Association 2010b, n.p.). The standards allowed an institute to apply for a waiver so that a "non-TA" could be permitted to see a trainee; institutes could potentially increase the number of trainees thereby.[7] The document, through providing for waivers, set in place a virtual standard. By adding the word "most" (it specified that the potentially waiverable non-TA analyst "must meet most of the eligibility requirements of IPA") and by stipulating that potentially waiverable non-TA analysts would be interviewed by the BOPS for their (undefined) "suitability," with decisions to be made on a case-by-case basis, this virtual standard, ostensibly posttheoretical, emphasizing the authority of an administrative procedure, would now function as an ideological placeholder for psychoanalysis proper. The waiver, that is, suspended the law but did not place it in question.[8] What had emerged as new standards was a system of law whose force would reside in the exception. Unwittingly, *the exception* would become a placeholder for psychoanalysis, installing a condition of simultaneous imperilment and promise for all who would strive to capture the status of psychoanalyst. In this impossible situation, a situation in which next to no one met the formal criteria that officially defined their practice, the new standards would govern conduct purely through the performative force of the concept of standards itself.[9]

"BE WHO I NEED YOU TO BE, DON'T JUST INTERPRET IT":
On the Reenchantment of Crisis

This shift to a system of virtual standards was viewed as a victory on both sides. It allowed for exceptions yet maintained the authority of the Board as the body that would grant these. As John Brandon remarked, "there is a crisis in terms of getting candidates; this has finally been brought out in public. One of the things in this new document is that it allows institutes to tailor many of these things in ways that will help them the most." One of the (self-denominated) dissidents announced with satisfaction that in his view "what was a conflict between the Local and the American is finally becoming a polarization we can work on locally. We are divided, and it's healthy that we are finally starting to be able to face it here."

When I described to John his older colleague Peter Shapiro's strong statement that the problem of recruiting patients to come four or five times per week derived from the analyst's unresolved countertransference issues, from the analyst's resistance to analysis, John stopped me. "The official frequency is an issue above all for candidates," he said. In his own case, once he graduated he "started doing it in accord with what patients would agree to." His statement turned out not to be entirely comprehensive, though, as he continued to describe his current practice and his hopes for his professional future. "Of course the official frequency *is* an issue," he added, "if you want to get immersion so you can go for certification, so what I am doing is kind of having two practices, one is my certification cases where I am really doing the official thing, and the other is my regular practice, where I am experimenting with frequency and being realistic about patients' reality issues and really learning how to be an analyst." He was doing a kind of double entry bookkeeping—official four-times-a-week cases on the one side, with the patient lying on the couch, and on the other side the cases in which he was being "realistic" about "reality issues" and "really" learning to be an analyst. By "really learning" he meant learning in an improvisatory way, without a protocol, seeing the patient at whatever frequency the patient desired, with the patient sitting up or lying on the couch. I asked

John if he noticed a difference in his work with his two categories of patients. "I am trying to pin that down," he said. "I do think there is a difference. Probably the certification patients react to my authority more, and the issues then are more often about their early histories of problems with authority and mistrust." The patient doesn't necessarily want to come four times a week but John must insist on it if he (John) is (professionally) to progress—and the patient reacts with understandable upset. The patient reacts to John's insistence, and John then must interpret her reactions in terms of her internal fantasies and fears about authority. He is doing the double entry bookkeeping to deal with the predicament of his double bind; it is a sort of adaptive lying that is necessary in order to constitute himself as an analyst. He is describing the tensions between institutional learning and his own notions of creative practice, auditing the boundary in a paradoxical bid to maintain himself as both a "real" analyst and an officially sanctioned analyst at the same time.

Penny Gould, who, like John, graduated in the early 1990s, concurred, saying that she had decided after graduating to distance herself from organized psychoanalysis because of this pressure: "It was affecting my work, coming out in how I functioned with my patients, and it wasn't worth it." But more than that, she said, "I think of everything I do as analysis. I'm an analyst, so what I do is analysis. I don't need anyone judging that and telling me what is or isn't analysis. I gave up on the formal definition even while I was in training—though of course one had to constantly be selective about what one presented to supervisors. That said, I really *did* want to learn the official way, even if I would never be able to do it, even if only to have something to bounce what I do do off of, so I wasn't totally cynical about it." In the face of the framing of the crisis of psychoanalysis in terms of "liberalization" versus "standards," Penny said she felt strongly that the only standard that mattered to her pertained to the analyst's ability to connect deeply with her patients. This couldn't, and shouldn't, be represented in the number of times one sees that patient each week. Like John, Penny was in favor of the director's proposal, which respected the integrity of the therapeutic relationship above all else.

At the intersection of the parties' competing visions an enchanted figure was emerging: the analyst as ontic presence, the analyst as *real person* as opposed to *transference figure.* Far from striving to reduce the patient's dependency—the agenda Franz Alexander strove to institute during the era of psychoanalysis's success through his experiments with shorter treatments—this analyst's job was, instead, to *become the indispensable, cen-*

tral ingredient in the patient's psychic functioning.[10] The analyst was to become the optimally responsive provider of the real emotional nourishment the patient needed for self-development. As the self psychologist Howard Bacal reported (1988, 130), a patient exhorted him in an explicit statement of this image of therapeutic personhood, "*Be* who I need you to be, don't just interpret it." Bacal went on in his now widely cited paper to specify that "most analysts know in their heart that this is a crucially therapeutic aspect of all analyses. But they seldom talk about it, and it is almost never written about, unless its absence produced significant dissonance between patient and analyst, in which case providing it is regarded as a 'parameter' and this is not properly psychoanalytic." Penny agreed with Bacal's exposing of this previously seldom-discussed truth of analysis. If original self psychology had focused on the self of the patient, relational self psychology brought back the object, the other. She noted the profession's tilt toward conceptualizing the old object—the imago of the parent of childhood as it showed up in the transference—as dangerous and pathogenic, while understanding the new object, the analyst in the present, as good, positive, loving, giving—and perhaps above all, separate, a separate "center of initiative." Accordingly, Penny called into question Kohut's vision of the role of frustration in fostering the structuring of the self. She problematized traditional analytic restraint, instead placing the curative force directly in the relationship with the analyst. Penny drew on a variety of extraanalytic sciences—cognitive neuroscience, child development, and the biology of attachment—to legitimate her skilled métier of affect attunement. She deployed this tool with an eye to helping the patient internalize her as good, new object.

I asked Penny to explain how she distinguished her notion of analysis as "about the relationship" from Mark's notion of cure by way of the analyst's interpretation of conflict.

> I think in the past, and still for some people, the focus was pretty exclusively on working through the old transferences, reengaging old objects. The analyst was really mostly a cipher, a screen for the patient's distortions and projections. The real difference is that we are building new, healthy object relationships in the present. And psychological skills. That's really my focus at the end of the day. I am not hanging back in the background, silently waiting for the patient's fantasies and then pointing out how she's distorting her image of me, I am actively sussing out her emotional needs, actively meeting them. Our relationship is front and center.

Focusing on objective need and its real satisfaction rather than subjective wish and its fantasied fulfillment, describing the patient's great need for her, she foregrounded the intense affects that coursed between her and her patients.[11] "We're all developmentalists now," she emphasized, noting the kinds of problems patients bring to analysts nowadays. "The trauma is earlier and deeper, which means longer and deeper treatments that directly focus on early attachment issues." The locus of pathology has shifted from infantile drives in conflict to developmental failure—failure at the hands of a failing other. The other comes into view, then, as the way of healing this. In this "developmental" theorization, the other is more deeply implicated in the self, both from the standpoint of having caused the original problems through faulty responsiveness and from the standpoint of healing them now, through accurate responsiveness. The therapeutic process can peel back later, pathological development to the zero point of original childhood injury, the juncture from which what Penny called "wholesome" new development could begin afresh in the relationship with the analyst.

In Kohut's own writing, the principal work of treatment was the analysis of the transference; the analyst did this through interpretation—albeit through the interpretation of the "selfobject" transference rather than the erstwhile Oedipal transference of ego psychology. The analyst's empathic immersion in the patient's subjective experience defined the domain of his work. He was not there as an objective observer or as an other but as a facilitator of the patient's self, an attuned listener to the patient's first-person plaint. Other than grasping and then explaining the patient's subjective experience, the analyst made no attempt to manage the clinical situation; he adduced no ancillary information from other sciences and no ancillary information about "reality" from what Kohut derided as "exteroceptive" perception or "sociological" observation. In discussing Kohut's legacy, analysts in Chicago have focused on the distinction he drew between interpretation and gratification. For Kohut's descendants, who have been working out the implications of his theories in the domain of the "object" as opposed purely to the domain of the self, perhaps the centrally contested question has been whether the analyst is exclusively to interpret empathic failures or whether she is to accent the healing qualities in the relationship itself in order to, in effect, be the new and better object for the patient. The stark difference with the classical ego psychological view is that the analyst treats the patient's demands for direct gratification not as resistances to insight but rather as legitimate attempts to receive needed supplies from the analyst. Terman, the Institute director who had proposed the opening up of training, himself one of Kohut's more prolific students, wrote that "it is the repetition of the presence [of help] that builds new structure. The repetition of the absence re-evokes the old patterns" (Terman 1988, 121). In this view of the therapeutic relationship, the psychoanalyst nurses the patient toward health with his presence. In contrast to this nutritive view, some of those opposed to such efforts to—as they saw it—"reparent" the patient viewed this as a contemporary revisiting of Alexander's concept of the corrective emotional experience; in their view this was role-playing, manipulation, and false promise. (Carrie's "New York analyst" had accused her of precisely this unanalytic "magic," of offering to be more for the patient than was healthy.)

The shift in the image of therapeutic personhood that renders the analyst an actual and indispensable provider of needed emotional supplies stems from a reading of Kohut by many contemporary self psychologists as, in essence, a theory of relationships. Some read it as a theory of "intersubjectivity," emphasizing the "field" between the two participants in treatment; others as a theory of object relations, in which the differentiation between the patient and his selfobject is eclipsed in favor of the relationship between the self and that fully external *other* who supplies the selfobject *function*. Both of these readings of Kohut have been hotly debated. Arnold Goldberg, for instance, responding to a question about whether Kohut's theory could be thought of as similar to that of the object relations theorist D. W. Winnicott, said: "Kohut's theory is not a theory of object relationship. . . . Kohut bent over backwards not to be involved with [relationships]. He was devoted to introspection and all of the data being from the intrapsychic point of view; what went on between people meant nothing except as a self experience. That's a big difference. . . . I don't think he is an heir in any way to Winnicott, and I personally think it's a tremendous waste of a lot of good effort to translate one theory into another."[12] In contrast to this reading of Kohut, in their book *Theories of Object Relations: Bridges to Self Psychology*, Howard Bacal and Kenneth Newman argued that it was the self *and* its object, not the self's purely internal experience of what went on between people, that should occupy the center of clinical attention. Their concern was that by occupying a purely "intrapsychic" stance, Kohut had lost sight of the *external object*, the *actual other* who provides the psychological assistance. They argued that the other's experience, in the case of analysis the analyst's countertransference, offered an important clue to the pathology of the patient—especially the seemingly unreachable, nonrelated, actively avoidant patient. This shift in focus accents the patient's need to be aware of the presence of others, aware of her impact on others. Moreover, now the *analyst's* subjective experience was an important element of the patient's treatment, underscoring the importance of the analyst's work on his or her own experience, his or her countertransference, as, literally, part of the treatment.

Newman himself took this even further, arguing that the analyst could *only* diagnose a patient's pathology by viscerally experiencing its force in himself. For instance, the analyst had to risk the real experience of denigration and rejection at the hands of the patient; the analyst had to be ready to accept the patient's accusations that he (the analyst) could do no right.[13] The analyst could then use these countertransference experiences of failure to diagnose the patient's pathologically "hypercathected self-sufficiency," a form of archaic omnipotence, a pathological "I don't need you" stance the patient held toward the world that prohibited her from embracing life—and analysis—fully. The analyst had to live through and then work through his intense countertransference states of feeling discarded, criticized, abused—and, most painfully of all, *not needed*—in order to inhabit the core of the patient's defensive system. It was only when the analyst experienced his own *uselessness* in this way that he could find in himself the patient's original pathogenic parent. Through finding the pathogenic parent in himself, he could identify the patient's original difficulties in receiving the help she needed to grow emotionally; then, through providing this positive help (as per David Terman), he could rectify the patient's condition. Inducing a deep clinical regression to the patient's earliest childhood was necessary in order for the analyst to develop the relevant countertransference and work through the impasse arising from his rejection by the "nonrelating" patient. By helping patients work through their defensive self-sufficiency, the analyst could help them come to grips with their dependency and embrace it as the privileged medium for renewed growth. Like other post-Kohutians, then, Newman describes a real relationship in which both analyst and patient are deeply connected to one another, though he accents the "negative transference" rather than the "positive" transference to a figure of help. Properly practiced, this approach could maintain patients in treatment for decades by wresting from them their omnipotent self-sufficiency, disallowing their *actual* rejection of the analyst before they had worked through their fears of true dependency on him. This circular theory could, as it happens, neatly make sense of patients' criticisms of analysis, of their threats to leave treatment. The process would of course necessitate longer analyses, often up to fifteen or twenty years long, so that the analyst could develop the relevant countertransference and work through the crises arising from the patient's rejection of him.

In tracing this shift toward a post-Kohutian risk-based, relational self psychology, it should be clear that I am pointing to a concomitant movement in the professional image of psychoanalytic personhood toward a far greater degree of personal and emotional involvement in work. The analyst's own "narcissism" is at risk—not only his competence, but his very survival is under threat. As Newman described in his 1999 article "The Usable Analyst: The Role of the Affective Engagement of the Analyst in Reaching Usability," "I realized that feeling insignificant can activate a sense of injury in me." To refrain from being overly interpretive in his work with a patient, he had, he wrote of his heroic efforts to cope with that painful feeling of injury, to "manage my countertransference reactions" (Newman 1999, 180). Carrie, for her part, too, described how she felt she was most susceptible to painful "narcissistic injury" when her patient withheld his needs for her, inducing in her the feeling that her efforts to help were "as useless and incompetent as the efforts of his parents, his original selfobjects." Her need for the patient and his need for her were deeply imbricated. The wider failure of psychoanalysis could now be experienced immediately in daily clinical work. Not only was Newman helping deeply isolated individuals, he was finding opportunity in failure. In the era of the success of psychoanalysis, top psychoanalysts like Gitelson had not needed the patient, either economically or (they believed) psychically. Patients were plentiful. As discussed in chapter 4, when the patient had a "negative transference" in Gitelson's office it was essentially a paranoid transference, a transference of fear and trembling at the analyst's great power and authority (even more than this, at the analyst's great power to reject those he did not want as "unanalyzable"). In contrast, the "negative transference" here is a dismissive, rejecting transference to failure—failure as embodied in the historical person of the analyst.

ON HISTORICAL PROBLEMATIZATION

One can see the professional image of psychoanalytic personhood shifting from dispenser of cure for a pathological patient (envisioned in a medical frame of reference) to provider of care for a psychologically deficient patient (envisioned in a developmental frame of reference). Here, as in other marginalized domains of work, affect and affective labor are currencies through which workers can acquire some sense of social utility, some sense of belonging, some means to stave off the relentless experience of margin-alization. On a flexible labor market the analyst's own therapeutic person-hood is understood as the ultimate healing property and a valued, labored, and indeed capitalized form of production. These relational laborers find, in this transformed image of their own subjectivity, a way to recuperate feelings of belonging and recognition. They are able to do this by means of an almost unlimited "optimally responsive" availability, overperforming their own usefulness. Theorizing their own use-value and demonstrating it in their case-talk, they are able to stage a scene of social usefulness and pub-lic value in the face of collective symbolic destruction.[14] The realness and the importance of the real analytic relationship thus conceived offers them a means of trafficking in good feeling, of staving off an engagement with real failure in exchange for the truncated (but workable, and theoretically rationalized) "failure of empathic responsiveness." Individuals can mediate their survival by skillfully manipulating what are understood to be psycho-logical powers of self-monitoring, expressive containment, repression of resentment, and management of role conflict. Meanwhile, collectively this relational work ethic serves to remoralize professional life in the face of the impossible demands for accountability pressing in on psychoanalysis from neoliberal medicine. Disembedding relational labor from its economic context, presenting it not only as personal but as moral, as animated by care and compassion, psychoanalysts disavow systemic failure. This allows their relational labor to appear as an act of generosity—one in which ne-gation of the self is the very condition of legitimacy. The analyst sees in the patient's attachment a spectral reflection of his own economy of desire. Performatively identifying "narcissistic" resistances *in oneself,* normalizing the use of *one's own* desire as the consummate diagnostic for the patient's pathology, lends itself handily to a set of neoliberal arrangements of power that are simultaneously liberating and regulating. This power is both laissez faire and normalizing, for it operates by playing up and then monitoring the verisimilitude of the real relationship, capillarizing and pluralizing a bond that looks, simply, natural.

Penny's discourse on the intimacy between patient and analyst sel-dom lingered on the kinds of workforce exclusions that moved her into these charged, *noninterpretive* activities of optimal responsiveness and care (Holinger 1999). Her erasure of the negative is crucial to the building of this neoliberal psychoanalysis, since this is how money and markets are in-tegrated into the daily work of care; the crisis of work is thus translated into what appears as opportunity. Penny sublimates her marginalization into an ethic of fulfilling real relationships and nonalienated labors. Grounded in a logic of despair, she is doubly dispossessed, aware of a crisis she feels is autonomous in respect to her own activity, victimized at the hands of the wider world, yet enabled by the succoring pleasures of cosuffering in rewarding real relationships that give her what Berlant calls an "approximation of belonging to a world that doesn't ... exist reliably anymore" (2008, 277).

I do not make the claim that the clinicians whose travails I have described are heroically "resisting" managed care in persisting in practicing (what they can think of as) psychoanalysis, nor that they are passive dupes of managed care, nor yet that they are practicing in bad faith in any simple sense. Rather, I am saying that they are contending with competing imperatives while trying at the same time to maintain themselves as both moral persons and successful professionals. They are doing all this in a broader system of medical neoliberalism into which they are daily interpellated, one in which their special work has no formal place.

In so maintaining themselves, they play, unwittingly, into a broader sociocultural process of what Michael Hardt calls "making up life from below" that scholars of biopolitics have described for our period of late modernity, of drawing "life itself" more deeply into the rationality of the market. In participating in this reorganization of human sociality in terms of a marketplace of vital affects—and in this case their affective labor is directed toward building up the attachment bond that makes up "life itself"—they give up the very dialectical traction that gives the Freudian analytic method its genius and its specificity. They give up *analysis* precisely in their efforts to maintain themselves *as psychoanalysts*, substituting an imaginary of objective need and its real satisfaction for an imaginary of wishful fantasy and its interpretative resolution, playing up the relationship and down the transference, maintaining themselves as analysts who do not *analyze* but instead *provide* vital emotional supplies. These biopolitical *dispositifs* are anchored in complex, consensual relations—coordinated, stratified, instituted relations—that cannot be reduced to the projection of a single sovereign power on passive individuals; instead, a multiplicity of powers act and react on each other according to relations of dependency, demand, desire, and obedience.[15]

So how do today's analysts maintain themselves as analysts when they do not—cannot—practice what they preach? What I found is that they do this, in Chicago, by bringing together what I discovered through my historical research to be a "Blitzstenite" emphasis on countertransference with an

The "real relationship" becomes the therapCⁱᵀ commodity. It becomes the "work."

Alexandrian emphasis on flexibility, with the figure of the real relationship as their condensation point, the place where these two previously irreconcilable elements converge. In a neat trick, this marriage allows today's analysts like Carrie to maintain themselves *as analysts* while they practice little of what they themselves think of as analysis. Further, it allows them rhetorically to ground what they are doing in classical terms of fathers and ancestral debates.[16] It is a genealogical reading of the divide between Blitzsten and Alexander, and then their students down through the generations, that allows one to recognize that the contemporary psychoanalyst has read and internalized both, and holds them in a constant and productive—if, now, biopolitically symptomatic—tension well past these ancestors' deaths. In effect, the contemporary analyst (Carrie, for instance, with her puzzling "half" patient) proclaims Blitzsten and acts Alexander. This allows her to make sense of the fact that "analysis" for her—the paradigm being her own training analysis—is something that takes place at a frequency of four weekly meetings, even as she can't manage to practice this herself with her own patients and must go through machinations, theoretically rationalized, to count as analysis what she actually does. In order to maintain this internal contradiction, the field has come to weave together the essential, yet previously apparently irreconcilable, aspects of the two imaginaries.

This marriage of previously irreconcilable historical elements is, I have argued, the profession's reflex to conserve work, one that deepens contradictions that are inherent in psychoanalysis as ontology. I have zeroed in on several baroque new imbrications of intimacy and commerce in the transformed proprietary/disciplinary space of knowledge production that is current psychoanalysis. Chief among these are those practices of "real relationship" that render the analyst's distress as a complementary and natural element of the patient's pathology. These practices thereby back a demand that the analyst diagnose the pathogenic parent *within himself or herself* in order to cure the patient. This demand, based on a particular reading of Kohut and a transmuting of self psychology into a kind of object relations theory, manifests itself semiotically in a tropism toward the analyst's interpretation of the patient's rejections of the analyst *and of analysis itself* as symptomatic of disordered attachment. I claim that these moves help psychoanalysts rationalize deep clinical regressions and longer and longer analyses; they magically translate the crisis of work and social belonging into what appears as opportunity. As such, they sublimate new forms of exclusion into an ethic of mutual obligation in deep, affect-laden, fulfilling relationships and nonalienated labors. It is through this bundling of enrollment and scientific problematization that I see psychoanalysis unwittingly contributing to the biopoliticization of contemporary U.S. society. I have shown how the very enrollment and retention of patients becomes a central clinical problematic; the real relationship is thus a way of making work, work that is psychoanalytic, even when there is no work. This is a moral economy that ostensibly exists in contrast to a market logic while in reality being constitutive of it. It is a market in flexible labor.

DESIRING PARITY: *Narcissism and the Parodies of Desire*

This kind of affective labor, Carrie's labor of creating succoring relationships, produces a particular form of biopolitical community in which economic production merges with social relations configured around the analyst's desire for work, and for work that is psychoanalytic, with the analyst's capitalized countertransference as currency. Within this network, the dichotomy of economy and society has broken down, leaving real relationships both dominated by and internal to capital. The symbolic value of "being needed" provides the switch point, for it is out of the analyst's experience of being *not needed*, not wanted, that she can now define the patient's pathology. As a form of sociality directly exploitable by capital and a form of governmentality geared to controlling a market by bundling enrollment and problematization, the real relationship creates the social bond itself.[17] In a redefinition of the production-consumption relationship, the real relationship literally *produces* subjectivity, society, and life; as a phenomenology of labor it serves as a pointed attempt to organize one's own work *and* one's own complex and highly ambiguous relations with larger corporate entities. Insurance did not originally underwrite this shift, but it has taken it on board and adapted it, driving these analysts' impulse to heights of self-valorization through, as I've shown, (highly theorized) self-devaluation. Corporate control over this form of relational work presupposes precisely the "free," creative, flexible, entrepreneurial activity of such workers, workers in direct competition with one another over what Mark so incisively called "being nice." As he said, meaning it as a criticism, "they want to be loved." Indeed, they want to be important. As the economic relationship becomes more deeply imbricated in the actual work, more thematized and psychologized, as consumption of therapy increasingly becomes grist for therapy, as patients in analysis are increasingly exclusively therapists and analysts, we can see an extension of governmentality over the psychologically—and economically—productive subject. Insurance adds yet another layer of contract to the traditional face-to-face contract of patient and doctor, a contract of citizen-and-corporation for the shared, actuarial underwriting of behavioral health. While still operating through the old *professional* contract, this newer contract casts on the old one a certain grave suspicion, transfiguring the relationship by installing in it an additional constraint, cutting the individual loose while binding him ever more tightly, as a member of a risk pool, to a world of social relations shaped by the market.

The state has progressively extended this form of "insurantial" social contract (to use Francois Ewald's term). Mental health parity law states that group health plans must treat psychiatric problems as equivalent to physical illnesses; the insurance industry states that mental health treatment must then be "medically necessary." The original 1996 Mental Health Parity Act required parity between mental and physical health insurance in annual and lifetime benefit limits. The 2008 Wellstone-Domenici Health Parity and Addiction Equity Act required parity in deductibles, co-pays, numbers of visits, lifetime caps, and annual caps and required that insurers place no "nonquantitative" limits on mental health treatment; any health insurance plan that provided mental health coverage could not have requirements that were more restrictive than the requirements applied to medical benefits. The 2008 Act applied only to group plans for employers with more than fifty employees.[18] The 2010 Patient Protection and Affordable Care Act ("Obamacare") goes beyond both of these, requiring that all plans cover mental health and substance abuse treatments and that these benefits must be on par with medical-surgical benefits.

These extensions of the insurantial contract have stimulated psychoanalysts to make multiple attempts to develop secure standards of judgment for their work, both within their collegium and beyond, by objectifying the relational ephemera at the center of what they do. Carrie described how intrusive the new medical necessity reviews were, where the reviewer, someone "clearly not trained," was making suggestions like "try group therapy." Her most recent review went "well," meaning her patient was granted twelve sessions because she translated what she was doing into DSM symptomatology, limited and concrete goals, and behavioral interventions. Playing with distinctions without a difference, products of a system that analyzes medical procedures by the cost of providing them and then conceives a quantifiable difference between 90806, 90807, and 90845—each a forty-five-minute conversation between two people in a room—she added:

"We still need to find causal not just thematic connections. What is it in the relationship that works?"

> We need more empirical research on how it works in what we do. We need to be able to say to people "x-y-z" [*sic*]. They need to be able to compare it to other treatments and we need to use best-evidence to tell them what we offer compared to other treatments. If we have the numbers, which we are starting to have, then we can make the argument. We need to standardize our concepts. If that problem can't be solved scientifically, we will have another century in which psychoanalysis can be accepted or rejected purely on the basis of people's taste.

Carrie is in almost all other aspects of her practice and theory opposed to the generalizing, positivizing impulse of the standards bearers. But even she is trying gamely to fit her real relationships into neoliberal strictures. Meanwhile her reading of the current situation is telling: she blames unnamed insurers for accepting or rejecting psychoanalysis arbitrarily, according to their taste, even as she tries to protect the realm in which the analyst's taste reigns supreme.

Another faculty member at the Chicago Institute who brought *taste* into her discussion spoke to the way changes to the DSM chipped away at psychoanalysis's territory in her 2010 blog entry "Requiem for a Diagnosis," writing that "much of the work of psychoanalysis and psychoanalytic psychotherapy is done in the land of personality disorders, so it is unsettling when 'our' terrain is profoundly altered" (Gourguechon 2010).[19] She delimited "our terrain" not by any generalizing standard but by comparing it to the distinction between ethnic food and fine dining: one of those "you know it when you see it" things. She was blogging about proposed changes in the forthcoming edition of the DSM (DSM V): the previous edition had eliminated neurosis, and now DSM V proposed to remove narcissism, "a diagnostic category that has been part of my thinking as a psychiatrist and then a psychoanalyst for, I don't know, almost 3 decades." Among the personality disorders, narcissism, added Jerry Kavka, a historian of psychoanalysis and a senior colleague of hers from the Institute, "has a special place in the history of Chicago." Narcissism, he said proudly, "is our own developmental line." Its removal from the DSM would be especially resonant because of the history of self psychology in Chicago (which, he added deferentially, "really was anticipated by Blitzsten"). Self psychology is centered on the treatment of problems in the area of narcissism, narcissism understood, as I've shown, in a very particular way. But, Kavka continued, it's not just about patients. Narcissism—both healthy and disordered—is "how we think about motivation in general." With the removal of narcissism from the DSM, the truths through which analysts could recognize themselves as objects of reflexive knowledge and as subjects capable of acting on others would lose their entire grounding in wider medicine.

One prominent commentator has suggested that the profession's shift from a focus on neurosis to a focus on narcissism in the 1980s was essentially a matter of an ideological fit between narcissism and the demands of a consumer society. (Recall that some ego psychologists argued that Kohut's technique of interpreting the patient's "narcissistic" needs exacerbated these rather than curbing them in accordance with the renunciative demands of "maturity.") But such an interpretation—essentially a culture and personality reading—is inadequate to the task of explaining the Chicago professional community's original acceptance of Kohut's ideas and their subsequent merging of those ideas with, and further development through, object relational ideas (Cushman 1995). Rather, analysts' broad shift to relational theories in Chicago, if not elsewhere, by making a kind of specialized competency an inalienable, personal quality, registers an institutional reflex to produce and conserve psychoanalytic authority. Possessing these ostensibly inalienable "personal" craft and connoisseurship values, the collegium stands to legitimate itself on its own terms in the face of neoliberal medicine's demands for standardization. The real relationship works at once with and against the economizing episteme of rationed care, resisting and fomenting the capitalization of therapy. It is simultaneously gift and commodity, experiential contradiction and fertile new problematization for work, a reflection of both large-scale processes of global economic and political change and local, place-based practices of self-authorization. The psychoanalysts in Chicago do not sit around proclaiming the horrors of dealing with Blue Cross Blue Shield to get reimbursed for their work. Rather, they turn their situation into a debate between ancestors and a complicated theoretical battle about the status of the therapeutic relationship. They internalize this debate in contradictory ways, such that one position in the debate comes out in their talk and the other in their action. Neatly, this maneuver of dividing talk and action, theory and practice, prevents them from having to be the object of (corporate medicine's) analysis, allowing them to maintain themselves *as analysts* even as they practice almost no analysis as they themselves define it.

I have indicated that the autonomy of psychoanalytic work is felt to be under threat from several sides, from within the patient-analyst relationship and from without, as this relationship is increasingly interpolated into broader regimes of accountability. The convergence of professional interest in the vicissitudes of countertransference and in the real relationship reflects such professional anxiety *in theory*. The recent professional literature offers accounts of clinical situations where patients threaten to leave therapy, fail to pay their bills, belittle the analyst, or otherwise stimulate the analyst's anxiety. In such reports, patients evoke third-person powers to make claims on the analyst's own emotional equilibrium, through interactional gambits that gesture at the crumbling frame of treatment, rendering that frame ever more perishable. I have described some of the ways analysts have come to inscribe an affectively charged relationship of mutual dependency between patient and analyst in the present situation, a situation characterized above all by the intensification of a historical condition of crisis around the decidability of psychoanalysis. These include a rationality of "attachment" that foregrounds childhood developmental lack as opposed to endogenous intrapsychic conflict; an epidemiology of disorders "deeper" than conventional neurosis; and a bundle of interpersonal micro-practices geared to filling in a patient's psychological deficit rather than interpreting her already-existing psychic conflicts. They also centrally include a form of "thinking by risk"—an intensification of risk problematization, anticipation, and planning geared to managing the hazards, as they are literally *felt by the analyst* in the countertransference, that deficient psychological structure will encounter in life. As a means of governing risk up close, the real relationship is an indigenous insurance policy that makes the analyst's vulnerability seem manageable, calculable; it is a way of spreading risk and doing so on the analyst's own theoretical terms. If neoliberal subjectivation blends distinctions between love, work, politics, and life itself, it is through such intimate, risky relationships that psychoanalysts, dreaming of security, come to imagine their world as one of uncommodified "real" care, their affective labor as a form of sociality that is prudentially able to calculate quasi-familial, "real" dependencies. I have suggested, then, that this charged relationship emerges into view in a compensatory embrace of the very neoliberal logics of accountability that lead the desiring professional

Clinician C-T becomes the handmaiden of the real self, centerpiece of the phsyical relationship between analyst and patient, which is in turn is embedded in the capitalization of therapy.

to remove the sexual, the drive, the unconscious, and the paternal law of desire from psychoanalysis, mutating it in a series of self-referential, self-authorizing labors of coordination with audit culture's ideology of the preferred provider. This relational ontology remoralizes collective professional organizational life in the face of unmeetable demands for accountability, embodying a steadily solidifying biopolitical fantasy that analysts can control human behavior, human experience, and *life itself*—including their own lives.

In reading the simultaneous allure and repulsion that neoliberal regulation holds for these psychoanalysts—containing both a promise of survival in a hostile world and a threat of subjective dissolution and betrayal of an ideal—I close then as I opened, with the narrative use of an envied, admired colleague, "Richard," whom I dub *the exception* for his special usefulness to the group as a vehicle for a socially productive and psychoanalytically specific *ressentiment*. Richard is the figure of plenty, the colleague with the full practice, about whom jealous, derisive, and admiring talk about "how he does it" is a constant. Richard incarnates an imaginary of practices that one wants to enjoy but to which one will never have empirical access. In realizing their own contrary desires through discursive practices of fiction, falsification, and outright attack on this colleague, analysts relate to his success phantasmatically, yet in a way that has real consequences for community life. In the absence of clear, externally imposed rules, an informal regulation has arisen around the person of the analyst. In their scandalous talk about Richard's capacity to produce value, it is as if he has special access to some unfathomable technology of success. It is his relational ability that is the real object of their envy, admiration, and derision (after all, he can't be doing "real psychoanalysis"); it is this relational techne that has become increasingly imaginable under neoliberal medicine, appearing in stories that describe a profoundly contradictory historical situation where potential and scarcity collide. Its figuration binds alterations in the global economy to the most local and specific of interpersonal events, in the most prosaic of terms, via intensely felt personal anxieties about daily work. These stories in the collegium attempt to rationalize, socialize, and stabilize the object of desire—psychoanalysis itself—as postideological, natural. As such they manifest a form of magical thinking that registers local anxieties about what the renowned anthropologist Edward Sapir— Lionel Blitzsten's friend from his Chicago days—dubbed "the business of getting a living." I have argued, following up on a conversation I imagine between Blitzsten and Sapir, that the business of getting a living and the work itself—the supposedly inviolate contents of expert knowledge—are inextricably intertwined, complicated by the anxieties and desires of the individual analyst. These anxieties and desires link the local world to translocal forces beyond individual control.

Situating himself within this collision of forces with a characteristically psychoanalytic form of self-reflection, Paul, the analyst whose story of thwarted desire I used to open the book, provocatively concluded our interview with a hopeful statement. I, too, shall end with it. "It is reasonable," he said, "to expect that the fact that we are discussing the vicissitudes of narcissism will be most helpful in working through the narcissistic issues involved in the process of discussion."

NOTES

INTRODUCTION

1 To protect the privacy of research subjects, I have changed the names of most of the people whose stories are described in this book. In some cases I have combined the stories of two or more people and changed certain identifying features to more thoroughly disguise individuals. While these efforts to disguise the identity of informants may somewhat distort the data, I have been concerned above all to anonymize research subjects sufficiently that those familiar with the locale not be able to identify the individuals. This has required some careful thinking and decision making about which ethnographic materials would best serve in the construction of a context or background against which other materials would be drawn out contrastively as analytically central. In some instances I have included a subject's real name and other identifying information; I have adopted this approach in particular for historical information in which living persons are not named or implicated directly.

2 For Freud, while transference itself appeared early on in a patient's analysis, the transference *neurosis* crystallized over the course of the treatment, enveloping the doctor in an organized web of significations representing the patient's intrapsychic conflicts of childhood. The transference neurosis was a cohesive "new edition" of the patient's childhood neurosis. As Freud described this development, "the transference thus creates an intermediate region between illness and real life through which the transition from the one to the other is made. The new condition has taken over all the features of the illness; but it represents an artificial illness which is at every point accessible to our intervention" (1914, 154). According to Freud's theory of psychoanalytic cure, "we regularly succeed in giving all the symptoms of the illness a new transference meaning and in replacing the ordinary neurosis by a 'transference neurosis' of which he [the patient] can be cured by the therapeutic work" (1914, 154).

3 Most psychoanalysts elsewhere, particularly Kleinian and Lacanian psychoanalysts in Europe and Latin America, did not draw such a distinction, preferring to see *all* aspects of the analysand's relation to the analyst as transference and, as such, as subject to analysis. There are American exceptions as well; see Brenner 1979.

4 Freud (1912, 105) referred to the "unobjectionable positive transference," the cooperative rapport of the trusting patient who believes in the doctor's helpfulness, as the very "vehicle of success in psychoanalysis." Unlike the *objectionable* erotic and aggressive transferences that were to be the focus of interpretive work, the unobjectionable positive transference was not itself to be analyzed. This brief statement was Freud's only reference to what came to be known among American analysts, variously, as the real relationship between doctor and patient, the working alliance (Zetzel 1956), the therapeutic alliance (Greenson 1967), the "nontransference relationship" (Greenson and Wexler 1969), or the "nontechnical personal relationship" (Lipton 1977). As Lipton (1977, 266) wrote in an exemplary declaration, "regardless of whether the phenomenon is called an alliance or a personal relationship, it exists."

5 For the history of the lawsuit, see Schneider and Desmond 1994; Wallerstein 2002c. The American Psychoanalytic Association, the oldest national psychoanalytic organization in the United States, was founded in 1911. Presently known by the acronym APsaA, the organization was previously referred to by American psychoanalysts as "The American" (in contradistinction to "The International," the International Psychoanalytical Association, presently known as the IPA).

6 Falk's statement is from his posting of June 27, 2010, to the Members List, a listserv for APsaA members to discuss issues of importance in American psychoanalysis; it is quoted with the author's written permission.

7 See Heinz et al. 2005 for an exemplary discussion of the transformation of the legal profession in the United States.

8 While undecidability generally refers to the aporetic nature of textual systems, in his later work Derrida made more explicit his consideration of the political and ethical implications of decision. For a historical and political analysis, see Bates 2005.

9 In pointing to the aura of the relationship I am of course invoking Walter Benjamin, and particularly his notion of the cultic object. Benjamin distinguished the cult value of a work of art, its place in the cult as a unique object often hidden from view, from its exhibition value, its worth as an object accessible to all. Technological reproduction, he argued, makes the cult value of an object recede in contrast to its public or exhibition value.

10 Foucault 1994, 818, from translation by Lemke 2005, 10 (Lemke quotes Foucault 1994, 818).

11 It is important to note that in this book I am using the term "relational" in the wider, commonsense use of the term, as it is used by the psychoanalysts in Chicago with whom I worked, rather than in the narrower sense of the largely

New York–based relational group of theorists associated with the New York University Postdoctoral Program in Psychotherapy and Psychoanalysis (authors like Lewis Aron, Jessica Benjamin, Irwin Hoffman, Steven Mitchell, Donnel Stern).

12 Over the course of Foucault's writing, psychoanalysis lost the heroic status it had in *Madness and Civilization* (with its strong critique of asylum psychiatry's repressive technologies) and in *The Order of Things* (where it showed up as one of the great modern counter-sciences), exemplifying, by the time of his final writings on "psychiatric power," the ultimate discipline that disciplines. This was a psychoanalysis with neither internal contradiction nor institutional specificity, unthinkable apart from a sovereign subjectivity that is fundamentally incompatible with the Freudian unconscious. It has been this psychoanalysis that Rose (1998, 1999b), Dean (1999), Lemke (2002), Hacking (1999), Young (1995), and others have taken up in their accounts of the "psy" disciplines in the post-Fordist welfare state, that setting for the "ideological crisis of liberalism" from which neoliberalism emerged. Much like Foucault, they, too, neglect the internal dynamics of "psy" institutions, so that, in spite of their claims about the centrality of the "psy complex" (Rose 1998) to modern governance, they too fall short in their efforts to produce a historically concrete analytics of the rationalities and practices that, as Hacking puts it, "make up" the modern self of psychoanalysis.

13 For a reading of the centrality of rationalization in the anthropology of postmodernity, see Ong 1991.

14 Derrida thematizes psychoanalysis's problematic undecidability throughout his work; see, especially, Derrida 1987, 1995, 1998. For a useful overview of the sweep of Derrida's engagement with psychoanalysis, see Sharpe 2004.

15 Derrida's sustained reading of the Freudian text in terms of its own resistances is to be found in Derrida 1998.

16 Freud alone distinguished five—and this despite his disavowal of a unitary concept for his science. He listed resistances proceeding from ego, id, and superego (from the ego come repression, transference, and the secondary gain of the symptom; from the id comes the repetition compulsion; from the superego comes the need to be punished and the intransigence of masochistic guilt).

17 For at least five decades the history of psychoanalysis in Chicago essentially *was* the history of the Chicago Institute for Psychoanalysis, and George Pollock (1977a), Jerome Kavka (1984), and Roy R. Grinker Sr. and Roy R. Grinker Jr. (1995) have each written commemorative essays on the history of this institution. Theirs are insider accounts, less inaccurate than they are narrow: none was interested in the anchoring of the psychoanalytic institution in wider fields of social action and cultural meaning; they simply documented "who was in charge when" (Jerome Kavka, archivist for the Chicago Institute for Psychoanalysis, personal communication, June 2007). In contrast, Douglas Kirsner (2000), a professional historian, examined the Chicago Institute comparatively, looking at how four institutes (Chicago, New York, Los Angeles, and Boston) have handled "the TA problem," the concentration of power among an elite group of

training analysts. Scholars have also written psychobiographies of various figures involved in psychoanalysis in Chicago: Erika Schmidt (2004, 2010) has written on Theresa Benedek and Franz Alexander; Susan Quinn (1987) and Jack L. Rubins (1978) on Karen Horney; Jerome Kavka (1991) on Lionel Blitzsten; and Charles Strozier (2001) on Heinz Kohut.

18 All of the names used in the book are pseudonyms except where otherwise noted; as a rule, I discuss historical figures and holders of appointed office without disguise. The limits of these sources and the analytically driven, selective use of interview materials mean that this research cannot claim to be a comprehensive, or a replicable, overview of psychoanalysis in Chicago.

CHAPTER 1. AN IMAGINARY OF THREAT AND CRISIS

1 For accounts of psychoanalysis in crisis, see Bornstein 2001; Hale 1995; Luhrmann 2000; Prince 1999; Shweder 2010; Summers 2008.

2 As Robin Chester (2003) writes, in the background of these discussions is the feared "demise of psychoanalysis." Chester identifies four main themes put forward as causes for the current crisis: cultural opposition to psychoanalytic ideas; a lack of new psychoanalytic ideas; the fracturing effect of a pluralistic field of ideas; rigidity in training institutions.

3 It should be noted that the psychoanalyst in this cartoon imaginary is always male. I use the male pronoun intentionally throughout much of the book (both for the analyst and for his patient), since for much of the history of psychoanalysis, despite its having been founded on the treatment of female hysterics, the analyst and the patient are characterized this way in the professional literature; it is only in later sections of the book that I begin to adopt gender-neutral language, corresponding with changing usage in the literature and with the feminization of the field.

4 Statements from the website http://www.digitaldiagnostics.com (accessed April 18, 2010).

5 Quoted interview material in this chapter is drawn from interviews with "Peter Shapiro," "John Brandon," "Bob Bosch," "Norm Peters," "Penny Gould," and "Carrie Janis." While the names of these individuals have been changed, the scenarios they describe in their interviews have not.

6 The training analysis is one of the three pillars of the "tripartite," or "Eitingon," model of training used in the United States (Max Eitingon, one of Freud's earliest followers, was the cofounder of the Berlin Polyclinic, the first center for treating patients with Freud's psychoanalytic method and the first training institute for analysts). The three requirements psychoanalytic trainees, or "candidates," undergo in training are a training analysis, several analyses of patients that are conducted under supervision ("control cases"), and a series of seminars. For a good description of the Eitingon model, see Schroter 2002.

7 For the history of crisis, one would need to start with Freud, whose autobiography is replete with observations about psychoanalysis's vulnerability to repression from without. A cogent statement of Freud's vision of the embattled status of psychoanalysis can be found in a letter to Ernest Jones where he writes: "What progress we are making! In the middle ages they would have burned me, nowadays they are content to burn my books" (Jones 1955, 181). See also Shamdasani 2002.

8 Though Leo Stone is credited with introducing this term in 1954, it wasn't until the later 1970s that the notion that psychoanalysis needed to address a wider range of patients became widely held.

9 The required frequency for analysis in APsaA institutes is, according to its bylaws, "five (or four) sessions per week." In the International Psychoanalytical Association bylaws the required frequency is three sessions per week. These are the required frequencies for *both* the candidate's own training analysis *and* for the "control" analyses the candidate conducts in training. While the use of session frequency as in itself defining of psychoanalysis has been problematized, organizationally it is still upheld as defining. Merton Gill, who in his early work was one of the framers of classical American ego psychology, later shifted his position on the definition of psychoanalysis, granting precedence to what he deemed its "intrinsic" factors (a focus on transference and defense) over its "extrinsic" factors (the number of sessions per week and the use of the couch). His position was never embraced by APsaA, which continues to uphold session frequency as the defining factor for determining a treatment to be psychoanalysis.

10 There is also a discourse of crisis around the *gender* of patients presenting for analysis. One training committee whose members I interviewed had to revisit over and again the seemingly unresolvable issue of whether a particular candidate could graduate having only analyzed female patients. A number of trainees had been unable to find male patients willing to undergo psychoanalysis and were therefore unable to graduate from training. Despite a broad movement away from Oedipal theory, in which sexual difference is binary and maturation involves a specific, prescribed relation to one's gender, it remains a requirement that trainees analyze both male and female control cases.

11 For the history of the lawsuit, see Schneider and Desmond 1994; Wallerstein 2002c.

12 According to my survey of all Chicago Institute graduates from 1935 to 2010, only one non-M.D.—an anthropologist, in 1978—graduated from training at the Institute before the 1989 lawsuit. The total number of graduates from 1935 to 2010 is 455, which means that 38 certificates have gone to non-M.D.s, 417 to M.D.s.

13 See Bartlett et al. 2005. Also noteworthy: over the course of the longer interval of 1946 to 2001, the average age of newly certified members increased from 36.2 years in 1946 to 50.2 years in 2001 (see table).

Summary of Candidates Admitted 1996–2002

Prof.	N	%	Avg. Age	Median	#	range
M.D.	307	41.6%	39.9 yrs.	37.9	236	(25–73)
Ph.D.	273	37.0%	45.7 yrs.	45.2	209	(28–68)
SW	99	13.4%	48.7 yrs.	48.2	80	(28–70)
Other	59	8.0%	47.0 yrs.	48.2	49	(24–60)

Average Age at Acceptance = 43.84 yrs.
Median Age at Acceptance = 43.80 yrs. (Sample size = 574)
Age Distribution: 20 to 30 = 3.3%; 30 to 40 = 34.0%; 40 to 50 = 36.9%; 50 to 60 = 23.0%; 60 to 70 = 23.0%; 70 to 80 = 0.3%

14 On the active contestation over the regulation of psychoanalysis, see Mosher 2006. Several states have recently created a new entry-level mental health profession called psychoanalysis with its own training and licensure requirements wholly separate from those established in the institutes of the APsaA. Another hotly debated area Mosher discusses is the externalization of credentialing; the central concerns for many in APsaA and the other self-consciously mainstream psychoanalytic organizations are to preserve the four-sessions-per-week frequency requirement and the special TA designation.

15 The Consortium is made up of the APsaA, the American Academy of Psychoanalysis, Division 39 of the American Psychological Association, and the American Association of Psychoanalysis in Clinical Social Work. Gray (2002) notes that some of these institutes make an end run around the APsaA, becoming affiliated directly with the International Psychoanalytical Association, while others are completely separate from either of these umbrella organizations. There is acrimony around the frequency issue in recent APsaA discussions of proposals that would allow IPA-trained analysts to join their organization, since, if this happened, APsaA would then house analysts trained under two different standards, one defining psychoanalysis in terms of a four-times-weekly frequency and the other a three-times-weekly frequency, a situation that, one of the chairs of the APsaA Board of Professional Standards wrote, "may result in generations of analysts being trained without adequate exposure to uniquely psychoanalytic experiences." Eric Nuetzel, unpublished letter, September 12, 2004, 1.

16 On the other side of the debate, the leading French psychoanalyst Andre Green (2000a, 46) writes that psychoanalysts give up what is uniquely psychoanalytic by complying with the positivist imperatives of EBM: "I came to the conclusion that the greater risk for the future of psychoanalysis is the decline and possible fall of the spirit of psychoanalysis, the specific mental state that inhabits the psychoanalyst during his or her work and thinking. Our task is to keep that spirit alive. I am not at all sure that this moral task can be better ensured by what is today called research in psychoanalysis." For an excellent study of the debate about research and the epistemic violence involved in legitimating psychoanalysis empirically, see Stormon 2004. Lynn Stormon describes how "in response to a widely acknowledged crisis in the psychoanalytic world, it has become commonplace to

assert that empirical research is urgently needed to legitimate psychoanalysis and that strategic interdisciplinary alliances must be forged or renewed with neighboring natural and behavioral sciences to ensure its very survival" (2004, 4).

17 The historical oscillation of biological and psychological construals of the object of psychiatric intervention exceeds my scope here, as does the history of the personal problems domain that grew out of early twentieth-century turf wars between mind cure, transcendentalism, Christian Science, pastoral counseling, and nascent psychiatry and neurology. For these histories, see Burnham 1988; Caplan 2001; Hirshbein 2009; Lunbeck 1994; Vogel and Rosenberg 1979.

18 See Callahan et al. 1995; R. G. Frank et al. 1999; Goldman 1995; Goldman et al. 1998; Grazier et al. 1999; Grazier and Eselius 1999. Through subcontracting to MBHOs, in the period between 1988 and 2000 MCOs brought down insurance payments for mental health services by 54% (while general health payments increased 7.4%). See Kaley et al. 1999.

19 For a signal early critique of the DSM, see Kirk and Kutchins 1992. See also Bollas and Sundelson 1995, who refer to therapists as "the new informants" in the regime of defensive medicine that the industrialization of health care has installed.

20 For the moment I simply want to flag the tension between naturalist, idealist, constructivist, and realist perspectives on medical dependency, a concept whose normative status has been debated at length in medical sociology.

21 William Pollack, quoted with permission from a February 22, 2010, APsaA Members List posting with the subject heading "The ethics and nostalgia generated by CPT codes—esp. 90807 which is meant to differentiate 'medical psychotherapy' from just 'talk psychotherapy.'"

22 Quoted with permission from an April 12, 2010, APsaA Members List thread.

23 "These resulting risks could be explained, in many cases, by the ways that the technical features of the treatment process of a psychoanalytic treatment plan noted above conflict with the conditions of review imposed on the treatment process by the third party." Cummings 1999.

24 See Phillips 2002; Stepansky 1999. Stepansky shows how Freud (like Fliess) saw the surgeon as the most active of physicians. Surgery became Freud's model for both the strengths and the weaknesses of medicine, though he began to wrestle with this metaphor before World War I, ultimately becoming convinced by the problem of war neurosis that a psychological rather than a medical metaphor was most apt for psychoanalysis.

25 The question of "lay analysis" has been extensively documented. See Mosher and Richards 2005; Lane and Meisels 1994; Wallerstein 1998.

26 For a useful history of the establishment of psychoanalysis in the United States and the politics of exclusion that characterized this effort, see Richards 1999.

27 For a useful overview of American ego psychology, see Blanck and Blanck 1994.

28 Freud's structural theory (id-ego-superego) replaced his earlier topographic theory (conscious-preconscious-unconscious). Structural theory was systematized and rationalized into what became known as ego psychology by, initially, Anna

Freud, and then by Heinz Hartmann. Roy Schafer described Hartmann's campaign for total systematization thus:

> It is evident that from the first Hartmann was keenly aware of the lack of elegance in psychoanalytic theory as it stood at the end of Freud's life. . . . He found the theory crude in every one of its metapsychological aspects. Dynamic propositions, especially those concerning aggression, were in a state of disorder: the many types of aims they covered were not hierarchically arranged, they were defined on many levels of abstraction, and they were not always clearly related to basic concepts concerning the driving forces of the personality; moreover, the conceptualization of these driving forces, especially the instinctual drives, was itself in need of considerable repair. The structural theory contained comparable weaknesses in its treatment of the development and functions of the id, ego and superego alike; especially intrasystemic issues had been neglected. The economic point of view (and, with it, the structural) was unworkable without considerable articulation and amplification of energic concepts. Genetic propositions were uncoordinated and unevenly developed, especially in the case of narcissism, aggression and pre-Oedipal development. Adaptive propositions concerning relations with the real world were lacking in theoretical stature and systematization, and required an approach through the biological concept of adaptation. (Schafer 1970, 429)

29 Crapanzano (1992) has written about the preference of psychoanalysis for referential language and semantics over pragmatics and linguistic function.

30 Eissler 1953. While Eissler's statement was particularly austere, it is nevertheless emblematic of the central tendency in ego psychology in the 1950s through the 1970s. In the late 1970s it was noted that Eissler's view of psychoanalysis by "interpretation alone" had been a distortion of Freud's own mature technique, which was far less severe. See, e.g., Lipton 1983.

31 Eissler (1953, 109) defined a parameter as "the deviation, both quantitative and qualitative, from the basic model technique, that is to say, from a technique which requires interpretation as the exclusive tool."

32 In 1915 Freud introduced the rule of abstinence in a discussion of transference resistance in "Observations on Transference-Love": "The treatment must be carried out in abstinence. By this I do not mean physical abstinence alone, nor yet the deprivation of everything that the patient desires, for perhaps no sick patient could tolerate this. Instead, I shall state it as a fundamental principle that the patient's need and longing should be allowed to persist in her, in order that they may serve as forces impelling her to do work and to make changes" (165). Anna Freud (1946, 13) further specified the implications of the principle of abstinence for psychoanalytic technique, writing that "we have to play a double game with the patient's instinctual impulses, on the one hand encouraging them to express themselves and, on the other, steadily refusing them gratification." Anna Freud's "double game" assisted in the transformation ("neutralization") of drive energy

from the pleasure-seeking primary sexual and aggressive instinctual demands of childhood into the reality-based, mature needs of adulthood that are realizable in socially acceptable "substitute satisfactions" (marriage, child-rearing, work, etc.).

33 It is indeed the case that Eissler argued that if his strictures about the use of parameters were adhered to one could, hypothetically, analyze a patient with a less than normal ego. He listed four criteria for the use of a parameter, however, if it were to fulfill the fundamental conditions of analysis: "(1) A parameter must be introduced only when it is proved that the basic model technique does not suffice; (2) the parameter must never transgress the unavoidable minimum; (3) a parameter is to be used only when it finally leads to its self-elimination; . . . the final phase of the treatment must always proceed with a parameter of zero . . . (4) the effect of the parameter on the transference relationship must never be such that it cannot be abolished by interpretation" (Eissler 1953, 111). In other words, if the parameter could not ultimately be zeroed out, then the patient could not be analyzed. "Every introduction of a parameter incurs the danger that a resistance has been temporarily eliminated without having been properly analyzed. Therefore . . . interpretation must become again the exclusive tool to straighten out the ruffle which was caused by the use of a parameter" (126).

34 Authors of other schools (in France, England, South America) considered psychoanalysis applicable to a wider range of patients, not only those who can establish an Oedipal transference neurosis in Zetzel's terms. For excellent comparative social histories of psychoanalysis, see Turkle [1978] 1992 (France); Zaretsky 2004 (US).

35 This idea originally comes from Sterba 1934. In Etchegoyen's (1991, 29) reading of analyzability, "those who could not complete these decisive steps in development will be unanalyzable, because they will continually tend to confuse the analyst as a real person with the imagos transferred on to him."

36 See Isakower 1992. For an appreciative retrospective on Eissler's parameter concept, see Garcia 2009. For an interpretation of Eissler's paper that is similar to my own, see Orgel 1995. Orgel writes that

> Eissler's paper must have had a "political" as well as a scientific mission at the time: to safeguard and preserve the scientific status of psychoanalysis against the then triple threats to it: first, from the emerging widening scope of patients whose pathology demanded that the parameters of the analytic situation be stretched, pulled, breached; second, the repeated seductive flowerings of techniques aiming for corrective emotional experiences under various names, which undermined the primary position of interpretation as the path toward insight; and third, the exponentially expanding practice of analytic-like psychotherapies which declared interactional processes themselves to be mutative. In stripping the human being (the patient and the analyst) into ideal fictions in imitation of the researches of other sciences, Eissler follows Freud's model of the analyst as surgeon working "ideally" in an aseptic field. This analyst violates the rules only in emergency situations provoked by the patient. (Orgel 1995, 556)

37 The social workers were willing to go along with their subordination to the psychiatrists, the psychologists less so. For an excellent study of these interprofessional dynamics, see Buchanan 2003. In a narrative from a social worker excited about incorporating psychoanalysis into her work, Joyce Edward delineates a typical ambition of psychoanalytically inclined social workers of that era, demonstrating the growing sense that members of that profession—much like psychoanalytically inclined psychologists—developed in the years leading up to the lawsuit that they, too, just as M.D.s, could master the techniques of "full" psychoanalysis, they too could "enter the realm of the unconscious," they needed no longer heed the admonition to limit their attention to the preconscious and conscious. Edward writes that

> as a psychoanalytic psychotherapist, I now began to enter the realm of the unconscious, to encourage my patients to free associate, and to deal with transference, counter transference and resistance. No longer did I have to heed Hollis' (1964) admonition to limit my focus to the preconscious or conscious and avoid encouraging "free association." If I heard a dream, I no longer was required to limit my attention to the manifest content, as Hollis had also advised social workers to do. Having seen how contemporary psychoanalysis could enrich my social work efforts, I was now to learn how much that background had prepared me for my role as a psychotherapist and to discover the influence it would have upon my clinical endeavors. (Edward 2009, 18)

38 Several theorists took part in this expansion. Most prominently in the United States, Kohut theorized the psychopathology and treatment of the narcissistic or self disorders, while Kernberg did the same for the borderline personality. Elsewhere Kleinians and others with an object relations perspective continued on a course that began well before the American "widening scope," treating psychotic patients and making little distinction between psychosis and neurosis with respect to suitability for analysis. For the disappearance of the neurotic and the conflation of this with a putatively epidemiological, historical shift, see, e.g., Acklin 1994; Bayer and Spitzer 1985; Kernberg 1980; Wallerstein 2000.

39 For an excellent study of the biologization of psychiatry and the tensions between psychiatry's "two minds," see Luhrmann 2000.

CHAPTER 2. ANALYSIS DEFERRED

1 In framing their conversation, I draw on Knorr-Cetina's notion of an *epistemic culture*, an internally referential system in which members "orient themselves more toward one another and previous system-states than toward the outside" (1999, 2). For Knorr-Cetina (2005, 70), "what is at stake in epistemic cultures is not simply the definition of subjects and objects but their reconfiguration in relation to the natural and social orders as they exist outside expert systems and in relation to each other."

2 A colleague of theirs described his solution to a form of social discomfort he regularly experienced: he had separate business cards printed up, one designating himself as a "Psychoanalyst," the other as a "Psychiatrist," so that he could manage the anxiety his troubled dual citizenship stirred up when he moved in different social worlds. His identity as psychoanalyst, which was indeed his preferred one, bore a stigma, he felt, among the successful businessmen, doctors, and lawyers in his social circle. (He, like Mark, has struggled to find any patients interested specifically in analysis.)

3 Jackson (2005, 2) deftly writes about his fieldwork anxieties that "to conduct fieldwork is to engage in a certain kind of research-based sincerity that is related to, but analytically distinct from, questions of ethnographic authenticity."

4 Many of today's TAs matriculated to that status before Certification involved an actual test of clinical competence (earlier Certification was pro forma and referred to an individual's having graduated from analytic training).

5 For the history of Certification, see Mosher and Richards 2005.

6 In Freud's reading of *Medusa's Head* (1922, 274), he argued that the displaying of the male organ has the apotropaic effect of warding off castration: "To display the penis (or any of its surrogates) is to say: 'I am not afraid of you. I defy you. I have a penis.' Here, then, is another way of intimidating the Evil Spirit."

CHAPTER 3. INSTITUTING PSYCHOANALYSIS IN CHICAGO

1 I borrow the concepts of the pedagogy of desire and the pedagogical imaginary from critical pedagogy studies, where they are used to analyze questions of cultural capital and canonicity in schools. See Guillory 1993; see also Jagodzinski 2002.

2 While a psychoanalytic institute offers formal training in psychoanalysis, a psychoanalytic society is a local membership organization for psychoanalysts (whether institute faculty or not). Typically a psychoanalytic society sponsors lectures or conferences.

3 Eisold offers a vivid introduction to the history of psychoanalytic schismogenesis.

> In the 1940s, two groups split off from the New York Psychoanalytic Society. . . . One of these groups, calling itself the Association for the Advancement of Psychoanalysis, itself suffered two schisms in turn: one group defected to form the William Alanson White Institute, and a second to form the Comprehensive Course in Psychoanalysis at the New York Medical College. The second group splitting off from the New York Psychoanalytic Society formed the Columbia Institute. At virtually the same time, the British Psycho-Analytical Society narrowly averted a split by agreeing to form virtually autonomous Kleinian and Freudian sub-groups; subsequently, a third, or "Middle Group," separated out. In the European institutes, schisms have occurred in Germany, Austria, France, Sweden and Norway (Eckhardt 1978). In France, the controversies surrounding Lacan produced at least four surviving institutes: The Freudian School, The Fourth Group, the Paris Institute and the French Psychoanalytical Association (Turkle 1978 [1992]). [Hannett]

Gitelson (1983), in addition, notes schisms that have occurred in Spain, Brazil, Mexico, Argentina and Venezuela, as well as, in the United States, in Washington/Baltimore, Philadelphia, Boston, Cleveland and Los Angeles. Arlow (1972) refers to half a dozen splits in the APsaA, as many narrowly-averted splits, and adds to the census of splits in the International Psychoanalytical Association, Colombia and Australia. (Eisold 1994, 785)

The historical literature suggests a number of explanations for the chronic schismogenesis of psychoanalytic institutions, most of them (perhaps understandably) psychological: Freud's own ambivalence about psychoanalysis; Freud's establishing of competitive sibling rivalries among his followers; the profession's collective failure to mourn Freud adequately; the potency of the forces of love and hate unleashed in psychoanalysis and the inherent difficulty of keeping them contained; surplus superego; incestuous power relationships; an inherent conflict between group affiliation and pair affiliation; a tendency among analysts to debase worldly organizations. See, e.g., Eckhardt 1978; Eisold 1994, 1998, 2003, 2007; Frosch 1991; Hale 1995; Kirsner 2000; Makari 2008; Reeder 2004; Roudinesco 1990.

4 McLean stated this in an unpublished filmed interview with Glenn Miller from the early 1970s (McLean n.d.). Psychiatry, she added, was what the second-rate students went into in the 1920s.

5 In France, Jacques Lacan attacked Alexander categorically, casting his own "return to Freud" and his efforts to institute a philosophically adequate psychoanalysis in France against the ego psychology that developed in Chicago.

6 For the founding of the APsaA and for Jones's alliance with Putnam and his rivalry with Brill, see Hale 1995.

7 Letter from Ernest Jones to Sigmund Freud, December 10, 1908, in Paskauskas 1995, 10–12.

8 Freud called his inner circle his Secret Committee (see Grosskurth 1992). For the strains and dynamics among Freud's closest epigones, see Berman 2004; Gay 2006; Jones 1955, 1957, 1972; Makari 2008; Roazen 1975.

9 Ernest Jones to Sigmund Freud, February 8, 1911, in Paskauskas 1995, 88. Jones was himself accused of sexually molesting a patient while he was in Toronto. He reported:

A severe hysteric whom I saw only a couple of times last September went to a woman doctor (Gordon), and after much pressing declared that I had had sexual relations with her "to do her good." Unfortunately Dr. Gordon had greatly interested herself in the stories, being the secretary of the local Purity League, so she went with the full batch to the President of the University and asked him to dismiss me, so that I should no longer pervert and deprave the youth of Toronto. The President took the matter very sensibly, although he is a parson, and referred it to Dr. Clarke, the Dean of the Medical Faculty, Professor of Psychiatry, and a close friend of mine. He investigated it as far as he could, naturally declared the stories a tissue of nonsense and gave his opinion that the patient was a paranoiac. (Ernest Jones to Sigmund Freud, February 8, 1911, in Paskauskas 1995, 88)

10 Ernest Jones to Sigmund Freud, February 8, 1911, in Paskauskas 1995, 88. Jones initiated a tradition of employing theoretical preference as a criterion of mental health, deeming psychotic those who were disloyal to Freud's doctrines.

11 Stuart Brent, the renowned Chicago book publisher, attended Blitzsten's famous Monday evening seminars as a young man and wrote about his experiences among Chicago's intelligentsia in his biography. I've used his colorful image of Blitzsten to open this chapter. Most of the other information on Blitzsten comes from his students' biographical accounts of his great influence as a teacher (many collected in a Festschrift edited by Robert Knight [1961b]), from the reflections of his former wife, Dorothy Blitsten, on his role in instituting psychoanalysis in Chicago, from obituaries, and from minutes of the APsaA. See Knight 1961b; Quinn 1987. (Dorothy Blitsten changed the spelling of her name after her divorce and went on to become a successful sociologist at Hunter College in New York.)

12 Blitzsten's students in the 1930s and 1940s make up a veritable Who's Who of 1940s and 1950s psychiatry in America. See Knight 1961b.

13 Dorothy Blitsten claims it was a "false myth" about Blitzsten that he was in analysis with Freud; Ira Blitzsten, Blitzsten's nephew, avers that he was. Orr (1961, 25–26) writes that "it was characteristic for Lionel to schedule his arrival in Vienna with a margin of only a couple of hours to get settled and get over to Freud's office." Apparently Blitzsten was not very amenable to Freud's Freudian reading of his behavior. Knight, in preparing the Blitzsten Festschrift and writing his introductory comments, describes asking Franz Alexander to help set the record straight on the matter of Blitzsten's pedigree. Knight reports that Alexander told him that he, Alexander, had been Blitzsten's sole analyst, and that while "there was talk about going to [Otto] Rank, actually he never had any treatment with Rank."

14 For Alexander at the Berlin Institute, see Schmidt 2010. For the contrasting cultures of the Berlin and Vienna institutes, see Berman 2004.

15 Brent writes of Blitzsten's "coterie" as including, among other literati, Studs Terkel, Nelson Algren, Saul Bellow, and Ben Hecht.

16 Unpublished memoir received from Susan Quinn, biographer of Karen Horney (housed in the Boston Psychoanalytic Institute archives).

17 Alexander would go on to develop a "vector theory of personality," holding that specific bodily symptoms were directly determined by specific unconscious drive conflicts. The formula for gastric cases, for example, was "intense receptive wishes which conflict with the patient's fight for his independence." Asthma revealed a conflict between aggressive-masculine and passive-feminine tendencies ("the patient in his asthma cries out for help from his mother and is afraid of separation from her"). Rheumatoid arthritis mostly affected women and was about "masculine protest." About the arthritic patient, Alexander's colleague Grotjahn wrote that "the patient's early history reveals dominating parents— mostly mothers—against whom the arthritic patients rebel, but to whom they

submit. This produced a kind of emotional strait jacket situation with the simultaneous innervation of extensor and flexor muscles." See Marmorston and
Stainbrook 1964, 227–231.

18 Alexander was accused of such "economic idylls" on several occasions; this is
from Eissler 1965, 192.

19 This event was reported in the 1933 Bulletin of the International Psychoanalytical
Association:

> On October 3, 1932, an Institute for Psycho-Analysis was inaugurated at
> 43 East Ohio Street, Chicago, Illinois. The Institute was empowered by the
> State authorities to open a Clinic and to conduct training. The President of
> the Board of Trustees is Dr. Alfred K. Stern. Dr. Franz Alexander and Dr.
> Karen Horney have been permanently appointed Director and Associate-
> Director respectively. In addition the teaching staff includes three analysts
> who work half-time (Dr. Thomas M. French, Dr. Helen McLean, Dr. Cath-
> erine L. Bacon) and also Dr. Leon J. Saul (permanently appointed). Two
> other medical men (Dr. Karl Menninger and Dr. Lionel N. Blitzsten) give
> courses of lectures. The work of The Institute is directed primarily to re-
> search and training. Research work at the present time consists in the in-
> vestigation of organ-neuroses (gastric, intestinal, and gynæcological cases).
> Work is also being done on the problem of neurotically conditioned crimi-
> nality. (Reports of the International Training Commission 1933)

20 "Psychodynamic" is code for psychoanalysis's "dynamic" conception of the
mind.

21 For a more general history of Prussian research institutes, see Servos 1993.

22 The plan to limit training to only a few is strongly emphasized in The Institute's
1932 founding mission statement.

23 Gregg's efforts followed changes in the Rockefeller Foundation's philanthropic
activities in the 1920s after the rededication of the Laura Spelman Rockefeller
Memorial, which shifted the foundation's overall emphasis toward a greater concentration on the social and behavioral sciences and a more intensive focus on
research (rather than education). See Bulmer and Bulmer 1981. Gregg and Stanley
Cobb would develop a center for psychosomatic research at Harvard; with Franz
Alexander, Gregg would develop the Chicago Institute, and with another leading academic psychiatrist he would develop a center in St. Louis. As Gregg would
write to his chief at the Rockefeller Foundation, "Stanley Cobb has ceased stut-
tering after being psychoanalyzed" (Brown 1987, 162). Stanley Cobb was one of
Gregg's mentors, and in one of Cobb's letters to Gregg, Cobb had written that
"what I feel is needed in psychiatry just now is cooperation between men who
know some organic things and those who are philosophers (albeit practical ones)
doing psychoanalysis" (Brown 1987, 162–163).

24 After several years of Alexander failing to secure a university affiliation for the
Chicago Institute, Gregg's relationship with him soured, and Gregg pulled the

funds from the Chicago project to put money into the New York and St. Louis projects, where university affiliations had been secured.

25 While Alexander cultivated links with the mental hygiene movement and with the social workers, writing books for a general public hungry for psychological knowledge, Blitzsten's group sought to make psychoanalysis the core of psychiatry, not part of an broader mental health system.

26 Viennese émigrés, Kurt and Ruth Eissler's antipathy toward Alexander drove them to leave Chicago after several apparently unbearably provincial years in the Midwest.

27 Statements from Blitzsten's followers quoted in Knight 1961a, 3–6.

28 In his eulogy, Orr (1961, 22) describes the famous "Blitzstenkrieg," Blitzsten's interpretive shock attack turned against a patient to break open a difficult case, prized by the "alpha chapter" of the "fraternity" of the "Sons of Blitzsten or S.O.B.s."

29 As Emch wrote in Blitzsten's obituary,

> Lionel Blitzsten has been called the most quoted analyst in America, but the quotations are almost invariably from seminars, supervisory sessions, letters, and conversations. He had a matchless gift for extemporizing, with a flair for the dramatic that ensured a lasting impression; but he could not with any ease bring himself to generalize from the particulars of his experience. He could only phrase his keen observations and clear insights in a living, particular interpersonal context. He had hoped to overcome this difficulty by writing about his supervisory experience, in which he had been so able to transmit the major tenets of his practice. . . . The work on paper remains unfinished. (Emch 1953, 154)

30 Theresa Benedek described the efforts to confirm Freud's theories with psychoanalytic clinical evidence: "The [Chicago] work on the female sexual cycle actually brought for the first time together Freud's ideas that libidinal theory and hormone physiology are closely interrelated." Quoted in Schmidt 2004, 225.

31 Blitzsten was "bitingly sarcastic, ruthless in the use of his penetrating skill for unmasking the pretenses and hidden motives of anyone who he happened to focus his attention on at a given moment, aggressively intrusive into the privacy of others" (Rubins 1978; Rubins added that "he could not bear to be alone, and he gathered an incredible number of people around him"). With a "glittering array of personal parlour talents," he was "a congenital psychoanalyst, examining motives, disguises" (Lucia Tower, in McLean and Tower n.d.). "He had an intuitive perception of how to hurt people, and he did it perfectly" (McLean n.d.). He was "a peeping Tom, fascinated with the life history of homosexuals" (McLean n.d.). He was "disruptive and seductive," holding forth "Buddha-like" in his salon (Lucia Tower, in McLean and Tower n.d.).

32 This comment by an esteemed senior analyst was made during a seminar titled "Failed Cases." The seminar was convened at the Institute by Arnold Goldberg during the 2009–2010 academic year.

33 Also called the depth or the action interpretation.

34 Gedo 1997, 7. On emergency interventions more generally, see Eissler 1965, 96.

35 For a Blitzstenite perspective on the political and organizational problem entailed by Alexander's flexibility, see Karl Menninger to Leo Bartemeier, February 16, 1943, in Faulkner and Pruitt 1995, 376–380.

36 A bit of organizational history is necessary to understand the ruling. In its effort to limit the IPA's reach in the United States, the APsaA had reorganized itself twice, in 1932 and then again in 1938, in order to leverage greater power over training standards.

37 Lionel Blitzsten to Karl Menninger, November 1936, in Faulkner and Pruitt 1988, 231.

38 Indeed, he amplified, psychoanalytic theory was "through psychosomatic channels [the possession] of the whole of medicine."

39 Lionel Blitzsten to Karl Menninger, November 1936, in Faulkner and Pruitt 1988, 231. The Vector is a reference to Alexander's psychosomatic vector theory of the personality, which identified personality based on physical types (the ulcer personality, the coronary personality, the arthritic personality, etc.); clearly Blitzsten found it asinine.

40 According to both Crowley and Emch, several of Blitzsten's analysands attempted to set up a separate institute; there is no record of their efforts beyond these mentions of it. See Crowley 1978; Emch 1953.

41 Maxwell Gitelson to Karl Menninger, March 31, 1958, in Faulkner and Pruitt 1995, 210.

CHAPTER 4. PROFESSIONALIZATION AND ITS DISCONTENTS

Second epigraph: a formula for the psychological assessment and selection of trainees for psychoanalysis during the 1950s, the era of its professionalization. Alexander and Ross 1952.

1 The U.S. Selective Service rejected over a million men on neurological and psychological grounds; during the war nearly 40 percent of all medical discharges were for neuropsychiatric reasons. See Plant 2005. Unlike during World War I, when recruits were turned away on the grounds of psychosis or intellectual insufficiency, rejections during World War II were typically on the grounds of neurosis, in terms, that is, of psychoanalytic nosology. The Veterans Administration coped with unprecedented numbers of neuropsychiatric casualties during World War II. See Burnham 1978; Herman 1995; Moskowitz 2001; Pols 1997; Zaretsky 2004.

2 This was the document that, following the war, would serve as the basis of the mental disorders section of the World Health Organization's *International Statistical Classification of Diseases* (1949) and of the first American Psychiatric Association's *Diagnostic and Statistical Manual of Mental Disorders* (1952).

3 In a 1939 letter to his brother Karl, William Menninger confided: "I do not know of any medical group that has as many queer birds . . . augmented now by a lot of emigrants." The emigrants he was referring to were the psychoanalysts fleeing Nazi persecution for new professional homes in the United States. In Europe they had been leaders of the psychoanalytic movement, proud of their proximity to Freud; in the U.S. they were rivals with American psychiatrists for the pool of patients, and they were foreigners, and most were not medical doctors, so they had to be corralled. The analysts were, on the whole, Menninger observed, a "bizarre group." Faulkner and Pruitt 1988, 1995. For a contemporary analysis of the relationship between sanity and social order, see Lasswell 1986. For the popular mental health movement and Hollywood's role in creating the image of mental illness as public enemy number one, see Gabbard 2001. For the role of psychological "experts" in sustaining democracy in the 1930s and 1940s, see Herman 1995; Lunbeck 1994; Rose 1999a.

4 Harry S. Truman to William Menninger, May 15, 1948, quoted in Plant 2005, 184. Truman's press secretary, Charles Ross, was the brother of Helen Ross, Franz Alexander's administrative director at the Chicago Institute and the woman who ran the organization behind the scenes.

5 These comments are from oral history interviews conducted by the author with Chicago psychoanalysts Mark Berger and Arnold Goldberg, respectively, on May 15, 2009, and April 28, 2009. Apart from close readings of all of the published writing by Institute faculty of this period, stories and impressions about the culture of the Institute in this chapter derive from interviews and conversations with senior Chicago psychoanalysts Jerome Beigler, Mark Berger, Bertram Cohler, Arnold Goldberg, Meyer Gunther, Jerome Kavka, George Klumpner, Sheldon Meyers, Leo Sadow, Henry Seidenberg, Arnold Tobin, Marian Tolpin, and Jerome Winer, and with senior Chicago social workers Marcia Adler, Mary Everett, Constance Goldberg, Joseph Palombo, and Colin Webber.

6 An unauthored report in the *Bulletin of the American Psychoanalytic Association* (American Psychoanalytic Association 1951, 213) quotes Gerhart Piers as writing the following update to the national organization about the Chicago Institute: "Beset by difficulties as much as any other psychoanalytic group, it takes justifiable pride in having maintained unity in discord, by neither suppressing 'dissenting' viewpoints nor permitting disruption through isolation. As the president indicated, the immediately preceding discussion was a case in point. It centered, at times rather acrimoniously, around the reports from the local and national Committees on Evaluation, presented by Joan Fleming and Maxwell Gitelson. Theresa Benedek and Gerhart Piers opened the debate which concerned itself mostly with the validity of the definition of psychoanalysis as presented by the Committee." The report in the *Bulletin* is confusing in that it is not clear where Gerhart Piers's words end and the un-named author of the APsaA report interpolates his (her?) own words (i.e., there are opening but no closing quotation marks). For a discussion of the history of splitting in American psychoanalytic institutes, see Eckhardt 1978; Kirsner 2000.

7 The members of this "school," a Chicago variant on ego psychology, were known locally as "the ego autonomy people."

8 "Maturity" and "normalization" are terms one sees over and again in the professional literature of this period. Heinz Kohut would call this a period of "maturity morality."

9 "Organize" is a word that crops up throughout Fleming's writing, just as "regulation" and "control" (and "adaptation") do throughout Hartmann's. These "superego values" were central to ego psychology; in fact, Schafer writes, "it was only after Hartmann... that the superego was fully established as an independent psychic structure equal in theoretical dignity to the id and ego" (Schafer 1970, 429).

10 From an interview conducted by the author with senior psychoanalyst Jerome Kavka, March 31, 2006. Kavka was supervised by Fleming during his training at the Institute.

11 Arnold Goldberg, interview with the author, April 28, 2009. In a video interview of Joan Fleming that was conducted by Lou Shapiro after she had retired (Shapiro was dean of education at the time he conducted this interview with his mentor and former teacher), Shapiro remarked that she hadn't told him quite how much of her time and effort the job actually took; she explained to him that she would stop seeing patients three full hours before and one hour after committee meetings so that she could do all the administrative work necessary. Fleming n.d. Several older analysts I interviewed also told me that she would hold the Admissions Committee and Selection Committee meetings at her house on Sunday mornings. Reflecting on the partisanship within the Institute, one older analyst who was a friend and colleague of Heinz Kohut's said that "Heinz didn't have anything to do with that. She [Fleming] was a real promoter of Henry, Sol, Max Forman—and none of them were therefore able to become Heinz's devotees. There was always tension with Heinz, because he was not going to be under anyone's thumb, and he was developing new ideas."

12 In the video interview with Shapiro, Fleming notes her admiration for Helen Ross, the Institute's administrative chief; while in structurally different positions, the two women shared a passion for administration and organization and in essence ran the Institute for nearly forty years.

13 Hartmann and Loewenstein 1962, 42. Their impression was that one group of analysts centralized the "superego," the moral agency of the psyche, whereas another group laid greater emphasis on the "ego," the executive agency of the psyche.

14 For the relation of the Rainbow Report to the Lewin and Ross field study, see Ekstein 1960; Wallerstein 1987; Weiss 1987. The 1910 Flexner Report was a comprehensive study of medical education in the United States. The report called on medical schools to adopt more rigorous educational standards and to conform to scientific inquiry, not "past traditions" (Flexner 1910, 9); numerous schools fell short of the standard it established and were shut down. The Flexner Report

is often invoked in debates about medical education to distinguish legitimate medicine from quackery or charlatanism, and its invocation by Wallerstein carries that resonance.

15 See, e.g., Hacking 1996, 1999; Lunbeck 1994; Milchman and Rosenberg 2006; Rose 1998; Rosenberg 1995. See also the chapter "Ethic of Honesty" in Rieff 1979.

16 From an interview conducted by the author with senior psychoanalyst Mark Berger, May 15, 2009.

17 Fleming used the male pronoun, writing as she was in an era when "he" represented the human universal. The sheer number of women applicants for psychoanalytic training—originally a field in which women had a markedly strong presence—dropped off markedly during the period of psychoanalysis's dominance in psychiatry. When psychoanalysis was at its peak, then, women were a definite minority. According to my survey of all Institute graduates, women made up fully a third of trainees in the 1930s (4 out of 19) and the 1940s (17 out of 53) and only one-tenth of trainees, 9 out of 111, in the 1950s. The numbers of female as compared to male trainees remained low in the 1960s (9 out of 72), 1970s (5 out of 59), and 1980s (9 out of 42), and then the numbers shifted dramatically in the 1990s. In the 1990s women made up nearly half of graduates (19 out of a total of 44). In the 2000s, more than four times as many women were trained as men; 40 women and 8 men were graduated in the decade 2000–2010.

18 For a contemporary analysis of this kind of bureaucratic thinking, see Shils 1982, 130, who wrote that the rational-legal form of "legitimacy dwells in the substance of the rule [that is] realized by the role, in the procedure of establishing the role, and in the procedure of appointing its incumbent."

19 Emch's point was that supervision offered an opportunity for an experience in multiple relationships, in contrast to the isolated, exclusive relationship that the training analysis offers. She felt that supervision represented an opportunity to contain splits in the political body by breaking up dyads—to bring about "mature" form of relating to the community as a whole rather than "infantile" forms of relating only to the analyst.

20 Jerome Kavka, interview with the author, May 20, 2009. Kavka also told me another great Joan Fleming story, about how much she and the other professional women appreciated having a cook making lunch for them so that they could focus on the important work of professionalizing psychoanalysis. It's an interesting story of the intersections of gender, race, class, and professionalization in this period and of one of the ways that a local elite was constructed.

> Fleming was a very smart woman, a bossy kind of woman; she was good for administrative work, and you know she became very important in the American because of it. She didn't marry. It [the story] connected up with the kitchen. We had a cook [at the Institute]; she made fabulous desserts, and the women analysts liked the idea they'd get their meal at lunch, they didn't have to cook and so forth—the women really appreciated it. Well, after that one left, I found the next cook, a black lady from Mississippi, Louella. OK, so it comes time the

other woman's quitting and I call Louella, I say, "I got a great job for ya, cooking for about thirty people." We had lunch every day. She said, "Oh, Dr. K, I can't cook for thirty people." I said, "Louella, I know what you can do, you can cook for thirty people." I said, "I'm sure you're gonna do OK." And the first day she gets on the job, it's Passover, and we all line up, all the Jew-boys line up for lunch, and she's got ham hocks and black-eyed peas. For lunch! I said, "Louella, what're ya doing, bunch of Jewish doctors there, they don't eat ham hocks and black-eyed peas." She said, "Well what should I make?" I says, "Look, Louella, it's Passover time, whatever else you do, get some matzeys. Get some matzo balls and soup for a Jewish holiday, you start off that way. And make Grivenes the first day." You know Grivenes? Its chicken skin, you fry it with onions in a frying pan with oil, it's the most delicious, it's like crackles, out of this world, my mother used to make it, Jewish women would make it all the time. So she said, "OK I'll make that." And I'll tell ya, they all went nuts! They loved it! [Long wistful pause] But the thing is, she wasn't good on desserts.

21 The "reports" themselves were not available, either because they were destroyed or lost, but Fleming's recommendations for reporting, including the list quoted here, are described in Fleming and Weiss 1987, 438.

22 The trainees were invariably people with whom the faculty had had prior professional contacts—former students, former residents, etc., so, according to Gitelson, the analyst had to work in strict incognito, observing strict personal anonymity in order to keep all extraanalytic contacts at a minimum and thereby "correct . . . the 'spoiling' which occur[ed] in the pre-analytic milieu." Gitelson 1973, 233. It is instructive to compare this postwar ideal of the anonymous blank screen analyst to an account of the training environment in 1920s Leipzig, where Fleming and Gitelson's colleague Theresa Benedek had trained. Benedek later described an informal environment, writing:

> Then, the same individuals whom I analysed five to six mornings of the week, also came to my house one evening a week to discuss psychoanalytic literature and learn theory from books. At that time it did not appear difficult to me or to them to change from one role to another. It seemed I did not speculate about my role as the leader of a study group conflicting with my role as an analyst. In the evening I was a student with my students; in the analytic session, if something came up in reference to or as a reaction to the interactions in the evenings, it was viewed either in the frame of the reality of the incident or interpreted in the transference. (Benedek 1969, 439)

23 For an account of his experience in analysis with Gitelson, and of Gitelson's efforts to interpret these pernicious cultural resistances, see Wolf 2002.

24 Gitelson famously commented about analysands who had dreams in which he (the analyst) appeared directly: "Such dreams are prognostic of a difficult if not impossible analytic situation, due to the fact that the analyst is quite literally

reacted to as if he were in fact an ancient and dangerous imago." The *literalness* of the reaction to the analyst was what boded ill. Gitelson 1954, 179.

25 Note that he calls his paper *therapeutic* problems in the analysis of the "normal" candidate, not *educational* problems; I understand that this distinction is where he and Fleming differed, despite their both being Blitzstenites. In an interview with the author on April 16, 2009, Henry Seidenberg reported that these two argued vigorously about the distinctions between therapeutic and educational functions, despite being great friends and close colleagues. (Seidenberg, who would later go on to be director of the Institute for a brief period, added: "We kids learned a ton from watching them go at it.")

26 It might be noted that Canguilhem (1991, 143), like Hartmann, privileged adaptation: "Taken separately, the living being and his environment are not normal: it is their relationship that makes them such." Interestingly, Gitelson is saying precisely the inverse.

27 Apparently John Gedo stated that he wouldn't accept a homosexual over his dead body (this is from an oral history interview conducted by the author with Gedo's colleague, Arnold Goldberg, on April 28, 2009; it has not been confirmed by discussion with Gedo).

28 Illegitimate according to Institute faculty, of course. In conceiving of the other as a place, Lacan (1977, 285) alluded to Freud's concept of psychical locality and Freud's description, in "The Interpretation of Dreams," of the unconscious as an "other scene" ("ein andere Schauplatz," Freud 1900, 535–536). I use the phrase playfully here, to allude to the idea that these repressions would return (in due time).

29 For a thoroughgoing account of the exclusions leading up to the lawsuit, and of the lawsuit and its sequelae, see Wallerstein 2000. The Giovacchini study group ultimately became a full-fledged (if short-lived) training program, as did the study group that formed the Chicago Center for Psychoanalysis, which would become a competitor institute for psychologists.

30 In the post–World War II period, when psychoanalysis was becoming popular, social work was becoming psychoanalytic. Martin Bergmann, an early lay analyst, wrote in his biography: "Many psychoanalysts at that time had the idea that patients not yet ready for psychoanalysis should be treated by a social worker, who would help them to cope with reality problems and prepare them for analysis." Bergmann 1988, 366. Social workers were seeing more and more clients (qua "patients") in psychiatric settings where M.D.s were unable to keep up with the demand, dispensing their own brand of "applied psychoanalysis." The social workers in child guidance settings originally had the responsibility for dealing with the social and environmental forces affecting the "disturbed" child; although they began as *intermediaries* between the child, the clinic, community resources, and the parents, they often observed that the child client's parents were more disturbed than the child himself was and that treating the parents was a necessary first step in helping the child: "The role of the psychiatric social worker began to shift to that of therapist for the parents, and often, because of a lack of

psychiatric personnel, to that of primary therapist for the child as well" (Philips 2009, 2). The experiences of these psychoanalytic therapists in community settings and then in private practice would, in turn, influence psychoanalysts in the professional communities where they practiced, nudging them toward "reality issues" and toward the role of the here-and-now relationship of patient and therapist in therapy.

31 Because of the dearth of émigré lay analysts in Chicago, this would take place much later than it had in New York or Los Angeles, cities with well-developed, self-consciously dissident, nonmedical psychoanalytic subcultures. Indeed, Chicago did not have a single prominent émigré lay analyst, whereas people like Erich Fromm or Erik Erikson played prominent roles in the psychoanalytic communities of New York and Boston.

32 For an account of the history of child psychoanalysis in Chicago, see Schmidt 2008.

33 Schmidt, in fact, views the child analysts' inability to establish themselves within the Institute during its first several decades as in part a function of their great success outside it (personal communication, June 25, 2008).

34 The rest of Knight's statement is worth reading for its clear articulation of the view that psychoanalysis is a medical procedure in need of medical safeguards:

> The 1938 resolution against the further training of laymen for clinical practice and the 1946 by-law requirement that all new members of the APsaA be physicians solidified th[e] official policy. At the present time there are seven lay analysts who are members of the APsaA, and about twenty-five others who have been given some kind of membership status in an affiliate society. It is not known how many other laymen are practicing psychoanalysis.... Many older analysts in this country, especially those who were trained in Europe, remain unconvinced that exclusion of laymen from training is a wise policy. They point to the highly esteemed contributions to theory and the successful clinical practice of the outstanding lay members of the APsaA and of its affiliate societies, and cite from their experience the eminent personal suitability for psychoanalytic work of many gifted psychologists who cannot now obtain official training. Those opposed to training laymen, who are in the great majority in the APsaA, admit the validity of these points, but are strongly of the opinion that therapy of sick patients is a medical function and must have medical safeguards ... result[ing] in overwhelming reaffirmation of the policy against accepting nonphysicians for official training. (Knight 1953, 201)

35 Not only did the Chicago Institute open a child care program and a teacher training program, it sponsored satellite institutes in Denver and St. Louis; in addition, trainees came to Chicago for weekend seminars from all over the Midwest and the South (from Cincinnati, Denver, St. Louis, Detroit, Indianapolis, Rochester, New York, Rochester, Minnesota, Syracuse, Oklahoma City, Milwaukee, Dallas, New Orleans, and Dayton.

36 Colin Pereira-Webber, April 29, 2009.

37 Marcia Adler, May 8, 2009. For an important study of the uses to which the idea of the primitive has been put in psychoanalysis, see Brickman 2003.

38 Joseph Palombo, April 1, 2009. Perhaps it should be noted that this individual, who went on to have a sterling career as a leading scholar in social work, was one of those rejected by the Institute's clinic as "unanalyzable." His antipathy is no doubt motivated by this experience of exclusion and pathologization.

39 Another senior social worker who worked at the Institute's clinic explained that "no one would even have the idea of going into private practice without their [the social work Private Practice Board's] approval; this was a totally new thing then." Interview with Constance Goldberg, April 13, 2009.

40 "Dayenu," concurred his compatriot Maurice Levine, invoking his own psycho-analytic orthodoxy in a 1953 article on the twin dangers of "flabby psychiatry and wild analysis" ("Dayenu" is the name of a traditional Passover song). Levine 1953, 51.

41 What is paradoxical, and fascinating, is that Gitelson, for all his criticisms of "applied" psychoanalysis, is doing precisely this. We must try to understand exactly what he meant, then, by *applied* in his effort to pin down psychoanalysis's proper domain.

42 I have transcribed this from an interview of Grinker by Brenda Solomon that was filmed in the 1970s; Film Archive, Chicago Institute for Psychoanalysis.

43 Note that Grinker also expressed disdain for the analytic scene in New York, with its high concentration of émigré analysts. "De–New Yorkating" analysis meant Americanizing it; he and his fellows saw the European love of theory as obfuscatory and academic and associated Gitelson's antiadaptationist arguments with European theory. (A dimension of the picture that is likely relevant here is their diverse Jewish roots—Grinker was a German Jew from an established Chicago family; Gitelson was a Russian Jew whose parents were immigrants; both grew up in Chicago, though they circulated in these very different Jewish cultural worlds.)

44 It should be noted that their historiographies of psychoanalysis differed as much as their sociologies of it. For Gitelson, psychoanalysis had reached the status of a Kuhnian normal science by the time the émigrés had fled Europe, but—given the interprofessional competitiveness in U.S. medicine at the time of their arrival in the United States—the further development of the science of psychoanalysis was disrupted. The growth of psychoanalysis in the United States had been too rapid, in his view, so local groups were no longer small enough to function with the trust and familiarity necessary for further scientific development; analysts, he observed, were anxiously waiting for a big breakthrough—rather than doing the less glamorous work of adding to the canon and strengthening the extant paradigm. Grinker, in contrast, felt that psychoanalysis had not yet reached the status of a normal science, but he believed that this development was imminent and that by allying itself with cybernetics psychoanalysis could soon reach that point.

45 See Maxwell Gitelson to Karl Menninger, May 23, 1955, in Faulkner and Pruitt 1995, 158–161. The Gitelson side (their position was much like Eissler's) views analysis as its own discipline, one that should be open to talented people regardless of background. The Grinker side, in contrast, is clear that since psychoanalysis is part of psychiatry, only M.D.s are entitled to train. (Needless to say, there is no neat breakdown of these sides in terms of labels like "conservative" or "liberal.")

CHAPTER 5. THE PLENTY OF SCARCITY

1 Regarding the industrialization of health care, Pollock wrote in 1972 that

the health care "industry" is considerably larger than the automotive industry, about 25 per cent smaller than the defense industry, and growing faster than both. There is increasing concern over the costs of this important sector of our economy. I feel certain that it will be but a short time before we have a nationalized system for the delivery of health services that will focus on treatment and prevention. . . . Questions will be asked of and about psychoanalysis as well as other fields of health care—and we will, in effect, be asked to pass a test of accountability to qualify for inclusion in such a national structure. If we are not included in a system of national health insurance, serious questions will be raised about our relevance. (Pollock 1972, 575)

2 For an excellent account of Pollock's administration, see Kirsner 2000. Grinker 1995 also provides a useful account.

3 "If our Association exclusively follows the path of the clinical application of psychoanalysis to treatment and its intimate coupling to psychiatry and a medical degree, then concerns of practice, licensure, health insurance, peer review, and certification will have to appropriately occupy more and more of our time, energy, money, and resources. These are the legitimate responsibilities of a professional organization, but the choice here may not allow us to use our resources in the systematic development of psychoanalysis as a basic science of man." Pollock 1977b, 30.

4 Oral history interview conducted by the author with Henry Seidenberg, April 16, 2009.

5 For the quotes in this paragraph, see American Psychoanalytic Association 1975, 872. About this group, a Chicago faculty member in his late eighties said to me that "Bob [Robert A.] LeVine has the distinction of being the only one of them who didn't go out and practice after having signed the waiver saying he wouldn't. The rest of them all did anyway." While factually untrue, his sentiment is noteworthy. Oral history interview with Jerome Beigler, February 28, 2007.

6 For the "Chicago Plan," see American Psychoanalytic Association 1974, 433. The Ph.D. program was never accredited, and after a year of training several students it was disbanded.

7 Oral history interview with John Demos conducted by the author on April 1, 2009.

8 Oral history interview with Jerome Winer conducted by the author on March 20, 2009.

9 Oral history interview with Robert LeVine conducted by the author on April 24, 2009.

10 The non-M.D.s include one anthropologist, who was trained to practice clinically, and seven other scholars trained to practice applied psychoanalysis in their research (one historian, two anthropologists, and four psychologists). Subsequent to the lawsuit, several of the psychologists who had earlier been trained as "research candidates" underwent a full, second training so that they could practice clinically.

11 Oral history interview with Constance Goldberg conducted by the author on April 13, 2009.

12 Oral history interview with Mary Everett conducted by the author on April 20, 2009. I am grateful to Ms. Everett for sharing with me some of the paperwork forms that were used in the clinic in the 1970s in the process of assessing patients' "analyzability."

13 "Good hysterics" were high-functioning women in all areas except their unsatisfactory sex lives. "Potential good hysterics" were similar but with some depressive tendencies. Both were analyzable, in contrast to "so-called good hysterics," women who, while attractive, had low self-esteem, rejected their femininity, and were passive and/or devaluing. Because these patients had impairments of ego functioning that made it difficult or impossible for them to trust the analyst, they were considered unlikely to be able to establish the therapeutic alliance necessary for analysis.

14 Kohut's was what Eve Sedgwick has called a reparative rather than a paranoid hermeneutic. See Sedgwick 2003.

15 In the classical view, "narcissism" described a pathology of extreme self-centeredness. The incapacity to love another—another as an *other*—was its defining feature. This problem, the problem of "object love" (as opposed to self-love), was therefore central. It was thought that narcissistic patients could not establish a transference and were therefore unanalyzable. Since they could not see outside themselves, they could not take in the analyst as a genuine "object" (or what we nowadays would call "subject"), and they could not experience him in terms of the Oedipal passions of love, rivalry, and the like.

16 A later nosological step would involve delimiting the stable, analyzable narcissistic personality from the less stable, unanalyzable, "borderline" personality; in Kohut's classification of self pathologies, the borderline patient was beyond the reach of psychoanalysis—though she could be helped through a supportive, stabilizing psychotherapy. Post-Kohutian self psychologists would later add the borderline patient to the list of those viewed as analyzable.

17 Gregory Rizzolo (personal communication March 28, 2013) notes that Kohut distinguished between a patient's "reality sense," which Kohut viewed as a prerequisite for being analyzed, and the "indirect reality" of the transference experience of the analyst: "Analysands whose sense of their own reality is comparatively

intact will allow themselves the requisite regression in the service of the analysis. They will thus be able to experience the . . . indirect reality of transference feelings" (Kohut 1971, 211). In this sense, the therapeutic "relationship" for Kohut did not refer to an interpersonal relationship between analyst and patient, nor was it a "therapeutic alliance" a la ego psychology; the "relationship" meant the patient's narcissistically invested experience of the analyst—i.e., from within the narcissistic nexus of a one-person psychology.

18 As he put this, "tolerable disappointments . . . lead to the establishment of internal structures which provide the ability for self-soothing and the acquisition of basic tension tolerance." Kohut 1971, 64. For the process of "structuralization," see also Terman 1988.

19 Kohut's list corresponded with some of the casework theories social workers had been working with that recognized that the *validation* of the client's perspective was central to helping them; his new nomenclature not only widened the scope of treatment, it also provided a unifying theoretical language for a widened scope of "psychoanalytic" practitioners.

20 Describing the excitement of that time, Bob LeVine, who studied under Kohut in the late 1960s, told me that he and the other academics "had no idea how far Kohut would go, hearing him in 1967, though in retrospect he was clearly starting out on something completely new." Robert A. LeVine, interviewed by the author April 24, 2009.

21 As Kohut (1972, 384) put it, "expressed differently: our defensive activity is primarily motivated by our shame concerning a defect in the realm of the omnipotent and omniscient grandiose self, not by guilt over the unconscious forbidden sexual or aggressive impulse which was revealed."

22 Kohut used the concept of narcissistic injury to describe the injuries to self-esteem that he viewed as primary motivators of even extreme social pathology.

23 In a fascinating account of the history of psychoanalytic publishing, Stepansky describes these as the last two "big books" to come out of psychoanalysis before the economic collapse of psychoanalytic publishing. See Stepansky 2009.

24 Goldberg (2002, 1) writes that "Kohut's original aim for self psychology, to have an established place within organized psychoanalysis, has given way to its rather surprising emergence embodied in a solid group of clinicians and investigators outside of the psychoanalysis that Kohut knew." Self psychology has been particularly embraced in Italy, Israel, and Australia.

25 A good example of this kind of anti-Kohut reaction can be found in Stein's 1979 comparison of Kohut with Freud:

> Kohut's work appears to be the product, *not so much of painstaking exploration*, of trial and error, and of attempts to test the truth, as of a more *purely subjective* and *inspirational* process, largely confined to the empathic-introspective method and relatively independent of other sources of knowledge—more akin to *revelation*. While we cannot expect to use the methods and criteria of science to the extent possible in more readily quantifiable and experimentally verifiable

fields of investigation, it would be a pity to move even further in the direction toward which he seems to be pointing . . . it is difficult to accept [Kohut's] as a genuine addition to psychoanalytic theory and practice. (Stein 1979, 680, emphases mine; I've chosen to highlight these portions because they exemplify a critique of narcissism that doesn't acknowledge its own grandiosity.)

26 Recall that "parameter" is Eissler's term for something the analyst does that is not analytic but that is, in dire situations, acceptable as long as it is later analytically undone or "resolved."

27 This was reported to me by one of this man's former analysands, a fourth-generation Blitzstenite who asked to remain anonymous.

28 Oral history interview with Arnold Tobin conducted by the author on February 28, 2007.

29 "Idiosyncratic to the Chicago scene, stemming as it does from Gitelson's contributions" (Schlessinger and Robbins 1983, 194), the concept of the defense transference has had no currency elsewhere. It is a thoroughly local doctrine, and Chicago psychoanalysts alone still teach it. Psychoanalysts elsewhere (especially followers of Winnicott, Ferenczi, and other object relations theorists) had already accepted the need for a more supportive, less suspicious approach to the patient, and "relational" theorists who followed them pushed this idea much farther than Gitelson or his group did, banishing any notion that the patient's relationship with the analyst might "contaminate" the transference.

30 For Gitelson, "characterological traits and defenses develop as an adaptive solution to separation-individuation problems and then serve as a defense against Oedipal conflicts. Their genetic roots require analytic exploration for effective re-solution of psychoneurotic conflicts." Gitelson 1973, 168. Gitelson and his followers therefore distinguished an *analytic* alliance from a merely *therapeutic* alliance; Oedipal patients alone were capable of an analytic alliance; sicker patients, those fixated at the level of developmentally earlier separation-individuation problems, could not.

31 Forman (1976, 65) conceded, "That some patients with Oedipal neuroses present pictures that resemble narcissistic disorders is true, but careful analytic work can distinguish between the two. It is also true that patients initially appearing to have Oedipal configurations—for instance, men who appear to have a phallic narcissistic neurosis—are often actually patients with narcissistic personality disorders. Women with regressions to phallic narcissistic and Oedipal fixation points, with much separation anxiety and penis envy, can initially present confusing pathologies because of the massiveness of the secondary narcissistic factors in the defense transference." Recall that for Freud the woman's wish for a penis and the man's fear of femininity were psychological bedrock, liable to cause suffering—and necessitate interminable analysis—even after the analyst had "penetrated through all the [other] psychological strata." Freud 1937a, 252.

32 After Pollock's ouster in the late 1980s, a closet full of *Annuals* was found by the new director, who also discovered that Pollock had suppressed Institute balance sheets that were dramatically in the red. Interview with Arnold Goldberg, April 28, 2009.

33 According to Kirsner, the 1991 APsaA site visitors were most impressed with the Committee on Committees idea, "the finest example of the changes brought about by the Reorganization." Kirsner 2000, 134.

34 Not only were there fewer applicants—and this despite the fact that after the lawsuit psychologists, social workers, and counselors could all train—there was more competition: a group of psychologists had set up an institute in Chicago that was attracting trainees who did not want to be associated with the medical history of the Institute, and distance-learning programs in New York, Los Angeles, and Washington, D.C., were attracting Chicago people interested in relational perspectives.

35 It is necessary to be clear here. While the analysts could readily find patients wishing once-weekly psychotherapy and able to afford a typical psychotherapy fee of $150 to $200 per session, finding patients willing and able to afford four times that (for four sessions per week) became well-nigh impossible; if a prospective patient could only afford $200 a week, it was clear that the analyst would recommend once-weekly therapy; in other words, the question could no longer be which treatment was going to be most helpful for the patient; it was which treatment did the analyst prefer to perform, given these economics.

36 I read this meeting along the lines of Victor Turner's approach to social drama (for his method, see Turner 1988). In introducing the speakers, Anderson announced that the meeting was being recorded, adding, with a note of humor that the audience clearly appreciated, "Don't say anything that you don't want to have on the tape." Anderson also generously provided me with copies of notes that several of the presenters had used to prepare their comments.

37 The idea of a "vertical split" is Kohut's, and it has been elaborated on by Goldberg (1999). Whereas Freud visualized a horizontal repression barrier between what was conscious and what was unconscious—Freud's repression barrier was not necessarily pathological—Kohut's vertical split was a pathological divide between different "selves" that were not in contact with one another. This latter kind of not-knowing is understood as *disavowal* rather than repression; the paradigmatic case of the vertical split is a high-functioning person who shoplifts compulsively and who, when confronted, genuinely feels she doesn't know why she does it.

CHAPTER 6. ON NARCISSISM

1 Goldberg and Shane have each mapped the several main strands of post-Kohutian self psychology. See Goldberg 2002; Shane and Shane 1993. Each identify a "mainline" group of writers intent on furthering Kohut's own theorizing, a group focusing on intersubjectivity, and a group focusing on the vicissitudes of the "object."

2 Quoted interview material in this chapter is drawn from interviews with "Peter Shapiro," "John Brandon," "Norm Peters," "Penny Gould," and "Carrie Janis."

3 As noted, session frequency had a long history at the center of debates surrounding training, and it remains a key criterion on which an institute's membership in the APsaA or the IPA turns. In the IPA bylaws the required frequency is three sessions per week, whereas in the APsaA it is "five (or four)." Unsurprisingly, there is acrimony around this differential in recent discussions of proposals that would allow IPA analysts to join the APsaA, since if this were to happen, in the words of one of the BOPS chairs in a 2004 letter to the International Psychoanalytical Association, "psychoanalysis could be reduced to a way of thinking, rather than the practice of a rigorous and unique clinical discipline." Eric Nuetzel, unpublished letter, September 12, 2004, 1.

4 BOPS representative at meeting with Chicago Institute, October 16, 2009. There was also much talk about "the public" needing these.

5 A Minor Revisions Task Force was given the assignment of looking at the current standards and trying to clean them up so that they could be more easily implemented. A Major Revisions Task Force was given the assignment of coming up with a proposal to substantially revise the existing processes and to deal with some of the central questions, for example, whether it should be possible to have people in full training in analysis with non-TAs and whether there should be routes to becoming a TA that would not involve the current certification process.

6 BOPS representative at meeting with Chicago Institute, October 16, 2009.

7 In Chicago the ratio of faculty to students was at an all-time high, almost four faculty for every one trainee.

8 The situation is even more baroque; the actual waiver goes to the institute, which is then allowed to count a given "couple" as engaged in an analysis that can lead to graduation. The waiver is, in this sense, specific to the couple, with the couple functioning under the dispensation that has been obtained by the Institute. Institutes had to choose whether they wanted to operate under the waiver-based system or the traditional system.

9 The ambiguity of the new standards statement prompted one blogger to write:

> Only Franz Kafka could fully illuminate the peculiar gyrations of the never-say-die BOPS folks who have generated an ever-expanding maze of "alternative pathways," verticalized "immersion requirements," tracks for three-times-a-weekers and four-times-a-weekers, post-certification rejection counseling, two-case inter-rater reliability studies, and a proposed penal colony for analysts who skype. . . . BOPS says it is being "flexible" and there's no reason to doubt its good intentions . . . but to anyone with sociological leanings, it looks more like a tribal attempt to hold onto power by co-opting as many constituencies as possible, all under the rubric of "standards," and with a capacity to generate new shapes and forms that might earn praise from old Proteus. (Charles Morgan, email posted to APsaA Members List, January 21, 2009, quoted with the author's permission)

10 Recall that Alexander aimed at avoiding "a too intensive dependent transference leading to an interminable analysis." Alexander 1950, 485.

11 In a recent study on "deepening" in psychotherapy, Servatius provides a first-person account much like Penny's.

> "I think depth means getting to the non-verbal and pre-verbal level of connecting, doing a lot of work non-verbally as well as verbally, depending on where the client is at. And it means using, basically, my whole self, because I think you only get half, you only get part of it through the overt verbal and physical goings on in the room. I also have to search what's happening inside me. So when I'm doing that and when the client is really letting me in—it's a very subjective kind of term—but then I know that there's something in-depth going on. And when I have a client and I'm having trouble feeling [connected], something is missing, then I feel like there's a way in which the client is really not connected to themselves very well and I am finding it much harder to connect. But that's still dealing with the in-depth of the treatment. (Servatius 2010, 64)

12 Goldberg, from a June 13, 1994, interview with Douglas Kirsner on the subject of whether Kohut can be thought of as an heir to Winnicott. Kirsner's unpublished data is cited with permission.

13 This is obviously much more complex, and I am emphasizing the particular facet of the argument that I am interested in, the reinstatement of the object's importance. See Newman 1999, 185:

> Neither Winnicott nor Kohut seemed to recommend the need for the analyst to be immersed in the countertransference to effect a facilitating environment conducive to therapeutic regression. Rather, they emphasized an empathic availability that was welcoming and receptive to the narcissistic transferences deployed onto them—essentially offering themselves as the good object to be used for creating expressions of the authentic self and for rewording the damaging effects of early trauma. They did not see themselves as inevitably being drawn into the countertransference as a necessary part of the therapeutic action. Of course, they addressed countertransference issues, but, for the most part, it was for the purpose of having the analyst recognize the impact the patient's way of "relating" or "nonrelating" was having on them. Grasping the patient's need for the analyst to accept the unique quality of his narcissistic use of the space, which often includes nonawareness of the analyst, is actually a crucial part of the holding environment. It requires management of one's own countertransference reactions to seemingly being nonsignificant, and, in fact, it is this capacity to hold the virtual relationship which becomes part of the facilitating environment. But the notion of becoming engaged affectively through the complex and mutual effects of transference/countertransference did not seem to be essential to Kohut's and Winnicott's work.

See also Newman 2007.

14 Gaining referrals is, no doubt, implicated in this face-work, since depictions of "real relationships" serve metapragmatically as signs of recognition that constitute speakers' competencies, generating and sustaining (transferable) intuitions of effective (and affective!) language use in context.

15 I follow Foucault ([1977] 1980, 194) in using *dispositif*, often translated as *apparatus*, to pick out "a thoroughly heterogeneous ensemble consisting of discourses, institutions, architectural forms, regulatory decisions, laws, administrative measures, scientific statements, philosophical, moral and philanthropic propositions—in short, the said as much as the unsaid." In Foucault's words, "The apparatus itself is the system of relations that can be established between these elements."

16 It is perhaps ironic that an increasingly "maternal" practice of curative care for "pre-Oedipal" disorder is grounded thus in a paternal discourse of legitimation.

17 It must be noted that this "market," the consumers of psychoanalysis, is made up increasingly exclusively of other therapists. On historical problematization, see also Osborne 2003.

18 Neither of these laws required that plans provide mental health/substance abuse coverage; they only specified that where such coverage is provided it must be on par with medical-surgical coverage.

19 Another leading figure in American psychiatry, the author of numerous articles and books put out by the American Psychiatric Association, shared his outrage at the proposed removal of narcissism from the new edition of the DSM. In an email interview on May 6, 2010, he wrote: "The problem is that the [DSM] Work Group feels there isn't enough empirical data to support the diagnosis. I have argued that the reason for that is simple—it's not a diagnosis that lends itself to diagnosis through a traditional research interview. If you ask a narso grosso [*sic*] person, 'Do you feel that you are entitled to special treatment?,' he/she will answer, 'No, of course not.' So you can't get data like you can for other diagnoses. Nonetheless, clinicians know it when they see it." He asked not to be quoted by name if I wished to use his "narso grosso" quip.

REFERENCES

Abbas, Ackbar. 1999. "Dialectic of Deception." *Public Culture* 11, 347–363.

Abbott, Andrew. 1988. *The System of Professions: An Essay on the Division of Expert Labor*. Chicago: University of Chicago Press.

———. 1993. "The Sociology of Work and Occupations." *Annual Review of Sociology* 19, 187–209.

———. 2001. *Chaos of Disciplines*. Chicago: University of Chicago Press.

Abraham, Nicolas, and Maria Torok. 1994. *The Shell and the Kernel: Renewals of Psychoanalysis*. Trans. Nicholas Rand. Vol. 1. Chicago: University of Chicago Press.

Acklin, Marvin W. 1994. "Psychodiagnosis of Personality Structure III: Neurotic Personality Organization." *Journal of Personality Assessment* 63, no. 1, 1–9.

Agamben, Giorgio. 1990. *Homo Sacer: Sovereign Power and Bare Life*. Stanford: Stanford University Press.

Akiskal, Hagop, S. Chen, G. Davis, V. Puzantian, M. Kashgarian, and J. Bolinger. 1985. "Borderline: An Adjective in Search of a Noun." *Journal of Clinical Psychiatry* 46, no. 2, 41–48.

Alexander, Franz. 1938. "Section Meeting on Culture and Personality." *American Journal of Orthopsychiatry* 8, no. 4, 587–626.

———. 1948. *The Fundamentals of Psychoanalysis*. New York: Norton.

———. 1950. "Analysis of the Therapeutic Factors in Psychoanalytic Treatment." *Psychoanalytic Quarterly* 19, 482–500.

———. 1960. *The Western Mind in Transition: An Eyewitness Story*. New York: Random House.

———. 1961. *The Scope of Psychoanalysis 1921–1961: Selected Papers of Franz Alexander*. New York: Basic Books.

Alexander, Franz, and Thomas French. 1946. *Psychoanalytic Therapy: Principles and Application*. New York: Ronald Press.

Alexander, Franz, and William Healy. 1935. *Roots of Crime*. New York: Knopf.

Alexander, Franz, and Helen Ross, eds. 1952. *Dynamic Psychiatry*. Chicago: University of Chicago Press.

————, eds. 1953. *20 Years of Psychoanalysis: A Symposium in Celebration of the Twentieth Anniversary of the Chicago Institute for Psychoanalysis*. New York: Norton.

Alexander, Franz, and Hugo Staub. 1957. *The Criminal, the Judge, and the Public*. Glencoe, IL: Free Press.

Alford, C. Fred. 2002. *Levinas, the Frankfurt School and Psychoanalysis*. Middletown, CT: Wesleyan University Press.

Allison, George. 2000. "The Shortage of Psychoanalytic Patients." *Psychoanalytic Inquiry* 20, 527–540.

Alperin, Richard M., and David G. Phillip, eds. 1997. *The Impact of Managed Care on the Practice of Psychotherapy: Innovation, Implementation, and Controversy*. New York: Brunner/Mazel.

American Psychiatric Association. 1952. *Diagnostic and Statistical Manual of Mental Disorders*. Washington, DC: American Psychiatric Association.

————. 2000. *Diagnostic and Statistical Manual of Mental Disorders*. 4th ed., text revision. Washington, DC: American Psychiatric Association.

American Psychoanalytic Association. 1951. "Events in the Psychoanalytic World." *Bulletin of the American Psychoanalytic Association*, no. 7, 203–228.

————. 1955. "Report of the Survey Steering Committee of the Board on Professional Standards." Unpublished report (known as the "Rainbow Report").

————. 1974. "Fall Meeting—December 12–16, 1973." *Bulletin of the American Psychoanalytic Association*, no. 30, 430–454.

————. 1975. "Annual Meeting—April 30–May 4, 1975." *Bulletin of the American Psychoanalytic Association*, no. 31, 867–889.

————. 1989. "Fall Meeting—December 14–18, 1988." *Bulletin of the American Psychoanalytic Association*, no. 45, 531–555.

————. 1994. "Practice Bulletin no. 2, Charting Psychoanalysis." Accessed December 11, 2013. http://www.apsa.org/About_APsaA/Practice_Bulletins.aspx.

————. 1996a. "Practice Bulletin no. 4, Charting Psychoanalysis, a Clarification." Accessed December 11, 2013. http://www.apsa.org/About_APsaA/Practice_Bulletins.aspx.

————. 1996b. "Practice Bulletin no. 5, Appointment Records." Accessed December 11, 2013. http://www.apsa.org/About_APsaA/Practice_Bulletins.aspx.

————. 1999. "Practice Bulletin no. 3, External Review of Psychoanalysis." Accessed December 11, 2013. http://www.apsa.org/About_APsaA/Practice_Bulletins.aspx.

————. 2001. "Practice Bulletin no. 6, Interacting with Third Parties." Accessed December 11, 2013. http://www.apsa.org/About_APsaA/Practice_Bulletins.aspx.

————. 2003. "Practice Bulletin no. 1, Informed Consent to Review." Revised. Accessed December 11, 2013. http://www.apsa.org/About_APsaA/Practice_Bulletins.aspx.

————. 2006. "Practice Bulletin no. 7, Psychoanalytic Clinical Assessment." Accessed December 11, 2013. http://www.apsa.org/About_APsaA/Practice_Bulletins.aspx.

———. 2009. "A Clarification Regarding the American Psychoanalytic Association's Training Analyst System." Board of Professional Standards. Unpublished memo.

———. 2010a. "Standards for Education and Training in Psychoanalysis." Accessed December 11, 2013. http://apsa.org/Portals/1/docs/Training/Standards.pdf.

———. 2010b. "Task Force on Educational Standards Revision (TFESR) Joint Task Force Meeting—January 9 & 10, 2010 Summary of Actions Taken." Unpublished memo.

Anders, Eric. 2000. "Disturbing Psychoanalytic Origins: A Derridean Reading of Freudian Theory." Ph.D. diss., University of Florida.

Anderson, Christopher. 2000. "Dealing Constructively with Managed Care: Suggestions from an Insider." *Journal of Mental Health Counseling* 22, no. 4, 343–353.

Apfelbaum, Bernard. 2005. "The Persistence of Layering Logic: Drive Theory in Another Guise." *Contemporary Psychoanalysis* 41, 159–161.

Appelbaum, Stephen A. 1992. "Evils in the Private Practice of Psychotherapy." *Bulletin of the Menninger Clinic* 56, no. 2, 141–149.

Arlow, Jacob A. 1972. "Some Dilemmas in Psychoanalytic Education." *Journal of the American Psychoanalytic Association* 20, no. 3, 556–566.

Aron, Lew. 2002. *A Meeting of Minds: Mutuality in Psychoanalysis*. Hillsdale, NJ: Analytic Press.

Austed, C. 1996. *Is Long-Term Psychotherapy Unethical? Toward a Social Ethic in an Era of Managed Care*. San Francisco: Jossey-Bass.

Bacal, Howard A. 1988. "Reflections on 'Optimum Frustration.'" *Progress in Self Psychology* 4, 127–131.

———, ed. 1998. *Optimal Responsiveness: How Therapists Heal Their Patients*. Northvale, NJ: Jason Aronson.

Bacal, Howard A., and Kenneth M. Newman. 1990. *Theories of Object Relations: Bridges to Self Psychology*. New York: Columbia University Press.

Baert, Patrick. 2005. *Philosophy of the Social Sciences: Towards Pragmatism*. Cambridge: Polity.

Baily, Mary Ann. 2003. "Managed Care Organizations and the Rationing Problem." *Hastings Center Report* 33, no. 1, 34–42.

Baker, Grace. (1947) 1988. "Letter from Grace Baker to William C. Menninger, 2 Dec. 1947." *The Selected Correspondence of Karl A. Menninger, 1919–1945.* Ed. Howard J. Faulkner and Virginia D. Pruitt. New Haven: Yale University Press.

Balint, M. 1954. "Analytic Training and Training Analysis." *International Journal of Psychoanalysis* 35, no. 2, 157–62.

Baranger, Madeleine, Willy Baranger, and Jorge Mom. 1983. "Process and Nonprocess in Analytic Work." *International Journal of Psychoanalysis* 64, 1–15.

Barnouw, Victor. 1985. *Culture and Personality*. 4th ed. Homewood, IL: Dorsey.

Barratt, Barnaby B. 1993. *Psychoanalysis and the Postmodern Impulse: Knowing and Being since Freud's Psychology*. Baltimore: Johns Hopkins University Press.

Barry, Andrew, Thomas Osborne, and Nikolas S. Rose. 1996. *Foucault and Political Reason: Liberalism, Neo-liberalism, and Rationalities of Government*. Chicago: University of Chicago Press.

Bartholomew, Robert E. 2000. *Exotic Deviance: Medicalizing Cultural Idioms: From Strangeness to Illness*. Boulder: University Press of Colorado.

Bartlett, Tom, Charles Morgan, and Paul Mosher. 2005. *Useful Demographics Committee White Paper (Range and Average Training Costs in APsaA Institutes; Salaries, as of January 5, 2005; Age at Time of Becoming Active Member of APsaA; Age at Time of Achieving APsaA Certification; Membership Stats; Candidate Demographics)*. New York: American Psychoanalytic Association.

Bass, Alan. 1997. "The Problem of 'Concreteness.'" *Psychoanalytic Quarterly* 66, 642–682.

———. 2000. *Difference and Disavowal: The Trauma of Eros*. Stanford: Stanford University Press.

———. 2006. *Interpretation and Difference: The Strangeness of Care*. Stanford: Stanford University Press.

Bass, Jeffrey. 2006. "In Exile from the Self: National Belonging and Psychoanalysis in Buenos Aires." *Ethos* 34, no. 4, 433–455.

Bates, David. 2005. "Crisis between the Wars: Derrida and the Origins of Undecidability." *Representations* 90, 1–27.

Bayer, Ronald, and Robert L. Spitzer. 1985. "Neurosis, Psychodynamics, and DSM III: A History of the Controversy." *Archives of General Psychiatry* 42, 187–196.

Beck, Ulrich. 1992. *Risk Society: Towards a New Modernity*. Trans. Mark Ritter. London: Sage.

Bellah, Robert N. 1999. "Max Weber and World-Denying Love: A Look at the Historical Sociology of Religion." *Journal of the American Academy of Religion* 67, no. 2, 77–304.

Benedek, Therese. 1969. "Training Analysis—Past, Present and Future." *International Journal of Psychoanalysis* 50, 437–445.

Benjamin, Jessica. 1995. *Like Subjects, Love Objects: Essays on Recognition and Sexual Difference*. New Haven: Yale University Press.

Benvenuto, Sergio. 1999. "Eyes Wide Shut: Is Psychoanalysis in Touch with the Real? Scientific Ideals, Hermeneutics and the Relation to the Real in Psychoanalytic Practice." *Journal of European Psychoanalysis* 8, no. 9, 43–66.

Berg, Marc. 1997. *Rationalizing Medical Work: Decision-Support Techniques and Medical Practices*. Cambridge, MA: MIT Press.

Bergmann, Martin, ed. 2004. *Understanding Dissidence and Controversy in the History of Psychoanalysis*. New York: Other Press.

Bergmann, Martin S. 1988. "Who Is a Lay Analyst?" *Psychoanalytic Review* 75, 361–172.

Berlant, Lauren, ed. 2000. *Intimacy*. Chicago: University of Chicago Press.

———. 2008. *The Female Complaint: The Unfinished Business of Sentimentality in American Culture*. Durham, NC: Duke University Press.

———. 2011. *Cruel Optimism*. Durham, NC: Duke University Press.

Berman, Emanuel. 2004. *Impossible Training: A Relational View of Psychoanalytic Education*. Hillsdale, NJ: Analytic Press.

Bernfeld, Siegfried. 1962. "On Psychoanalytic Training." *Psychoanalytic Quarterly* 31, 453–482.

Bersani, Leo. 1986. *The Freudian Body: Psychoanalysis and Art*. New York: Columbia University Press.

Betan, Ephi, Amy Kegley Heim, Carolyn Zittel Conklin, and Drew Westen. 2005. "Countertransference Phenomena and Personality Pathology in Clinical Practice: An Empirical Investigation." *American Journal of Psychiatry* 162, 890–898.

Beutler, Larry E., and Mary L. Malik, eds. 2002. *Rethinking DSM: A Psychological Perspective*. Washington, DC: American Psychological Association.

Biehl, João. 2005. *Vita: Life in a Zone of Social Abandonment*. Berkeley: University of California Press.

Birenbaum, Arnold. 1997. *Managed Care: Made in America*. Westport, CT: Praeger.

Blackman, Jerome S. 2004. *101 Defenses: How the Mind Shields Itself*. New York: Brunner-Routledge.

Blanchot, Maurice. 1988. *The Unavowable Community*. Trans. Pierre Joris. Barrytown, NY: Station Hill.

Blanck, Gertrude. 1998. "Lay Analysis in the Postwar Years." *Journal of the American Psychoanalytic Association* 46, no. 4, 1243–1245.

Blanck, Gertrude, and Rubin Blanck. 1994. *Ego Psychology: Theory and Practice*. New York: Columbia University Press.

Bleger, José. 1967. "Psychoanalysis of the Psycho-analytic Frame." *International Journal of Psychoanalysis* 48, 511–519.

Blitzsten, N. Lionel, Ruth S. Eissler, and K. R. Eissler. 1950. "Emergence of Hidden Ego Tendencies during Dream Analysis." *International Journal of Psychoanalysis* 31, 12–17.

Blitzsten, N. Lionel, and Joan Fleming. 1953. "What Is a Supervisory Analysis?" *Bulletin of the Menninger Clinic*, July.

Blum, Harold P. 2004. "The Wise Baby and the Wild Analyst." *Psychoanalytic Psychology* 21, 3–15.

Bollas, Christopher. 1983. "Expressive Uses of the Countertransference—Notes to the Patient from Oneself." *Contemporary Psychoanalysis* 19, 1–33.

Bollas, Christopher, and David Sundelson. 1995. *The New Informants: The Betrayal of Confidentiality in Psychoanalysis and Psychotherapy*. London: Karnac Books.

Borch-Jacobsen, Mikkel. 1988. *The Freudian Subject*. Stanford: Stanford University Press.

Bornstein, Robert F. 2001. "The Impending Death of Psychoanalysis." *Psychoanalytic Psychology* 18, 3–20.

Bos, Jaap, David W. Park, and Petteri Pietikainen. 2005. "Strategic Self-Marginalization: Case of Psychoanalysis." *Journal of the History of the Behavioral Sciences* 41, no. 3, 207–224.

Bourdieu, Pierre. 1977. *Outline of a Theory of Practice*. Trans. Richard Nice. Cambridge: Cambridge University Press.

——. 1984. *Distinction: A Social Critique of the Judgement of Taste*. Trans. Richard Nice. Cambridge, MA: Harvard University Press.

——. 1985. "The Social Space and the Genesis of Groups." *Theory and Society* 14, no. 6, 723–744.

——. 1988. *Homo Academicus*. Trans. Peter Collier. Stanford: Stanford University Press.

Bourdieu, Pierre, and Loïc J. D. Wacquant. 1992. *An Invitation to Reflexive Sociology*. Chicago: University of Chicago Press.

Bowlby, John. 1982. *Attachment and Loss*. Vol. 1. 2nd ed. New York: Basic Books.

Boyer, Dominic. 2006. "Conspiracy, History, and Therapy at a Berlin *Stammtisch*." *American Ethnologist* 33, no. 3, 327–339.

Brauer, Lee David, Samuel Brauer, and David I. Falk. 2008. *Report on the 2006 Survey of Analytic Practice*. New York: American Psychoanalytic Association.

Brenneis, Donald. 2008. "Telling Theories." *Ethos* 36, no. 1, 155–169.

Brenner, Charles. 1974. *An Elementary Textbook of Psychoanalysis*. New York: Anchor.

——. 1979. "Working Alliance, Therapeutic Alliance, and Transference." *Journal of the American Psychoanalytic Association* 27, 137–157.

Brent, Stuart. 1989. *The Seven Stairs: An Adventure of the Heart*. New York: Simon and Schuster.

Breuer, Joseph, and Sigmund Freud. 1895. *Studies in Hysteria*. Trans. A. A. Brill. Boston: Beacon.

Brickman, Celia. 2003. *Aboriginal Populations in the Mind: Race and Primitivity in Psychoanalysis*. New York: Columbia University Press.

Brint, Steven. 1994. *In an Age of Experts: The Changing Role of Professionals in Politics and Public Life*. Princeton: Princeton University Press.

Brodwin, Paul. 2008. "The Coproduction of Moral Discourse in Community Psychiatry." *Medical Anthropology Quarterly* 22, no. 2, 127–147.

Bromberg, Philip M. 1998. *Standing in the Spaces: Essays on Clinical Process, Trauma, and Dissociation*. Hillsdale, NJ: Analytic Press.

Bronner, Stephen Eric. 2002. *Of Critical Theory and Its Theorists*. 2nd ed. New York: Routledge.

Brown, Norman O. 1986. *Life against Death: The Psychoanalytical Meaning of History*. Middletown, CT: Wesleyan University Press.

Brown, Phil. 1995. "Naming and Framing: The Social Construction of Diagnosis and Illness." *Journal of Health and Social Behavior* 35, 34–52.

Brown, Theodore M. 1987. "Alan Gregg and the Rockefeller Foundation's Support of Franz Alexander's Psychosomatic Research." *Bulletin of the History of Medicine* 61, no. 2, 155–182.

Brown, Wendy. 1995. *States of Injury: Power and Freedom in Late Modernity*. Princeton: Princeton University Press.

Browner, C. H. 1999. "On the Medicalization of Medical Anthropology." *Medical Anthropology Quarterly* 13, no. 2, 135–140.

Browning, Don S. 1997. "Can Psychoanalysis Inform Ethics? If So, How?" *Journal of Religion* 77, no. 2, 278–282.

Buchanan, Roderick D. 2003. "Legislative Warriors: American Psychiatrists, Psychologists, and Competing Claims over Psychotherapy in the 1950s." *Journal of the History of the Behavioral Sciences* 39, no. 3, 225–249.

Bulmer, M., and J. Bulmer. 1981. "Philanthropy and Social Science in the 1920s: Beardsley Ruml and the Laura Spelman Rockefeller Memorial, 1922–1929." *Minerva* 19, 347–407.

Bunzl, Matti. 2004. "Boas, Foucault, and the 'Native Anthropologist': Notes toward a Neo-Boasian Anthropology." *American Anthropologist* 106, no. 3, 435–442.

Burchell, Graham. 1996. "Liberal Government and Techniques of the Self." *Foucault and Political Reason: Liberalism, Neo-Liberalism, and Rationalities of Government.* Ed. Andrew Barry, Thomas Osborne and Nikolas Rose, 19–36. Chicago: University of Chicago Press.

Burchell, Graham, Colin Gordon, and Peter Miller, eds. 1991. *The Foucault Effect: Studies in Governmentality.* Chicago: University of Chicago Press.

Burnham, John C. 1978. "The Influence of Psychoanalysis upon American Culture." *American Psychoanalysis: Origins and Development.* Ed. J. Quen and E. T. Carlson, 52–72. New York: Brunner/Mazel.

———. 1988. "Psychology and Counseling: Convergence into a Profession." *The Professions in American History.* Ed. Nathan O. Hatch, 181–198. South Bend, IN: University of Notre Dame Press.

Buse, William. 1999. "The Alternate Session: Memory and Membership in a Psychoanalytic Society." Ph.D. diss., Columbia University.

Butler, Judith. (1987) 1999. *Subjects of Desire: Hegelian Reflections in Twentieth-Century France.* New York: Columbia University Press.

———. 1997a. *Excitable Speech: A Politics of the Performative.* New York: Routledge.

———. 1997b. *The Psychic Life of Power: Theories in Subjection.* Stanford: Stanford University Press.

———. 1999. *Gender Trouble: Feminism and the Subversion of Identity.* New York: Routledge.

———. 2005. *Giving an Account of Oneself.* New York: Fordham University Press.

———. 2006. *Precarious Life: The Powers of Mourning and Violence.* New York: Verso.

Cabaniss, Deborah L., Nicholas Forand, and Steven P. Roose. 2004. "Conducting Analysis after September 11: Implications for Psychoanalytic Technique." *Journal of the American Psychoanalytic Association* 52, 717–734.

Callahan, J. J., D. S. Shepard, R. H. Beinecke, and M. J. Larson. 1995. "Mental Health / Substance Abuse Treatment in Managed Care." *Health Affairs* 3, 173–184.

Canguilhem, Georges. 1991. *The Normal and the Pathological.* Trans. Carolyn R. Fawcett. New York: Zone Books.

Caplan, Eric. 2001. *Mind Games: American Culture and the Birth of Psychotherapy.* Berkeley: University of California Press.

Castells, Manuel. 2000. *The Rise of the Network Society.* Malden, MA: Blackwell.

Castoriadis, Cornelius. 1984. *Crossroads in the Labyrinth*. Trans. Kate Soper and Martin H. Ryle. Cambridge, MA: MIT Press.

———. 2005. *The Imaginary Institution of Society*. Trans. Kathleen Blamey. Cambridge: Polity.

Chandler, James, Arnold I. Davidson, and Harry Harootunian, eds. 1994. *Questions of Evidence: Proof, Practice, and Persuasion across the Disciplines*. Chicago: University of Chicago Press.

Chapman, P. D. 1988. *Schools as Sorters: Lewis M. Terman, Applied Psychology, and the Intelligence Testing Movement, 1890–1930*. New York: New York University.

Chester, Robin. 2003. "Psychoanalysis and Crisis." *Psychoanalysis Downunder*, no. 4, n.p.

Chicago Institute for Psychoanalysis. 1947. *Institute for Psychoanalysis, Report of the Five Year Period 1942–1947*. Chicago: Chicago Institute for Psychoanalysis.

———. 1960. *The Chicago Institute for Psychoanalysis/1960*. Chicago: Chicago Institute for Psychoanalysis.

———. n.d. *Interview with Helen McLean (Glenn Miller)*. Chicago Institute for Psychoanalysis Library, Film Archive. Unpublished film.

———. n.d. *Interview with Helen McLean and Lucia Tower (Glenn Miller)*. Chicago Institute for Psychoanalysis Library, Film Archive. Unpublished film.

———. n.d. *Interview with Joan Fleming (Louis Shapiro)*. Chicago Institute for Psychoanalysis Library, Film Archive. Unpublished film.

———. n.d. *Interview with Roy R. Grinker (Brenda Solomon)*. Chicago Institute for Psychoanalysis Library, Film Archive. Unpublished film.

Chodorow, Nancy J. 1999. *The Power of Feelings: Personal Meaning in Psychoanalysis, Gender, and Culture*. New Haven: Yale University Press.

Chrysanthou, Marc. 2002. "Transparency and Selfhood: Utopia and the Informed Body." *Social Science and Medicine* 54, no. 3, 469–479.

Clemens, Norman. 2003. "HIPAA: A Report from the Front Lines." *Journal of Psychiatric Practice* 9, no. 3, 237–239.

Cocks, Geoffrey, ed. 1994. *The Curve of Life: Correspondence of Heinz Kohut, 1923–1981*. Chicago: University of Chicago Press.

Cohen, J., J. Marecek, and J. Gillham. 2006. "Is Three a Crowd? Clients, Clinicians, and Managed Care." *American Journal of Orthopsychiatry* 76, no. 2, 251–259.

Colarusso, Calvin. 1985. "A Developmental View of the Psychoanalytic Process. Follow-Up Studies and Their Consequences. (Emotions and Behavior Monograph 1.): By Nathan Schlessinger, M.D., and Fred P. Robbins, M.D. New York: International Universities Press, Inc., 1983. 228 pp." *Psychoanalytic Quarterly*, no. 54, 281–286.

Cole, Jonathan R. 1970. "Patterns of Intellectual Influence in Scientific Research." *Sociology of Education* 43, 377–403.

Comaroff, Jean. 2007. "Beyond the Politics of Bare Life: AIDS and the Global Order." *Public Culture* 19, no. 1, 197–219.

Comaroff, Jean, and John Comaroff. 1992. *Ethnography and the Historical Imagination*. Boulder: Westview.

———. 1999. "Occult Economies and the Violence of Abstraction: Notes from the South African Postcolony." *American Ethnologist* 26, no. 2, 279–301.

———. 2000. "2000 Millennial Capitalism: First Thoughts on a Second Coming." *Public Culture* 12, no. 2, 291–343.

———. 2003. "Ethnography on an Awkward Scale: Postcolonial Anthropology and the Violence of Abstraction. *Ethnography* 4, no. 2, 291–324.

Cooper, Melinda. 2008. *Life as Surplus: Biotechnology and Capitalism in the Neoliberal Era*. Seattle: University of Washington Press.

Cooper, Steven H. 2007. "Alexander's Corrective Emotional Experience: An Objective Turn in Psychoanalytic Authority and Technique." *Psychoanalytic Quarterly* 76, 1085–1102.

Coopersmith, Sy. 2005. "Determinants of Licensing in Psychoanalysis: Exclusivity and Pluralism." *Psychoanalytic Review* 92, no. 6, 895–905.

Copjec, Joan, ed. 1994. *Supposing the Subject*. London: Verso.

Couch, Arthur. 1999. "Therapeutic Functions of the Real Relationship in Psychoanalysis." *Psychoanalytic Study of the Child* 54, 130–168.

Crane, Diana. 1969. "Social Structure in a Group of Scientists: A Test of the 'Invisible College' Hypothesis." *American Sociological Review* 34, no. 3, 335–352.

———. 1972. *Invisible Colleges: Diffusion of Knowledge in Scientific Communities*. Chicago: University of Chicago Press.

Crapanzano, Vincent. 1992. *Hermes' Dilemma and Hamlet's Desire: On the Epistemology of Interpretation*. Cambridge, MA: Harvard University Press.

Crawford, R. 1980. "Healthism and the Medicalization of Everyday Life." *International Journal of Health Services: Planning, Administration, Evaluation* 10, no. 3, 365–388.

Crowley, Ralph M. 1978. "Psychiatry, Psychiatrists, and Psychoanalysts: Reminiscences of Madison, Chicago and Washington-Baltimore in the 1930s." *Journal of the American Academy of Psychoanalysis* 6, 557–567.

Cummings, Nicholas A., Michael S. Pallak, and Janet L. Cummings, eds. 1996. *Surviving the Demise of Solo Practice: Mental Health Practitioners Prospering in the Era of Managed Care*. Madison, CT: Psychosocial Press.

Cushman, Philip. 1995. *Constructing the Self, Constructing America: A Cultural History of Psychotherapy*. Reading, MA: Addison-Wesley.

Danziger, Paula, and Elizabeth Welfel. 2001. "The Impact of Managed Care on Mental Health Counselors: A Survey of Perceptions, Practices, and Compliance with Ethical Standards." *Journal of Mental Health Counseling* 23, no. 2, 137–150.

Davidson, Tim, Jeanette Davidson, and Sharon Keigher. 1999. "Managed Care: Satisfaction Guaranteed. Not!" *Health and Social Work* 24, no. 3, 163–169.

Davies, James. 2009. *The Making of Psychotherapists: An Anthropological Analysis*. London: Karnac Books.

Davis, Douglas A. 1994. "A Theory for the 90s: Traumatic Seduction in Historical Context." *Psychoanalytic Review* 81, 627–639.

Davis, Elizabeth Anne. 2012. *Bad Souls: Madness and Responsibility in Modern Greece*. Durham, NC: Duke University Press.

Dean, Jodi. 2008. "Beginning Biopower." *I Cite*, December 30. http://jdeanicite .typepad.com/i_cite/2008/12/beginning-biopower.html.

———. 2009. "The Birth of Biopolitics (1): Liberalism Is Not a Dream." *I Cite*, January 5. http://jdeanicite.typepad.com/i_cite/2009/01/the-birth-of-biopolitics-1 -the-crisis-of-liberalism.html.

———. 2010. "Drive as the Structure of Biopolitics, Economy, Sovereignty, and Capture." *Krisis: Journal of Contemporary Philosophy*, no. 2, 2–15.

Dean, Mitchell. 1999. *Governmentality: Power and Rule in Modern Society*. London: Sage.

Decker, Hannah. 2013. *The Making of DSM-III®: A Diagnostic Manual's Conquest of American Psychiatry*. New York: Oxford University Press.

Deleuze, Gilles, and Felix Guattari. 1983. *Anti-Oedipus: Capitalism and Schizophrenia*. Trans. Robert Hurley, Mark Seem, and Helen R. Lane. Minneapolis: University of Minnesota Press.

———. 1987. *A Thousand Plateaus: Capitalism and Schizophrenia*. Trans. Brian Massumi. Minneapolis: University of Minneapolis Press.

Demos, John. 1978. "Oedipus and America: Historical Perspectives on the Reception of Psychoanalysis in the United States." *Annual of Psychoanalysis* 6, 23–39.

Derrida, Jacques. 1987. *The Post Card: From Socrates to Freud and Beyond*. Trans. Alan Bass. Chicago: University of Chicago Press.

———. 1992. "Force of Law: 'The Mystical Foundation of Authority.'" *Deconstruction and the Possibility of Justice*. Ed. Drucilla Cornell and Michael Rosenfeld, 3–67. New York: Routledge.

———. 1994. *Specters of Marx: The State of the Debt, the Work of Mourning and the New International*. Trans. Peggy Kamuf. New York: Routledge.

———. 1995. *Archive Fever: A Freudian Impression*. Trans. Eric Prenowitz. Chicago: University of Chicago Press.

———. 1998. *Resistances of Psychoanalysis*. Trans. Peggy Kamuf, Pascale-Anne Brault, and Michael Naas. Stanford: Stanford University Press.

———. 2005. *The Politics of Friendship*. Trans. George Collins. London: Verso.

———. 2007. *Psyche: Inventions of the Other*. Vol. 1. Ed. Peggy Kamuf and Elizabeth Rottenberg. Stanford: Stanford University Press.

———. 2008. *Psyche: Inventions of the Other*. Vol. 2. Ed. Peggy Kamuf and Elizabeth Rottenberg. Stanford: Stanford University Press.

Derrida, Jacques, and Giovanna Borradori. 2003. "Autoimmunity: Real and Symbolic Suicides." *Philosophy in a Time of Terror*. Ed. Giovanna Borradori. Chicago: University of Chicago Press.

Derrida, Jacques, and Anne Dufourmantelle. 2000. *Of Hospitality*. Trans. Rachel Bowlby. Ed Mieke Bal and Hent de Vries. Stanford: Stanford University Press.

Derrida, Jacques, and Jeffrey Mehlman. 1972. "Freud and the Scene of Writing." *Yale French Studies* 48, 74–117.

Devereux, George. 1978. *Ethnopsychoanalysis: Psychoanalysis and Anthropology as Complementary Frames of Reference.* Berkeley: University of California Press.

Dews, Peter. 2002. "Imagination and the Symbolic: Castoriadis and Lacan." *Constellations* 9, no. 4, 516–521.

Doctors, Shelley R. 1996. "Notes on the Contribution of the Analyst's Self-Awareness to Optimal Responsiveness." *Progress in Self Psychology* 12, 55–63.

Doidge, Norman. 1999. "How to Preserve Psychoanalysis: Introduction to Gunderson and Gabbard." *Journal of the American Psychoanalytic Association* 47, no. 3, 673–676.

Doidge, Norman, B. Simon, L. A. Gillies, and R. Ruskin. 1994. "Characteristics of Psychoanalytic Patients under a Nationalized Health Plan: DSM-III-R Diagnoses, Previous Treatment, and Childhood Trauma." *American Journal of Psychiatry* 151, 586–590.

Donald, A. 2001. "The Wal-Marting of American Psychiatry: An Ethnographic Study of Psychiatric Practice in the Late Twentieth Century." *Culture, Medicine, and Psychiatry* 25, no. 4, 427–439.

Dorn, Robert M., Howard F. Stein, and Burness E. Moore. 2006. "Genealogy in Psychoanalytic Education: Reinforced Adherence or Useful Aids toward Individuation?" *Psychoanalytic Psychology* 23, 8–29.

Dranove, David. 2000. *The Economic Evolution of American Health Care: From Marcus Welby to Managed Care.* Princeton: Princeton University Press.

Dufresne, Todd. 2002. "What's Next for Psychoanalysis?" *Semiotic Review of Books* 13, no. 1, 1.

———. 2003. *Killing Freud: Twentieth-Century Culture and the Death of Psychoanalysis.* London: Continuum.

———. 2007. "Psychoanalysis Eats Its Own: Or, the Heretical Saint Roazen." *Psychoanalysis and History* 9, no. 1, 93–109.

Dumit, Joseph. 2003. *Picturing Personhood: Brain Scans and Biomedical Identity.* Princeton, NJ: Princeton University Press.

Dumont, Louis. 1977. *From Mandeville to Marx: The Genesis and Triumph of Economic Ideology.* Chicago: University of Chicago Press.

———. 1986. *Essays on Individualism: Modern Ideology in Anthropological Perspective.* Chicago: University of Chicago Press.

Dunn, Jonathan. 1995. "Intersubjectivity in Psychoanalysis: A Critical Review." *International Journal of Psychoanalysis* 76, 723–738.

Dupuy, Jean Pierre. 2000. *The Mechanization of the Mind: On the Origins of Cognitive Science.* Princeton: Princeton University Press.

Eagleton, Terry. 1996. *The Illusions of Postmodernism.* Malden, MA: Blackwell.

Easser, Barbara Ruth, and Stanley R. Lesser. 1965. "Hysterical Personality: A Reevaluation." *Psychoanalytic Quarterly* 34, 390–405.

Eckhardt, M. H. 1978. "Organizational Schisms in American Psychoanalysis." *American Psychoanalysis: Origins and Development*. Ed. J. M. Quen and E. J. Carlson, 141–161. New York: Brunner/Mazel.

Edward, Joyce. 2009. "When Social Work and Psychoanalysis Meet." *Clinical Social Work Journal* 37, no. 1, 14–22.

Edward, Joyce, and Jean Sanville. 1996. *Fostering Healing and Growth: A Psychoanalytic Social Work Approach*. Northvale, NJ: Jason Aronson.

Ehrenberg, Darlene Bregman. 1992. *The Intimate Edge: Extending the Reach of Psychoanalytic Interaction*. New York: Norton.

Ehrenreich, Barbara. 2004. *Global Woman: Nannies, Maids, and Sex Workers in the New Economy*. New York: Owl Books.

Ehrenwald, Jan, ed. 1976. *The History of Psychotherapy: From Healing Magic to Encounter*. New York: Jason Aronson.

Eisold, Kenneth. 1994. "The Intolerance of Diversity in Psychoanalytic Institutes." *International Journal of Psychoanalysis* 75, 785–800.

———. 1998. "The Splitting of the New York Psychoanalytic Society and the Construction of Psychoanalytic Authority." *International Journal of Psychoanalysis* 79, 871–885.

———. 2003. "The Profession of Psychoanalysis: Past Failures and Future Possibilities." *Contemporary Psychoanalysis* 39, 557–582.

———. 2007. "The Erosion of Our Profession." *Psychoanalytic Psychology* 24, no. 1, 1–9.

Eissler, Kurt. 1950. "The Chicago Institute of Psychoanalysis and the Sixth Period of the Development of Psychoanalytic Technique." *Journal of General Psychology*, no. 42, 103–159.

———. 1953. "The Effect of the Structure of the Ego on Psychoanalytic Technique." *Journal of the American Psychoanalytic Association*, no. 1, 104–143.

———. 1965. *Medical Orthodoxy and the Future of Psychoanalysis*. New York: International Universities Press.

———. 1979. "A Possible Endangerment of Psychoanalysis in the United States." *International Review of Psychoanalysis* 6, 15–21.

Eist, Harold I. 1997. "Managed Care: Where Did It Come From? How Does It Survive? What Can Be Done about It?" *Psychoanalytic Inquiry* 17, supp. 1, 162–181.

Ekstein, Rudolf. 1960. "A Historical Survey on the Teaching of Psychoanalytic Technique." *Journal of the American Psychoanalytic Association* 8, 500–516.

Elias, Norbert. 2001. *The Society of Individuals*. Reissue ed. New York: Continuum.

Emch, M. 1955. "The Social Context of Supervision." *International Journal of Psychoanalysis* 36, no. 4–5, 298–306.

Emch, Minna. 1953. "N. Lionel Blitzsten: 1893–1952." *International Journal of Psychoanalysis* 34, 153–154.

———. 1955. "The Social Context of Supervision." *International Journal of Psychoanalysis* 36, 298–306.

————. 1961. "Obituary: Lionel Blitzsten." N. *Lionel Blitzsten, M.D.: Psychoanalyst, Teacher, Friend.* Ed. Robert P. Knight, 15–20. Madison, CT: International Universities Press.

Ennis, James G. 1992. "The Social Organization of Sociological Knowledge: Modeling the Intersection of the Specialities." *American Sociological Review* 57, 259–265.

Esposito, Roberto. 2008. *Bios: Biopolitics and Philosophy.* Trans. Timothy Campbell. Minneapolis: University of Minnesota Press.

Etchegoyen, Horacio. 1991. *The Fundamentals of Psychoanalytic Technique.* Trans. Patricia Pitchon. London: Karnac Books.

Ewing, Katherine P. 1990. "The Illusion of Wholeness: Culture, Self, and the Experience of Inconsistency." *Ethos* 18, no. 3, 251–278.

Falzeder, Ernst. 1998. "Family Tree Matters." *Journal of Analytical Psychology* 43, 127–154.

Farquhar, Judith. 1994. *Knowing Practice: The Clinical Encounter of Chinese Medicine.* Boulder: Westview.

————. 2005. "Biopolitical Beijing: Pleasure, Sovereignty, and Self-Cultivation in China's Capital." *Cultural Anthropology* 20, no. 3, 303–327.

Fassin, Didier. 2007. *When Bodies Remember: Experiences and Politics of AIDS in South Africa.* Berkeley: University of California Press.

Faulkner, Howard J., and Virginia D. Pruitt, eds. 1988. *The Selected Correspondence of Karl A. Menninger, 1919–1945.* New Haven: Yale University Press.

————, eds. 1995. *The Selected Correspondence of Karl A. Menninger, 1946–1965.* Columbia: University of Missouri Press.

Featherstone, Mike. 1991. "The Body in Consumer Culture." *The Body: Social Process and Cultural Theory.* Ed. Mike Featherstone, Mike Hepworth, and Bryan S. Turner, 170–196. London: Sage.

Feigenbaum, Janet. 2007. "Dialectical Behaviour Therapy: An Increasing Evidence Base." *Journal of Mental Health* 16, no. 1, 51–68.

Fenichel, Otto. 1945. *Psychoanalytic Theory of Neurosis.* New York: Norton.

Ferenczi, Sándor. 1988. "Confusion of Tongues between Adults and the Child—the Language of Tenderness and of Passion." *Contemporary Psychoanalysis* 24, 196–206.

Ferro, Antonino. 2002. *In the Analyst's Consulting Room.* Trans. Philip Slotkin. Hove, UK: Brunner-Routledge.

Fine, Reuben. 1977. *History of Psychoanalysis.* Lanham, MD: Jason Aronson.

Fineman, Stephen. 2000. *Emotion in Organizations.* London: Sage.

Fink, Bruce. 1995. *The Lacanian Subject: Between Language and Jouissance.* Princeton: Princeton University Press.

————. 1997. *A Clinical Introduction to Lacanian Psychoanalysis: Theory and Technique.* Cambridge, MA: Harvard University Press.

Finn, Molly. 1997. "In the Case of Bruno Bettelheim." *First Things* 74, 44–48.

Fish, Allison. 2006. "The Commodification and Exchange of Knowledge in the Case of Transnational Commercial Yoga." *International Journal of Cultural Property* 13, no. 2, 189–207.

Flax, Jane. 1990. *Thinking Fragments: Psychoanalysis, Feminism, and Postmodern in the Contemporary West*. Berkeley: University of California Press.

Fleming, Joan. 1961. "What Analytic Work Requires of an Analyst: A Job Analysis." *Journal of the American Psychoanalytic Association* 9, 719–729.

———. n.d. *Interview with Joan Fleming (Louis Shapiro)*. Chicago Institute for Psychoanalysis Library, Film Archive. Unpublished film.

Fleming, Joan, and Theresa Benedek. 1966. *Psychoanalytic Supervision: A Method of Clinical Teaching*. New York: Grune and Stratton.

Fleming, Joan, and Stanley S. Weiss. 1987. *The Teaching and Learning of Psychoanalysis: Selected Papers of Joan Fleming, M.D.* New York: Guilford Press.

Flexner, Abraham. 1910. "Medical Education in the United States and Canada." *Bulletin Number Four*. The Carnegie Foundation for the Advancement of Teaching. Accessed December 11, 2013. http://www.carnegiefoundation.org/sites/default /files/elibrary/Carnegie_Flexner_Report.pdf.

Fonagy, Peter. 1999. "Paul Williams Interviews Peter Fonagy: The Implications of Contemporary Neuroscience, Psychology and the 'Cognitive Revolution' for Psychoanalysis." *International Psychoanalytical Association Newsletter* 8, no. 2, 195–212.

———. 2001. *Attachment Theory and Psychoanalysis*. New York: Other Press.

Fonagy, Peter, Arnold M. Cooper, and Robert S. Wallerstein, eds. 1999. *Psychoanalysis on the Move: The Work of Joseph Sandler*. London: Routledge.

Fonagy, Peter, Gyorgy Gergely, Elliot L. Jurist, and Mary Target. 2002. *Affect Regulation, Mentalization, and the Development of the Self*. New York: Other Press.

Fonagy, P., H. Kächele, R. Krause, E. Jones, and R. Perron. 1999. *An Open Door Review of Outcome Studies in Psychoanalysis*. London: International Psychoanalytical Association.

Forman, Max. 1976. "Narcissistic Personality Disorders and the Oedipal Fixations." *Annual of Psychoanalysis* 4, 65–92.

Forrester, John. 1991. *The Seductions of Psychoanalysis: Freud, Lacan and Derrida*. Cambridge: Cambridge University Press.

———. 1997. *Dispatches from the Freud Wars: Psychoanalysis and Its Passions*. Cambridge, MA: Harvard University Press.

Fosshage, James L. 1997. "'Compensatory' or 'Primary.'" *Progress in Self Psychology* 13, 21–27.

Foucault, Michel. (1964) 1988. *Madness and Civilization: A History of Insanity in the Age of Reason*. New York: Vintage Books.

———. (1966) 1995. *The Order of Things: An Archaeology of the Human Sciences*. New York: Vintage Books.

———. 1975. *Discipline and Punish: The Birth of the Prison*. New York: Vintage Books.

———. (1977) 1980. "The Confession of the Flesh." *Power/Knowledge: Selected Interviews and Other Writings, 1972–1977*. Ed. Colin Gordon, 194–228. New York: Pantheon Books.

———. (1978) 1990. *The History of Sexuality*. Vol. 1. Trans. Robert Hurley. New York: Vintage Books.

———. 1988. *Technologies of the Self: A Seminar with Michel Foucault*. Ed. Luther H. Martin, Huck Gutman, and Patrick H. Hutton. Amherst: University of Massachusetts Press.

———. 1994. *Dits et Écrits: 1954–1988*. 4 vols. Bibliothèque des Sciences Humaines. Paris: Editions Gallimard.

———. 1998. *Essential Works of Foucault, 1954–1984*. Vol. 1: *Ethics: Subjectivity and Truth*. Ed. Paul Rabinow. New York: New Press.

———. 1999. *Essential Works of Foucault, 1954–1984*. Vol. 2: *Aesthetics, Method, and Epistemology*. Ed. James D. Faubion. New York: New Press.

———. 2001. *Essential Works of Foucault, 1954–1984*. Vol. 3: *Power*. Trans. Robert Hurley. Ed. James D. Faubion. New York: New Press.

———. 2003. *"Society Must Be Defended": Lectures at the Collège de France, 1975–1976*. Trans. David Macey. Ed. Mauro Bertani and Alessandro Bertani. New York: Picador.

———. 2008. *The Birth of Biopolitics: Lectures at the Collège de France, 1978–1979*. Trans. Graham Burchell. Ed. Michel Senellart. New York: Picador.

———. 2009. *Security, Territory, Population: Lectures at the Collège de France, 1977–1978*. Trans. Graham Burchell. Ed. Michel Senellart. New York: Picador.

Frank, R. G., and T. G. McGuire. 1997. "Savings from a Medicaid Carve-Out for Mental Health and Substance Abuse Services in Massachusetts." *Psychiatric Services* 48, no. 9, 1147–1152.

Frank, R. G., T. G. McGuire, S. L. Normand, and H. H. Goldman. 1999. "The Value of Mental Health Care at the System Level: The Case of Treating Depression." *Health Affairs* 18, no. 5, 71–88.

Frattaroli, Elio. 1992. "Orthodoxy and Heresy in the History of Psychoanalysis." *Educating the Emotions: Bruno Bettelheim and Psychoanalytic Development*. Ed. Nathan M. Szajnberg and Bruno Bettelheim, 121–150. New York: Plenum.

Freeman, Lucy. 1956. *Hospital in Action: The Story of Michael Reese Medical Center*. New York: Rand McNally.

Freidson, Eliot. 1984. "The Changing Nature of Professional Control." *Annual Review of Sociology* 10, 1–20.

———. 1994. *Professionalism Reborn*. Chicago: University of Chicago Press.

French, Thomas M. 1964a. "Franz Alexander." *Behavioral Science* 9, no. 2, 97–100.

———. 1964b. "In Memoriam: Franz Alexander, M.D." *Psychosomatic Medicine* 26, no. 3, 203–206.

———. 1970. *Psychoanalytic Interpretations: The Selected Papers of Thomas M. French, M.D.* Chicago: Quadrangle Books.

Freud, A. 1946. *The Ego and the Mechanisms of Defense*. New York: International Universities Press.

Freud, Sigmund. 1900. "The Interpretation of Dreams." In Freud 1953–1974, vols. 4–5, ix–627.

———. 1901. "The Psychopathology of Everyday Life." In Freud 1953–1974, vol. 6, vii–296.

———. 1905a. "Jokes and Their Relation to the Unconscious." In Freud 1953–1974, vol. 8, 1–247.

———. 1905b. "Fragment of an Analysis of a Case of Hysteria." In Freud 1953–1974, vol. 7, 1–122.

———. 1905c. "Three Essays on the Theory of Sexuality." In Freud 1953–1974, vol. 7, 123–246.

———. 1912. "The Dynamics of Transference." In Freud 1953–1974, vol. 12, 97–108.

———. 1913. "Totem and Taboo." In Freud 1953–1974, vol. 13, vii–162.

———. 1914. "Remembering, Repeating, and Working Through." In Freud 1953–1974, vol. 12, 145–156.

———. 1915. "Observations on Transference-Love (Further Recommendations on the Technique of Psycho-analysis III)." In Freud 1953–1974, vol. 12, 157–171.

———. 1916. "On Transience." In Freud 1953–1974, vol. 14, 303–307.

———. 1919. "Lines of Advance in Psycho-analytic Therapy." In Freud 1953–1974, vol. 17, 157–168.

———. 1921. "Group Psychology and the Analysis of the Ego." In Freud 1953–1974, vol. 23, 65–144.

———. 1922. "Medusa's Head." In Freud 1953–1974, vol. 23, 273–274.

———. 1923. "The Ego and the Id." In Freud 1953–1974, vol. 19, 1–66.

———. 1926. "Inhibitions, Symptoms and Anxiety." In Freud 1953–1974, vol. 20, 75–176.

———. 1930. "Civilization and Its Discontents." In Freud 1953–1974, vol. 21, 57–146.

———. 1937a. "Analysis Terminable and Interminable." In Freud 1953–1974, vol. 23, 209–254.

———. 1937b. "Constructions in Analysis." In Freud 1953–1974, vol. 23, 255–270.

———. 1953–1974. *The Standard Edition of the Complete Psychological Works of Sigmund Freud.* 24 vols. Trans. and ed. James Strachey. London: Hogarth.

Friedman, Lawrence. 1978. "Trends in the Psychoanalytic Theory of Treatment." *Psychoanalytic Quarterly* 47, 524–567.

Friedman, Lawrence, and Kevin Kelly. 1994. "K. R. Eissler's (1953) 'The Effect of the Structure of the Ego on Psychoanalytic Technique.'" *Journal of the American Psychoanalytic Association* 42, no. 3, 875–882.

Friedman, Lawrence J. 1990. *Menninger: The Family and the Clinic.* New York: Knopf.

Fromm, Erich. 1971. *The Crisis of Psychoanalysis: Essays on Freud, Marx and Social Psychology.* London: Jonathan Cape.

Frosch, John. 1987. "Journal of the American Psychoanalytic Association: A Retrospective (1953–1972)." *Journal of the American Psychoanalytic Association* 35, no. 2, 303–336.

————. 1991. "The New York Psychoanalytic Civil War." *Journal of the American Psychoanalytic Association* 39, 1037–1064.

Furedi, Frank. 2004. *Therapy Culture: Cultivating Vulnerability in an Uncertain Age*. London: Routledge.

Furlong, Allannah. 2005. "Confidentiality with Respect to Third Parties: A Psychoanalytic View." *International Journal of Psychoanalysis* 86, 375–394.

Gabbard, Glen O. 1995a. "Countertransference: The Emerging Common Ground." *International Journal of Psychoanalysis* 76, 475–485.

————. 1995b. "The Early History of Boundary Violations in Psychoanalysis." *Journal of the American Psychoanalytic Association* 43, 1115–1136.

————. 1995c. "Transference and Countertransference in the Psychotherapy of Therapists Charged with Sexual Misconduct." *Journal of Psychotherapy Practice and Research* 4, 10–17.

————. 1999. "Irene Chiarandini Interviews Glen O. Gabbard: Psychoanalysis and Research; Future or Illusion? *International Psychoanalytic Association Newsletter* 8, no. 2. Accessed May 2, 2004. http://eseries.ipa.org.uk/prev/newsletter/99-2/E3.htm.

————. 2001. *Psychoanalysis and Film*. London: Karnac Books.

————. 2009. "Transference and Countertransference Developments in the Treatment of Narcissistic Personality Disorder." *Psychiatric Annals* 39, no. 3, 129–136.

Gabbard, Glen O., and Thomas H. Ogden. 2009. "On Becoming a Psychoanalyst." *International Journal of Psychoanalysis* 90, 311–327.

Gaines, A. D. 1992. "From DSM-I to III-R; Voices of Self, Mastery and the Other: A Cultural Constructivist Reading of U.S. Psychiatric Classification." *Social Science and Medicine* 35, no. 1, 3–24.

Galatzer-Levy, Robert M. 1988. "Heinz Kohut as Teacher and Supervisor: A View from the Second Generation." *Progress in Self Psychology* 4, 3–42.

Galatzer-Levy, Robert M., Henry Bachrach, Alan Skolnikoff, and Sherwood Waldron, Jr. 2000. *Does Psychoanalysis Work?* New Haven: Yale University Press.

Gamwell, Lynn, and Nancy Tomes. 1995. *Madness in America: Cultural and Medical Perceptions of Mental Illness before 1914*. Ithaca: Cornell University Press.

Gane, Nicholas. 2004. *Max Weber and Postmodern Theory: Rationalization versus Re-enchantment*. New York: Palgrave.

Gann, Erik. 2002. "What the 2001 Practice Survey Means to You." *American Psychoanalyst* 36, no. 1, 37–38.

Garber, Benjamin. 2006. "A History of the Barr-Harris Children's Grief Center." Chicago: Chicago Institute for Psychoanalysis.

Garcia, Emanuel E. 2009. "Enduring Relevance: An Introduction to the Clinical Contributions of K. R. Eissler." *Psychoanalytic Quarterly* 78, no. 4, 1109–1126.

Gardner, Howard. 1987. *The Mind's New Science: A History of the Cognitive Revolution*. New York: Basic Books.

Gay, Peter. 2006. *Freud, a Life for Our Time*. New York: Norton.

Gediman, Helen K. 1999. "The Inner World in the Outer World: Psychoanalytic Perspectives." *International Journal of Psychoanalysis* 80, 402–406.

Gedo, John E. 1972. "The Dream of Reason Produces Monsters." *Journal of the American Psychoanalytic Association* 20, 199–223.

———. 1975. "To Heinz Kohut: On His 60th Birthday." *Annual of Psychoanalysis* 3, 313–322.

———. 1979. *Beyond Interpretation*. New York: International Universities Press.

———. 1984. *Psychoanalysis and Its Discontents*. New York: Guilford Press.

———. 1997. *Spleen and Nostalgia: A Life and Work in Psychoanalysis*. Northvale, NJ: Jason Aronson.

———. 2005. *Psychoanalysis as Biological Science: A Comprehensive Theory*. Baltimore: Johns Hopkins University Press.

Gedo, John E., and Arnold Goldberg. 1973. *Models of the Mind: A Psychoanalytic Theory*. Chicago: University of Chicago Press.

Gedo, John E., and George H. Pollock, eds. 1976. *Freud, the Fusion of Science and Humanism: The Intellectual History of Psychoanalysis*. New York: International Universities Press.

Gehrie, Mark J. 1993. "Psychoanalytic Technique and the Development of the Capacity to Reflect." *Journal of the American Psychoanalytic Association* 41, no. 4, 1083–1111.

Gellner, Ernest. 2003. *The Psychoanalytic Movement: The Cunning of Unreason*. London: Wiley-Blackwell.

George, M. S., E. M. Wasserman, W. A. Williams, A. Callahan, T. A. Ketter, P. Basser, M. Hallett, and R. M. Post. 1995. "Daily Repetitive Transcranial Magnetic Stimulation (rTMS) Improves Mood in Depression." *Neuroreport* 6, 1853–1856.

Gergen, Kenneth J. 1999. *Realities and Relationships: Soundings in Social Construction*. Cambridge, MA: Harvard University Press.

———. 2000. *The Saturated Self: Dilemmas of Identity in Contemporary Life*. New York: Basic Books.

Gill, Merton. 1991. "Psychoanalysis and Psychotherapy." *International Journal of Psychoanalysis* 72, 159–161.

Gill, Merton M. 1988. "Converting Psychotherapy into Psychoanalysis." *Contemporary Psychoanalysis* 24, 262–274.

Gilman, Sander L. 1998. *Creating Beauty to Cure the Soul: Race and Psychology in the Shaping of Aesthetic Surgery*. Durham, NC: Duke University Press.

Giovacchini, Peter L. 1990. *Tactics and Techniques in Psychoanalytic Therapy*. 3 vols. Northvale, NJ: Jason Aronson.

———. 1993. *Borderline Patients, the Psychosomatic Focus, and the Therapeutic Process*. Northvale, NJ: Jason Aronson.

———. 2000. *Impact of Narcissism: The Errant Therapist on a Chaotic Quest*. Northvale, NJ: Jason Aronson.

Gitelson, Maxwell. 1948. "Problems of Psychoanalytic Training." *Psychoanalytic Quarterly* 17, 198–211.

———. 1953. "N. Lionel Blitzsten: 1893–1952." *Bulletin of the American Psychoanalytic Association* 9, 189–192.

———. 1954. "Therapeutic Problems in the Analysis of the 'Normal' Candidate." *International Journal of Psychoanalysis* 35, 174–183.

———. 1956. "Psychoanalyst U.S.A., 1955." In Gitelson 1973, 239–253.

———. 1960. "Psychoanalytic Education in the United States: By Bertram D. Lewin and Helen Ross. New York: W. W. Norton & Co., 1960. 478 Pp." *Psychoanalytic Quarterly* 29, 559–567.

———. 1961. "Obituary: Lionel Blitzsten." *N. Lionel Blitzsten, M.D.: Psychoanalyst, Teacher, Friend.* Ed. Robert P. Knight, 9–14. Madison, CT: International Universities Press.

———. 1962a. "Communication from the President about the Neoanalytic Movement." In Elizabeth R. Zetzel, "Report of the 22nd International Psychoanalytical Congress." *Bulletin of the International Psycho-analytical Association* 43, 373–375.

———. 1962b. "The Curative Factors in Psychoanalysis." *International Journal of Psychoanalysis* 43, 194–205.

———. 1963. "On the Present Scientific and Social Position of Psychoanalysis." In Gitelson 1973, 342–359.

———. 1964. "On the Identity Crisis in American Psychoanalysis." *Journal of the American Psychoanalytic Association* 12, 451–476.

———. 1973. *Psychoanalysis: Science and Profession.* New York: International Universities Press.

Glover, Edward. 1964. "Freudian or Neofreudian." *Psychoanalytic Quarterly* 33, 97–109.

Goggin, James E., and Eileen Brockman Goggin. 2001. "Politics, Ideology, and the Psychoanalytic Movement before, during, and after the Third Reich." *Psychoanalytic Review* 88, no. 2, 155–193.

Goldberg, Arnold. 1975. "A President Looks Back—and Forward: An Interview with Dr. George Pollock." *Journal of the American Psychoanalytic Association* 9, no. 4, 4–5.

———. 1999. *Being of Two Minds: The Vertical Split in Psychoanalysis and Psychotherapy.* New York: Routledge.

———. 2002. "Self Psychology since Kohut." *Progress in Self Psychology* 18, 1–13.

———. 2004. *Misunderstanding Freud.* New York: Other Press.

———. 2011. *The Analysis of Failure: An Investigation of Failed Cases in Psychoanalysis and Psychotherapy.* New York: Routledge.

Goldman, Dana P. 1995. "Managed Care as a Public Cost-Containment Mechanism." *Rand Journal of Economics* 26, no. 2, 277–295.

Goldman, W., J. McCulloch, and R. Sturm. 1998. "Costs and Use of Mental Health Services before and after Managed Care." *Health Affairs* 17, no. 2, 40–52.

Goldstein, Jan. 2002. *Console and Classify: The French Psychiatric Profession in the Nineteenth Century.* Chicago: University of Chicago Press.

Gostin, Lawrence O. 2000. "At Law: Managed Care, Conflicts of Interest and Quality." *Hastings Center Report* 30, no. 5, 27–28.

Gourguechon, Prudence. 2010. "DSM IV—Requiem for a Diagnosis." *The President's Corner* (blog), American Psychoanalytic Association, May 1. http://www.apsa .org/.

Graeber, David. 2001. *Toward an Anthropological Theory of Value: The False Coin of Our Own Dreams.* New York: Palgrave.

Gray, Sheila Hafter. 1996. "Developing Practice Guidelines for Psychoanalysis." *Journal of Psychotherapy Practice and Research* 5, 213–227.

———. 2002. "Evidence-Based Psychotherapeutics: Presidential Address to the American Academy of Psychoanalysis on May 6, 2001, New Orleans, Louisiana." *Journal of the American Academy of Psychoanalysis and Dynamic Psychiatry* 30, 3–16.

———. 2009. "Evidence and Narrative in Contemporary Psychiatry." *Journal of the American Academy of Psychoanalysis and Dynamic Psychiatry* 37, no. 3, 415–420.

Grazier, Kyle L., and Laura L. Eselius. 1999. "Mental Health Carve-Outs: Effects and Implications." *Medical Care Research and Review* 56, no. 2, 37–59.

Grazier, Kyle L., Laura L. Eselius, Teh-wei Hu, Karen K. Shore, and William A. G'Sell. 1999. "Effects of a Mental Health Carve-Out on Use, Costs, and Payers: A Four-Year Study." *Journal of Behavioral Health Services and Research* 26, no. 4, 381–389.

Green, Andre. 2000a. "Science and Science Fiction." *Clinical and Observational Psychoanalytic Research: Roots of a Controversy.* Ed. Joseph Sandler, Anne Marie Sandler, and R. Davies, 41–72. London: Karnac Books.

———. 2000b. "What Kind of Research for Psychoanalysis?" *Clinical and Observational Psychoanalytic Research: Roots of a Controversy.* Ed. Joseph Sandler, Anne Marie Sandler, and Rosemary Davies, 32–37. London: Karnac Books.

Greenacre, Phyllis. 1954. "The Role of Transference—Practical Considerations in Relation to Psychoanalytic Therapy." *Journal of the American Psychoanalytic Association* 2, 671–684.

———. 1961. "A Critical Digest of the Literature on Selection of Candidates for Psychoanalytic Training." *Psychoanalytic Quarterly* 30, 28–55.

———. 1966a. "Memorial Tribute: Maxwell Gitelson." *International Journal of Psychoanalysis* 47, 440–445.

———. 1966b. "Problems of Training Analysis." *Psychoanalytic Quarterly* 35, 540–567.

Greenberg, Jay R. 1986. "Heinz Hartmann and Drive Theory: A Reevaluation." *Psychoanalytic Inquiry* 6, 523–541.

Greenberg, Jay R., and Stephen A. Mitchell. 1983. *Object Relations in Psychoanalytic Theory.* Cambridge, MA: Harvard University Press.

Greenhouse, Steven. 2008. *The Big Squeeze: Tough Times for the American Worker.* New York: Knopf.

Greenson, Ralph R. 1965. "The Working Alliance and the Transference Neurosis." *Psychoanalytic Quarterly* 34, 155–181.

———. 1967. *The Technique and Practice of Psychoanalysis*. New York: International Universities Press.

Greenson, Ralph R., and Milton Wexler. 1969. "The Non-transference Relationship in the Psychoanalytic Situation." *International Journal of Psychoanalysis* 50, 27–39.

Gremillion, Helen. 2003. *Feeding Anorexia: Gender and Power at a Treatment Center*. Durham, NC: Duke University Press.

Grinker, Roy R., Sr. 1965. "Identity or Regression in American Psychoanalysis?" *Archives of General Psychiatry* 12, no. 2, 113–125.

———. 1975. "Reminiscences of Dr. Roy Grinker." *Journal of the American Academy of Psychoanalysis and Dynamic Psychiatry* 3, 211–221.

———. 1977. "Twenty Years of Psychoanalysis: Retrospect and Prospect." *Journal of the American Academy of Psychoanalysis and Dynamic Psychiatry* 5, 79–93.

———. 1994. "Training of a Psychiatrist-Psychoanalyst." *Journal of the American Academy of Psychoanalysis*, no. 22, 343–350.

———. n.d. *Interview with Roy R. Grinker (Brenda Solomon)*. Chicago Institute for Psychoanalysis Library, Film Archive. Unpublished film.

Grinker, Roy R., Sr., and Roy R. Grinker Jr. 1995. "The History of Psychoanalysis in Chicago, 1911–1975." *Annual of Psychoanalysis* 23, 155–195.

Grinker, Roy R., Sr., Sandor Rado, and Franz Alexander. (1963) 1964. "The Open Window Policy in Psychoanalysis." Letter printed in Elizabeth R. Zetzel, "125th Bulletin of the International Psycho-analytical Association." *Bulletin of the International Psycho-analytical Association* 45, 618–625.

Grosskurth, Phyllis. 1992. *Secret Ring: Freud's Inner Circle and the Politics of Psychoanalysis*. New York: Addison-Wesley.

Grotjahn, Martin. 1954. "About the Relation between Psycho-analytic Training and Psycho-analytic Therapy." *International Journal of Psychoanalysis* 35, 254–262.

Grunbaum, Adolf. 1985. *The Foundations of Psychoanalysis: A Philosophical Critique*. Berkeley: University of California Press.

———. 1993. *Validation in the Clinical Theory of Psychoanalysis: A Study in the Philosophy of Psychoanalysis*. Madison, CT: International Universities Press.

———. 2006. "Is Sigmund Freud's Psychoanalytic Edifice Relevant to the 21st Century?" *Psychoanalytic Psychology* 23, no. 2, 257–284.

———. 2007. "The Reception of My Freud-Critique in the Psychoanalytic Literature." *Psychoanalytic Psychology* 24, no. 3, 545–576.

Guillory, John. 1993. *Cultural Capital: The Problem of Literary Canon Formation*. Chicago: University of Chicago Press.

Gunderson, John G., and Glen O. Gabbard. 1999. "Making the Case for Psychoanalytic Therapies in the Current Psychiatric Environment." *Journal of the American Psychoanalytic Association* 47, 679–704.

Hacking, Ian. 1996. "Normal People." *Modes of Thought: Explorations in Culture and Cognition*. Ed. David R. Olson and Nancy Torrance, 59–71. Cambridge: Cambridge University Press.

———. 1999. "Making Up People." *The Science Studies Reader*. Ed. Mario Biagioli, 161–171. London: Routledge.

Hale, Nathan G., Jr. 1995. *The Rise and Crisis of Psychoanalysis: Freud and the Americans, 1917–1985*. New York: Oxford University Press.

Hall, Bernard H., ed. 1947. *A Psychiatrist for a Troubled World: Selected Papers of William C. Menninger, M.D.* New York: Viking Press.

Hall, Jane. 2006. "The Importance of Psychoanalytic Psychotherapy Training: A Tale of Two Programs." *Psychologist-Psychoanalyst* 26, no. 1, 1–21.

Hamilton, Victoria. 1996. *The Analyst's Preconscious*. Hillsdale, NJ: Analytic Press.

Hannett Gitelson, Frances. 1983. "Identity Crises, Splits or Compromises." *The Identity of the Psychoanalyst*. Ed. Edward D. Joseph and Daniel Widlocher, 157–180. New York: International Universities Press.

Hardt, Michael. 1999. "Affective Labor." *Boundary* 26, no. 2, 89–100.

Hardt, Michael, and Antonio Negri. 2001. *Empire*. Cambridge, MA: Harvard University Press.

Hartmann, Heinz. 1956. "The Development of the Ego Concept in Freud's Work." *International Journal of Psychoanalysis* 37, 425–438.

———. 1968. *Ego Psychology and the Problem of Adaptation*. Trans. David Rapaport. New York: International Universities Press.

Hartmann, Heinz, and Rudolph Loewenstein. 1962. "Notes on the Superego." *Psychoanalytic Study of the Child* 17, 42–81.

Haynal, Andre, and Ernst Falzeder. 1991. " 'Healing through Love'? A Unique Dialogue in the History of Psychoanalysis." *Free Associations* 21, no. 2, 1–20.

———, eds. 1994. *100 Years of Psychoanalysis: Contributions to the History of Psychoanalysis*. London: Karnac Books.

Hedges, Lawrence E., Robert Hilton, Virginia Wink Hilton, and O. Brandt Caudill Jr. 1998. *Therapists at Risk: The Perils of the Intimacy of the Therapeutic Relationship*. Northvale, NJ: Jason Aronson.

Heinz, John P., Robert L. Nelson, Rebecca L. Sandefur, and Edward O. Laumann. 2005. *Urban Lawyers: The New Social Structure of the Bar*. Chicago: University of Chicago Press.

Herman, Ellen. 1995. *The Romance of American Psychology: Political Culture in the Age of Experts*. Berkeley: University of California Press.

Hiltner, Seward. 1961. "Psychoanalytic Education: A Critique." *Psychoanalytic Quarterly* 30, 385–403.

Hindess, Barry. 1996. *Discourses of Power from Hobbes to Foucault*. Oxford: Blackwell.

———. 2005. "Politics as Government: Michel Foucault's Analysis of Political Reason." *Alternatives* 30, 389–414.

Hirsch, Irwin. 1995. "Changing Conceptions of Unconscious." *Contemporary Psychoanalysis* 31, 263–276.

Hirshbein, Laura D. 2009. *American Melancholy: Constructions of Depression in the Twentieth Century*. New Brunswick, NJ: Rutgers University Press.

Hochschild, Arlie Russell. 2003. *The Commercialization of Intimate Life: Notes from Home and Work*. Berkeley: University of California Press.

Hoffman, Irwin Z. 1998. *Ritual and Spontaneity in the Psychoanalytic Process: A Dialectical-Constructivist View*. Hillsdale, NJ: Analytic Press.

Hofstadter, Richard. 1965. *The Paranoid Style in American Politics and Other Essays*. New York: Vintage Books.

Hoit, Michael. 1999. "Response to Kenneth Newman's 'The Usable Analyst.'" *Annual of Psychoanalysis* 26, no. 195–200.

Holinger, Paul C. 1999. "Noninterpretive Interventions in Psychoanalysis and Psychotherapy: A Developmental Perspective." *Psychoanalytic Psychology* 16, no. 2, 233–253.

Hollis, Florence. 1964. *Social Casework: A Psychosocial Therapy*. New York: Random House.

Holzman, Philip S. 1985. "Psychoanalysis: Is the Therapy Destroying the Science?" *Journal of the American Psychoanalytic Association* 33, 725–770.

Honneth, Axel. 2008. *Reification: A New Look at an Old Idea*. Ed. Martin Jay. Berkeley Tanner Lectures. Oxford: Oxford University Press.

Hopper, Kim. 1997. "On Contract Knowing: Notes toward a Taxonomy of Foreclosed Inquiry." *Anthropology News* 38, no. 6, 34–35.

———. 2001. "Commentary: On the Transformation of the Moral Economy of Care." *Culture, Medicine, and Psychiatry* 25, no. 4, 473–484.

Horn, Margo. 1989. *Before It's Too Late: The Child Guidance Movement in the United States, 1922–1945*. Philadelphia: Temple University Press.

Horney, Karen. 1950. *The Collected Works of Karen Horney*. 2 vols. New York: Norton.

Horwitz, Allan V. 2003. *Creating Mental Illness*. Chicago: University of Chicago Press.

Hunter, Virginia. 1992. "An Interview with Ernest Wolf Part II: The Analytic Years to 1990." *Psychoanalytic Review* 79, 481–507.

Hurley, James S. 1998. "Real Virtuality: Slavoj Žižek and 'Post-ideological' Ideology." Review of *The Plague of Fantasies*. *Postmodern Culture* 9, no. 1.

Hurst, Andrea. 2008. *Derrida vis-a-vis Lacan: Interweaving Deconstruction and Psychoanalysis*. New York: Fordham University Press.

Hustead, Edward, and Paul Mosher. 1993. "Insuring Psychoanalysis." *Contingencies*, no. 93, 55–57.

Hutchins, Robert Maynard. 1953. *The University of Utopia*. Chicago: University of Chicago Press.

Imber, Jonathan B. 2004. *Therapeutic Culture*. New Brunswick: Transaction.

Inderbitzin, Lawrence B., and Steven T. Levy. 2000. "Regression and Psychoanalytic Technique: The Concretization of a Concept." *Psychoanalytic Quarterly* 69, 195–223.

International Psycho-analytical Association. 1933. "Reports of the International Training Commission." *Bulletin of the International Psycho-analytical Association* 14, 459–462.

Isakower, Otto. 1992. "Preliminary Thoughts on the Analyzing Instrument." *Journal of Clinical Psychoanalysis* 1, 184–194.

Jackson, Anthony, ed. 1987. *Anthropology at Home*. London: Tavistock.

Jackson, John L., Jr. 2005. *Real Black: Adventures in Racial Sincerity*. Chicago: University of Chicago Press.

Jackson, Stanley W. 1999. *Care of the Psyche: A History of Psychological Healing*. New Haven: Yale University Press.

Jacobson, Lawrence. 1997. "The Soul of Psychoanalysis in the Modern World: Reflections on the Work of Christopher Bollas." *Psychoanalytic Dialogues* 7, 81–115.

Jacoby, Russel. 1986. *The Repression of Psychoanalysis: Otto Fenichel and the Political Freudians*. Chicago: University of Chicago Press.

———. 1997. *Social Amnesia: A Critique of Contemporary Psychology*. Piscataway, NJ: Transaction.

Jagodzinski, Jan. 2002. *Pedagogical Desire: Authority, Seduction, Transference, and the Question of Ethics*. Westport, CT: Praeger.

Jaye, Chrystal, Tony Egan, and Sarah Parker. 2006. "'Do as I Say, Not as I Do': Medical Education and Foucault's Normalizing Technologies of Self." *Anthropology and Medicine* 13, no. 2, 141–155.

Johnson, Barbara. 1988. "The Frame of Reference: Poe, Lacan, Derrida." *The Purloined Poe: Lacan, Derrida, and Psychoanalytic Reading*. Ed. John P. Muller and William J. Richardson, 213–241. Baltimore: Johns Hopkins University Press.

Jones, Ernest, ed. 1949. *Sigmund Freud: Collected Papers*. Vol. 11. London: Hogarth.

———. 1955. *The Life and Work of Sigmund Freud*. Vol. 2: *Years of Maturity, 1901–1919*. New York: Basic Books.

———. 1957. *The Life and Work of Sigmund Freud*. Vol. 3: *The Last Phase 1919–1939*. London: Hogarth.

———. 1972. *The Life and Work of Sigmund Freud*. Vol. 1: *The Young Freud 1856–1900*. London: Hogarth.

Jones, Kathleen W. 1999. *Taming the Troublesome Child: American Families, Child Guidance, and the Limits of Psychiatric Authority*. Cambridge, MA: Harvard University Press.

Joseph, Betty. 1985. "Transference: The Total Situation." *International Journal of Psychoanalysis* 66, 447–454.

Kahr, Brett. 2002. "The Provocative Renaissance Man: The Contributions of John Gedo." *British Journal of Psychotherapy* 19, no. 2, 247–253.

Kalberg, Stephen. 1994. *Max Weber's Comparative-Historical Sociology*. Chicago: University of Chicago Press.

Kaley, Harriette, Morris N. Eagle, and David L. Wolitzky. 1999. *Psychoanalytic Therapy as Health Care: Effectiveness and Economics in the Twenty-First Century.* Hillsdale, NJ: Analytic Press.

Katz, Jay. 1963. "On Primary Gain and Secondary Gain." *Psychoanalytic Study of the Child* 18, 9–50.

Kaufman, Eleanor. 2001. *The Delirium of Praise: Bataille, Blanchot, Deleuze, Foucault, Klossowski.* Baltimore: Johns Hopkins University Press.

Kavka, Jerome. 1974. "Empathy in the Beginning Analyst: The First Case Report." *Annual of Psychoanalysis* 2, 293–307.

———. 1976. "The Analysis of Phallic Narcissism." *International Journal of Psychoanalysis* 3, 277–282.

———. 1984. "Fifty Years of Psychoanalysis in Chicago: A Historical Perspective." *Psychoanalysis: The Vital Issues.* Ed. George H. Pollock and John Gedo, 465–493. New York: International Universities Press.

———. 1991. "N. Lionel Blitzsten, M.D., 1893–1952: The Theories of a Pioneer American Psychoanalyst." *Annual of Psychoanalysis* 19, 213–230.

Kaye, Howard L. 1991. "A False Convergence: Freud and the Hobbesian Problem of Order." *Sociological Theory* 9, no. 1, 87–105.

———. 1992. "Rationalization as Sublimation: On the Cultural Analyses of Weber and Freud." *Theory, Culture and Society* 9, no. 4, 45–74.

Keane, Webb. 1997. *Signs of Recognition: Powers and Hazards of Representation in an Indonesian Society.* Berkeley: University of California Press.

Kernberg, Otto. 1980. "Neurosis, Psychosis, and the Borderline States." *Comprehensive Textbook of Psychiatry.* Ed. A. M. Freeman, H. I. Kaplan, and B. J. Sadock, 845–850. Baltimore: Wilkins and Wilkins.

———. 1986. "Institutional Problems of Psychoanalytic Education." *Journal of the American Psychoanalytic Association* 34, 799–834.

———. 1998. *Ideology, Conflict, and Leadership in Groups and Organizations.* New Haven: Yale University Press.

———. 1999. "Psychoanalysis, Psychoanalytic Psychotherapy and Supportive Psychotherapy: Contemporary Controversies." *International Journal of Psychoanalysis* 80, 1075–1091.

———. 2000. "A Concerned Critique of Psychoanalytic Education." *International Journal of Psychoanalysis* 81, 97–120.

———. 2006. "The Coming Changes in Psychoanalytic Education: Part I." *International Journal of Psychoanalysis* 87, 1649–1673.

Kieffer, Christine C. 2007. "Emergence and the Analytic Third: Working at the Edge of Chaos." *Psychoanalytic Dialogues* 17, no. 5, 683–703.

Kirk, Stuart A., and Herb Kutchins. 1992. *The Selling of DSM: The Rhetoric of Science in Psychiatry.* New York: de Gruyter.

Kirsner, Douglas. 1999. "Life among the Analysts." *Free Associations*, no. 7, 416–436.

———. 2000. *Unfree Associations: Inside Psychoanalytic Institutes.* London: Process.

Kleinke, J. D. 2001. *Oxymorons: The Myth of a U.S. Health Care System*. San Francisco: Jossey-Bass.

Kligerman, Charles. 1984. "Memorial for Heinz Kohut, M.D., October 31, 1981." *Annual of Psychoanalysis* 12, 9–15.

Klossowski, Pierre. 1997. *Nietzsche and the Vicious Circle*. Trans. Daniel W. Smith. Chicago: University of Chicago Press.

Knight, Robert P. 1953. "The Present Status of Organized Psychoanalysis in the United States." *Journal of the American Psychoanalytic Association* 1, no. 2, 197–221.

———. 1961a. "Memorial Address: Chicago Psychoanalytic Society." In Knight 1961b, 3–8.

———, ed. 1961b. *N. Lionel Blitzsten, M.D.: Psychoanalyst, Teacher, Friend*. Madison, CT: International Universities Press.

Knorr Cetina, Karin. 1992. "The Couch, the Cathedral and the Lab: On the Relationship between Experiment and Laboratory Science." In *Science as Practice and Culture*, 113–38. Chicago: University of Chicago Press.

———. 1995. "Culture in Global Knowledge Societies: Knowledge Cultures and Epistemic Cultures." *The Blackwell Companion to the Sociology of Culture*. Ed. Mark Jacobs and Nancy Weiss Hanrahan, 65–79. Oxford: Blackwell.

———. 1999. *Epistemic Cultures: How the Sciences Make Knowledge*. Cambridge, MA: Harvard University Press.

Kohler, Robert E. 2002. *Landscapes and Labscapes: Exploring the Lab-Field Border in Biology*. Chicago: University of Chicago Press.

Kohut, Heinz. 1959. "Introspection, Empathy, and Psychoanalysis: An Examination of the Relationship between Mode of Observation and Theory." *Journal of the American Psychoanalytic Association* 7, no. 3, 459–483.

———. 1962. "The Psychoanalytic Curriculum." *Journal of the American Psychoanalytic Association* 10, 153–163.

———. 1966. "Forms and Transformations of Narcissism." *Journal of the American Psychoanalytic Association* 14, no. 2, 243–272.

———. 1971. *The Analysis of the Self: A Systematic Approach to the Psychoanalytic Treatment of Narcissistic Personality Disorders*. New York: International Universities Press.

———. 1972. "Thoughts on Narcissism and Narcissistic Rage." *Psychoanalytic Study of the Child* 27, 360–400.

———. 1977. *The Restoration of the Self*. New York: International Universities Press.

———. 1979. "The Two Analyses of Mr Z." *International Journal of Psychoanalysis* 60, 3–27.

———. 1982. "Introspection, Empathy, and the Semi-circle of Mental Health. Int. J. Psycho-anal., 63:395–407." *International Journal of Psychoanalysis* 62, 395–407.

Kohut, Heinz, and Paul H. Ornstein. 1978. *The Search for the Self: Selected Writings of Heinz Kohut, 1950–1978*. Vol. 2. New York: International Universities Press.

Kramer, Charles H. 1967. "Maxwell Gitelson: Analytic Aphorisms." *Psychoanalytic Quarterly* 36, 260–270.

Kramer, Paul. 1965. "Maxwell Gitelson: 1902–1965." *Psychoanalytic Quarterly* 34, 441–444.

Kristeva, Julia. 2001. *Melanie Klein*. Trans. Ross Guberman. Ed. Lawrence D. Kritzman. New York: Columbia University Press.

Kroskrity, Paul V., ed. 2000. *Regimes of Language: Ideologies, Politics, and Identities*. Santa Fe: School of American Research Press.

Kuhn, Thomas. 1996. *The Structure of Scientific Revolutions*. Chicago: University of Chicago Press.

Kuklick, Henrika. 1998. "Review: Speaking with the Dead." *Isis* 89, no. 1, 103–111.

Lacan, Jacques. 1977. *Ecrits: A Selection*. Trans. Alan Sheridan. London: Norton.

———. 1988a. *The Ego in Freud's Theory and in the Technique of Psychoanalysis, 1954–1955*. Trans. Sylvana Tomaselli. Ed. Jacques-Alain Miller. The Seminar of Jacques Lacan, book 2. New York: Norton.

———. 1988b. *Freud's Papers on Technique, 1953–1954*. Trans. John Forrester. Ed. Jacques-Alain Miller. The Seminar of Jacques Lacan, book 1. New York: Norton.

———. 1992. *The Ethics of Psychoanalysis, 1959–1960*. Trans. Dennis Porter. Ed. Jacques-Alain Miller. The Seminar of Jacques Lacan, book 7. New York: Norton.

———. 1993. *The Psychoses, 1955–1956*. Trans. Russell Grigg. Ed. Jacques-Alain Miller. The Seminar of Jacques Lacan, book 3. New York: Norton.

———. 1998a. *The Four Fundamental Concepts of Psychoanalysis*. Trans. Alan Sheridan. Ed. Jacques-Alain Miller. The Seminar of Jacques Lacan, book 11. New York: Norton.

———. 1998b. *On Feminine Sexuality: The Limits of Love and Knowledge, 1972–1973*. Trans. Bruce Fink. Ed. Jacques-Alain Miller. The Seminar of Jacques Lacan, book 20. New York: Norton.

———. 2006. *The Other Side of Psychoanalysis*. Trans. Russell Grigg. The Seminar of Jacques Lacan, book 17. New York: Norton.

Lachicotte, William S., and Suzanne R. Kirschner. 2001. "Managing Managed Care: Habitus, Hysteresis and the End(s) of Psychotherapy." *Culture, Medicine and Psychiatry* 25, no. 4, 441–456.

Lain, Robert C., and Murray Meisels, ed. 1994. *A History of the Division of Psychoanalysis of the American Psychological Association*. Hillsdale, NJ: Lawrence Erlbaum.

Lakoff, Andrew. 2005. *Pharmaceutical Reason: Knowledge and Value in Global Psychiatry*. Cambridge: Cambridge University Press.

———. 2010. *Disaster and the Politics of Intervention*. New York: Columbia University Press.

Lakoff, Andrew, and Stephen J. Collier. 2008. *Biosecurity Interventions: Global Health and Security in Question*. New York: Columbia University Press.

Lammers, John C., and Patricia Geist. 1997. "The Transformation of Caring in the Light and Shadow of 'Managed Care.'" *Health Communication* 9, no. 1, 45–60.

Lane, Christopher. 2000. "The Experience of the Outside: Foucault and Psychoanalysis." *Lacan in America*. Ed. Jean-Michel Rabate, 309–347. New York: Other Press.

Lane, Robert C., and Murray Meisels, eds. 1994. *A History of the Division of Psychoanalysis of the American Psychological Association*. New York: Erlbaum.

Laplanche, Jean. 1986. *Life and Death in Psychoanalysis*. Baltimore: Johns Hopkins University Press.

———. 1999. *Essays on Otherness*. London: Routledge.

Laplanche, Jean, and J. B. Pontalis. 1974. *The Language of Psychoanalysis*. New York: Norton.

Lasch, Christopher. 1978. *The Culture of Narcissism: American Life in an Age of Diminishing Expectations*. New York: Norton.

Lasswell, Harold D. 1935. *World Politics and Personal Insecurity*. New York: McGraw-Hill.

———. 1946. "Psychiatric Testing Urged for Leaders to See if They Are Fit to Wield Power." *New York Times*, May 13, 2.

———. 1986. *Psychopathology and Politics*. Midway Reprints. Chicago: University of Chicago Press.

Latour, Bruno. 1988. *The Pasteurization of France*. Trans. Alan Sheridan and John Law. Cambridge, MA: Harvard University Press.

———. 1993. *We Have Never Been Modern*. Trans. Catherine Porter. Cambridge, MA: Harvard University Press.

———. 2005. *Reassembling the Social: An Introduction to Actor-Network-Theory*. New York: Oxford University Press.

Latour, Bruno, and Peter Weibel, eds. 2005. *Making Things Public: Atmosphere of Democracy*. Cambridge, MA: MIT Press.

Latour, Bruno, and Steve Woolgar. 1979. *Laboratory Life: The Social Construction of Scientific Facts*. Beverly Hills: Sage.

Lave, Jean, and Etienne Wenger. 1991. *Situated Learning: Legitimate Peripheral Participation*. Cambridge: Cambridge University Press.

Layton, Lynne. 1998. *Who's That Girl? Who's That Boy? Clinical Practice Meets Postmodern Gender Theory*. Northvale, NJ: Jason Aronson.

Lazzarato, Maurizio. 1996. "Immaterial Labour." *Radical Thought in Italy: A Potential Politics*. Ed. Michael Hardt and Paolo Virno, 133–147. Minneapolis: University of Minnesota Press.

———. 2002. "From Biopower to Biopolitics." *Pli: The Warwick Journal of Philosophy* 13, 99–113.

———. 2009. *Expérimentations Politiques*. Paris: Éditions Amsterdam.

Lear, Jonathan. 1990. *Love and Its Place in Nature: A Philosophical Interpretation of Freudian Psychoanalysis*. New York: Noonday.

———. 2005. *Freud*. London: Routledge.

Leavey, John P. 1989. "Destinerrance: The Apotropocalyptics of Translation." *Deconstruction and Philosophy: The Texts of Jacques Derrida*. Ed. John Sallis, 33–46. Chicago: University of Chicago Press.

Leicht, Kevin, and Mary L. Fennell. 1997. "The Changing Organizational Context of Professional Work." *Annual Review of Sociology* 23, 215–231.

Lemke, Thomas. 2002. "Foucault, Governmentality, and Critique." *Rethinking Marxism: A Journal of Economics, Culture & Society* 14, no. 3, 49–64.

———. 2005. "Biopolitics and Beyond: On the Reception of a Vital Foucauldian Notion." Accessed December 11, 2013. http://www.biopolitica.cl/docs/Biopolitics_and_beyond.pdf.

———. 2011a. "Beyond Foucault: From Biopolitics to the Government of Life." *Governmentality: Current Issues and Future Challenges*. Ed. Susanne Krasmann, Thomas Lemke, and Ulrich Bröckling, 165–184. New York: Routledge.

———. 2011b. *Biopolitics: An Advanced Introduction*. New York: New York University Press.

Levey, Mark. 2009. "Common Analytic Process Goals: A Clinical Model of Analytic Change." Accessed December 11, 2013. http://internationalpsychoanalysis.net/2009/02/23/common-analytic-process-goals-a-clinical-model-of-analytic-change-by-mark-levey/.

Levin, Carol B. 2007. "'That's Not Analytic': Theory Pressure and 'Chaotic Possibilities' in Analytic Training." *Psychoanalytic Inquiry* 26, no. 5, 767–783.

Levin, Fred. 2000. "Learning, Development, and Psychopathology: Applying Chaos Theory to Psychoanalysis." *Annual of Psychoanalysis* 28, 85–104.

Levine, Maurice. 1953. "The Impact of Psychoanalysis on Training in Psychiatry." *Twenty Years of Psychoanalysis*. Ed. Franz Alexander and Helen Ross, 50–83. New York: Norton.

Levy, Steven T. 2000, ed. *The Therapeutic Alliance*. Madison, CT: International Universities Press.

Levy, Steven T., and Lawrence B. Inderbitzin. 2000. "Suggestion and Psychoanalytic Technique." *Journal of the American Psychoanalytic Association*, no. 48, 739–758.

Lewin, Bertram D., and Helen Ross. 1960. *Psychoanalytic Education in the United States*. New York: Norton.

Leys, Ruth. 2000. *Trauma: A Genealogy*. Chicago: University of Chicago Press.

Lightbody, Richard. 2008. "The History and Status of Social Workers in the American Psychoanalytic Association." *Clinical Social Work Journal* 37, no. 1, 23–31.

Lindon, John A. 1994. "Gratification and Provision in Psychoanalysis: Should We Get Rid of 'the Rule of Abstinence'?" *Psychoanalytic Dialogues* 4, no. 4, 549–582.

Lipton, Samuel D. 1977. "The Advantages of Freud's Technique as Shown in His Analysis of the Rat Man." *International Journal of Psychoanalysis* 58, 255–273.

———. 1983. "A Critique of So-Called Standard Psychoanalytic Technique." *Contemporary Psychoanalysis*, no. 19, 35–45.

Litowitz, Bonnie E. 2007. "The Second Person." *Journal of the American Psychoanalytic Association* 55, no. 4, 1129–1149.

Livingston, James. 2001. *Pragmatism, Feminism, and Democracy: Rethinking the Politics of American History*. New York: Routledge.

Loewenstein, Rudolph. 1972. "Ego Autonomy and Psychoanalytic Technique." *Psychoanalytic Quarterly* 41, 1–22.

Lopez, Steven R., and Peter J. Guarnaccia. 2000. "Cultural Psychopathology: Uncovering the Social World of Mental Illness." *Annual Review of Psychology* 51, 571–598.

Luhrmann, T. M. 2000. *Of Two Minds: The Growing Disorder in American Psychiatry*. New York: Knopf.

———. 2001. "Commentary." *Culture, Medicine, and Psychiatry* 25, 467–472.

Lunbeck, Elizabeth. 1994. *The Psychiatric Persuasion: Knowledge, Gender, and Power in Modern America*. Princeton: Princeton University Press.

Lupton, Deborah. 1996. "Consumerism, Reflexivity and the Medical Encounter." *Social Science and Medicine* 45, no. 3, 373–381.

Magid, Barry, ed. 1993. *Freud's Case Studies: Self-Psychological Perspectives*. Hillsdale, NJ: Analytic Press.

Makari, George. 2000. "Change in Psychoanalysis: Science, Practice, and the Sociology of Knowledge." *Changing Ideas in a Changing World: The Revolution in Psychoanalysis; Essays in Honour of Arnold Cooper*. Ed. Joseph Sandler, Robert Michels, and Peter Fonagy, 255–262. New York: Karnac Books.

———. 2008. *Revolution in Mind: The Creation of Psychoanalysis*. New York: Harper Perennial.

Malcolm, Janet. 1982. *Psychoanalysis: The Impossible Profession*. New York: Vintage Books.

Marcus, George E. 2005. "Review Essay: Family Firms amidst the Creative Destruction of Capitalism." *American Ethnologist* 32, no. 4, 618–621.

Margolis, Marvin. 2001. "The American Psychoanalytic Association: A Decade of Change." *Journal of the American Psychoanalytic Association* 49, 11–25.

Marill, Irwin H., and Everett R. Siegel. 2004. "Success and Succession." *Journal of the American Psychoanalytic Association* 52, 673–688.

Markell, Patchen. 2003. *Bound by Recognition*. Princeton: Princeton University Press.

Martin, Emily. 2007. *Bipolar Expeditions: Mania and Depression in American Culture*. Princeton: Princeton University Press.

Mayes, Rick, and Allan V. Horwitz. 2005. "DSM-III and the Revolution in the Classification of Mental Illness." *Journal of the History of the Behavioral Sciences* 41, no. 3, 249–267.

McLean, Helen. 1965. "Franz Alexander—1891–1964." *International Journal of Psychoanalysis* 46, 247–250.

———. n.d. *Interview with Helen McLean (Glenn Miller)*. Chicago Institute Library, Film Archive. Unpublished film.

McLean, Helen, and Lucia Tower. n.d. *Interview with Helen McLean and Lucia Tower (Glenn Miller)*. Chicago Institute Library, Film Archive. Unpublished film.

Mechanic, David. 1986. *From Advocacy to Allocation: The Evolving American Health Care System*. New York: Free Press.

——. 1989. *Mental Health and Social Policy*. 3rd ed. Englewood Cliffs, NJ: Prentice Hall College Division.

——. 2007. "Mental Health Services Then and Now." *Health Affairs* 26, no. 6, 1548–1550.

Menninger, W. 1946. "Remarks on Accepting Nomination for Presidency of the American Psychoanalytic Association." *Psychoanalytic Quarterly* 15, 413–415.

Messer, Stanley B., Louis A. Sass, and Robert L. Woolfolk, eds. 1990. *Hermeneutics and Psychological Theory: Interpretive Perspectives on Personality, Psychotherapy, and Psychopathology*. New Brunswick, NJ: Rutgers University Press.

Metzl, Jonathan. 2003. "'Mother's Little Helper': The Crisis of Psychoanalysis and the Miltown Resolution." *Gender and History* 15, no. 2, 240–267.

Micale, Mark S. 1995. *Approaching Hysteria: Disease and Its Interpretations*. Princeton: Princeton University Press.

Milchman, Alan, and Alan Rosenberg. 2006. "A Foucauldian Analysis of Psychoanalysis: A Discipline That 'Disciplines.'" Accessed December 11, 2013. http://www.academyanalyticarts.org/milch&rosen.htm.

Miller, J. Hillis. 2006. "Derrida's Destinerrance." *Modern Language Notes* 121, no. 4, 893–910.

Miller, Jule P. 1985. "How Kohut Actually Worked." *Progress in Self Psychology* 1, 13–30.

Minton, Henry. 1988. *Lewis M. Terman: Pioneer in Psychological Testing*. New York: New York University Press.

Mitchell, Stephen. 1997. *Influence and Autonomy in Psychoanalysis*. Hillsdale, NJ: Analytic Press.

Mitchell, Stephen A. 1998. "The Analyst's Knowledge and Authority." *Psychoanalytic Quarterly* 67, 1–31.

Mitchell, Stephen A., and Lewis Aron. 1999. *Relational Psychoanalysis: The Emergence of a Tradition*. Hillsdale, NJ: Analytic Press.

Mitchell, Stephen A., and Margaret J. Black. 1995. *Freud and Beyond: A History of Modern Psychoanalytic Thought*. New York: Basic Books.

Molino, Anthony, ed. 2004. *Culture, Subject, Psyche: Dialogues in Psychoanalysis and Anthropology*. Middletown, CT: Wesleyan University Press.

Molino, Anthony, and Christine Ware, eds. 2001. *Where Id Was: Challenging Normalization in Psychoanalysis*. Middletown, CT: Wesleyan University Press.

Moreno, Jonathan D. 2001. *Undue Risk: Secret State Experiments on Humans*. New York: Routledge.

Morreim, E. Haavi. 1995a. *Balancing Act: The New Medical Ethics of Medicine's New Economics*. Washington, DC: Georgetown University Press.

——. 1995b. "Lifestyles of the Risky and Infamous: From Managed Care to Managed Lives." *Hastings Center Report* 25, no. 6, 5–12.

Morris, Rosalind. 2007. "Legacies of Derrida: Anthropology." *Annual Review of Anthropology* 36, 355–389.

Mosher, Paul W. 1999. "Managed Care for the Perplexed." *Journal of the American Psychoanalytic Association* 47, 921–928.

———. 2002. "APsaA Age Trends." *Task Force on Communication and Information*, New York: American Psychoanalytic Association.

———. 2006. "Monopoly Is Over: Now Its Time for Risk." *Bulletin of the Association for Psychoanalytic Medicine* 40, 60–70.

Mosher, Paul W., and Arnold Richards. 2005. "The History of Membership and Certification in the APsaA: Old Demons, New Debates." *Psychoanalytic Review* 92, no. 6, 865–894.

Moskowitz, E. S. 2001. *In Therapy We Trust: America's Obsession with Self-Fulfillment*. Baltimore: Johns Hopkins University Press.

Muller, John P. 1999. "Modes and Functions of Sublimation." *Annual of Psychoanalysis* 28, 103–125.

Muller, John P., and Joseph Brent, eds. 2000. *Peirce, Semiotics, and Psychoanalysis*. Baltimore: Johns Hopkins University Press.

Muller, John P., and William Richardson, eds. 1988. *The Purloined Poe: Lacan, Derrida, and Psychoanalytic Reading*. Baltimore: Johns Hopkins University Press.

Murphy, Ann V. 2011. "Corporeal Vulnerability and the New Humanism." *Hypatia* 26, no. 3, 575–590.

Nancy, Jean-Luc. 1991. *The Inoperative Community*. Minneapolis: University of Minnesota Press.

Negri, Antonio. 2008. "The Labor of the Multitude and the Fabric of Biopolitics." *Mediations*, no. 2, 9–26.

Nelson, Robert L., David M. Trubek, and Rayman L. Sullivan, eds. 1992. *Lawyers' Ideals/Lawyers' Practices: Transformations in the American Legal Profession*. Ithaca: Cornell University Press.

Newman, Kenneth M. 1999. "The Usable Analyst: The Role of the Affective Engagement of the Analyst in Reaching Usability." *Annual of Psychoanalysis* 26, 175–194.

———. 2007. "Therapeutic Action in Self Psychology." *Psychoanalytic Quarterly* 76S, 1513–1546.

———. 2009. *Therapeutic Action in Self Psychology, with Special Focus on Two Dimensions of Selfobject Failure*. Chicago: Chicago Psychoanalytic Society.

Nierenberg, Ona. 2007. "The Lay and the Law: Legislating the 'Impossible Profession.'" *Psychoanalysis, Culture and Society* 12, 65–75.

Nobus, Dany. 2000. *Jacques Lacan and the Freudian Practice of Psychoanalysis*. New York: Routledge.

Norton, Anne. 2004. *Leo Strauss and the Politics of American Empire*. New Haven: Yale University Press.

Ogden, Thomas. 1983. "The Concept of Internal Object Relations." *International Journal of Psychoanalysis* 64, 227–241.

———. 1992. *The Primitive Edge of Experience*. New York: Jason Aronson.

———. 1993. *The Matrix of the Mind: Object Relations and the Psychoanalytic Dialogue*. New York: Jason Aronson.

———. 1994. "The Analytic Third: Working with Intersubjective Clinical Facts." *International Journal of Psychoanalysis* 75, 3–19.

———. 1997. *Reverie and Interpretation*. Lanham, MD: Jason Aronson.

———. 2007. "Reading Harold Searles." *International Journal of Psychoanalysis* 88, 353–369.

Olesko, Kathryn M. 1993. "Tacit Knowledge and School Formation." *Osiris* 8, 16–29.

Ong, Aiwa. 1991. "The Gender and Labor Politics of Postmodernity." *Annual Review of Anthropology* 20, 279–309.

Orgel, Shelley. 1995. "A Classic Revisited: K. R. Eissler's 'The Effect of the Structure of the Ego on Psychoanalytic Technique.'" *Psychoanalytic Quarterly* 64, 551–567.

———. 2002. "Some Hazards to Neutrality in the Psychoanalysis of Candidates." *Psychoanalytic Quarterly* 71, 419–443.

Ornstein, Paul, ed. 1990. *The Search for the Self: Selected Writings of Heinz Kohut, 1978–1981*. Vol. 1. Madison, CT: International Universities Press.

Orr, Douglas. 1961. "Lionel Blitzsten, the Teacher." *N. Lionel Blitzsten, M.D.: Psychoanalyst, Teacher, Friend*. Ed. Robert P. Knight, 21–69. Madison, CT: International Universities Press.

Ortner, Sherry B. 2006. *Anthropology and Social Theory: Culture, Power, and the Acting Subject*. Durham, NC: Duke University Press.

Osborne, Thomas. 1993. "Mobilizing Psychoanalysis: Michael Balint and the General Practitioners." *Social Studies of Science* 23, no. 1, 175–200.

———. 2003. "What Is a Problem?" *History of the Human Sciences* 16, no. 4, 1–17.

Oshana, Marina. 2007. "Autonomy and the Question of Authenticity." *Social Theory and Practice* 33, no. 3, 411–429.

Parad, Howard J. 1958. *Ego Psychology and Dynamic Casework: Papers from the Smith College School for Social Work*. New York: Family Service Association of America.

Paris, Bernard. 1994. *Karen Horney: A Psychoanalyst's Search for Self-Understanding*. New Haven: Yale University Press.

Paris, Joel. 2005. "The Diagnosis of Borderline Personality Disorder: Problematic but Better Than the Alternatives." *Annals of Clinical Psychiatry* 17, no. 1, 41–46.

Parker, Ian. 2007. "The State of Psychotherapy and the Place of Psychoanalysis." *Psychoanalysis, Culture and Society* 12, 76–82.

Parsons, Michael. 2006. "The Analyst's Countertransference to the Psychoanalytic Process." *International Journal of Psychoanalysis* 87, 1183–1198.

Paskauskas, Andrew. 1995. *The Complete Correspondence of Sigmund Freud and Ernest Jones 1908–1939*. Cambridge, MA: Belknap Press.

Perkin, Harold J. 1989. *The Rise of Professional Society: England since 1880*. London: Routledge.

Peterson, Mark A. 1998. *Healthy Markets? The New Competition in Medical Care*. Durham, NC: Duke University Press.

Petryna, Adriana, Andrew Lakoff, and Arthur Kleinman, eds. 2006. *Global Pharmaceuticals: Ethics, Markets, Practices*. Durham, NC: Duke University Press.

Philips, David G. 2009. "Clinical Social Work and Psychoanalysis: Introduction to the Special Issue." *Clinical Social Work Journal* 37, no. 1, 1–6.

Philipson, Ilene. 1993. *On the Shoulders of Women: The Feminization of Psychotherapy*. London: Guilford Press.

Phillips, James. 2002. "Review Essay: The Vicissitudes of Freud's Surgical Metaphor." *Psychoanalytic Dialogues* 12, no. 3, 485–497.

Pickering, Andrew. 1995. *The Mangle of Practice: Time, Agency, and Science*. Chicago: University of Chicago Press.

Pinch, T. J. 1997. "Kuhn, the Conservative and Radical Interpretations: Are Some Mertonians 'Kuhnians' and Some Kuhnians 'Mertonians'?" *Social Studies of Science* 27, 465–482.

Plant, Rebecca Jo. 2005. "William Menninger and American Psychoanalysis, 1946–48." *History of Psychiatry* 16, no. 2, 181–202.

Pollack, Michael. 1988. "The Shapes of Scientific Rivalry: Careers, Resources and Identities." *Poetics Today* 9, no. 1, 29–40.

Pollock, George H. 1960. "The Role and Responsibilities of the Psycho-analytic Consultant." *International Journal of Psychoanalysis* 41, 633–636.

———. 1961. "Mourning and Adaptation." *International Journal of Psychoanalysis* 42, 341–361.

———. 1972. "What Do We Face and Where Can We Go? Questions about Future Directions." *Journal of the American Psychoanalytic Association*, no. 20, 574–590.

———. 1975. "On Mourning, Immortality, and Utopia." *Journal of the American Psychoanalytic Association* 23, no. 2, 334–362.

———. 1976. "Chicago Selection Research: The Selection Process and the Selector." *Annual of Psychoanalysis* 4, 309–331.

———. 1977a. "The Chicago Institute for Psychoanalysis: From 1932 to the Present." *Annual of Psychoanalysis* 5, 3–22.

———. 1977b. "The Mourning Process and Creative Organizational Change." *Journal of the American Psychoanalytic Association* 25, no. 1, 3–34.

———. 1983. "The Presence of the Past." *Annual of Psychoanalysis* 11, 3–27.

Pols, J. C. 1997. "Managing the Mind: The Culture of American Mental Hygiene, 1910–1950." Ph.D. diss., University of Pennsylvania.

Povinelli, Elizabeth. 2001a. "Radical Worlds: The Anthropology of Incommensurability and Inconceivability." *Annual Review of Anthropology* 30, 319–334.

———. 2001b. "Sexuality at Risk: Psychoanalysis Metapragmatically." *Homosexuality and Psychoanalysis*. Ed. Tim Dean and Christopher Lane, 387–411. Chicago: University of Chicago Press.

Prince, Robert M. 1999. *The Death of Psychoanalysis: Murder? Suicide? Or Rumor Greatly Exaggerated?* New York: Jason Aronson.

Quinn, Susan. 1987. *A Mind of Her Own: The Life of Karen Horney*. New York: Summit Books.

———. n.d. "Interview with Dorothy Blitsten." Karen Horney papers, Boston Psychoanalytic Society. Unpublished interview.

Rabinow, Paul. 1996. *Essays on the Anthropology of Reason*. Princeton: Princeton University Press.

Rabinow, Paul, and Nikolas Rose. 2006. "Biopower Today." *Biosocieties* 1, 195–217.

Rachman, Arnold. 1997. "Sándor Ferenczi and the Evolution of a Self Psychology Framework in Psychoanalysis." *Progress in Self Psychology* 13, 341–365.

Radden, Jennifer, ed. 2000. *The Nature of Melancholy: From Aristotle to Kristeva*. New York: Oxford University Press.

Rado, Leslie. 1987. "Cultural Elites and the Institutionalization of Ideas." *Sociological Forum* 2, no. 1, 42–66.

Raffensperger, John G., and Louis G. Boshes, eds. 1997. *The Old Lady on Harrison Street: Cook County Hospital, 1833–1995*. New York: Peter Lang.

Rand, Nicholas, and Maria Torok. 1997. *Questions for Freud: The Secret History of Psychoanalysis*. Cambridge, MA: Harvard University Press.

Rangell, Leo. 1986. "The Executive Functions of the Ego: An Extension of the Concept of Ego Autonomy." *Psychoanalytic Study of the Child* 41, 1–37.

Reed, Gail. 1994. *Transference Neurosis and Psychoanalytic Experience*. New Haven: Yale University Press.

Reed, Ralph, and Daryl Evans. 1987. "The Deprofessionalization of Medicine." *Journal of the American Medical Association* 258, no. 22, 3279–3282.

Reeder, Jurgen. 2004. *Hate and Love in Psychoanalytical Institutions: The Dilemma of a Profession*. New York: Other Press.

Renik, Owen. 1996. "The Perils of Neutrality." *Psychoanalytic Quarterly* 65, 495–517.

———. 1998. "The Analyst's Subjectivity and the Analyst's Objectivity." *International Journal of Psychoanalysis* 79, 487–497.

Reppen, Joseph, Jane Tucker, and Martin Schulman, eds. 2004. *Way beyond Freud: Postmodern Psychoanalysis Observed*. London: Open Gate.

Rhodes, Loma A. 2004. *Total Confinement: Madness and Reason in the Maximum Security Prison*. Berkeley: University of California Press.

Richards, Arnold. 1999. "A. A. Brill and the Politics of Exclusion." *Journal of the American Psychoanalytic Association* 47, 9–28.

———. 2008. "Jews in the Development of American Psychoanalysis: The First Fifty Years." *Encyclopedia of American Jewish History*. Ed. Stephen Harlan Norwood and Eunice G. Pollack, 775–776. Santa Barbara: ABC-CLIO.

Richards, Arnold David, and Arthur A. Lynch. 2008. "The Identity of Psychoanalysis and Psychoanalysts." *Psychoanalytic Psychology* 25, no. 2, 203–219.

Richardson, Theresa. 1989. *The Century of the Child: The Mental Hygiene Movement and Social Policy in the United States and Canada*. Albany: State University of New York Press.

Ricoeur, Paul. 1970. *Freud and Philosophy: An Essay on Interpretation*. Trans. Denis Savage. New Haven: Yale University Press.

Rieff, Philip. 1979. *Freud: The Mind of the Moralist*. Chicago: University of Chicago Press.

———. 1987. *The Triumph of the Therapeutic: Uses of Faith after Freud*. Chicago: University of Chicago Press.

Rieff, Philip, and Jonathan B. Imber. 1990. *The Feeling Intellect: Selected Writings*. Chicago: University of Chicago Press.

Riles, Annelies. 2001. *The Network Inside Out*. Ann Arbor: University of Michigan Press.

Riley, Denise. 2000. *The Words of Selves: Identification, Solidarity, Irony*. Stanford: Stanford University Press.

Roazen, Paul. 1975. *Freud and His Followers*. New York: Knopf.

Robertson, Brian M., and Joel Paris. 2005. "The Place of Psychoanalysis in Academic Psychiatry: A Debate." *Canadian Journal of Psychoanalysis* 13, 333–355.

Robins, Cynthia S. 1999. *The Corporate Practice of Medicine: Competition and Innovation in Health Care*. Berkeley: University of California Press.

———. 2001. "Generating Revenues: Fiscal Changes in Public Mental Health Care and the Emergence of Moral Conflicts among Care-Givers." *Culture, Medicine, and Psychiatry* 25, no. 4, 457–466.

Rorty, R. 1986. "Freud and Moral Reflection." *Pragmatism's Freud: The Moral Disposition of Psychoanalysis*. Ed. Joseph H. Smith and William Kerrigan, 1–27. Baltimore: Johns Hopkins University Press.

Rose, Nikolas. 1998. *Inventing Ourselves: Psychology, Power, and Personhood*. New York: Cambridge University Press.

———. 1999a. *Governing the Soul: The Shaping of the Private Self*. London: Free Association.

———. 1999b. *Powers of Freedom: Reframing Political Thought*. Cambridge: Cambridge University Press.

———. 2007. *The Politics of Life Itself: Biomedicine, Power, and Subjectivity in the Twenty-First Century*. Princeton: Princeton University Press.

Rose, Nikolas, and Peter Miller. 1992. "Political Power beyond the State: Problematics of Government." *British Journal of Sociology* 43, no. 2, 173–205.

———. 2008. *Governing the Present*. Cambridge: Polity.

Rosenberg, Charles. 1995. *The Care of Strangers: The Rise of America's Hospital System*. Baltimore: Johns Hopkins University Press.

Rosenberg, Edie, and David Ray DeMaso. 2008. "A Doubtful Guest: Managed Care and Mental Health." *Child and Adolescent Psychiatry Clinics of North America* 17, no. 1, 53–66.

Roth, Michael S., ed. 1998. *Freud: Conflict and Culture*. New York: Vintage Books.

Rothman, David J. 2002. *The Discovery of the Asylum: Social Order and Disorder in the New Republic*. New York: de Gruyter.

Rothstein, Arnold. 1997. "Psychoanalytic Technique and the Creation of Analytic Patients." *North American Psychoanalytic Association* 45, 630–633.

Rotmann, Johann M. 1994. "Third-Party Payment: Can Its Transference Significance Be Analyzed?" *Annual of Psychoanalysis* 22, 145–170.

Roudinesco, Elisabeth. 1990. *Jacques Lacan & Co.: A History of Psychoanalysis in France, 1925–1985.* Trans. Jeffrey Mehlman. Chicago: University of Chicago Press.

———. 2008. "Lacan, the Plague." *Psychoanalysis and History* 10, no. 2, 225–235.

Roustang, Francois. 1986. *Dire Mastery: Discipleship from Freud to Lacan.* Trans. Ned Lukacher. Washington, DC: American Psychiatric Press.

Rowe, Crayton E., Jr. 1981. "Psychoanalytic Theory and Social Work Practice. Herbert S. Strean. New York: The Free Press, 1979. 212 Pp." *Psychoanalytic Review* 68, 451–452.

Rubins, Jack. 1978. *Karen Horney: Gentle Rebel of Psychoanalysis.* New York: Summit Books.

Rubovits-Seitz, Philip F. D., in collaboration with Heinz Kohut. 1999. *Kohut's Freudian Vision.* New York: Routledge.

Rudnytsky, Peter L. 2002. *Reading Psychoanalysis: Freud, Rank, Ferenczi, Groddeck.* Ithaca: Cornell University Press.

Rustin, Michael. 2001. *Reason and Unreason: Psychoanalysis, Science, and Politics.* Middletown, CT: Wesleyan University Press.

Sackett, David L., Sharon E. Straus, W. Scott Richardson, William Rosenberg, and R. Brian Haynes. 2000. *Evidence-Based Medicine: How to Practice and Teach EBM.* 2nd ed. New York: Churchill Livingstone.

Safouan, Moustapha. 2000. *Jacques Lacan and the Question of Psychoanalytic Training.* Trans. Jacqueline Rose. New York: St. Martin's.

Safran, Jeremy D. 2009. "Interview with Lewis Aron." *Psychoanalytic Psychology* 26, no. 2, 99–116.

Samuel, Lawrence R. 2013. *Shrink: A Cultural History of Psychoanalysis in America.* Lincoln: University of Nebraska Press.

Samuelsen, Helle, and Vibeke Steffen. 2004. "The Relevance of Foucault and Bourdieu for Medical Anthropology: Exploring New Sites." *Anthropology and Medicine* 11, no. 1, 3–10.

Sanchez-Pardo, Esther. 2003. *Cultures of the Death Drive: Melanie Klein and Modernist Melancholia.* Durham, NC: Duke University Press.

Sandler, Joseph, Anne-Marie Sandler, and Rosemary Davies, eds. 2001. *Clinical and Observational Psychoanalytic Research: Roots of a Controversy.* Madison, CT: International Universities Press.

Sanville, Jean, Joyce Edward, and Elaine Rose. 1999. *The Social Work Psychoanalyst's Casebook: Clinical Voices in Honor of Jean Sanville.* Hillsdale, NJ: Analytic Press.

Sapir, Edward, and David Goodman Mandelbaum. 1949. "Psychiatric and Cultural Pitfalls in the Business of Getting a Living." In *Edward Sapir: Culture, Language and Personality*, 578–589. Berkeley: University of California Press.

Saul, Leon J. 1957. "The Psychoanalytic Diagnostic Interview." *Psychoanalytic Quarterly*, no. 26, 76–90.

———. 1964. "Franz Alexander—1891–1964." *Psychoanalytic Quarterly*, no. 33, 420–423.

Schachter, Joseph. 2005. "Contemporary American Psychoanalysis: A Profession? Increasing the Role of Research in Psychoanalysis." *Psychoanalytic Psychology* 22, 473–492.

Schafer, Roy. 1970. "An Overview of Heinz Hartmann's Contributions to Psychoanalysis." *International Journal of Psychoanalysis* 51, 425–446.

———. 1994. "A Classic Revisited: Kurt Eissler's 'The Effect of the Structure of the Ego on Psychoanalytic Technique.'" *International Journal of Psychoanalysis* 75, 721–728.

Schaler, Jeffrey A., ed. 2004. *Szasz under Fire: The Psychiatric Abolitionist Faces His Critics*. Chicago: Open Court.

Schlessinger, Nathan. 1990. "A Developmental View of Converting Psychotherapy to Psychoanalysis." *Psychoanalytic Quarterly* 10, 67–87.

Schlessinger, Nathan, and Fred P. Robbins. 1983. *A Developmental View of the Psychoanalytic Process: Follow-Up Studies and Their Consequences*. New York: International Universities Press.

Schmidt, Erika. 2004. "Therese Benedek: Shaping Psychoanalysis from Within." *Annual of Psychoanalysis* 32, 217–232.

———. 2007. "The Complex Legacy of Franz Alexander." Paper presented at Chicago Psychoanalytic Society Scientific Program, November 27.

———. 2008. "Child Psychoanalysis and Child Psychotherapy in Chicago, 1932–2008." *Annual of Psychoanalysis* 36, 45–61.

———. 2010. "The Berlin Tradition in Chicago: Franz Alexander and the Chicago Institute for Psychoanalysis." *Psychoanalysis and History* 12, 69–83.

Schneider, Ann W., Kathryn Hyer, and Marilyn Luptak. 2000. "Suggestions to Social Workers for Surviving in Managed Care." *Health and Social Work* 25, no. 4, 276–279.

Schneider, Arnold Z., and Helen Desmond. 1994. "The Psychoanalytic Lawsuit: Expanding Opportunities for Psychoanalytic Training and Practice." *A History of the Division of Psychoanalysis of the American Psychological Association.* Ed. Robert C. Lain and Murray Meisels, 313–335. Hillsdale, NJ: Lawrence Erlbaum.

Schor, Juliet B. 1992. *The Overworked American: The Unexpected Decline of Leisure*. New York: Basic Books.

Schore, Allan. 1994. *Affect Regulation and the Origin of the Self: The Neurobiology of Emotional Development*. New York: Erlbaum.

Schorske, Carl E. 1981. *Fin-de-Siecle Vienna*. New York: Vintage Books.

Schröter, Michael. 2002. "Max Eitingon and the Struggle to Establish an International Standard for Psychoanalytic Training (1925–1929)." *International Journal of Psychoanalysis* 83, no. 4, 875–893.

———. 2008. "The Dissemination of the Berlin Model of Psychoanalytic Training: A Sketch of the International Training Commission 1925–1938." *Psychoanalysis and History* 10, 205–223.

Scull, Andrew, ed. 1989. *Social Order/Mental Disorder: Anglo-American Psychiatry in Historical Perspective.* Berkeley: University of California Press.

Sedgwick, Eve Kosofsky. 1990. *Epistemology of the Closet.* Berkeley: University of California Press.

———. 2003. *Touching Feeling: Affect, Pedagogy, Performativity.* Durham, NC: Duke University Press.

Seitz, Philip. 1974. " 'Reality Is a Stone-Cold Drag': Psychoanalytic Observations of Hippies, with a Selected List and Annotated Index of References on Adolescent Problems." *Annual of Psychoanalysis* 2, 387–410.

Servatius, Joan M. 2010. "Clinical Social Workers, Psychoanalytic Theory, and Deepening the Treatment." Ph.D. diss., Institute for Clinical Social Work, Chicago.

Servos, J. 1993. "Research Schools and Their Histories." *Osiris* 8, 3–15.

Shamdasani, Sonu. 2002. "Psychoanalysis." *Semiotic Review of Books* 13, no. 1, 5.

Shamdasani, Sonu, and Michael Munchow, eds. 1994. *Speculations after Freud: Psychoanalysis, Philosophy and Culture.* London: Routledge.

Shane, Morton, and Estelle Shane. 1993. "Self Psychology after Kohut: One Theory or Many?" *Journal of the American Psychoanalytic Association* 41, 777–797.

———. 1996. "Self Psychology in Search of the Optimal: A Consideration of Optimal Responsiveness, Optimal Provision, Optimal Gratification, and Optimal Restraint in the Clinical Situation." *Progress in Self Psychology* 12, 37–54.

Shane, Morton, Estelle Shane, and Mary Gales. 1997. *Intimate Attachments: Toward a New Self Psychology.* New York: Guilford Press.

Shapiro, Elizabeth L., and Rachel Ginzberg. 2003. "To Accept or Not to Accept: Referrals and the Maintenance of Boundaries." *Professional Psychology: Research and Practice* 34, no. 3, 258–263.

Sharpe, Matthew. 2004. "Psychoanalysis." *Understanding Derrida.* Ed. Jack Reynolds and Jonathan Roffe, 63–74. London: Continuum.

Shedler, Jonathan. 2002. "A New Language for Psychoanalytic Diagnosis." *Journal of the American Psychoanalytic Association* 50, no. 2, 429–456.

Shelby, Dennis, and Denise Duval. 2009. "Psychoanalytic Identity Project." Poster presentation, American Psychoanalytic Association, New York.

Sherman, Murray H. 1965. "*Medical Orthodoxy and the Future of Psychoanalysis.* By K. R. Eissler." *Psychoanalytic Review* 52D, 147–149.

Shils, Edward. 1982. *The Constitution of Society.* Reprint. Chicago: University of Chicago Press.

Shore, Cris. 2008. "Audit Culture and Illiberal Governance." *Anthropological Theory* 8, no. 3, 278–298.

Shore, Cris, and Stephen Nugent. 2002. *Elite Cultures: Anthropological Perspectives.* London: Routledge.

Shore, Cris, and Susan Wright. 1997. *Anthropology of Policy: Critical Perspectives on Governance and Power*. London: Routledge.

———. 1999. "Audit Culture and Anthropology: Neo-Liberalism in British Higher Education." *Journal of the Royal Anthropological Institute* 5, 557–575.

Shorter, Edwin. 1997. *A History of Psychiatry: From the Era of the Asylum to the Age of Prozac*. New York: Wiley.

Shweder, Richard. 2010. "Freud's Friends and Enemies One Hundred Years Later." *Psychology Today Cultural Commentary*. February. Accessed December 11, 2013. http://www.psychologytoday.com/blog/cultural-commentary/201002/freuds -friends-and-enemies-one-hundred-years-later-part-1-0.

Silverman, Doris K., and David Wolitzky, eds. 2000. *Changing Conceptions of Psychoanalysis: The Legacy of Merton M. Gill*. Hillsdale, NJ: Analytic Press.

Silverstein, Michael. 1998. "The Improvisational Performance of Culture in Real-time Discursive Practice." *Creativity in Performance*. Ed. K. Sawyer, 265–312. Greenwich, CT: Ablex.

———. 2003. *Talking Politics: The Substance of Style from Abe to "W."* Chicago: Prickly Paradigm.

———. 2004. "Boasian Cosmographic Anthropology and the Sociocentric Component of Mind." *Significant Others: Interpersonal and Professional Commitments in Anthropology*. Ed. Richard Handler, 131–157. Madison: University of Wisconsin Press.

Silverstein, Michael, and Greg Urban, eds. 1996. *Natural Histories of Discourse*. Chicago: University of Chicago Press.

Sklansky, Morris. 1991. "N. Lionel Blitzsten, M.D. (1893–1952): The Theories of a Pioneer American Psychoanalyst." *Annual of Psychoanalysis* 19, 230–234.

Skolnikoff, Alan Z. 2000. "Seeking an Analytic Identity." *Psychoanalytic Inquiry* 20, 594–610.

Smaller, Mark D. 1993. "Louis B. Shapiro: Dean of Chicago Analysts." *American Psychoanalyst* 27, no. 1, 26–27.

Smith, Barbara Herrnstein. 2005. *Scandalous Knowledge: Science, Truth, and the Human*. Durham, NC: Duke University Press.

Smith, Joseph H., and William Kerrigan, eds. 1984. *Taking Chances: Derrida, Psychoanalysis, and Literature*. Baltimore: Johns Hopkins University Press.

Spencer, James H., Jr., and Leon Balter. 1990. "Psychoanalytic Observation." *Journal of the American Psychoanalytic Association* 38, no. 2, 393–421.

Star, Susan Leigh, and James R. Griesemer. 1989. "Institutional Ecology, 'Translations' and Boundary Objects: Amateurs and Professionals in Berkeley's Museum of Vertebrate Zoology, 1907–39." *Social Studies of Science* 19, no. 3, 387–420.

Starr, Paul. 1882. *The Social Transformation of American Medicine: The Rise of a Sovereign Profession and the Making of a Vast Industry*. New York: Basic Books.

Stein, Martin H. 1979. "*The Restoration of the Self*. By Heinz Kohut. New York: International Universities Press, 1977, Xxii + 345 Pp., $17.50." *Journal of the American Psychoanalytic Association* 27, 665–680.

Stein, Ruth. 1991. *Psychoanalytic Theories of Affect*. London: Karnac Books.

———. 1997a. "Analysis as a Mutual Endeavor—What Does It Look Like?" *Psychoanalytic Dialogues* 7, no. 6, 869–880.

———. 1997b. "The Shame Experiences of the Analyst." *Progress in Self Psychology* 13, 109–123.

Steinmetz, George. 2006. "Bourdieu's Disavowal of Lacan: Psychoanalytic Theory and the Concepts of 'Habitus' and 'Symbolic Capital.'" *Constellations* 13, no. 4, 445–464.

Stepansky, Paul. 1999. *Freud, Surgery, and the Surgeons*. Hillsdale, NJ: Analytic Press.

———. 2009. *Psychoanalysis at the Margins*. New York: Other Press Professional.

Sterba, Richard. 1934. "The Fate of the Ego in Analytic Therapy." *International Journal of Psychoanalysis*, no. 15, 117–126.

Stern, Daniel. 1998. *The Interpersonal World of the Infant*. London: Karnac Books.

Stern, Donnel B. 1996. "The Social Construction of Therapeutic Action." *Psychoanalytic Inquiry* 16, no. 2, 265–293.

———. 1997. *Unformulated Experience: From Dissociation to Imagination in Psychoanalysis*. Hillsdale, NJ: Analytic Press.

Stern, Steven. 2008. "Analytic Identity and the Definition of Psychoanalysis." Paper presented at Chicago Psychoanalytic Society Scientific Program, February 12.

———. 2009. "Session Frequency and the Definition of Psychoanalysis." *Psychoanalytic Dialogues* 19, 639–655.

Stevens, Rosemary. 1998. *American Medicine and the Public Interest*. Berkeley: University of California Press.

Stewart, Kathleen. 1996. *A Space on the Side of the Road: Cultural Poetics in an "Other" America*. Princeton: Princeton University Press.

———. 2007. *Ordinary Affects*. Durham, NC: Duke University Press.

Stokes, T. D., and J. A. Hartley. 1989. "Coauthorship, Social Structure and Influence within Specialties." *Social Studies of Science* 19, 101–125.

Stolorow, Robert D. 1990. "Converting Psychotherapy to Psychoanalysis: A Critique of the Underlying Assumptions." *Psychoanalytic Inquiry* 10, 119–130.

———. 1994. "Kohut, Gill, and the New Psychoanalytic Paradigm." *Progress in Self Psychology* 10, 221–226.

Stone, Alan A. 1995. "Where Will Psychoanalysis Survive? What Remains of Freudianism When Its Scientific Center Crumbles?" *Harvard Magazine* 99, no. 3, 34–39.

Stone, Leo. 1954. "The Widening Scope of Indications for Psychoanalysis." *Journal of the American Psychoanalytic Association* 2, 567–594.

———. 1961. *The Psychoanalytic Situation: An Examination of Its Development and Essential Nature*. New York: International Universities Press.

Stormon, Lynn. 2004. *Transgressing Aggression: Making Time, Creating Space, Hearing Voices*. Ph.D. diss., Pacifica Graduate Institute.

Strathern, Marilyn. 2000. *Audit Cultures: Anthropological Studies in Accountability, Ethics, and the Academy*. London: Routledge.

———. 2004. *Partial Connections*. Walnut Creek, CA: AltaMira.

Strati, Antonio. 1998. "Organizational Symbolism as a Social Construction: A Perspective from the Sociology of Knowledge." *Human Relations* 51, no. 11, 1379–1402.

———. 1999. *Organization and Aesthetics*. London: Sage.

Strean, Herbert S. 1979. *Psychoanalytic Theory and Social Work Practice*. New York: Free Press.

Strenger, Carlo. 1989. "The Classic and the Romantic Vision in Psychoanalysis." *International Journal of Psychoanalysis* 70, 593–610.

———. 1991. *Between Hermeneutics and Science: An Essay on the Epistemology of Psychoanalysis*. Madison, CT: International Universities Press.

———. 1998. *Individuality, the Impossible Project: Psychoanalysis and Self-Creation*. Madison, CT: International Universities Press.

———. 2002. *The Quest for Voice in Contemporary Psychoanalysis*. Madison, CT: International Universities Press.

Strozier, Charles B. 1985. "Glimpses of a Life: Heinz Kohut (1913–1981)." *Progress in Self Psychology* 1, 3–12.

———. 2001. *Heinz Kohut: The Making of a Psychoanalyst*. New York: Farrar, Straus and Giroux.

Sullivan, Dale L. 1999. "Beyond Discourse Communities: Orthodoxies and the Rhetoric of Sectarianism." *Rhetoric Review* 18, no. 1, 148–161.

Sullivan, Harry Stack. 1997. *The Interpersonal Theory of Psychiatry*. New York: Norton.

Sullivan, William. 1999. "What Is Left of Professionalism after Managed Care?" *Hastings Center Report* 29, no. 2, 7–13.

Sulloway, Frank J. 1991. "Reassessing Freud's Case Histories: The Social Construction of Psychoanalysis." *Isis* 82, no. 2, 245–275.

Summers, Frank. 2005. "The Self and Analytic Technique." *Psychoanalytic Psychology* 22, no. 3, 341–356.

———. 2008. "Theoretical Insularity and the Crisis of Psychoanalysis." *Psychoanalytic Psychology* 25, no. 3, 413–424.

Sunder Rajan, Kaushik. 2005. "Subjects of Speculation: Emergent Life Sciences and Market Logics in the United States and India." *American Anthropologist* 107, no. 1, 19–30.

———. 2006. *Biocapital: The Constitution of Post-genomic Life*. Durham, NC: Duke University Press.

Tansey, Michael J. 1992. "Psychoanalytic Expertise." *Psychoanalytic Dialogues* 2, 305–316.

Tansey, Michael J., and Walter F. Burke. 1989. *Understanding Countertransference: From Projective Identification to Empathy*. Hillsdale, NJ: Analytic Press.

Taylor, Charles. 1991. *The Ethics of Authenticity*. Cambridge, MA: Harvard University Press.

———. 1993. *Philosophy and the Human Sciences: Philosophical Papers II.* Cambridge: Cambridge University Press.

———. 1995. *Human Agency and Language: Philosophical Papers I.* Cambridge: Cambridge University Press.

———. 2004. *Modern Social Imaginaries.* Durham, NC: Duke University Press.

Taylor, Eugene. 1999. *Shadow Culture: Psychology and Spirituality in America.* Washington, DC: Counterpoint.

Teicholz, Judith Guss. 1999. *Kohut, Loewald, and the Postmoderns: A Comparative Study of Self and Relationship.* Hillsdale, NJ: Analytic Press.

Terman, David M. 1984. "The Self and the Oedipus Complex." *Annual of Psychoanalysis* 12, 87–104.

———. 1988. "Chapter 8 Optimum Frustration." *Progress in Self Psychology*, no. 4, 113–125.

———. 2009. "Letter from Chicago." *International Journal of Psychoanalysis* 90, 205–207.

Tessman, Lora. 2003. *The Analyst's Analyst Within.* Hillsdale, NJ: Analytic Press.

Thomä, Helmut. 2004. "Psychoanalysts without a Specific Professional Identity: A Utopian Dream?" *International Forum of Psychoanalysis* 13, no. 4, 213–236.

Thompson, Clara. (1950) 2003. *Psychoanalysis: Evolution and Development.* New Brunswick, NJ: Transaction.

Thompson, M. Guy. 2000. "The Crisis of Experience in Contemporary Psychoanalysis." *Contemporary Psychoanalysis* 36, 29–56.

Timmermans, Stefan, and E. S. Kolker. 2004. "Evidence-Based Medicine and the Reconfiguration of Medical Knowledge." *Journal of Health and Social Behavior* 45 (suppl.), 177–193.

Timms, Edward, and Naomi Segal. 1988. *Freud in Exile: Psychoanalysis and Its Vicissitudes.* New Haven: Yale University Press.

Tower, Lucia, and Helen McLean. n.d. *Interview with Helen McLean and Lucia Tower (Glenn Miller).* Chicago Institute for Psychoanalysis Library, Film Archive. Unpublished film.

Tuckett, David. 2008. "Does Anything Go? Towards a Framework for the More Transparent Assessment of Psychoanalytic Competence." *International Journal of Psychoanalysis* 86, no. 1, 31–49.

Turkle, Sherry. (1978) 1992. *Psychoanalytic Politics: Jacques Lacan and Freud's French Revolution.* 2nd ed. London: Free Association Books.

Turner, Victor. 1988. *The Anthropology of Performance.* New York: PAJ.

Tyrer, P. 1999. "Borderline Personality Disorder: A Motley Diagnosis in Need of Reform." *Lancet* 354, no. 9196, 2095–2096.

Van Haute, Philippe. 2002. *Against Adaptation: Lacan's "Subversion" of the Subject.* Trans. Paul Crowe and Miranda Vankerk. New York: Other Press.

Vassalli, Giovanni. 2001. "The Birth of Psychoanalysis from the Spirit of Technique: What Have We Learned? How Can We Apply It?" *International Journal of Psychoanalysis* 82, 3–25.

Vatter, Miguel. 2009. "Biopolitics: From Surplus Value to Surplus Life." *Theory & Event* 12, no. 2. Accessed December 11, 2013. http://muse.jhu.edu.

Vaughan, Susan C., and Steven P. Roose. 1995. "The Analytic Process: Clinical and Research Definitions." *International Journal of Psychoanalysis* 76, 343–356.

Viderman, Serge. 1979. "The Analytic Space: Meaning and Problems." *Psychoanalytic Quarterly* 48, 257–291.

Vogel, Morris, and Charles Rosenberg, eds. 1979. *The Therapeutic Revolution: Essays in the Social History of American Medicine*. Philadelphia: University of Pennsylvania Press.

Von Unwerth, Matthew. 2005. *Freud's Requiem: Mourning, Memory, and the Invisible History of a Summer Walk*. New York: Riverhead Books.

Wagner, Laurel Bass. 2007. "The Culture of Psychoanalysis in the United States: The Use of State and Federal Government to Advance Psychoanalysis." *Psychoanalysis, Culture and Society* 12, 51–64.

Wallerstein, Robert S. 1987. "Foreword." *The Teaching and Learning of Psychoanalysis: Selected Papers of Joan Fleming, M.D.* Ed. Stanley S. Weiss, vii–xii. New York: Guilford Press.

———. 1995. *The Talking Cures: The Psychoanalyses and the Psychotherapies*. New Haven: Yale University Press.

———. 1997. "Merton Gill, Psychotherapy, and Psychoanalysis: A Personal Dialogue." *Journal of the American Psychoanalytic Association* 45, 230–256.

———. 1998. *Lay Analysis: Life inside the Controversy*. Hillsdale, NJ: Analytic Press.

———. 2000. "Where Have All the Psychoanalytic Patients Gone?" *Psychoanalytic Inquiry* 20, 341–373.

———. 2002a. "The Growth and Transformation of American Ego Psychology." *Journal of the American Psychoanalytic Association* 50, no. 1, 135–168.

———. 2002b. "The Trajectory of Psychoanalysis: A Prognostication." *International Journal of Psychoanalysis* 83 (pt. 6), 1247–1267.

———. 2002c. "Wallerstein on Lay Analysis and the Lawsuit." *Journal of the American Psychoanalytic Association* 50, 639–642.

———. 2005. "Will Psychoanalytic Pluralism Be an Enduring State of Our Discipline?" *International Journal of Psychoanalysis* 86, 623–626.

Wallerstein, Robert S., and Edward M. Weinshel. 1989. "The Future of Psychoanalysis." *Psychoanalytic Quarterly* 58, 341–373.

Wang, Wen-Ji. 2003. "*Bildung* or the Formation of the Psychoanalyst." *Psychoanalysis and History* 5, no. 2, 91–118.

Ware, Norma C., William Lachiocotte, Suzanne Kirschner, Dharma E. Cortes, and Bryon Good. 2000. "Clinician Experiences of Managed Mental Health Care: A Rereading of the Threat." *Medical Anthropology Quarterly* 14, no. 1, 3–27.

Warner, Michael. 2002. *Publics and Counterpublics*. Cambridge, MA: Zone Books / MIT Press.

Wax, Craig M. 2010. "E H R: The Grand Illusion." *Internal Medicine News* 43, no. 5, 14–15.

Weber, Samuel. 2000. *The Legend of Freud*. Stanford: Stanford University Press.

Weinshel, E. M. 1970. "The Ego in Health and Normality." *Journal of the American Psychoanalytic Association* 18, 682–735.

Weiss, Stanley S., ed. 1987. *The Teaching and Learning of Psychoanalysis: Selected Papers of Joan Fleming, M.D.* New York: Guilford Press.

Welch, Bryant, and Stockhamer Nathan. 2003. "The Lawsuit from the Plaintiffs' Perspective." *Journal of the American Psychoanalytic Association* 51S, 283–300.

Wenger, Etienne. 1998. *Communities of Practice: Learning, Meaning, and Identity*. Cambridge: Cambridge University Press.

Whitaker, Robert. 2010. *Anatomy of an Epidemic: Magic Bullets, Psychiatric Drugs, and the Astonishing Rise of Mental Illness in America*. New York: Crown.

Whitebook, Joel. 1996. *Perversion and Utopia: Studies in Psychoanalysis and Critical Theory*. Cambridge, MA: MIT Press.

———. 2004. "Hans Loewald: A Radical Conservative." *International Journal of Psychoanalysis* 85, no. 1, 97–115.

Wille, Robbert S. 2008. "Psychoanalytic Identity: Psychoanalysis as an Internal Object." *Psychoanalytic Quarterly* 77, 1193–1229.

Winer, Jerome A., and James William Anderson, eds. 2001. *Sigmund Freud and His Impact on the Modern World*. Hillsdale, NJ: Analytic Press.

Winer, Jerome A., James William Anderson, Bertram J. Cohler, and R. Dennis Shelby, eds. 2002. *Rethinking Psychoanalysis and the Homosexualities*. Hillsdale, NJ: Analytic Press.

Winnicott, D. W. 1949. "Hate in the Counter-transference." *International Journal of Psychoanalysis* 30, 69–74.

———. 1955. "Metapsychological and Clinical Aspects of Regression within the Psycho-analytical Set-Up." *International Journal of Psychoanalysis* 36, 16–26.

———. 1956. "On Transference." *International Journal of Psychoanalysis* 37, 386–388.

———. 1958. "The Capacity to Be Alone." *International Journal of Psychoanalysis* 39, 416–420.

———. 1968. "Playing: Its Theoretical Status in the Clinical Situation." *International Journal of Psychoanalysis* 49, 591–599.

———. 1969. "The Use of an Object." *International Journal of Psychoanalysis* 50, 711–716.

Wolf, E. S. 2002. "Traveling into Inner Space—an American Psychoanalytic Odyssey: From Ego Psychology to Pluralism and Diversity." *Psychoanalytic Inquiry* 22, no. 1, 124–143.

Wood, Edwin C., and Constance D. Wood. 1990. "Referral Issues in Psychotherapy and Psychoanalysis." *American Journal of Psychotherapy* 44, no. 1, 85–94.

World Health Organization. 1949. *International Statistical Classification of Diseases*. Geneva: World Health Organization.

Young, Allan. 1995. *The Harmony of Illusions: Inventing Post-traumatic Stress Disorder*. Princeton: Princeton University Press.

Zaretsky, Eli. 2004. *Secrets of the Soul*. New York: Knopf.

Zelman, Walter A., and Robert A. Berenson. 1998. *The Managed Care Blues and How to Cure Them*. Washington, DC: Georgetown University Press.

Zetzel, Elizabeth. 1956. "Current Concepts of Transference." *International Journal of Psychoanalysis* 37, 369–375.

Zetzel, Elizabeth R. 1962. "Report of the 22nd International Psycho-analytical Congress." *Bulletin of the International Psycho-analytical Association* 43, 363–375.

———. 1963a. "122nd Bulletin of the International Psycho-analytical Association." *Bulletin of the International Psycho-analytical Association* 44, 384–386.

———. 1963b. "Editorial Comment." *Bulletin of the International Psycho-analytical Association* 44, 521.

———. 1964. "125th Bulletin of the International Psycho-analytical Association." *Bulletin of the International Psycho-analytical Association* 45, 618–625.

———. 1966. "Maxwell Gitelson: 1902–1965." *Journal of the American Psychoanalytic Association* 14, no. 1, 3–8.

———. 1968. "The So Called Good Hysteric." *International Journal of Psychoanalysis* 49, 256–260.

Žižek, Slavoj. 1999. *The Ticklish Subject: The Absent Centre of Political Ontology*. London: Verso.

———. 2003a. *Jacques Lacan: Critical Evaluations in Cultural Theory*. New York: Routledge.

———. 2003b. *The Puppet and the Dwarf: The Perverse Core of Christianity*. Cambridge, MA: MIT Press.

———. 2004. "Four Discourses, Four Subjects." *Cogito and the Unconscious*. Ed. Slavoj Žižek, 74–116. Durham, NC: Duke University Press.

———. 2009. *The Parallax View*. Cambridge, MA: MIT Press.

Zolberg, Vera L. 1986. "Review: Taste as Social Weapon." *Contemporary Sociology* 15, no. 4, 511–515.

INDEX

abstinence, technique of, 43, 64, 196n32

adaptation: of the ego, 106, 108, 116, 119, 134; of psychoanalytic practice, 4, 26, 124, 125, 150, 160, 196n28, 206n9, 209n26

Adler, Marcia, 205n5

Adorno, Theodor W., 119

Aetna, 28, 29, 33

affective labor, 7, 62, 177, 179, 181, 185

Agamben, Giorgio, 8

aggression, 137, 140

Alexander, Franz: as analyst of Bitzsten, 77, 201n13; and association with Healy, 80; Blitzsten's critique of, 83, 87, 90; Blitzsten's followers' critique of, 85–86, 132; as Chicago Institute leader, 51–52, 80–82, 91, 94, 97, 99, 202n19; ego psychologists' critique of, 44, 83–84; and fee-splitting scandal, 80; Freud's support for, 80, 92; and Grinker's debate with Gitelson, 112, 115, 117; and interest in criminology, 78, 80, 82; Lacan's critique of, 200n5; Pollock compared to, 123, 126; psychoanalysis popularized by, 82–83, 87; psychoanalytic approach of, contrasted with Blitzsten's, 81–94, 164, 179–80, 203n25; publica-

tions of, 83, 86, 87; Sachs as analyst of, 85; Schmidt's psychobiography of, 192n17; on scientific status of psychoanalysis, 88–89; as student of Freud, 77; therapeutic technique developed by, 7, 44, 82–84, 90–91, 92–93, 107, 163, 172, 175; as University of Chicago professor, 78–80; and vector theory of personality, 201–2n17, 204n39

alliance: analytic, 145, 146, 215n30; therapeutic, 37, 38, 44, 45, 90, 190n4, 213n13, 214n17, 215n30

Altschul, Sol, 101

American Academy of Psychoanalysis, 113

American Association of Psychoanalysis in Clinical Social Work, 194n15

American Medical Association (AMA), 30, 34

American Psychiatric Association, 96, 123

American Psychoanalytic Association (APsaA): and age of members, 25, 193–94n13; Alexander's technique criticized at, 83, 91; Blitzsten's activity at, 82, 83, 86, 90, 91; Board of Professional Standards (BOPS) of, 58, 101, 165, 169, 170, 217n9; and

American Psychoanalytic Association
(APsaA) (*continued*)
Certification of training analysts,
58; Chicago Institute's relations
with, 91, 100, 101, 130, 151, 167; and
children's therapy, 110, 112; Committee on Psychoanalytic Education
(COPE) at, 102; and disciplinary autonomy of psychoanalysis, 82; and
distinction between psychoanalysis
and psychotherapy, 42–43; and ego
psychology, 44, 52, 83; founding of,
190n5; and frequency of sessions,
22, 91, 193n9, 194nn14–15; and full
vs. applied training, 42, 46, 47;
IPA's relations with, 41–42, 91, 167,
204n36, 217n3; Jones as founder
of, 75; Kohut as president of, 136;
and liberalization of TA system, 165,
169–70; and M.D. requirement, 3,
24, 41, 47, 109, 210n34; William
Menninger as head of, 96; multitiered training system of, 42–43;
and number of patients, 23; Pollock
as head of, 123; and practice bulletins, 37–40; and practice surveys,
22–23; Rainbow Report at, 101–2;
research training program at, 129;
schisms avoided at, 97–98; and
third-party mediation, 37–40
American Psychological Association
(APA), 26, 194n15
American style of psychoanalysis, 48,
75–77, 98, 211n43
analyzability of patients, 43–46, 48, 95,
101, 108–9, 110, 111, 131–32, 197n35,
211n38, 213nn15–16
Anderson, James, 151
Annual of Psychoanalysis, 127, 148,
215n32
anthropology, 6, 8, 55, 128,
186
antipsychiatry movement, 48

anxiety: pharmacological treatments
for, 29, 32; professional, 5, 185; short-
term therapy for, 32
applied psychoanalysis, 42, 46, 60, 110,
114, 127, 129, 209n30, 211n41, 213n10
apraxias, in self psychology, 168–69
Arlow, Jacob, 42
audits, health-care, 19, 26, 28, 29, 30, 33,
34, 40, 54
authority, psychoanalytic, 14, 45, 48,
73, 74, 84, 107, 117, 118–20, 123, 177
autonomy: of the ego, 99–100, 119, 141,
144; of psychoanalysis, 8, 20, 31, 32,
33, 41, 48, 73, 82, 95, 100, 185

Bacal, Howard, 173, 175
Baker, Grace, 95
Bartemeier, Leo, 78
Bateson, Gregory, 114
behavioral science, 26
behavior modification, 60
Beigler, Jerome, 205n5
Benedek, Theresa, 104, 192n17, 203n30,
205n6, 208n22
Benjamin, Walter, 190n9
Berger, Mark, 205n5
Bergmann, Martin, 209n30
Berlin Institute, 81
Berlin Polyclinic, 192n6
Bernfeld, Siegfried, 118
Bettelheim, Bruno, 109
biopolitics, 6, 8, 9, 10, 11, 13, 179, 181
biopower, 6–7, 15
Blitsten, Dorothy, 78, 201n11, 201n13
Blitzsten, Lionel: Alexander as analyst
of, 77, 201n13; Alexander's work
criticized by, 83, 87, 90; at APsaA,
82, 83, 86, 90; as Chicago Psychoana-
lytic Society founder, 73–74, 78, 83,
84–85; Emch's obituary of, 203n29;
Fleming's relations with, 101, 104,
105; followers of, 84–88, 101, 103–4,
105, 115, 136, 162, 203n31, 209n25;

and Gitelson's debate with Grinker, 112, 115; Kavka's psychobiography of, 192n17; psychoanalytic approach of, contrasted with Alexander's, 81–94, 164, 179–80, 203n25; psychoanalytic training of, 76–77; and relations with Freud, 77, 201n13; and relations with patients, 89–90; and rivalry with Alexander at Chicago Institute, 93–94; seminars of, 77–78, 86, 87, 201n11; technical purism of, 92–93; as training analyst, 77, 86, 88

Blue Cross, 28

Bolgar, Hedda, 85

Borowitz, Gene, 109

Boston, psychoanalytic practice in, 80, 210n31

Brenner, Charles, 42

Brent, Stuart, 73, 78, 86, 201n11

Brill, Abraham, 75

Bulletin of the International Psycho-analytical Association, 117, 205n6

Canguilhem, Georges, 209n26

castration complex, 45, 78, 136, 140, 143, 145, 146, 199n6

cathexis, 140, 148, 150

Center for Psychoanalytic Study, 127

Certification of training analysts, 58, 199n4

Chester, Robin, 192n2

Chicago, psychoanalytic practice in, 7, 14, 191–92n17; and Alexander's work at University of Chicago, 78–80; and Blitzsten's seminars, 77–78; and children's therapy, 110, 111; and dearth of émigré analysts, 210n31; and dissident groups, 109; dual psychiatric-psychoanalysis training program in, 113; and 2009 IPA Congress, 163, 169; and Jones's visit, 75–76; and number of patients, 23; and relational analysis, 184

Chicago Center for Psychoanalysis, 209n29

Chicago Institute for Psychoanalysis: Alexander as leader of, 51–52, 80–82, 91, 94, 97, 99, 100, 202n19; APsaA's relations with, 91, 100, 101, 130, 151, 169; Blitzsten's followers at, 92–94, 101, 103–4; and Blitzsten's rivalry with Alexander, 93–94; and children's therapy, 111–12, 128, 210n33, 210n35; and definition of psychoanalysis, 5; democratization of, 150–60; exclusionary practices at, 108–9; Fleming's work at, 100–101, 103, 206nn11–12; and integration of psychoanalysis with psychiatry, 96, 98–99; literature on, 191–92n17; M.D.s vs. non-M.D.s at, 127, 129–31, 193n12, 213n10; meeting to discuss Pollock's ouster at, 151–59; Menninger brothers as graduates of, 95; number of graduates of, 193n12; Ph.D. program at, 127, 129–31, 212n6; Piers as leader of, 99, 100–101, 205n6; Pollock as leader of, 123–31, 146–60; Pollock's misuse of funds at, 126, 150–60; Pollock's patronage system at, 125, 127, 147, 148, 151, 153, 155, 160; psychosomatics studied at, 82; renown of, 51; research vs. education at, 100; Ross as administrator at, 205n4, 206n12; satellite institutes of, 210n35; schisms avoided at, 94, 97–98; social workers' screening of applicants at, 131–32; and Stern's philanthropy, 81; training program of, 81, 99–100, 102–4, 128–32, 151, 152, 210n35; university affiliation sought by, 80–81, 82, 91, 202–3n24; university model adopted by, 126–27, 156

Chicago Psychoanalytic Society, Blitzsten as leader of, 73–74, 78, 83

child development, 135, 174, 185
children, psychoanalysis of, 110–12, 128,
    209–10n30, 210n33, 210n35
Cobb, Stanley, 202n23
codes, DSM and CPT, 27, 30, 33–37, 39,
    182, 183, 195n21
Cohler, Bertram, 205n5
Combined Psychiatric Faculties of
    Chicago, 113
Consortium, 25, 194n15
constipation, 79
consultant, psychoanalyst as, 147
conversion, from psychotherapy to
    psychoanalysis, 167
corporate health care: consolidation
    of, 27; DSM standards for, 30; and
    third-party mediation, 31–40, 185;
    traditional psychoanalysis chal-
    lenged by, 3–5
costs: health-care, 29–30, 123, 195n18; of
    psychoanalytic sessions, 169, 216n35
couch, use of, in psychoanalytic prac-
    tice, 20, 56, 57, 61, 124
countertransference: and Blitzsten's
    work, 88, 92, 104, 162; in ego
    psychology, 45; in object relations
    theory, 175–77, 218n13; and super-
    visory analysis, 104; and third-party
    mediation of care, 185; and unana-
    lytic modes of practice, 64
Crapanzano, Vincent, 196n29
criminology, 78, 80, 82
crisis of psychoanalysis, 3–5, 8, 19–22,
    49–50, 192n2; and coding system,
    27, 30, 33–37, 39; and deskilling, 25;
    and DSM standards, 30–31, 36–37;
    and evidence-based medicine (EBM),
    3, 4, 26, 27–28, 32, 37, 194n16;
    and frequency of sessions, 22–23,
    171–72, 193n9; Freud on, 21, 193n7;
    and gender of patients, 193n10; and
    industrialization of health care, 27;
    and insurance system, 32–40; inter-

viewees' experience of, 1, 52, 63–69,
    171–79; and lay analysis, 41–48; and
    managed care, 29–30, 179; and num-
    ber of patients, 1, 4, 7, 20, 22–24;
    and number of trainees, 24; Pollock's
    response to, 123–26, 146–50, 212n1;
    and qualifications of trainees, 24–25;
    and quantification of practice, 26–
    27; and relational analysis, 1, 2, 4, 7,
    173–77; and synthesis of Alexander's
    and Blitzsten's approaches, 179–
    80; and third-party mediation, 28,
    30–40
cultic object, 190n9
cybernetics, 115, 116, 211n44

Dean, Jodi, 9, 191n12
definition of psychoanalysis: and
    Derridean double bind, 65; and
    frequency of sessions, 166–67, 193n9,
    194n15, 217n3; and intrinsic vs.
    extrinsic factors, 193n9; and transfer-
    ence, 57, 61, 74
denial, 28, 148
dependency, in psychoanalytic relation-
    ship, 7, 62, 68, 69, 91, 134, 142, 144,
    172, 185, 195n20
depression: pharmacological treatments
    for, 29, 32; short-term therapy for, 32
depth psychology: empathy in, 133;
    removed from DSM, 31
Derrida, Jacques, 4, 8, 10–13, 51, 65, 66,
    68, 69, 190n8, 191nn14–15
deskilling, 25
diagnosis, DSM standards for, 30–31, 183
Diagnostic and Statistical Manual of
    Mental Disorders (DSM), 30–31, 36–
    37, 182, 183, 195n19, 219n19
diatrophic bond, 141, 142, 146
Digital Diagnostics, 19
dissident groups, 109, 117–18, 120,
    210n31
Dollard, John, 78

double bind of analysis, 57, 65, 68, 69, 172

dreams, 12, 76, 140, 198n37, 208–9n24

drive theory, 43, 87, 125, 133, 134, 135, 140, 146, 148, 166, 196n28

DSM. *See Diagnostic and Statistical Manual of Mental Disorders*

Dufresne, Todd, 21

Easser, Barbara Ruth, 131

EBM. *See* evidence-based medicine

eclecticism, in psychoanalytic practice, 54, 59, 60, 65, 113, 115

education, psychoanalytic, 100, 101–2, 104–5. *See also* training programs

Edward, Joyce, 198n37

ego: and Alexander-Blitzsten debate, 91, 164; autonomy of, 99–100, 119, 141, 144; and Gitelson-Grinker debate, 119; post-Freudian critiques of, 119; and work-ego, 101, 103, 119

ego psychology, 2, 42–46, 83, 109, 119, 124, 125, 193n9, 195–96n28, 214n17; in competition with self psychology, 140–46, 153–59

Eisold, Kenneth, 199–200n3

Eissler, Kurt, 43–44, 83–84, 90, 196nn30–31, 197n33, 197n36, 215n26

Eissler, Ruth, 138

Eitingon, Max, 192n6

Emch, Minna, 86, 104, 203n29, 207n19

émigré psychoanalysts, 205n3, 210n31, 211n43

empathy, in self psychology, 133

epistemic culture, 198n1

Erikson, Erik, 210n31

Etchegoyen, Horatio, 197n35

ethics: of analyst-patient relationship, 63; of coding system, 35

ethnography, 7–8, 10, 13, 14, 54

evidence-based medicine (EBM), 3, 4, 26, 27–28, 32, 37, 194n16

Ewald, Francois, 182

exceptionalism of psychoanalysis, 4, 42, 49, 65–66

exclusionary practices, 108–9, 211n38

Falk, David, 3–4, 190n6

Federal Employees Health Benefits Program, 28

Ferenczi, Sándor, 64, 215n29

Fleming, Joan, 100–101, 103–6, 109, 132, 205n6, 206nn9–12, 207–8n20, 207n17, 208nn21–22, 209n25

Flexner Report, 102, 206–7n14

Fordism, 48

Forman, Max, 101, 145, 146, 206n11, 215n31

Forrester, John, 41

Foucault, Michel, 6, 8–9, 103, 191n12, 219n15

French, Thomas, 78, 83, 93, 100, 106, 202n19

frequency of psychoanalytic sessions, 22–23, 56, 91, 124, 151, 166–67, 171–72, 193n9, 194nn14–15, 216n35, 217n3

Freud, Anna, 46, 133, 136, 141, 161, 195–96n28, 196n32

Freud, Sigmund: on American reception of psychoanalysis, 41; American students of, 76–77; on authority, 123; on civilization, 73; and correspondence with Jones, 75–76; and crisis of psychoanalysis, 21, 193n7; Derrida's reading of, 10–13; and frequency of sessions, 166; Gitelson's invocation of, 113–15; Grinker analyzed by, 82; on group psychology, 114, 123, 149; Kohut compared to, 214–15n25; on lay analysis, 47; on mourning, 148; on patient loyalty, 41, 43; on penis display, 199n6; Pollock's invocation of, 127–28; on principle of abstinence, 196–97n32; and relations with Alexander, 77, 80, 92; and relations with Blitzsten,

Freud, Sigmund (*continued*)
77, 92, 201n13; on repression barrier,
216n37; on resistance, 191n16; and
schisms within psychoanalysis,
200n3; on social relations, 114; surgery metaphor used by, 38, 195n24;
on transference, 2, 189n2, 190n4; on
transience, 124
Fromm, Erich, 210n31
Fromm, Erika, 109
frustration, as vehicle for structuring of
self, 134–35, 173

Garber, Benjamin, 128
Gedo, John, 168, 209n27
gender: of patients, 193n10; of psychoanalysts, 192n3, 207n17
Gerard, Margaret, 78, 93
Gill, Merton, 42, 109, 193n9
Giovacchini, Peter, 109, 209n29
Gitelson, Maxwell, 94, 97, 99, 104,
106–8, 109, 148, 205n6, 208–9nn22–
26, 211n41, 211n43; and debate with
Grinker, 112–19, 211n44, 212n45;
film archive named for, 127; on
preparatory phase of analysis, 142–
43, 215nn29–30; and psychoanalytic
authority, 117–20, 177; as training
analyst, 139, 144
Glabbard, Glen, 26
Global Claims Services, 33
Goldberg, Arnold, 156, 158, 175,
205n5, 206n11, 209n27, 214n24,
216n37
Goldberg, Constance, 205n5
Gourguechon, Prudence, 183
government health-care programs, 28,
29, 30, 31, 123, 181–82
gratification, 103, 135–36, 144, 168, 174,
196n32
Gray, Sheila, 25
Green, Andre, 194n16
Gregg, Alan, 81, 82, 202–3nn23–24

Grinker, Roy, 79, 80, 82, 97, 191n17,
211nn42–43; and debate with Gitelson, 112–19, 211n44, 212n45
Grotjahn, Martin, 201–2n17
group psychology, 114, 123, 149, 156–58
Gunther, Meyer, 205n5

Hacking, Ian, 9, 191n12
Hannett, Frances, 85–86, 119–20
Hardt, Michael, 179
Hartmann, Heinz, 42, 101, 108, 136,
196n28, 206n9, 209n26
Healy, William, 80
Hecht, Ben, 77
Hollis, Florence, 198n37
homosexuality, 108, 209n27
Horney, Karen, 84, 192n17, 202n19
humanism, 48, 141, 143, 144
Hutchins, Robert Maynard, 78
hysteria, 45, 132, 143, 192n3, 213n13

id-centered psychoanalysis, 75
Illinois Psychiatric Association, 123
Illinois Psychoanalytic Association,
123
industrialization of health care, 27,
195n19
insurance industry: and costs of health
care, 195n18; and industrialization
of health care, 27; and mental health
coverage, 28–30, 182, 219n18; psychoanalysts' negotiations with, 32–40;
psychotherapists' relations with, 47;
therapeutic relationship affected by,
181–82
International Psychoanalytical Association (IPA), 41, 47, 77, 91, 136, 190n5,
193n9, 194n15, 204n36, 217n3; 2009
Congress of, 163, 169
interpretation: in ego psychology,
43–44, 45, 47, 83, 167, 196n30; in self
psychology, 168–69
intersubjectivity, 10, 55, 175, 216n1

negative transference, 59, 106, 176, 177

Negri, Antonio, 8

neoliberalism: Foucault's critique of, 9, 10; health-care model of, 4, 13–14, 26, 30, 147, 162, 178, 179, 183, 185, 186

neurosis: and Alexander's psycho-analytic practice, 91; and Blitzsten's psychoanalytic practice, 81, 91; in ego psychology, 44–45, 145–46; and military medicine, 204n1; psychoanalysis as preferred treat-ment for, 65; removed from DSM, 31, 183; in self psychology, 133; and transference, 2, 57, 61, 145–46, 161, 166, 189n2

Newman, Kenneth, 175–77, 218n13

New York, psychoanalytic practice in, 77, 82, 91, 110, 191n11, 199–200n3, 210n31, 211n43

Nixon administration, health-care plan of, 123

normality, 99–100, 102–3, 106–8, 119, 209n25

Northwestern University Medical School, 77

"not analysis," psychotherapeutic prac-tices viewed as, 5, 7, 13, 59, 63, 64, 69, 215n26

"not splitting," 97–98

Nuetzel, Eric, 194n15, 217n3

Obamacare (Patient Protection and Affordable Care Act), 30, 182

Oberndorf, 91

objectivism, psychoanalytic, 133, 134

object relations, 109, 132, 175–77, 180, 215n29, 218nn12–13

obsessive-compulsive disorder, 32, 45

Oedipus complex: and analyzability of patients, 131–32; in ego psychol-ogy, 44–45, 141, 143, 144–46, 215, 215nn30–31; and Foucault's biopolitics, 9; and gender of patients,

193n10; relational analysis's shift from, 167–68, 174; and schisms in psychoanalytic groups, 120; in self psychology, 136, 140, 143, 144–46

Orgel, Shelley, 197n36

Orr, Douglas, 201n13

Palombo, Joseph, 205n5

parameters, in ego psychology, 43, 46, 143, 173, 196n31, 197n33, 215n26

parapraxes, 137

Patient Protection and Affordable Care Act, 30, 182

patients: analyzability of, 43–46, 48, 95, 101, 108–9, 110, 111, 131–32, 197n35, 211n38; frequency of sessions attended by, 162, 171–72; gender of, 193n10; number of, 1, 4, 7, 20, 22–24, 131–32; and shift in therapeutic personhood, 173–77

pedagogy: and Alexander-Blitzsten rivalry, 73, 85, 86, 88, 164; of desire, 73, 164, 199n1; and Fleming's work, 103, 104; and Pollock's work, 130

penis, display of, 65, 199n6

penis envy, 140, 146, 215n31

personhood, therapeutic, 172–77, 178

pharmaceuticals: cost-effectiveness of, 29, 32; incentivizing of, 30; and industrialization of health care, 27; therapeutic efficacy of, 32

philanthropy, 81, 202n23

Piers, Gerhart, 99–100, 205n6

political relations: and Alexander's departure from Chicago Institute, 100; and Blitzsten's followers, 84, 85; and medical coding system, 35; and problem of lay analysis, 47–48. *See also* biopolitics

Pollack, William, 195n21

Pollock, George H.: as Chicago Institute leader, 123–31, 146–60; compared to Alexander, 123, 126;

self psychology (*continued*)
    competition with ego psychology,
    140–46, 153–59; relational, 173–77;
    synthesized with object relations
    theory, 175–77, 180, 218nn12–13
Servatius, Joan M., 218n11
sexuality, in psychoanalytic theory, 9,
    76, 92, 108, 135, 137, 145
Shapiro, Louis, 101, 132, 206nn11–12
Shils, Edward, 207n18
social relations: and children's therapy,
    111–12; Freud's works on, 114; self
    psychology's exclusion of, 134
social science, 78–79, 82
social workers: and children's therapy,
    111–12, 209–10n30; patients screened
    by, 131–32; as psychoanalytic train-
    ees, 24–25, 46, 47, 109, 128, 198n37
Solomon, Brenda, 211n42
Spitz, Rene, 143
standards, traditional, in psychoanaly-
    sis, 161–72, 183
Stein, Martin H., 214–15n25
Stepansky, Paul, 195n24, 214n23
Stern, Alfred, 81, 82, 202n19
Stern, Steven, 53–54
Stone, Leo, 46, 193n8
Stormon, Lynn, 194–95n16
Strozier, Charles, 192n17
structural theory (id-ego-superego),
    42–43, 195–96n28
subjectivism, psychoanalytic, 133,
    134
SubmitPatientForms, 34
Sullivan, Harry Stack, 46, 109, 111
superego, 101, 206n9, 206n13
supervisory analysis, 104
surgery, psychoanalytic treatment com-
    pared to, 38–39, 45, 165–66, 195n24,
    197n36
surveys, practice, 22–23
syncretism, in psychoanalytic educa-
    tion, 105

Terman, David M., 163, 168, 174–75
therapeutic alliance, in ego psychology,
    44, 45
third-party mediation, 28, 30–40
Thompson, Clara, 161
Tobin, Arnold, 156–57, 158
Tolpin, Marian, 139, 205n5
Tracy, Mark, 22
trainees, psychoanalytic: age of, 24, 25,
    193–94n13; analyzability of, 108–9;
    and ego, 103, 106; full vs. applied
    training for, 42, 46, 47; gender of,
    24, 46, 207n17; as guaranteed pool
    of patients, 23, 46; immersion as cri-
    terion for, 53, 151; and liberalization
    of TA system, 159, 160, 161, 163–72;
    normalcy of, 99–100, 102–3, 106–8;
    number of, 24, 151; psychologists
    as, 24, 25, 46, 47, 109, 128, 198n37;
    qualifications of, 24–25, 152, 159, 160;
    social workers as, 24–25, 46, 47, 109,
    128, 198n37; standardized selection
    of, 101, 102; and supervisory analysis,
    104; and transference, 104, 105–6
training analysts (TAs), 20, 194n14;
    Blitzsten as, 77, 86, 88; Certification
    of, 58, 199n4; and Eitingon model,
    192n6; and frequency of sessions,
    22–23, 167, 193n9; and gender of pa-
    tients, 193n10; and liberalization of
    TA system, 159, 160, 161, 163–72; and
    number of patients, 23; and number
    of trainees, 24
training programs: at Berlin Institute,
    81; at Chicago Institute, 81, 99–100,
    102–4, 128–32, 210n35; and child
    analysis, 110–11; at Combined
    Psychiatric Faculties of Chicago, 113;
    syncretism in, 105; traditional stan-
    dards defended in, 161–72, 183
transference: defense, 141, 144–45,
    215n29; and definition of psycho-
    analysis, 57, 61, 74; in ego psychol-

ogy, 2, 43, 44, 45, 83, 141, 144–45,
193n9; erotic, 12, 190n4; and evaluation of psychoanalytic trainees, 104,
105–6; and frequency of sessions,
91, 166; Freud on, 2, 189n2, 190n4;
manipulation vs. analysis of, 43, 44,
64, 83, 90; and narcissism, 213n15,
214n17; negative, 59, 106, 176, 177;
and neurosis, 2, 57, 61, 145–46,
161, 166, 189n2; in object relations
theory, 175–77; and reality sense,
213–14n17; and relational analysis,
172, 173, 174; and selfobject, 136,
174; and supervisory analysis, 104;
undermined by third-party mediation, 33, 34
transition pathology, 148
Truman, Harry S., 96
trust, patient's, in relation to analyst,
44, 45, 62, 103, 132, 142–43, 167,
190n4, 213n13
Turner, Victor, 216n36

unconscious, 8, 9, 11, 39–40, 64, 84,
114–15, 117, 147, 149, 150, 186, 191n12,

198n37, 201n17, 209n28, 214n21,
216n37
undecidability of psychoanalysis, 4–5,
8, 10, 73, 190n8, 191n14
University of Chicago, 75, 78–80,
82

vertical split, Kohut's concept of, 154–
55, 158, 216n37
virtual standard, in psychoanalytic
training, 170–71

Wallerstein, Robert, 26, 47, 102
Webber, Colin, 205n5
Wellstone-Domenici Health Parity and
Addiction Equity Act, 182
Winnicott, Donald, 109, 175, 215n29,
218nn12–13
Wolf, Ernest, 139, 144
work-ego, 101, 103, 119

Young, Allan, 9, 191n12

Zetzel, Elizabeth, 44, 132
Žižek, Slavoj, 21